DATE DUE			

BEFORE I FORGET

Burton Rascoe

BEFORE I FORGET

THE LITERARY GUILD OF AMERICA, INC.

New York   *1937*

PRINTED AT THE *Country Life Press*, GARDEN CITY, N. Y., U. S. A.

FOR HAZEL

Alors il croit pourtant
Le burlesque croit, la hâche à la main
Il va equarrir son rêve dans les cœurs
Bâtir son rêve fanatique avec des morts
Et deux vivants peut-être.

—JEAN DE BOSSCHÈRE

Acknowledgments

I WISH to express special gratitude to Mr John Craig, of Doubleday, Doran & Co., for the unusual pains he took to verify verifiable matter in this book, for his careful copyreading, and for the valuable suggestions he gave me. The chapter heads are, in the main, his. I wish also to express my thanks to: Captain Joseph Medill Patterson of the Chicago Tribune Company and of the New York *Daily News* for permission to quote reviews and excerpts covered by the Chicago *Tribune's* blanket copyright and for permission to quote from his book, *The Notebook of a Neutral;* Captain Rupert Hughes for permission to republish his "Anti-Cabellum"; to Mr James Branch Cabell for permission to republish his "Ultra Crepidam" and "Epilogue"; and Mr John Farrar for permission to republish certain articles I wrote anonymously for a book now out of print, entitled *The Literary Spotlight,* edited by Mr Farrar.

Reflections on Aim and Intention

BY BURTON RASCOE

THE EXCUSE for anyone's writing an autobiography is in Dr Samuel Johnson's pronouncement that every man has at least one great book in him if he should tell the truth about himself. The man's station in life matters not at all, according to the good Doctor. He may be humble, undistinguished, lacking in glamor or conspicuous ability; he may have never strayed beyond the confines of his own village, fought no battles, witnessed no great events. But if he should know the truth about himself and have the courage and the words to tell it, then will he produce a masterpiece which all will acclaim, for he will have told a universal truth about the life of man, and he will have awakened the emotion of recognition in the breast of every man; for the truth about any man is in a large measure the truth about every man.

I do not flatter myself that I have written an autobiography such as Dr Johnson had in mind. My aim is modest. Although I have long taken heed of Socrates' injunction, "Know thyself," I confess I have not yet attained full knowledge of myself. I know some aspects of myself; I can be truthful and reasonably accurate about phases of my life, because my memory is good and I have no vanity which would prompt me to make myself out otherwise than I have been, no false pride which would conceal my ignorance or the faults of my temperament, the facts of my origin or the facts of

[ix]

my experience; but it is quite possible that some will see the truth about myself better from the record I have attempted than I myself have divined.

The record, such as it is, is there. Let him who can, and will, pronounce judgment upon me, interpret my character, teach me about myself. My modest aim is so to reveal myself, so to set down my impressions of the visible and tangible world, so to state my reactions to a given experience at a given moment, that you will find something of yourself, if only to reflect with satisfaction how different you are from me.

The truth about oneself is one of the most difficult things to get at and, even if you know the truth, it is very difficult to express it; for no matter how clever you are, how articulate, how easily the right words spring into your consciousness, those words often have a disconcerting way, once they are written down, of being not at all adequate to what you know and feel and want to express. They may omit no factual detail, each separate sentence may be an exact truth; and yet the sum of these truths may be untrue; they may add up to an essentially false impression; they may be comment upon the experience rather than a true reflection of the emotion engendered by the experience when it occurred.

I know how true this is, because there is one episode in *Before I Forget* which I have been trying for nearly three years, off and on, to get right in the telling. As it stands, the episode is related in less than five hundred words. It is so brief that most readers probably will not notice it; but anyone who has an instinct for these matters will sense that there is something wrong in the telling there, that it may have truth in it but that it isn't true. I feel this. I know this. But I don't know how to make it true; for I have tried, perhaps half a hundred times and in half a hundred ways. The results, after all these trials, have not conveyed what the experience meant to me at the time it occurred; it has sounded ridiculous, but there was nothing ridiculous about the experience when it occurred. On the contrary, it was beautiful, elevating, saddening and painful. It was anguishing and bewildering.

Elsewhere I have tried to tell and (I think) have more or less succeeded in telling the pertinent and cogent truths about the world I found myself in and my response to contacts with the people and events of that world in boyhood, adolescence and young manhood, as a lad in a peaceful and leisured Kentucky village, as a boy and youth in the newly pioneered, bustling, progressive and rapidly changing Oklahoma Territory, and as a student, newspaperman and literary journalist in Chicago during one of the most spectacular of Chicago's recurrent outbursts of cultural activity.

This book, as I conceive it, is in a way the story of the Education of One Man, emotionally and intellectually, who has, confessedly, a vast deal yet to learn and has only begun to scratch the surface of real knowledge. It is the story of a process of education through study and self-instruction, but more so by struggle and experience, by fruitful contacts with people and by the contemplation of men and events.

I have tried to deal with each phase of my past as the contemporary experience seemed to me then and not as I think of it now. For instance, the boy I once was, so feverishly eager and aspiring, so full of illusions and energy, is so remote from me now that I have had to be extremely careful not to make the stupid and cruel adult mistake of laughing at that youth's coltish bewilderments and entanglements, his great seriousness and unflagging belief in an exciting, high destiny.

I have tried not to betray that boy by writing of him in the light of what I now think and feel instead of as he saw and felt; of picturing him as I think he should have been, or as I would like him to have been, instead of as he was. Fortunately he has helped me; for he contracted the diary-keeping habit early from reading Ralph Waldo Emerson, his first heady stimulant toward finding in books some key to the door of knowledge, because Emerson kept a journal. I have been able to draw from this diary and, by referring to it, correct any distorted image or any romanticized memory of the boy. There were times when he seems to me self-righteous and a prig, self-centered and selfish, vain, impatient with the conduct of others; but he was also eager and easily moved emotionally, friendly, independent, industrious, fascinated by the spectacle of life and by the promise of life. There was a long period after he had passed his youth, had married and had entered upon a career of sorts, when he was so fascinated by the spectacle of life, so intense upon the promise of life, that he scarcely took time to think of himself at all, but was absorbed in contemplation of the personalities and the work of those around him.

This, then, is a remembrance of things past, a reconstruction of childhood and youth, a record of things seen, impressions gained, people known, admired and liked, windmills tilted against with fury, phantom enemies challenged with sanguine intrepidity, real enemies created and staunch friends made. And it is a history, also, of an almost frantic avoidance of a philosophy, out of an experience and belief that one can have a philosophy about an action only when it is too late to be of any good and that life is an adventure so unpredictable that to espouse an intransigent system of thought and belief is either to confuse one's life with unsupportable conflicts and contradictions or so to delude oneself as to give the appearance of hypocrisy. This does not prevent me from having convictions passionately held and fought for, the necessary prejudices of sentient but fallible humankind. Nor does it prevent me from pursuing the dream, perhaps grotesquely and fanatically.

BURTON RASCOE.

New York City
March 31, 1937.

Contents

CONTENTS

CONTENTS

CONTENTS

[xvi]

CONTENTS

CONTENTS

[xviii]

CONTENTS

PART I

Souvenirs of Childhood

CHAPTER I

Out of the South

A Vehement Lack of Pride in Family. My Father's Kin.
Grandfather and Grandmother Rascoe. My Father a "Bound"
Boy. Grim-visaged Grandfather Burton.

T HE SURNAME, IT APPEARS, is not Rascoe. At least it was not that
originally. I don't know this of my own research or knowledge or
from anything I ever heard from any of my kinsfolk. I have it only
on the word of an amateur genealogist, Mr Harvey Dann, who once
wrote me that we have a common ancestor. To prove this he supplied me with a very brief, inconsecutive and not altogether convincing genealogical chart, which is the only one I ever possessed.

In fact, until this moment I have never looked at this chart with
close attention. In revolt against a circumstance in my boyhood
which I found foolish, unsocial and inconsistent, I cultivated a
vehement lack of pride in family. Born a Southerner, I have encountered too many professional Southerners who cultivate all the
worst traits of Southern manner and point of view and take offensive pride in their peculiarity; born a Kentuckian, I have encountered too many professional Kentuckians who might give
residents of other states the notion that Kentucky is exclusively
populated by feeble-minded and distasteful persons; and born of
a union of family of property and a family of none, I came to loathe
the artificial distinctions which made my mother's people and my
father's people hostile to one another when they should have been
friendly. I have counted it (perhaps too readily) against those I

have met when they disclosed with obvious pride, as though it counted much in their favor, that they inherit family names associated with property or distinction; for I believe that one should take care to cultivate whatever one holds to be the good values in life and not to imagine that the character and deeds of one's ancestors, however great, compensate for sloth, boorishness or incompetence in oneself. If I knew for a fact that I had for an ancestor a great or famous man, I should ask myself whether I could be sure he was proud of his descendant before I bruited the matter about.

On the other hand men of great, even the greatest, abilities have sometimes had this little vanity in pride of lineage. Shakespeare, so the legend has it, made his application to the Heralds' College for a coat of arms in 1596, alleging that one of his ancestors "for valiant and faithful service" had been rewarded by King Henry VII. The coat of arms was granted him, though the most careful research has been unable to confirm the claim in the application, and of the whole Shakespearean line he is the only one who bore the name with renown. Victor Hugo, although a humanitarian and a republican, did not hesitate to invent a noble lineage for himself. Caesar claimed descent from Aeneas, Alexander from Apollo.

Even in my own time I have seen on the walls of H. L. Mencken's home the framed gloomy prints of heavy, formidable and highly unprepossessing-looking individuals whom, because they bear the name of Mencken (or something resembling it), Mencken chooses to regard as his ancestors, after some hasty research among the print shops of Germany. And in the reception hall of James Branch Cabell's home there is an artistic eyesore in the form of a gigantic and detailed family tree, patiently hand-painted by Cabell himself, after years of work among the public records of Virginia.

When Cabell and Mencken, who are unique in their respective lines, yield to the harmless vanity of ancestral devotion, I am persuaded that no great harm will be done if I glance more closely at the brief memorandum, so full of lacunae, so vague, so inconclusive and yet somehow, at this moment, so provocative and take some halfhearted stock in what it tells me.

From this chart it would seem that the name is not Scots-Irish or North English, as I had vaguely imagined it to be, but French Huguenot. It was originally spelled Rauscoue or Rouscoue. It is a name that has suffered many sea changes because of the illiteracy of those who bore it and because of the negligence of clerks who wrote it into records from the way it sounded to them.

According to my genealogical relative, the name has been variously spelled Rauscoue, Rouscoue, Rascoe, Ruscoe, Rasco, Resco, Reskew, Raskow; but never Roscoe, which would confuse it with the North English people who have a name which sounds something like that. The genealogist is wrong in this, because my father's elder brother got tired of correcting people about the spelling of his name and so humored them by changing it to Roscoe without asking the government's permission to do so.

Something I know and something I read in history give an air of plausibility to my kinsman's chart. My father's immediate ancestors came from North Carolina (possibly in that great train of migration into Tennessee in 1765 which saw a thousand wagons pass through Hillsboro, North Carolina, within a year, in one of which wagons was the family of Andrew Jackson), and, as we know from history, the Carolinas were originally settled by French convicts, religious refugees and political prisoners. The chart is silent about this, but whether because of the compiler's ignorance or pride I know not. It would have been so facile for him, I should think, to admit that the early Rascoes were French convicts, but to point out that in those days, as in this, it was easy to become a convict simply by sharing a minority opinion or by holding to a faith that was numerically at a disadvantage.

From there I should think it would also be easy for him to rig up a really imposing chart showing that we Rascoes are descendants of Henry of Navarre (I have known so many men who claim descent from that romantic and dashing Huguenot), and to claim that although the blood of our ancestors flowed on St Bartholomew's Night, the princely swords of the Rascoes flashed valorously against the terror of sinister Catherine's perverted thirst for blood. He might easily have made the Rascoes, of the remote past, splendid.

He did not. He is so drably factual I begin to believe him:

The family came from Sawbridgeworth, Herts, England. Earliest name found there, 1545, John Rouscoue, alien. Flemish or Dutch Flemish

[5]

name of Huguenot origin, variously Rauscoue and Rouscoue. Name rare in England and not the same as Roscoe. Roger Ruscoe (Rescoe) b 1585, d 1618. William Ruscoe, b 1593, came to New England 1635 on the ship *Increase,* aged 41. His wife Rebecca, aged 40. They had four children, Nathaniel, John, Samuel, William [etc., etc., etc.].

There follows a short, uninspiring account from the records of births, marriages and deaths of common men, adherents to the Protestant faith and its subsequent schisms and branches—Methodists, Baptists, Congregationalists and Presbyterians.

My father's kin—all that I have ever known of them—have been, at least since the Civil War, largely of that indeterminate class common in the South, never very poverty-stricken, always fed and sheltered by their own labor and resource (even the poorest of them) and never very well off—small farmers, large landholders with cash income scarcely sufficient to pay and board their help and maintain themselves, middle-class artisans and small-town merchants.

One of my father's brothers was a sculptor, but despite the many monuments to Confederate generals, the profession of sculpture does not flourish in the South. My uncle earned his living in the North by modeling wax figures to be used in the display windows of department stores. When he died he was the head modeler and designer of such figures in a large fixture supply factory in Lansing, Michigan.

My father's other brother was a musician, but his trade was that of a carpenter. He played the violin, the accordion, the banjo, the mandolin, the jew's-harp and the foot organ without ever having taken a lesson. He raised a large family of girls and housed them in a home he had built with his own expertness as a carpenter; he fed them, clothed them, educated them and saw to it that they were given music lessons, although it was not the desire of any of them to be musicians and the lessons were almost a total loss. Then he left them. Vanished.

Something happened to this musician-carpenter. No one ever found out just what. When all of his daughters were of an age to have had some schooling, he disappeared. He said he was going to Memphis on a business matter, and it is known that he took a fair-sized roll of money with him—money he had made in fulfilling a building contract. He was never heard of after that, although the search for him, continued a year or more, occupied much space in the columns of the Southern newspapers and impoverished my father through the expense of helping the police to try to find my uncle and running down false information that he had been seen in various towns in the South.

There were stories that he had been a spender in the red-light district on his arrival in Memphis. And there was a sensational story about his having "wined and dined," as the newspapers reported, a pretty young woman whose reputation was not good. The newspapers did not know the name of this woman. The wine, the newspapers said, was sherry; and so the young woman became known as the "Sherry Girl" in the baffling mystery.

That was more than twenty-five years ago. My aunt still confidently believes that her husband will someday return to her, although she long ago collected the insurance upon his life when the courts declared that he was officially dead.

Because presently I shall write at length about my father, I shall not speak of him now beyond saying that he was neither a musician nor a sculptor, like his brothers, but that he could fix anything whatever, do any manual work from carpentry to dressing hogs, better than anyone I ever knew, and that he had the greatest natural wit I have ever encountered in life or in books. I will also add that I have never encountered anyone who had such an innate sense of the proper way to get along with, and to treat, one's fellow human beings; no one, while giving much, got more out of life.

It was not until just before my father's death in 1930 that I ever developed any curiosity about his immediate ancestry. It was then too late, for his mother was long since dead, and my father had had apparently no more curiosity about his origins than I.

The only definite information he could give me, in fact, was that his people were originally from North Carolina, his mother was a Davis, and his grandfather was the first Baptist circuit rider west of the Alleghanies. This preacher grandfather of mine, he said, was a man of learning, courage and piety, who traveled on horseback, combining the roles of evangelist, educator and physician. He would go from settlement to settlement, remaining for a brief time in one community, ministrating to the sick with his homeopathic medicines, establishing reading and spelling classes in districts where there were no schools, instructing and exhorting the faithful in the Baptist version of the religion of the New Testament, and baptizing by total immersion in the warm or icy waters of creeks and muddy rivers the converts drawn to him among the Indians and the "heathen" settlers.

My father never knew or saw his father; for while my father was being born in Henry County, Tennessee, his mother and those attending her could hear the boom of the cannon in the attack upon Fort Donelson, and my grandfather was already in the gray uniform of the Confederacy in which, presumably, he died. He was reported to have been taken prisoner and to have succumbed to the horrible conditions of the Federal prison and to have died in action at the battle of Shiloh, and there may be truth in either of these reports, for those on both sides who fought at Shiloh were veterans of the battle of Fort Donelson; and because he joined the Confederate army near by, his baptism of fire probably was at Fort Donelson.

My grandfather Rascoe was a private infantryman who never achieved higher rank. It was, therefore, one of my father's jests that his father until his death must have been the only common soldier in the Confederate army, since, at annual reunions, all the veterans of the War between the States, for as long as he could remember, had been captains, majors or colonels. My grandfather on my father's side never came back from the war, nor did my grandfather on my mother's side who fought in the Union army with his father and his son.

But my grandmother Rascoe believed that her husband came back to her, not in the flesh but in the spirit, and indeed at the very moment his spirit left his body.

She used to tell me, when I was a child, the whole circumstances of this visitation. She was standing on the front porch of the farmhouse he had built, and which he had left in a prosperous and happy state, when she spied her husband trudging down the country road toward the house in a ragged and blood-spattered uniform. She ran forward to the front gate to greet him, and he spoke to her wearily, saying, "I am wounded unto death." She embraced him and he was gone.

As my grandmother grew old in years—she lived an incredibly active life to the age of eighty-two—she declined to retell or to elaborate upon this incident, and for reasons which enshrouded the incident in a deeper mystery to me then and to me now. For she would say to me in her late seventies, "I have given all that up."

I had heard from my mother and from my aunts, but never from my father, strange stories of Grandmother Rascoe's "psychic" demonstrations in her younger years. They told me that they had seen her lift a heavy dining-room table five feet off the floor simply by touching her fingers to the top of it, and that in darkened rooms she had caused recognizable faces and voices of the departed to appear. There were other curious reports of my grandmother's abilities, varying in nature and in incredibility according to whether the testatrix liked or disliked my grandmother. Those who disliked her, including my mother, said it was known that in her girlhood or young womanhood my grandmother had made a pact with the devil, and that this was the reason why she "gave up," when she grew old, the uncanny abilities the devil had granted her, in what they considered a vain and too long delayed effort to save her soul from hell. We must not take too much stock in this matter of a "pact."

Whatever may have been the truth of the matter, my grandmother was distinguished from her sisters and her daughters by her complete lack of their somewhat excessive Baptist religiosity and pious zeal. Not even in the years when she was supposed to have given up her commerce with the devil and to be preparing herself for a blissful future life was she known to enter the church wherein her sisters and her daughters and even daughters-in-law interested themselves in an active and highly vocal manner.

My grandmother's conversation with, and admonitions to, me were never prefaced by, or attended with, those proverbs from, or references to, the Bible, which were so much the parts of speech of her sisters. She never talked religion to me or set me upon a way of life, except by the most rationalist and common-sense of advice. She was, I suspect, like my father, neither religious nor irreligious, but broadly tolerant to all groups and beliefs, for I never heard her saying anything impious or blasphemous, or anything to show that she was affected by, or that she took part in, those seething prejudices which animated the warring sects of Protestantism in the South. She did, however, dip snuff. There is no warrant in the Bible for that, so it was a pampering of the flesh not indulged in by her sisters and frowned upon by them, visibly.

That conflict between the Protestant sects in the South is the more incongruous in that it is heatedly internecine and yet solidly united against Catholicism and Judaism. My grandmother, for instance, would never have been guilty of the unconscious non sequitur of the words of her sister to me once when she said, concerning a young man who boarded at her house, "He is a Catholic, but a good Christian boy just the same."

My grandmother was literate and well read in the classics and in the books current before the Civil War, and it is some measure of the devastation and blight of war that my father had only four weeks of schooling, had to be taught by my mother, after he was married, to spell and read and figure, and that to the end of his days he never read a dozen books through from first page to last.

For, as you will see presently, my father had the most agile, alert, logical and vocally articulate brain I ever watched function—the sort of brain which caused him to be elected three times to a judgeship, which he did not want, by the almost unanimous vote of the community and in defiance of the law he was called upon to dispense. The law of the state wherein he presided expressly forbade a justice to take or hold office unless he had been admitted to the bar. My father never opened a lawbook in his life, but he was elected and kept in office by the demand of a community which held him to be a wise and just man. Under the law no decision he ever made had any legal validity, but there was no case during his term in office wherein the legality of his status was questioned (though every lawyer who came before him knew the situation), nor was there any incident wherefrom his judgment was appealed.

I have often wondered how my grandmother, left at home on a remote farm with three small boys and three young girls to take care of, managed to survive when her husband did not return from the war. I have wondered what resources she had to sustain her. There was produce from the farm, of course, but there was no one except herself to sow and reap the harvest, to slaughter the hogs and do the other manual labor reserved for men on a farm. Besides this, she was subjected to the constant pillage of the guerrillas who carried on their ghoulish enterprises while the menfolk of the farms were away to the war. Only women, old men and very young boys were left at home. The guerrillas, or border bandits belonging to neither of the contending armies, prowled the countryside in armed bands, taking by force or intimidation cattle, provisions, silverware, implements and exchangeable goods away from the defenseless. They stripped farms as tent caterpillars strip sapling cherry trees.

Those years of, and immediately following, the war must have been for my grandmothers, whose men fought on opposite sides, years of great misery which taxed their resources to the utmost. I think of this often and reproach myself for my minor frets at the hazards, handicaps and disappointments of the comparatively easy, even luxurious and indolent, life I have known. Thoughts of these grandmothers shame me.

My father's two older brothers, aged eight and ten, remained at home to help my grandmother with the farm, but at the age of seven, after only a few weeks of schooling, my father was "bound out"—that is, he was inducted into a form of slavery as terrible as any that existed before the Emancipation. He was required to arise at three in the morning, do chores about the house until sunup and work in the fields until long after sundown. His pay was his keep and, unlike an apprentice in a trade, no pledge was given him that he would ever acquire any sort of a partnership in the work he learned to do or even that he would be paid at any time in cash for his labors. His rations were not those of the family but those of other "bound" boys, quartered in shacks formerly occupied by Negro slaves. The diet mainly was of salt pork, corn bread, molasses and such vegetables as the boys were allowed to forage for themselves.

The boys were never given butter to eat or milk to drink. Milk and butter were articles marketable in town for cash. The surplus beyond the immediate family needs was, therefore, conserved for this use. I learned of this once when I asked my father to explain to me why he could never eat creamed things or meats fried in butter, and never ate butter or drank milk. He told me the story. Having been deprived of milk and butter after leaving his mother's home, he came to want them greatly. It was a greedy obsession with him. His idea of luxury was to eat as much butter and drink as much milk as he wanted. Then one day this privilege was open to him. At a Baptist camp meeting, a religious affair at which farmers of a whole section would gather and camp for a week to hear an itinerant evangelist, he ate a great quantity of butter and further filled his stomach with milk. It was an extremely hot day, and he was violently ill from his indulgence. He was never able to eat butter or drink milk after that or to bear the taste of either in cooking.

Those camp meetings, which ordinarily lasted a week, were about the only forms of entertainment or recreation "bound" boys like my father were permitted to enjoy, at least during the sowing and harvesting seasons. In the winter, of course, there were corn huskings and occasional social gatherings called candy pulls. The central features of these events were the making and pulling of molasses candy and the making of popcorn balls with molasses.

My father told me that while he was a "bound" boy he *nearly* saw a circus once. The man for whom he worked told him and another boy one spring that if they worked hard all season he would give them fifty cents apiece to go into Paris to see the circus when it came in the summer. He explained to the boys what a circus was like, and in anticipation of the strange animals and other wonders unfolded to them they worked with ferocious activity until the day came when the two of them were to mount, bareback, an old riding mare and ride eleven miles into town.

In those days circus posters were not spread through the country-side but were confined to billboards around the city square. The boys had never seen these posters and, indeed, had been taken into town on only one or two occasions. They hitched their mare to one of the public hitching posts of the town and started in search of the circus.

They were confronted, as they reached the city square, by a

marvelous sight. In dazzling colors there were pictures of giraffes, elephants, rhinoceroses and zebras, and pictures also of beautiful men and women in ballet costumes and tights performing wonders of equilibrium on trapezes and high, tight wires. The boys gaped at these in an ecstasy of admiration and delight, reluctant to move from one to another to see them all. Since there was almost a square block of these billposters, they were a very long time in absorbing and enjoying them. When they came at last to the very end of these delights and there were no new posters to be seen, the boy who was with my father turned to him and asked, "Who do we pay?"

A tall Negro standing by, who had been watching them, said, "Pay me, boys." Each handed over his fifty-cent piece; they went to their horse, mounted it, and rode home happily, recounting and reliving every detail of their adventure. It was not until five years after that, my father told me, that he learned that he had never seen a circus. He had always believed he had.

At sixteen my father ran away from the farm on which he was bound and hired himself out for pay as a hand on a farm in Fulton County, Kentucky, across the state line and perhaps forty miles from the farm on which he had been indentured. By that time he was already not only a skilled farmhand but an expert dresser of hogs, maker of sausage, cook, carpenter, blacksmith, teamster and horse groom. He also knew the ways of the woods and streams.

It was while working on this latter farm that my father met my mother at a church social in a country meeting house. They fell in love that day. My mother, Bettie Burton, was a town girl, living in Fulton, and on that occasion was merely visiting with her mother on a large farm which her father owned but rented on shares, or for which he had an overseer; I can't remember which.

When my mother returned to town, my infatuated father followed her. His first job was that of a hostler and driver in my grandfather Burton's vast livery barn where he kept horses and carriages for hire and stabled and groomed horses belonging to people who did not have stables of their own or did not want to take care of their horses themselves. The livery stable was only one of my grandfather Burton's many enterprises, and it was in charge of his eldest son. There were living quarters in the stable for the hired help, and so this was my father's home for some time while he was adapting himself to the ways of town fellows.

My grandfather Burton was very strict with his daughters; in fact, an irascible tyrant concerning them and all of his possessions. Moreover, he was not at all free of class consciousness and the petty feelings of caste, but rather was bound by them. My mother knew that she would not be permitted to keep company with a hired man like my father. Nor, indeed, would she be permitted to keep company with him even if his station in life were considerably higher than it was. Grandfather Burton demanded to approve of the suitors of his daughters, and his approval involved matters not only of income and property but of family.

Therefore, for a very long time even the fact that my mother and father were acquainted with one another any more than a servant and mistress are acquainted was kept by them a secret. The horse she rode sidesaddle was kept in the big barn, of course, and you can be sure that this horse did not suffer from lack of care. The family carriages were also kept in the barn. My mother developed a mad passion for horsemanship and a rapt concern for the polish of the carriages and the condition of the harness. And, although her home was on a hilltop not more than five hundred yards away from the stables, the two lovers corresponded.

The elaborate device evolved by them for this communication is an example of the sweets of secrecy where love is concerned, and of the happy foolishness which lovers indulge in; for to post and receive these letters they each had to go about two miles to where they had a confederate, in on their secret, who was post office for them. They could have avoided delays by using Uncle Cabbage, my grandfather's Negro manservant, or one of the Negro houseboys as message bearers: the boys would have enjoyed doing this for the lovers. But simplicity, expedition and efficiency have no value where love is concerned.

In time, of course, the secret became an open one, as most secrets unfortunately do, and at last it reached the ears of my grandfather Burton. There was an explosion.

I can imagine what it was like, for I remember my grandfather all too distinctly, and that memory of him, carried from the age of four, when he flung a quarter across the room at me and told me to get out of his house (the brat of "Fate" Rascoe* was not allowed in his house, although I did not know this), is full of distaste. He was a medium-height, muscular, well-knit man, without an ounce of fat, with a face all in sharp planes, square-jawed, square-foreheaded, grim-visaged, with bushy eyebrows and fierce black mustachios.

He had been a very young officer, reaching a majority, in the Union army during the Civil War; his father, who had also served as an officer in the war with Mexico, and his grandfather had been killed in that war, his father in action and his grandfather, a feeble old man, brutally shot down, while he fed his hogs, by drunken guerrillas. He had been unusually successful as a farmer, a trader, a cattleman and a speculator, and had acquired and lost wealth, and won wealth again, as wealth went in that region, with such concentration of energy that it had taken great toll upon his nerves, his temper and his sentiment.

He was a lonely and pathetic man when he treated me so badly as a child, but only years have enabled me to understand this. I hated him then with that puzzled dread which is the nearest akin to hate a child can have, and when, four years later, he died and I was at last admitted, along with my mother and father, into the big house to view his remains and listen to the dreary sermon about his virtues, I could feel no sentiment except one of relief, and, because I thought I was called upon to exhibit a grief I did not feel, I rubbed my knuckles into my eyes until they burned with pain and reddened; and I was even shameless enough to squeeze onion juice to streak my cheeks with tears.

*My father's full name was Matthew Marquis de Lafayette Rascoe. His mother must have had an admiration for the gallant Frenchman who so helped the American colonies in their revolt against English rule. But she could only have known about him from books or hearsay. My father, until I told him, had only a vague notion about his namesake. People always called him "Fate" for short, except my mother, who always called him "Mr Rascoe," pronouncing it "Mistroskoe." She never spoke about him or addressed him in any other way; but that is a common thing among women of the older generation in the South. It was a sign of respect women had in return for the tradition which put women on a pedestal.

CHAPTER II

Father and Mother

Four Funerals. My Father and Mother Elope Melodramatically, despite Grandfather Burton. My Father a Kindly Bismarck in His Last Years. A Picture of My Mother.

I WAS NINE when my grandfather Burton died. Although I recall the funeral vividly and the family reunion it occasioned, I do not recall my grandfather as pleasantly as those older than I recall him, because I so rarely saw him, and seeing him was accompanied by fear and dread. The funeral was on a cold and rainy day in early spring. Many carriages followed the black hearse, drawn by white horses, on the long procession four miles to the cemetery.

On the Burton lot George Wade Burton's sons and daughters, close relatives and Uncle Cabbage stood in the drizzling rain while the words of the final prayer were said, the coffin was lowered into the grave, the muddy earth was filled in to make a mound, the rain-soaked flowers were piled upon it in abundance.

At this funeral my mother's youngest brother caught a cold, developed pneumonia rapidly, and just one week later to a day his body was buried alongside that of his father. Within a month my grandmother Burton, broken by grief, had taken her place beside her husband in the shadow of the tall stone obelisk, set on an oblong base of dappled marble, on which were marked their names, the years of their births and the years of their deaths.

Not very long after that Uncle Cabbage died also, and the funeral for him was attended by more people than was either of the other three funerals. All of the remote relatives, as well as the immediate sons, daughters, and in-laws of my grandfather, and all the children attended this funeral. Negro friends of Uncle Cabbage and their children from Nigger Town filled not only all the carriages from my grandfather's stables but most of the other carriages available in the town also.

I do not know whether Uncle Cabbage had a full name or not. He had been my great-grandfather's slave and, although given his freedom along with others before the Emancipation, he, because he was a house servant, remained in my great-grandfather's house and joined the Union forces as orderly to my grandfather. He lost his left arm from a shell wound in battle, but this did not incapacitate him for the chores he was called upon to do when he and my grandfather returned to civil life. He had been born into the Burton family some ten years before my grandfather was born into it, and he had remained in it during the last nine years of his life largely as nursemaid to the Burton grandchildren. He took care of me as a baby when my mother and father would go away to Memphis or Louisville, and he took care of my cousins, as they came along, in the same capacity, living sometimes in the servant houses in the rear of our houses but having his home really, and his duties, in the big house. His duties there were largely confined to making mint juleps for my grandfather.

I know little about my grandfather Burton except that his people came from Virginia somewhere around Lynchburg, that he served in the Civil War, that he married a Bellew, that he had five sons and one adopted son and three daughters, that he made and lost several fortunes, being worth at one time about half a million dollars, and that he died from overstrain not long after he had paid back all of his creditors following the panic of 1897, in which time of panic he refused to take advantage of the bankruptcy laws. His enterprises were numerous, but his main one was that of buying beeves, hogs and sheep on the hoof, and selling them in carload lots in the stockyards of East St. Louis, Chicago and Louisville. He also bought and sold grain and other produce and gambled in futures in corn, wheat, tobacco and cotton on the New Orleans and Louisville exchanges. On his large farm the principal selling crop was tobacco, which, cured in large barns, his tenants sold in the local Fulton market. He had smokehouses, too, for the curing of hams and bacon, from the hogs he raised.

From the time of my mother's marriage until his death my grandfather did not speak to my mother or my father. As soon as my grandfather learned of the love affair of my father and mother, his first step to break it up was to strike at my father economically by discharging him. His second was to send my mother away to visit relatives. My father got a job as short-order cook and day manager in a restaurant alongside division headquarters of a railroad. The restaurant was something like a modern Tierney diner. One of his regular customers was a young man, S. P. Freeling, who was working as a brakeman on the Illinois Central, educating his sister in music abroad and saving his money for a course in law at Harvard University. Twenty years later he was attorney general of Oklahoma.

The more my grandfather tried to separate my father and mother, the more determined were they to get together. They eloped in good old melodramatic fashion. My mother was a devoted reader of the novels of Mrs Southworth, E. P. Roe, Charles Major, G. W. Cable and other romantic writers of the period, and it was probably her suggestion for the plans they carried out. She sneaked out of the house with the connivance of the servants; my father had a carriage, hitched to a fast trotting mare, waiting, and they raced (though there was no one trying to catch them) a few miles across the state line where there was a preacher, a license certificate and a few witnesses ready for their marriage.

If my mother believed that my grandfather merely had a gruff exterior and that beneath it he had a heart of soft gold, she had many years to reflect upon her error. If she expected, when she sent word to him that she was married, a message from him asking her to return, all was forgiven, she got a surprise when notified that she was never to set foot in his house again or even to attempt to speak to him if she encountered him on the street. He deeded a small house and lot to her from among some property he owned, across the street from the houses he had deeded, one to his eldest married son and one to his married daughter. Then he revised his will, leaving her out of it. Thus he was done with his favorite child.

My father was twenty-five and my mother was eighteen. He was six feet tall, straight as an arrow, quick in his movements, full of nervous energy, given much to pleasant laughter, alternately lighthearted and grave. He had a high broad forehead, surmounted with a stiff pompadour of coal-black hair, a black mustache, white even teeth, a chin more rounded than square, a long neck, an oval head which looked smaller than it was on account of his height, and eyes of clear deep blue, never speckled or dimmed before his death at the age of seventy. In his last years he bore a remarkable resemblance to Bismarck, although more kindly disposed in appearance.

He always remained at about the same weight, never gaining flesh. He looked thin, but this thinness was deceptive; his muscles were like finely cured leather, extremely pliable but also extremely strong. At the age of sixty he could do more work in the fields, cotton picking, pitching hay, plowing, or cutting sugar cane, than any of his younger hired hands, including Negroes. When my brother George returned from a vacation after two years at West Point, he tried to demonstrate to my father one day not only what soldiering and calisthenics had done for him but also what his wrestling instructor had taught him. He and my father were of a size and weight. My brother tried some tricks of wrestling which only made my father laugh at him. After breaking all my brother's holds, he finally got tired of the play, said, "This is the way to rassle," and threw my brother so hard and so quick that it knocked the wind out of him and mildly crippled him for about a week.

In his youth and young manhood my father chewed tobacco and smoked cigars. He never smoked cigarettes, which he always referred to as "coffin nails," and until the day of his death he had a violent moral antipathy toward them. Reading "dime" novels (which really cost a nickel) and smoking cigarettes were the only vices he warned me against and expressly forbade me.

I do not remember ever having seen my father use tobacco in any form, for, as I learned after I had grown up, he had taken the "cure" for the tobacco habit in the early years of his married life, having spent some weeks in Hot Springs, Arkansas, taking the baths and drinking the waters to remove the traces of his indulgence. After that he gave up tobacco entirely, with never a relapse.

This has always struck me as being curious, for he never troubled to take the "cure" for alcohol, in which he indulged mildly, and sometimes overindulged, throughout his life. Why he and my mother should have considered tobacco more deleterious to his health or morally more reprehensible than alcoholic drinks, I do not know, unless it was that the members of the No-Tobacco and the Anti-Cigarette leagues were more active, vocal and inflammatory at that period than were the crusaders for prohibition. It is certain that those who crusaded against tobacco had so effectively pictured the horrors, disintegration and death caused by the use of tobacco that my father never escaped the superstitions, whereas he was never disturbed by the effects of alcohol upon his own system or that of anyone else.

To check up on my memory of my mother as she was when I was a child, I have just been looking at some photographs of her taken shortly before her marriage. There she stands, in one of them, with her sister, Janie, both looking self-conscious, stiff and coiffed to absolute perfection. There is a gate (which has no yard attached to it) between them, and their poses are taken against a property hedge and a backdrop of canvas, on which is painted a not very realistic sylvan scene. They are in costumes which, I think, they would never have worn on an outing in the woods.

Mother there is strong-looking, not buxom, five feet seven perhaps, and I should say about 135 pounds in weight, but the leg-o'-mutton sleeves, the bustle and the vast accumulation of underthings and crisp taffeta of her overthings gave her a rather solid appearance. She is not what you might call pretty in that picture, though my father, at the time, would probably dispute me on that point. She has, rather, character—almost too much of it. There is the "Burton frown" on her countenance, prominently. I am cursed with it, and so are my brothers, and, most unfortunately, my daughter has it also. All of the Burtons whose pictures I have seen have it. It gives us a look of being continually in pain, even when we are happiest. It is represented by two deep ridges between the eyebrows, which are visible even when our eyebrows are not the least bit knitted.

It is curious, but I do not know my mother of that picture. She must have remained pretty much like that for a long time after I was born. I remember her as she looks in the family-reunion picture, taken on the occasion of the funeral of my grandfather. She looks almost exactly like that now. Even though I have grown gray around the temples, her hair is still that auburn-tinted brown I have always known.

Even now she laughs nervously and with difficulty, as if to laugh were an indiscretion, to be checked by quick remembrance of the seriousness of life. Duty, obligation, subjection of self to the comfort, security and happiness of others have been my mother's vices. And, like all vices, they have rendered accounts fiscally and in sum total to date. If she has ever been happy I have known perhaps not more than a dozen instances in which she has visibly expressed happiness. And she has always cried on those occasions, weeping and smiling at the same time.

What goes on in her head, of course, I don't know, and I have never known. It has always been a puzzle to me. Her favorite axiom is, "Actions speak louder than words." I have never known anybody to act more thoroughly in accordance with an axiom than she does. Never, so long as I can remember, has she ever complimented me, praised me or even said that something I had done was even "pretty good." The most she has been able to grant to me in the way of expressing approval for anything I have ever done is an "Umn," uttered rather resignedly but with a pained air of mitigated approval, accompanied by a sudden flash of her eyes which changes so suddenly to one with a preoccupation with other things that I treasure it only as one treasures the sight of a shooting star.

For many years I was vain enough to send her pieces I had written for the newspapers and magazines. I did this to impress her with the notion that I was getting on in the world and that she had reason to be proud of me. However she may have felt about it, I got no encouragement from her to continue the course I was pursuing. I never even got an acknowledgment of the clippings or books I had written, which I had sent her. When I was on the New York *Tribune* (later the *Herald Tribune*) I put her on the mailing list to receive the book section which I edited and for which I wrote.

The only indication I ever had from her that she read it was a letter asking me to discontinue sending it to her. In "The Bookman's Daybook" I had recorded in all innocence and honesty that I had driven to Boston in an automobile with a young woman, the wife of a friend of mine and both of them friends of my wife; that the car had broken down and we had had to camp on the roadside until a truck came by in the morning. I should have thought that common sense would have told anyone that if I had anything on my conscience about that trip I should have been discreet enough not to record it in my printed diary. But my mother did not reason that way: what I had done was so offensive to her sense of the rightness of things that she did not wish to read any more public accounts of my doings. What is more, she didn't want to have the newspaper section to which I contributed around as a temptation to learn of such goings on. When I asked her permission to dedicate *Prometheans* to her I was actually fearful that she would refuse me on the grounds that she could not sanction the views expressed in that book. For some strange reason she read *Jurgen* over and over again. She must have read it more times than I have. And yet she reads it (apparently) only to censure me for being the dedicatee of such a book.

I am less in favor with my mother than either of my two brothers; and this is because I have been least dependent upon her. The one of us who will let her do the most for him—washing, ironing, cooking, mending, waiting on, advancing money to, doing favors for, getting out of trouble or making life indolent and dependent upon her—that one she is most devoted to. I began to earn my own living at thirteen, and at fourteen I began to support myself, living in quarters away from home. It annoyed me that she wanted to wash out shirts for me when I could get them laundered by the Chinese laundryman for three cents apiece; it did not seem right to me that she, with all the other work she had to do, should attend me like a valet to an invalid or an especially irresponsible cretin. Moreover, I did not like the conflict of her being automatically opposed to any idea I expressed if she had not implanted the idea in my head in the first place. I breathed easier away from her.

And so, I think, did she. But she was, and is, one constituted to serve, to make rather a martyrdom of serving, those closest to her. When one declines to be served, the outward manifestations of her devotion become invisible. And yet I do not think that she loves me less than either of my brothers. Certain I am that materially, in gifts and favors, she makes no distinctions among us. Rather, indeed, it has been my earnest counsel (now that I am older and can speak with the air of a man of prudence and experience and not as a child even to my mother) that she should cease impoverishing herself by material gifts to us and cease to worry about the welfare of three sons, all of whom have at no time neglected their own selfish interests to make things easier for her.

CHAPTER III

Childhood in Fulton, Kentucky

Dulcie Murphy. My Teacher Breaks My Heart. I Finance the Purchase of an Elaborate Valentine—and Give up Women. Buffalo Bill's Wild West Show. I Enter Carr's Institute at Six. My Father a Good Cook and Entrepreneur of a Barbecue and a Magic Show. Smokehouses in Fulton. A Horseless Carriage Whizzes through Fulton. My Father Builds a Trapeze for Me.

Fulton is in the southwestern part of Kentucky, on the Tennessee line. Part of the town, indeed, sprawls over into the adjoining state; hence there are two separate governments for a town tiny in size, and it is a convient matter for those of the criminal or misdemeanor cast of mind to set up difficult legal barriers against their apprehension simply by walking from one side to the other of an invisible but well-established border line.

According to the latest census, only one hundred people live on the Tennessee side. There were certainly more than that when I was a boy: I must have had half that many relatives living south of State Line Street. My uncle George Creedle's coal and lumber yard was over there, and the love of my life when I was six and seven years old, Dulcie Murphy, lived on the south side of the highway dividing the town.

In Dulcie's yard there was a red-haw tree. I used to carry her books home from school. She was too delicate to be weighted down with such a burden. In fact, there were pale and skinny lads lugging home primers, spelling books, geographies, slates and tablets for husky damsels twice their weight and strength because some forms of chivalry still pervaded in the South, making happy monkeys out of all of us males.

Dulcie was imperious for a child of six. She could command without saying anything. She caused me to shin up the red-haw tree and pull down berries for her without asking me to, and then when she had got them she would thank me with her eyes in such a manner—I can't describe it—that I would wish I could shin up a hickory tree and pull her down pomegranates just to see that approving flash in the eyes. It said, "You'll do." That was all it said. But I would run home, lickety-split, slowing down as I passed through the business section of the town, and, on reaching home, I would saddle my pony, ride out to Dick Thomas' field, drive home the milk cow and wonder if Dulcie really loved me as much as I loved her.

She had an oval face, black eyebrows, full lips always slightly apart, as if she were vaguely annoyed not only with me and her teacher and the rest of the pupils but with the whole unprepossessing mess she, at the age of six, had got herself into.

Dear Dulcie, wherever you are now, I wonder if you know how much you fixed yourself in my childish mind. There was a rivalry between you and Lillian Fields, and it was not a rivalry between you for me or for Lancy Savage or for Bert Cecil or Giltner Prestwood, but simply a rivalry between you and Lillian. Lillian died, didn't she, when she was a very young bride, of tuberculosis? And it was probably that unknowable fierce fear in Lancy and me that she might perish that we (Lancy and I) should have had that keen rivalry for Lillian's favor.

You were sweet, Dulcie. Your parents did not misname you; for Dulcie is from the Latin, meaning "sweet." There must have been a lover of the classics in your family. But you found school lessons a bore. In spelling classes we stood in line. The one who had worked himself to the head of the class took his position at the end of the class and worked himself up again. I rarely got to the head of the class, and here is the reason: I would be asked to spell a word. You would be next to me. I would whisper to you, without moving my lips, the correct spelling, and then I would purposely misspell it myself. You would spell it correctly and pass ahead of me. On the formation of the line I would always step back and urge you in ahead of me. You could not get to the top because there were individualists ahead of you who were not in love with you. They did not care what became of you. I did. I always wanted you to be just slightly ahead of me.

You were, because I saw to it that you were. But it cost me a summer's vacation. Miss Nichols, our third-grade teacher, who looked almost exactly like you, except that she was about seventeen years older, had to drill me and grade me in the courses in spelling I had flunked in order that you might get ahead. I fell just as violently in love with Miss Nichols as I had been with you. I pretended I couldn't spell, so I could keep going to her house for lessons; and the kinder she was to me, the unhappier I became. And she was extremely kind. She made fudge for me when I came for my lessons, and on very hot days she would serve lemonade or she would make ice cream in her hand-turned freezer. Lessons with her were a joy—a joy so great I could not endure it without my heart filling with sadness. Her house was a square, dumpy frame structure, set on large square pegs. I took lessons from her in the kitchen, across an oilcloth-covered table. In my knee pants and wide-collared shirt I would hurry home to bury myself in the hayloft and cry because I loved Miss Nichols.

That same summer Miss Nichols broke my heart. She destroyed an illusion for me. I did not know it was an illusion, so I was angered as well as hurt: I was not philosophical about it. It happened at a street fair and carnival. I was riding a horse on a merry-go-round. Miss Nichols got into a gondola just in front of me with a tall and very old man. He must have been at least twenty-five. She hadn't noticed me. She had seemed to be all wrapped up in this fellow and to find him very entertaining. I wondered if he could "skin the cat" on the trapeze, as I could, or walk on his hands or turn cart wheels. I felt like getting off the horse and telling Miss Nichols to watch me while I turned cart wheels. But just at that moment my heart sank and misery went swimming around in my brain. The man put his arm around Miss Nichols, and there, where anybody could see, he kissed her. Only once, as I remember; but she laughed and shook her finger at him, looking up into his eyes—and allowed him to keep his arm around her.

That finished me with Miss Nichols. But I was not angry with

Miss Nichols, only angry and displeased with myself. It seemed unjust to me that I should be so little, so ineffectual. It dawned upon me that I could not set up as a rival of this man. He would probably marry her and take her away, or go to live in her house, and she would make ice cream and fudge for him, not for me; and he would take her for rides on merry-go-rounds. I feared and envied him, and, later, every time I saw him in the drugstore or on the street, blood rushed to my face, my heart pounded and my lips quivered in fear and resentment.

He was a clerk in a men's clothing store. I noticed that he did not have a horse or pony. At least I never saw him riding one. This gave me courage—the courage to be in his presence and not feel small and insignificant. I would curry and brush Prince, my pony, until he was a glossy brown, and bridling and saddling him I would ride up in front of the store with a flourish and make Prince rear up on his hind legs, then let him down into a fast gallop. I hoped my successful rival would be looking.

I don't know how it was I lost Dulcie; but I believe it was because her parents took her away in her third year at school and I did not see her again. Meanwhile the tender worship that Lancy Savage and I had toward Lillian Fields intensified. It intensified to such an extent that we ultimately had a fight on her account. We had come to an honorable arrangement about Lillian. It was to be a fair competition. We would each ask to carry her books home on alternate days. Both of us were afraid of Lillian's father. Just why, I don't know, except that we thought he might resent and punish us for any designs we might have about stealing away his daughter. Neither of us ever carried Lillian's books all the way home. We would carry them within sight of her house or to a spot where we might be visible from her front yard or porch, hand over the books and walk negligently or briskly, as the occasion seemed to demand, in a direction which would not lead us past her house. Clandestine we were.

On an Eve of St Valentine's I saw in Cohn's general store, on the notion counter, an elaborate valentine in pink celluloid. It was star-shaped, in a box a foot square. Every other prong of the star was folded in and caught with pink ribbon. In the center was painted a dove, which carried in its mouth a riband reading, in magnificent penmanship, "To My Valentine." It was valued at a great deal of money. The price tag said "25¢." There were elegant ones at five and ten cents apiece. But this was something extraordinary. It stood out as the especially precious and costly heart offering it was.

How to get a quarter was a problem. A new catcher's mit, of soft leather padded and laced with leather thongs, had cost me only that much. When I was sent to the butcher's I got a sirloin steak large enough for the family and servants for fifteen cents, and dog bones and cat liver were thrown in. A new cap cost only fifteen cents. Yes, twenty-five cents was not an amount of money you could get simply by asking for it—especially so soon after having been bought a bicycle. It must be acquired by exchange of goods or services. It would take some time to find enough boys with a nickel apiece who would be in want of articles such as tops, boxes of tiger-eye agates and Belgian hares I might dispose of. I was being paid five cents a week to drive the milk cow home from the pasture, but most of this went for hokey-pokey ice cream at one cent a stick. The man came around in a horse-driven cart of which the side boards and the containers were covered with white oilcloth. For a headdress the horse wore a miniature bell tower, and with each step forward the horse nodded his head: this kept the bell tinkling constantly, because even when the horse stood still his head was in motion in a pathetic effort to combat the flies.

There were no chores about the house or barn which I could do that did not embrace the duties of Uncle Cabbage. The only thing I could do was to ask my father for the loan of twenty-five cents and ask him to pay himself back by giving me only five cents a week until the debt was discharged. That was the proposition I put up to him. He chuckled and handed over the quarter, saying, "Here you are, Horsefly."

(Why my father used "Horsefly" as a term of endearment, I do not know; he called me that as a child, and later he called my son that. He called the brother next to me "Hammerhead," and my younger brother whose name is Henry he called "Hen-rye," which he thought was the French pronunciation of Henri. My father had an infinite knowledge of homely things and of home-folk, but throughout his life he was unacquainted with the ways and affairs of the great world, even though he had attended both the World's Columbian Exposition and the World's Fair at St Louis. When my brother George was page in the Oklahoma legislature my father went up to Oklahoma City to visit him. Hoping to give my father a treat, my brother took him to a Chinese restaurant. After glancing at the bill of fare, my brother said he was going to have some chop suey and asked my father if he would have some. My father said, "Don't be a country boy all your life. That ain't a dish. That's the son-of-a-bitch's name. I seen it when I come in—Chop Suey Restaurant." My brother explained; but nevertheless my father ordered ham and eggs. . . . Years later, when my father was living in San Francisco, he and I motored down to Hollywood, and on our first evening there we called upon my aunt and cousin and took them to a restaurant famous for fried chicken. On our way back to the house we passed Sid Grauman's Chinese Theater. My cousin said there was a famous opening that night—it was the first showing of the first talkie musical comedy—and that all Hollywood would be there. He invited us to see the spectacle. My father, who hitherto had been cheerful and full of fun, suddenly took on the most woebegone expression. He said he was "awfully sick" and that he had to go home. We were all very solicitous, because it looked as though he would cave in any minute. He allowed himself to be fed bismuth and bicarbonate of soda, but said what he needed most was a toddy. He wanted hot water and sugar but said he would fix it himself. Into the water and sugar he poured half a tumbler of bourdon and told us to go along to the show; he would be all right. Next morning he seemed full of health. It was not until we were halfway back to San Francisco that I dragged the truth out of him. "I didn't want to hear a lot of gongs and chatter I don't understand," he said. I asked him where he expected to hear a lot of gongs and chatter he did not understand. He said, "At that show you went to last night." I told him it was a movie in English and that I didn't hear any gongs. "It said on the outside, 'Chinese Theater'; that's what it was, wasn't it?" I told him no, that was just Hollywood's idea of being tony when they put up a picture show house. Then it came out. My brother George had taken him to a Chinese drama, acted by Chinese in San Francisco, and it had bored my father. It had bored him so acutely that in mere remembrance of it and at the threat of having to undergo it again he had simulated a violent illness.)

With the twenty-five cents I purchased the valentine. It was so precious I was afraid to entrust it to the mails, and I should not have been able to mail it, anyhow, because parcel post had not been established at that time and postage would have cost me too much. I waited until about an hour after nightfall and went across town to Lillian's house. I stood outside until I was sure no one was approaching and that no one was on the porch or in the yard. I sneaked up to the front door, opened the screen, dropped the package inside and tiptoed away.

Next morning Lillian came up to me in the hallway at school, smiling sweetly and said, "Thank you very much for the lovely valentine. You *did* send it to me, didn't you?" I had not put my name on it, because I thought it should be obvious that I had sent it. Coyly I answered, "No. It wasn't me." I expected her to see through the fib and tease me into admission. This would prolong the ecstasy of pleasing her. That was my mistake. She took me to be a man of my word and, with her face slightly clouding, she said, "Then Lancy must have sent it." She waited for Lancy to come in, which he did presently. I waited, too. She asked Lancy if he had sent her a valentine. The damned little liar said yes.

There was nothing, in honor, I could do about this situation—at the moment. I went resolutely into the classroom, but all day long my thoughts were not on my books. After school was out I followed Lancy out of earshot of teachers and told him to put down his books because I was going to beat the stuffin' out of him. . . . I think it is on the records that in a manner of speaking I did. He was not keyed up for the fight as I was by a tigerish resentment which energized every resource of my body. We pummeled each other, tore each other's clothes, scratched, bit and kicked; and when finally I had Lancy down and was sitting on top of him he kept yelling, "Uncle! Uncle!" until I let him up. You had to let a boy up when he yelled "Uncle," because that signified he acknowledged defeat.

[30]

Shortly after that I gave up women. One usually begins to give up women at the age of eight and keeps on giving them up, off and on, to the age of eighty. As a usual thing your normally constituted male doesn't turn woman hater at the age of eight; that comes usually in the seventeenth year, when he also becomes cynical and world-weary; at eight he is just indifferent to women and considers them a nuisance. When you are going camping or playing Indian or when you get on a baseball nine, you can't have girls tagging around.

All thoughts of girls went entirely out of my mind and the tenderer sentiments forsook me after Buffalo Bill's Wild West Show came to town. The expert rifle shooting of Colonel Cody himself and of the bespangled Annie Oakley did not impress me because what they did—riding at full speed, they shattered tinsel balls with rifle fire as fast as they were thrown into the air—was not something I could imitate. I had a twenty-two rifle and I had a pony; but I did not have any tinsel balls to shoot at.

What did impress me and all my playmates was the cowboy and Cossack riding, where you hung away from the saddle, head down, with one leg around the saddle horn and the other caught in the stirrup under the horse's belly, and where you swung around from one side of the saddle to the other by going under the horse's throat, all while the horse was at full gallop. Giltner and Russell Prestwood both had ponies (their father ran a livery stable); Lancy had a pony, and I had one. We practised these stunts and got to be pretty good at it, after getting rather badly bunged up from falls.

In the Wild West Show the cattle thieves were caught with lassoes and dragged on their bellies around the tanbark. Learning to use the lasso is easy, and in no time we were catching anything and everybody in sight. Swinging the open loop around our heads, we would lasso calves, cows, horses, dogs, fence posts, Uncle Cabbage, nigger kids, girl cousins and callers, including the minister, indiscriminately. Cecil Johnson didn't have a pony, so he was the cattle thief. He put on a pair of padded football pants which hung down over his knees and stuffed a pillow under his sweater. One of us would lasso him, and with the end of the lasso tied to the saddle horn we would drag Cecil (who held onto the rope and tried to keep from rolling over on his side or back) around the barnyard or through the cockleburs and thistles of Dick Thomas' pasture.

The *pièce de résistance* of Buffalo Bill's Wild West Show was a realistic depiction of Custer's Last Fight. The preliminaries included the parade of the covered wagons before camp was pitched for the night. Then the Indian warriors with spears and bows and arrows, in feathers and war paint, raced around the enclosure, uttering bloodcurdling yells. Then the Indians had a war dance. Then they circled the little band headed by Custer, set fire to the covered wagons and the battle was on. The horses of Custer and his men lay down to be used as breastworks from which to shoot at the circling Indians. Braves, brought to bite the dust by Custer's fire, would pitch from their horses, mortally wounded, but not too mortally wounded to scurry back out of sight through the enclosure entrance. Custer's men would stagger and fall prone across their horses until Custer himself (played by Colonel Cody) was left alone—and when he was finally done for, the war whoops were terrific.

Adley Morris had a very docile, old, white, one-eyed mule. Adley could make him kneel on his forelegs like the circus horses; but what was more important, Adley could make him lie down to be used as a breastwork. So Adley was General Custer, and Dick Casey was his band of men. Giltner, Russell, Lancy, Cecil Johnson and I were the Indians. Cecil didn't have a pony, and he didn't have a bow and arrow, but he wanted to be an Indian, so he sat behind me on my pony's rump clutching the back of my saddle while we raced in a circle around Adley, Dick and the mule, yelling war whoops at the top of our lungs and shooting arrows at them, while they defended themselves with popguns and continual shouts of "Bang! Bang!"

One of Giltner's arrows went wild and hit my pony in the rump. Prince at once left the scene of battle and started for home as fast as he could gallop. He had never run away with me before, and I knew I would lose face with my father if he learned that I had not known how to handle him. We reached State Line Street, with Cecil holding onto me for dear life and with me drawing the reins as hard as I could and yelling, "Whoa, Prince! Whoa! Whoa!" Somebody was hauling a telephone pole which stuck out twenty feet or more from the rear of a wagon. The driver had come into State Line Street from a side road, and in order to turn had had to cross clear over to the other side of the road. The projecting telephone pole was therefore a hurdle. Prince cleared it with a foot or so to spare, bouncing Cecil up to my neck. I had been taught to try to turn a runaway horse out of the course he was adopting, and so, as we approached the small bridge across the creek at the fork of the highway, I pulled with all my might on the left rein, hoping to turn Prince out of his beeline home and start him up the hill by the Christian Church. He seemed to be going that way, and so I released the rein. He swerved so quickly to the right that he hurled Cecil against the rotting handrail across the bridge; the post gave way, and Cecil rolled down the bank into the creek. Meanwhile Prince raced through Lake Street, making people scurry to the sidewalk. He came to an abrupt stop at the gate. I dismounted, tied the reins, cut me a willow switch, remounted and, switching him furiously, I ran him out into the country until he was white with lather and breathing heavily.

He never ran away with me again; but my problem was to keep it a secret that he had run away with me the first time. At breakfast next morning my father asked me if I had been eating any green apples yesterday. I told him I hadn't. He said that was curious, because I had talked a lot in my sleep and had said something about Prince running away with me. I confessed that Prince had run away with me. So my father confessed that I had not talked in my sleep. Dr Marshall had seen Cecil flying through the air and had, indeed, fished him out of the creek and taken him home; the poor lad's side was badly bruised where he had collided with the handrail post.

"It is a shame and a disgrace," my mother said, "to have a wooden bridge across that creek right there on Lake Street. It ought to be concrete. And with a rotten handrail, too! Why, somebody is liable to fall in there."

"Cecil Johnson did," observed my father dryly, "yesterday."

I was a precocious child at six when I entered the first grade at Carr's Institute. That was the public school, a two-story brick building with ample playground around it, adjoining Carr's Park, a wooded bit of acreage donated to the town by the same public-spirited citizen who had given the town a school site and a school. I don't know anything about Mr Carr except that he had two sons, both lawyers, both graduates of Vanderbilt, and the younger of these two brothers, in the best-looking clothes I had ever seen anybody wear, addressed a graduating class in my second year. The Carrs lived in a brick mansion, with a back yard which swept all the way down to State Line Street. Everything about the place was pretty.

Going to Carr's Institute was a tremendous experience for me. It was away across the other side of town. I knew almost nobody in my class. My acquaintance had been limited to my cousins who lived on the same street. These girl cousins were like sisters, only worse. Claudice and I were in rivalry, and once she hurled a sprinkler at me while I was tightrope walking on the front banister. It hit me in the right forehead, and I was knocked down and out for hours. When I recovered I went over to her house and tramped down all the walls, furniture, dolls and appurtenances of a four-room doll house her father had bought her. Next to Dulcie, Lillian, Miss Nichols and a Cohn girl—who was simply too beautiful for me to entertain any ideas about—Claudice was about the loveliest thing I had laid eyes upon. And I hated her like poison.

Fulton was a division point on the Illinois Central and also on the Louisville & Nashville Railroad. That branch of the L. & N. has since been absorbed by the I. C. In my boyhood the crews of both lines were changed there; and the lay-overs, therefore, made the quick-lunch restaurant, the boarding house and the cheaper-class hotel businesses worth engaging in.

Being a division point also gave Fulton a certain metropolitan cast in other ways. It was a convenient stop-over town for barn-storming opera troupes and for traveling salesmen who peddled their wares in hired gigs along the countryside. Knight's Hotel arose as a dream against the demand of people who were used to the best in overnight accommodation. It was a brick structure, four stories high, with bathrooms attached to suites, an ornate dining room in red plush and gilt, a lobby approached from above in a spectacular spreading staircase, a bar paved in marble, a barber shop, and a sidewalk shaded by maples and bedecked with

chairs for the populace as well as for patrons of the hotel. A permanent fixture also was an aged blind Negro who sat on a bench
under the trees all day in spring and summer, reading aloud from
a Bible in Braille.

My father ran the bar of the hotel, and in time he was to graduate to the management of the hotel. He had shown that tolerance
for the weakness of other human beings, that ability to settle a
quarrel without recourse to force, that amiable indifference which
masks as good-fellowship that a bartender needs. He was also
not without those resources in duplicity which recommend themselves to employers.

In the South, for instance, one of the delicacies especially regarded by the working classes (as well as the leisured classes) is
scrambled brains and eggs. Hog brains are used, not calf brains.
Fresh hog brains. They are not always easy to come by. They
spoil quickly. One had to buy them at the slaughterhouse each
morning early, and not every day was a day for slaughtering hogs.
This fact is not borne in mind by the brakemen, firemen, engineers
and conductors who, along with baggagemen and freight handlers,
constituted the bulk of the morning's patronage in the short-order
restaurant over which my father presided. They wanted brains
and eggs every morning. Some intuition flashed into my father's
mind, one morning when he had an order for brains and eggs and
there were no brains in the icebox, that boiled oatmeal (the same
ordinarily used as a cereal) tasted, when properly salted and
peppered, very much like scrambled hogs' brains. He scrambled
his eggs, plopped in a saucerful of cooked oatmeal, mixed the
two hurriedly, browning the latter slightly, and dished it out. His
customer thought it was the best dish of brains and eggs he had
ever eaten and promptly ordered another. Thereafter my father
did not bother to go down to the slaughterhouse at five o'clock in
the morning to get a day's mess of hog brains.

There are, of course, cooks and cooks. My father was a cook. A
good cook seems not only to have a knack, inborn and unteach-
able, of making dishes tasty, but also, it would appear, of giving
something of themselves in the preparation of a dish which makes
all the difference in the world between fodder (or vitamins) and
good eating. Strindberg has a crazy play about servants which, I

am convinced after many experiences, is not as crazy as it reads or acts. The point in this play is that paid servants extract all the nourishment, all the taste out of the food they prepare, and so leave their employers and their children undernourished. A subtle hate, unconscious but none the less malignant, governs the preparation of their dishes for those they, at heart, despise for being their employers; and this hate takes out most of the food value as well as the savoriness of the food they prepare.

Those who look upon cooking as a repugnant duty (as most intransigeant wives do) can take all the savor out of the food they prepare, even when they are preparing it with an eye to making an impression. There is a metaphysical subtlety there which I am not prepared to elaborate upon. Nor am I prepared to answer any questions you may want to ask. I only know within my heart it is so.

Food, like a sonnet, must be concocted with a maximum of detachment. The impulse to prepare it must be there, and the divine sense that this, within its prescribed limitations, must be the best, or at least a peer, in its line. But food, like a sonnet, will not admit, without disastrous results, interruptions of an emotional nature.

My father could broil a steak—that seems simple enough—in a way that you would think you could broil it also. But try it. I have. My mother has. The results were not by any means as tasty as the way my father did it. I am not the only witness to what I am about to tell you: there are, still, perhaps hundreds who would bear me out.

Have you ever eaten barbecued mutton, beef, lamb or pig? My father, an entrepreneur, used to arrange social affairs centering upon the barbecuing of meats. The advertisement for them was simply, "Barbecue." There would follow, on the handbills, information as to the date and place. In Fulton the place was usually Carr's Park. The affair lasted a full week. It took place in the summer. From miles around the farmers gathered in, pitching tent, some of them, as well as the petit bourgeois of the town.

There were concessions at these barbecues. Concessionaires paid my father a small fee against the fee he had to pay for renting the park and for guaranteeing against all damage to the grounds and trees; and they set up lemonade stands, coffee stands, candy wheels, palmistry tents, magic-lantern shows, hokey-pokey ice cream stands, and merry-go-rounds.

My father always had two attractions of his own at these gatherings. He had a barbecue stand and a magic show in a tent. He was barker for this latter attraction also. He told the people out in front that inside the tent they would see a lady turned into stone for one dime, the tenth part of a dollar—"Satisfaction guaranteed! One of the Seven Wonders of the World! Something you can tell your grandchildren about! A beautiful lady turned into stone right before your very eyes, and brought back to blood-pulsing, happy, gay young life again! Satisfaction guaranteed! And if what you are called upon to pay your dime, one tenth part of a dollar, for is not as represented by me before you here, all you need to do is come back to the box office, state your grievance and get a bash on the beezer. Step right up, ladies and gents—no pushing, no shoving, no crowding. We are all ladies and gentlemen here, except for a few plug-uglies I see out there in front of me, including my old friend Jeff Wheeler out there, who hasn't washed below his chin since the day he was baptized—have you, Jeff? Now don't crowd; there's room for all; ten cents a ticket, a tenth part of a dollar. Step right up. The little lady at the ticket booth here is a right bit nervous, but she will hand you out the right change— or split the difference with me. Shin-plasters or Confederate money is not accepted here. The young lady won't take it. You must have ready for your tickets the genuine coin of the realm, ten cents, the tenth part of a dollar. Ready to go now; the show's about to begin."

Behind a complex arrangement of mirrors my mother and my aunt, or two other females, cousins or aunts (because they liked to do it), sat on stools and alternately lighted, gradually, or dimmed two kerosene lamps at their left and their right hands. The illusion produced was that a porcelain figure, not in the likeness of either of them, came to life, with the gradations of the reflections in the mirrors and then went back into porcelain again. It was the old Medusa trick.

As a child this did not interest me much, but the barbecue pits of my father did. The pits were six feet long, three feet wide and four feet deep. They were dug into the ground. Crossbars of iron were laid at four-inch intervals across them. A great fire was built of wood shavings and hickory wood before the dressed meat was laid on the crossbars. The fire was bellowed into flame until there was a deep bedding of wood ash glowing with red embers. A small flame was maintained, but not a scorching one. The meat was turned with a prong while it sizzled and crackled over the heat of the pit.

My father basted the meat constantly with a concoction of vinegar, salt and pepper, soaked into a muslin wad and attached to the end of a green hickory stick. When the meat was thoroughly done, it was sliced and served on slices of white bread. Other people with other pits tried to serve barbecue the same way, with bastings in vinegar as my father instructed them; but my father got most of the trade. They patronized the other barbecuers only when his meat gave out.

He also made a sausage I have been trying these twenty years, when fall comes around, to imitate. City folks, especially Northern city folks, don't know what sausage is. When you ask for it in the meat market, it is the cheapest meat you can get. That is because it is made up of waste cuttings of pork, beef and lamb, with a peppering of powdered sage. It isn't sausage, in the true sense, at all. I don't know what fried bathmats would be like, but I think it would be like the stuff Northern butcher shops sell for sausage.

For good sausage you need fresh pork from the late-fall killings, after the November frosts have set in. My father used the tenderloins, the shoulder meat, and what was left after hams, bacons, salt pork and spareribs were accounted for. He grew his own sage and his own red peppers, both parched crisp in the sun. Into the sausage grinder he fed sage, red pepper and salt; meantime he fed the pork. The knack of doing this so as to get the right flaxor, I never learned, studiously as I watched him doing it; but, even so, I can make better sausage than anybody else, Cudahy, Swift, Armour, Jones, or the Mennonites of Norfolk, Va., not excepted. I must add that you cannot make *very* good sausage with frozen or refrigerated pork. And the flavor of sausage is enriched by its being hung in the cold, open air, packed in corn husks or muslin bags until much of the fat's moisture has evaporated.

Smokehouses began to vanish from Fulton when I was about

eight years old. Hitherto nearly all of the middle-class homes had them, just as they had shacks for Negro servants in the back, barns, coal and wood sheds, and privies plangently announced with festoons of hollyhocks and sunflowers. The chemical curing of meats seemed to have come in at about the same time as the telephone and indoor plumbing.

We had a smokehouse on the property on which I was born, but not on the fancy place adjoining, which, when my father grew prosperous enough, he purchased from the family physician who had gained enough in years and savings to wish to retire and live with his married daughter in Louisville. When you had a smokehouse you raised your own hogs and cured your own meat. You had a vegetable garden and, besides radishes, onions, peppers, tomatoes, lettuce, beets, cabbage, beans, turnips, watermelons, cantaloupes, and muskmelons, you also grew sweet corn, to be served on the cob when young and fed to the hogs when it matured. You also had a cow and, as an accessory to her, a churn—so you could have butter and buttermilk. Usually you had two cows, because one of them had a biological habit of going dry at seasonal intervals.

You killed hogs when you were quite sure there would be no more warm weather; for you had no refrigerators, and your fat pork must not only be salted and packed against disintegration, but your hams, bacons and sausages must be cured with hickory smoke against invasion by midges and worms. You hung up these edibles, suspending them from rafters in the smokehouse. The flooring of the smokehouse was of native earth. You built a fire of hickory shavings and fed that fire (or rather your Negro handy man did) with chopped logs of hickory, never enough to have it burst violently into flame but enough to keep it smoldering. There was a small vent in the roof to draw the smoke upward and keep the fire from dying down altogether. But the door was kept closed, except for refuelling, to prevent drafts which would smite the embers into flame.

Somebody invented a chemical with which you could paint a fresh ham and keep it free from insects and thus cure it—not as well or as tastily, perhaps, as you could cure it by hickory smoke, but more rapidly. And speed was becoming a desideratum. I was sixteen years old before I ever saw an automobile, and that was after we had moved to Shawnee, Oklahoma; but when I was nine years old there was an exceedingly well-attested "fact" that one of those horseless carriages had whizzed through the streets of Fulton at two hundred and fifty miles an hour.

Across the street from our house there was a woman who had seen it. She was an extremely reliable person, not given to exaggeration. Her husband ran a gristmill. She was ordinarily taciturn and unsociable, and people weren't inclined to seek her opinion or testimony on many matters, but after she had seen that horseless carriage going lickety-split right through the very town and not caring a bit for life or limb, she had a large, insistent and credulous audience. Of which I was one. What, I asked, did it look like?

"That I can't tell you. I never seen the like in all my born days. I was leaning right out yonder over that thar picket fence and calling to Nell's baby, you know Nell, of course, she's my daughter and her baby's her baby, my grandson. Goodness gracious me, I don't have to explain all that to you, do I? You ain't much bigger than he is, if I do say it myself. Well, as I was telling you, I was leaning over that picket fence and calling to my grandchild, my daughter's baby, and it's a good thing I did it just at the time I did, or he might have been run over and killed right before my very eyes and never known what struck him, poor lamb. Wouldn't that have been awful? My only grandson, a mere baby, killed right before my very eyes! I don't think I could have stood it. Might as well take me while they are at it, and not a poor innocent baby like my grandchild. Well, as I was saying, I looked and there it was a-coming. And I looked and there it was gone. Like a ball of fire it was, chugging and spitting flame. They ought to be a law against them things, I say, scaring everybody and the horses and all and 'dangering life and limb."

Mrs Nealy thereby achieved sudden fame in the town. She was the first to see one of those horseless carriages which had been written about in the Louisville *Courier-Journal* and the *Saturday Blade and Chicago Ledger*. At least she was the first to let her imagination play over what she had read and give creative life to the vision of an automobile paying its respects to Fulton, Kentucky, by streaking through it like a bat out of hell. I remember it to my mother's credit that she did not claim to have seen this apparition, but put her faith in the veracity of Mrs Nealy and thereby took vicarious civic pride in the fact that she knew a woman who had seen one of those horseless carriages which had gone through the streets of Fulton so fast you couldn't tell whether it was coming or going.

But before we went tony by acquiring the big house next door, our place was small. We had no parlor. (We acquired a parlor when we moved into the adjoining house. A parlor was a place where you had all your best furniture, hermetically sealed against any trespass. Shutters were closed around it, admitting no light. A thick Brussels carpet, under which dry straw and paper crackled and slithered as you walked over it, covered the flooring. It had a musty smell, odoriferous of camphor balls and calla lilies. It was thrown open for marriages, deaths and family reunions. There were conch shells under glass in this room, and souvenirs from the World's Columbian Exposition.) We had no parlor. . . . We had, instead, a living room with a fireplace, a kitchen, a dining room, a room in which Mother and Father slept and a room in which I slept. Out back Uncle Cabbage had a mean shed, probably ten feet by six in dimension, with two windows, a door and a cot.

In that first place there was a barn, there was a horse, there were two cows, there was a vegetable garden, there was Uncle Cabbage's shack, there was a smokehouse, a grape arbor, a privy and our house. There was also, alongside the house, a possession which all the boys of my age envied me in the town. My father had taken me to a circus and had noticed my interest in the trapeze performers, an interest which had caused me to rig up, on the limb of an apple tree, my own trapeze. My father was indulgent. He purchased two telephone poles and had them set up in our yard. A good carpenter himself, he installed the crossbar connecting them and suspended from them, properly secured, twisted ropes. At the end of these he fastened iron rings, made at his direction by the local blacksmith, taped and padded them, and contrived a crossbar of steel to connect them and so form a trapeze. Thus I had both flying rings and a flying trapeze and, from falling upon my head into the soft sand my father had arranged for two feet beneath me, I learned some feats to astonish the other lads, in none of which could any of them excel me.

In summer we children went barefoot, of course. There was trouble in our house arising over differences of opinion between my mother and me as to when summer had officially begun. She was afraid of pneumonia—so afraid, indeed, that I used to go swimming with the other boys and carry my shoes and stockings two miles back from the swimming hole and put them on under the railroad culvert just before reaching home, so she would not have occasion to scold me.

When it was really permissible to go barefoot, however, another crisis developed between my mother and me. It was almost a nightly unpleasantness. There was a hydrant out in front, and I was supposed to wash my feet off before going to bed. Even when I did this I was not likely to do it to my mother's satisfaction. I would turn the water on. It would be cold. No matter how hot the day had been, I would shiver. I wouldn't bother to get my feet and legs clean—or even dry. I would hop into bed, streaking the sheets with mud. When the beds were made next morning I would hear of this.

CHAPTER IV

More Memories of Fulton

The Town Drunkard and a "Dope Fiend." Dick Thomas, the Dude. Camping Trips. Books in My Home. I Explore the Arctic. Norma Collins Reads to Me. Parson Weems's *Life of Washington* Makes Me Want to Cut Down a Cherry Tree. My Father Investigates Business Prospects in Oklahoma Territory. A Medley of Memories of Fulton. We Leave Fulton.

THE ADULTS OF THE TOWN I remember most vividly, aside from relatives and the Negro help, were Tom Loftis, the town drunkard; Dick Thomas, the town dude who owned a drugstore and a pasture in which our cows grazed and to which we boys went on camping excursions; Miss Hetty Collins, the prim and severe teacher of the fifth grade at school; Dr Marshall, our family doctor from whom my brother got his middle name; Mr Prestwood, who owned the opera house and gave Giltner, Russell and me gallery tickets to the road-company shows which played there; Henry Knight, who inherited Knight's Hotel; my mother's uncle John, whose farm we visited in summer; "Professor" Craig, the school principal; and a woman who had the reputation of being a "dope fiend."

The reason these people stand out in my memory, now that I think of it, is that they alone, among those with whom I came in contact, differed distinctly in personality from the other people in the town. My curiosity, of course, was aroused about the woman who was alleged to be a morphine addict because I heard her talked about so much by my mother and aunts. She was reported to be "dead to the world" most of the time. I used to go several blocks out of my way in order to pass her house and get a glimpse of her. She lived in a fine brick house with white pillars on the front porch. I saw her only once. She was a red-haired woman, pale and very pretty.

Tom Loftis looked like the conventional chromos of Enoch Arden, or like Joseph Jefferson in the last act of *Rip Van Winkle*. He had a long, scraggly gray beard and unkempt white hair. His clothes were torn, patched and nondescript. He never wore a coat or hat even in the coldest weather. His immunity from colds and infections was miraculous. When he was of a mind to he slept in the hayloft of my grandfather's livery barn, but he also slept in ditches, under culverts or wherever sleep overtook him, unmindful of and impervious to rain or sleet. My father told me that Tom had once gone to sleep in a ditch and next morning was found with his hair and beard frozen to the ground, so that it was necessary to cut him free with shears. But this did not harm Tom. He did no work of any kind. Nor was he molested. People liked to hear him sing, which he did at the top of his voice. He was gentle with children and would spend hours fashioning slingshots, bows and arrows and stilts for them without compensation, but he would work for no one except bartenders, for whom he would mop a floor or remove beer cases and kegs for drinks of whisky. He lived entirely on sandwiches people would bring to him and on whisky. He was supposed to be a black sheep of the Loftis mail-order diamond people of Chicago, but townsmen probably made that up.

Dick Thomas, the dude, wore fancy, embroidered waistcoats, high collars with loud ascot ties, tight-fitting jackets and striped trousers. He was always immaculate, his shoes highly polished, his clothes pressed and his hat set at a rakish angle. He was a bachelor of means and property, youngish and handsome; but, strangely enough, he dressed for himself, not to impress the young women. He was not a lady-killer. When he drove his surrey through the streets on a Sunday or holiday, his elderly, tiny, white-haired aunt, in black taffeta and white ruching, was beside him, not one of the town belles. We boys liked him and admired him not only because he was a splendid sight to see, with his fine clothes, horseshoe sparkler in his cravat, gold watch chain and pearl derby, but also because he permitted us to use his great enclosed pasture of several acres for any play use we wished to make of it, so long as we kept the gate closed after passing through it.

There was a stream of clear water through Dick Thomas' field which had a fine swimming hole, fifty feet wide and about five feet deep, at a bend under an oak tree. When we went camping, our mothers would provide for us a frying pan, a coffeepot, forks, Irish and sweet potatoes, slices of ham and bacon, sliced bread and jars of preserves. We ourselves sewed gunny sacks or flour sacks together for tents and took with us hatchets, ropes, matches and jackknives. We would pitch tent or cut down saplings and build lean-tos, with piles of leafed branches for thatch. Watermelons and cantaloupes were plentiful in Dick Thomas' field, and he allowed us to take all we wanted of them, because he grew them only for his own use: there was no market for them.

The attraction of these camping trips have for small boys is profound and readily explainable. It is not merely that their imaginations are so vivid that they can make of these excursions great adventures and readily share the dangers, adventures and exploits such as they read about in books like *Famous Frontiersmen, Pioneers and Scouts* (which was our favorite), but it is also because these are the first real opportunities a boy has to be independent and self-reliant, away from the admonitory and overcautious solicitude of parents. "Don't do this, don't do that," he is told every minute.

On camping trips, away from adults, we could experience a sense of individual and collective achievement. We would stretch our tents or build lean-tos, make our beds of leaves, build our fires for cooking in enclosures of stones we had gathered, fry our meats, serve and eat, and wash our utensils in the stream. If we were lucky we would have fried perch we had caught with hook and line and had scaled and dressed ourselves. We would swim naked and tell what we wanted to be when we got big and recount the stories we had read about Daniel Boone, Kit Carson, Sam Houston and Buffalo Bill.

I was able to read long before I entered first grade at school. In fact, if you are to believe my mother and my aunts, what I have heard many times about me is true: that I knew my alphabet and could spell simple words before I was able to walk. Inasmuch as my own son was not able to talk, let alone read, until he was four years old, I have always doubted this precocity of mine. But since my mother says it is true, it is possibly true.

The explanation is this: My grandmother Rascoe lived with us during the first few years of my life, and it appears that she was not only doting but eager to force my co-ordination every minute, drilling me in speech and articulation constantly. We subscribed to the Louisville *Courier-Journal* as well as to the Fulton *Daily Leader,* and it seems that I learned my letters from the headlines and mastheads of these newspapers and that when I was still in arms I could read off the lettering on the freight cars when asked to do so.

There were few books in our home except the Bible, a pharmacopoeia, a translation of Dante's *Inferno,* illustrated by Doré, Longfellow's *Hiawatha,* some books of verse and some girls' finishing-school books of my mother's, some novels by E. P. Roe, Charles Major and G. W. Cable, Hostetter's Almanac, and the books my parents bought for me, like *Famous Frontiersmen, Pioneers and Scouts,* Frederic Remington's book of pictures of the Wild West, *Our Presidents,* and *Little Men* and *Little Women* and some of the Elsie Dinsmore series. The Doré book fascinated and frightened me and caused me to dream terrified dreams. Only one of these books did I like, and that was the *Famous Frontiersmen, Pioneers and Scouts.* We did not have, and I never read, any fairy stories, such as Andersen's and those of the brothers Grimm, until I was grown up—nor any other "juveniles" beyond those I mention.

Next door to us, however, there lived a Collins family, and I spent much time with Miss Norma, who was fond of me and told me stories by the hour, read to me aloud from books and helped me to learn to read from the considerable shelf of books she had. Among the books of hers which I came to know almost by heart was an illustrated book on arctic exploration.

This book was the instrument of my becoming a monstrous liar during the very first week I was in school. I had to walk nearly two miles to Carr's Institute. The teachers there and most of the pupils were unknown to me. I knew only those who lived in my neighborhood or whom I had met at Sunday School. I was frightened of them all, for I had not yet become acquainted with the boys who were to be my constant playmates—the Prestwood boys, Lancy Savage and Cecil Johnson.

They all seemed to be more sure of themselves than I felt; they seemed to know more and to have seen more. I thought it was advisable to establish myself as a personage in their eyes, so when the teacher asked me where I lived, how old I was and whether I had been born in Fulton, I wished to compete with the boy who said he was born in Montreal, Canada. I told the teacher (and the class) that I was born in Fulton but that I had been on an arctic exploration.

This surprised the teacher and piqued her curiosity. She asked me to tell the class about it. I described our preparations, our boat, our fur clothes, our spears, dog sleds, firearms; how the native Esquimaux harpooned fish and lived in igloos—in fact, I recited as much as I could remember of the exploration book. They were all fascinated, no one more so than the indulgent teacher. She asked me to make drawings on the blackboard of the igloos, the harpoons, the dog sleds and spears, which I did with prideful avidity.

If this teacher saw through my elaborate fib she never gave me away or reproached me for it. And if she had something on me, I later had something on her.

She was young and sweet, a local girl not long out of normal school herself and not versed in the ways of the world. There had been two things (as I have said before) which my father had forbidden me—one was to smoke cigarettes and the other was to read nickel novels.

There was a middle-aged vagabond who worked as a porter and man of all work for my father and who lived in the attic of our house. He smoked hand-rolled cigarettes incessantly, and he bought all the pulp-paper novels as fast as they were displayed on the drugstore counter. In his room he had stacks of copies of *Liberty Boys of '76, Diamond Dick* and the Frank Merriwell series. The four-colored covers of these magazines thrilled me and, because they were forbidden me, my curiosity was great concerning their contents.

It was the custom of our first-grade teacher to read aloud to us from some book of fiction for about an hour each morning. She read *Little Men* and *Little Women,* with which I was already familiar, and then read from Hawthorne's *Tanglewood Tales,* which is boring and incomprehensible to children in the primary grades. She asked us if any of us had books at home we should like to have read. I held up my hand and said I did and that I would bring them in the morning.

I brought her five copies of *Liberty Boys of '76.* She apparently thought they were authentic history in fiction form and patriotic reading besides. She read from *Liberty Boys of '76* all year. We were enchanted and exalted.

And thereby I learned what was in nickel novels without disobeying my father. I myself did not read them. They were read *to me.* I could not imagine then, and I cannot imagine now, why these stirring yarns, so exemplary in their portrayal of noble motives in action—so *moralistic*—should have been considered bad influences on the minds of youngsters.

Miss Collins read to me from Dumas and Dickens, *Tom Brown's Schooldays* and Weems's *Life of Washington,* and I would read them over on my own account. Of the latter I remember more vividly what she told me about the book itself than about its contents. She told me that this book, the one she actually had in her hands, was the first book Abraham Lincoln ever owned. He had borrowed it from a neighbor, she said, and had read it by the light of a log fire while lying on his stomach before the hearth. He had stuck it between the logs of the cabin in a place where the chinks had fallen out; a rainstorm had come up, ruining the part of the book exposed to the rain; and Lincoln had worked for thirty days splitting logs to pay for the book. She gave the book to me.

I have it now, and I have read and heard the legend about Lincoln's copy of Weem's *Life of Washington* many times since then. The book in its cover of black cloth had been damaged, certainly, by water. From the upper right-hand corner to within an inch of the lower left-hand corner the upper left triangle had been water-soaked. Miss Collins never told me how she came into possession of this biography. I have just taken it out and looked at it. Its title* is:

The Life/of George Washington,/with/Curious Anecdotes/Equally Honorable to Himself/and Exemplary to His Young Countrymen/

> *A life how useful to his country led!*
> *How loved! while living!—how revered! now dead!*
> *Lisp! lisp! his name, ye children yet unborn!*
> *And with like deeds your own great names adorn.*

/Embellished with Six Engravings/By M. L. Weems/Formerly Rector of Mount Vernon Parish/

The author has treated this great subject with admirable

"Success in a new way. He turns all the actions of Washington, to the encouragement of virtue, by a careful application of numerous exemplifications drawn from the conduct of the founder of our republic from his earliest life"

H. Lee, Major-General, Army U. S.

/Philadephia:/Published by Joseph Allen/and sold by Lippincott, Grambo & Co./No. 14 North Fourth Street.

There are faint pencil markings, some running into the destroyed portions: "A.," "Boo," "Mathew," "A. G. Shott," "op," "July," "I."

*Copy editor, J. C., to B. R.: "Curiously enough, the American Dictionary of Biography, reputedly scholarly, gives the title as *The Life and Memorable Actions of George Washington*. But I assume you copied it accurately from your edition of the book." B. R. to J. C.: "There were many editions of this book, including pirated ones. The American Dictionary of Biography is in error. *The Life and Memorable Actions of George Washington* was a pamphlet written by Weems during Washington's lifetime and published by George Keating, 207 Market Street, Baltimore, in 1800, a few months after Washington's death. The cherry-tree story does not appear in it. Weems expanded the pamphlet into a 'biography' entitled *The Life of George Washington,* to take sales advantage of interest created in the subject by Washington's death. It has not been settled whether the first edition of the expanded 'Life' was the one published in Georgetown in 1800 or the one published in Philadelphia in the same year. The original pamphlet was expanded into a 'Life' merely by Weems's packing in more lies and 'exemplary anecdotes' invented by himself. The cherry-tree story did not appear until the 'fifth' edition in 1806. Cf. *A Book Hunter's Holiday,* by A. S. W. Rosenbach, 1936."

During my childhood I did not permit myself to doubt that this was the very book Abraham Lincoln as a boy had read and worked to pay for. But skepticism has since corroded my credulity, and I now doubt not only that the book is what Miss Collins told me it was, but that the Lincoln story is any more than a legend, like the dreadful stuff Parson Weems wrote about young Washington and the cherry tree. The misguided parson believed that in inventing these yarns about Washington he was relating "anecdotes exemplary to his [Washington's] young countrymen."

One result of the example of that book set me was that I wanted to hack down a cherry tree and see what my father would do about it when I told him the truth. We had no cherry tree, so I chopped down a peach sapling. My father didn't do anything about it. He wasn't home when it happened. My mother did not ask me whether I had done it or not. She knew I had. She caught me at it just when the tree crashed to the ground. She did not ask me anything; she just cut a limb off the sapling and gave me a thrashing.

I imagine there have been welts on the backsides of thousands of youngsters as a result of their reading Parson Weems's exemplary anecdote.

I was handicapped in my enjoyment of Weems's *Life of Washington* by the fact that we did not live in a log cabin and our house was lighted by kerosene lamps. Moreover, although we had a fireplace in the living room it was sealed up as being too expensive and too troublesome to keep a fire going in it and as giving out less heat than a large, ornamental base-burner stove did, anyhow. There was a grate in my room, however, and I would gather kindling and stovewood for it (although it was meant to burn coal), blow out the light and read Weems while lying on my stomach.

I regret to record that I got no enjoyment out of Weems commensurate with the trouble I took to read him in the manner Lincoln was supposed to have done. I found him a tedious bore. I read page after page without absorbing the meaning. My mind would fly away from the page to dwell on the image of young Lincoln splitting rails and reading by the light of fire logs; I would think what I would like to have for breakfast and what I intended to do next day; I would see Daniel Boone stalking through the forests and Kit Carson barely escaping from an ambush of Indians. And I would reproach myself for not being as studious or ambitious as Lincoln.

We had several horses, a buggy, a trap, a phaeton and a dogcart for a Shetland for my younger brothers—George, who is seven years younger than I; and Henry, who is nine years younger. I had as pets a Newfoundland dog, two Belgian hares, an alligator, a horned toad and a garter snake. Electric lights had been installed in the house (a process which seemed almost to require demolition), and the telephone, no longer a toy, hung on our living-room wall so one could listen in on conversations of the neighbors or engage in conversations your neighbors could listen in on. (You turned a crank like a coffee-grinder three times, and when the operator answered you said, "Hello, Central! Give me three-four-two." General use of the telephone, even in small towns, gave inspiration for an endemic popular song, "Hello, Central! Give Me Heaven.")

The conversations I had heard my elders indulge in concerned the imprisonment of Dreyfus on Devil's Island and his trial; the fiendish murder of a little girl by the Ponsonby boy in Boston; the blowing up of the *Maine* and the subsequent war, which brought troop trains through the town carrying away three of my male relatives; the poisoned-beef scandal of the war; the Indian outbreaks in Minnesota; the assassination of Governor Goebel at the state capital; the Galveston flood; the trial of Caleb Powers for the assassination of Goebel; the campaign of Bryan for the presidency; the Pan-American Exposition at Buffalo (which my parents attended); and the assassination of President McKinley by Czolgosz.

I remember marching in a body with the other school children to the town park to attend the vicarious funeral ceremony performed in McKinley's honor. And I remember being held aloft by my father to see Admiral Dewey as he stood on the back platform of a Pullman car, and likewise in the same manner to see Captain Richmond Pearson Hobson who commanded the collier *Merrimac* and sank her in Santiago harbor and got kissed by so many women for his exploit. But I can't say I remember much else about world happenings as a boy in Fulton.

[51]

BEFORE I FORGET

The Cherokee Strip in Oklahoma Territory was purchased from the Indians and thrown open to settlement nearly a year before I was born, but my father did not become interested in the Western migration until 1903. He had emerged from the panic and depression of 1897 without any perceptible change in his fortunes that a child could see, and at the turn of the century his prosperity seems to have reached its peak for a long time to come.

In 1903 my father went out to investigate business prospects in Oklahoma Territory. By that time he was definitely committed to the saloon business as a vocation, although his avocations were horse trading, auctioneering, and conducting barbecues. Opposition to the liquor business was growing in Kentucky, the home of bourbon and mint juleps, and my father felt it was certain Hickman County would go dry at the next local-option election—and it did.

He anticipated this by a year, selling out his business and his home and auctioning off all his household goods and chattels himself, except a large framed oleo in full color of the painting, "Custer's Last Fight," a work of art furnished all saloons of the time which used the Anheuser-Busch Brewing Company's beer. On the day we left Fulton there were two photographs taken of the house and family, one with us standing in front of the fence and one with us standing behind it, the house and grape arbor covered with sleet and icicles. My mother, my father, my grandmother, my two brothers and I are in them. In one of the pictures the lower parts of our bodies are cut off by that framed work of art. My father wanted that photograph. That's why my mother insisted upon another being taken—without the artistic foreground.

On a preliminary survey of the Oklahoma scene, my father had been present during the mushroom growth of Lawton, a boom town which grew in two weeks' time from an arid spot of sagebrush prairie into a town of 14,000 with banks, hotels, gambling joints and stores under tents; drinking water at twenty cents a glass, a tent cot at five dollars a night and chuck-steak dinners at five dollars each.

My father did not choose Lawton, thank God, but moved on to another boom town, Snyder, which was just springing up. He bought two lots. Luckily he did not choose to stay there to watch his property grow in value. The town was blown away twice—completely—by cyclones. He picked Shawnee as a likely spot to begin life anew again, and it was to Shawnee that we moved.

For the rest my memory of Fulton is a medley of picnics and barbecues, horseback riding, camping and fishing, circuses and Wild West shows (witnessed and of my own organizing); of Hallowe'en nights with wheelbarrows atop barn gables and front gates hung on the crossbars of telephone poles; of hay rides in autumn and sleigh rides in winter; of a slightly older girl cousin's apprising me of the physiological differentiation between boys and girls; of learning to shoot with a Flobert rifle and to fish minnows with a bent pin; of attending a Baptist camp meeting with my parents and a party of Fultonians who acted as though the fervent conversions and total immersion of baptisms were a comic spectacle; of shooting a meadowlark with my new rifle and of burying it tenderly with tears of contrition afterward; of learning to dive and swim, and of taking a chew of tobacco and swallowing the juice according to an older boy's directions and of being deathly sick and afraid to tell my mother, and of taking a fervent oath upon the family Bible, hidden away on a table in the shuttered and musty parlor, that if God would forgive me I would never, never, never take a chew of tobacco again (which oath I have kept: I get sick now at the thought of that episode); of being ill of the measles in a darkened room and of my eyes paining me; of having mumps with a lump under the jaw and of having whooping cough that nearly strangled me and could be heard for blocks away; of stirring up a hornet's nest with disastrous results; of being caught in a whirlpool in a swollen river and of going down four times in defiance of tradition, only to come up and be rescued by a husky farmhand; of being taken to a hootchy-kootchy dance at the Paducah street fair and being both excited by, and disgusted with, and ashamed of my father for laughing at it; of enjoying the Yellow Kid comics and thinking the horse races the prettiest of sports; of drinking "pot likker" and scraping the pan when batter cakes were made; of wading in rain puddles with new rubber boots and carrying posies and apples to the then most beautiful woman in the world, Miss Nichols; of chewing slippery-el-um and

crunching sugar cane; of picking muscadines from the roadside and
of wetting noses for cooling drinks from bubbling springs; of killing black snakes and copperheads and water moccasins; of playing
pillow and post office and of kissing Edith Blythe with such thrilling pleasure it seemed as if I could never kiss her enough; of bear-
ing a shocked love, respect and admiration for Giltner and Russell
Prestwood's mother for affectionately calling the three of us "little
piss-ants"; of a boy, whose name I forget, being put in the re-
formatory for exposing his privates to girls in the third grade and
of being glad because he was always twisting the wrists or pulling
the ears of us smaller boys; of going to Sunday School and singing
in the choir and getting starchly dressed for Sunday School picnics;
of being vainly forbidden to play with Adley Morris because he
was "poor white folk," although I admired Adley more than anybody else, for he was allowed to do as he pleased and smoked
Sweet Caporals and could blow smoke through his nose, just as in
the Wild West show, and of being taken by Adley once during
summer vacation into the girls' water closets at school and being
appalled by the verse and drawings he showed me on the walls
there—so much more explicit than the drawings and scrawlings in
the boys' water closets; of thinking Aunt Mattie radiantly beautiful
and the kindest, gayest and most generous woman anywhere, and
of wondering why my mother and my other aunts spoke harshly of
her and why Uncle Labron had shot three men on account of her;
of rummaging through old toys and pictures and books in the attic
on rainy days, and of rattling sticks along fence palings and making
people angry who whitewashed their fences instead of painting
them, for the sticks scraped off the whitewash; of hopping the back
step of the ice wagon for a ride and of putting my feet on the
handle bars of a bicycle and coasting down the long hill near the
cemetery; of smoking whipstock and dried corn silk and of playing
baseball by "choosing up;" of swanking it with a thick new red
sweater on a hot day and a new catcher's mask, mitt, flannel knickers
and visored cap my father had bought for me; of being held aloft for
a view of a long-haired fat man called Bryan in a black coat and with
waving arms who talked from the observation platform of a railway car; of studying arithmetic and geography under a large reading lamp on a big round table near a grate fire before which slept

a Shepherd dog; of making a parachute by tying the staves of a wagon umbrella and leaping successfully from the barn roof, and of reciting "The day is done and the darkness . . ." at graduating exercises; of disarranging ant hills and watching the ants build them up again; of eating watermelons in the field by bursting them open and gouging out the heart with my fingers; of watching Tom Loftis, the town drunkard, reel down the street, shouting; of playing hooky to deepen the cave in the clay gulley near the rock quarry; of playing charades, and of making molasses candy and popcorn balls; of cracking hickory nuts and walnuts with a hammer over an inverted flatiron held between the knees; of saying prayers on cold nights by kneeling under the covers in bed; of washing dirty bare feet under the front hydrant before coming in to supper; of always getting the pulley-bone and liver of fried chicken except when there was company; of pumping in the swing with Alice Blythe and running under when she sat down to swing; of going to be an Indian fighter like Kit Carson, and of going to be President by getting a job driving a team on the towpath of the Erie Canal; of throwing a lawn-hose nozzle at my cousin, Claudice, and cutting a gash in her scalp after she had pushed me off a banister on which I was "tightrope walking," and of being very sorry afterward, for I loved Claudice; of going to the Opera House with my parents to see *Faust, East Lynne, Midnight in Chinatown, The Wizard of Oz, If I Were King, The Great Divide, Shenandoah,* Richard Mansfield in *Cyrano de Bergerac,* Sarah Bernhardt in a gibberish play I thought very silly, and Joseph Jefferson in a play I thought very grand, called *Rip Van Winkle,* and of liking *Midnight in Chinatown* and *The Wizard of Oz* the best of all, although the devil in *Faust,* who could make electric sparks come out of his tail when he wrote with the tip of it on a big book, seemed to me pretty fine; of hating to part with my pony and with Shep and with the bay mare, and of regretting to leave behind the two big elm trees, grape arbor, the attic and the barn loft; of pressing my nose against the window-pane of the Pullman car for a last look at the trestle south of town, where I had often sat on a buttress, watching trains from the other road approach from afar off, throwing up a white spirt of steam, to be followed a moment later by the tardy sound of the whistle which the spirt announced; and of being so excited by the prospect

of new and strange adventure that I could not get to sleep but
stared at the curving roof of the car and at the faint light that came
over the curtain pole of the berth, until I imagined that the
rhythmic sound of the wheels passing over the rail jointures were
framing the words, Ken-tuc-kee, Ken-tuc-kee, Ken-tuc-kee.

CHAPTER V

Shawnee, Oklahoma

Shawnee and Its Settlers. The Indian Reservations Near By.
Shawnee's Breath-Taking Development. Boyhood Reading.

Before we left fulton, "Professor" Craig, principal of Carr's Institute (all male teachers, musicians, and piano tuners in the South at that time were called professors), had called me into his office and had told me that my parents were making a grave mistake in taking me out to the wilds of Oklahoma. He said I was a bright and promising lad and that association with savages, rough and ill-mannered people would be very bad for me, and that I would grow up coarse and uneducated.

I for my part believed that the West, which would be my new home, was really untamed and that I should find conditions there as exciting as I had seen them portrayed in the Wild West shows and in the melodramas at the Opera House. For this reason I took pains to include, in the few belongings I took with me, my twenty-two rifle, an old horse pistol an uncle had given me, a deck of cards which I did not know how to play, and a pair of dice which I did not know how to shoot. I thought it would be up to me to learn how to play poker, shoot crap and handle a pistol as soon as I could master these arts.

Professor Craig's ideas of Oklahoma were typical of the simple, provincial, ingrown outlook of the citizenry of Fulton. Shawnee turned out to be intellectually much more alive and in all things more alert than the sleepy little town of Fulton, which had no library, no bookstore, no magazine distribution except the *Saturday Blade and Chicago Ledger,* the *War Cry* of the Salvation Army, nickel novels, and the *Saturday Evening Post.* The people who had settled Shawnee, on the other hand, were mostly of the educated and adventurous-minded sort who had struck out for a new life from towns and cities in all parts of the country east of the Mississippi. Even when we arrived in Shawnee the town was already supporting a small public library which was later to be housed in one of the standard yellow brick buildings supplied by the Carnegie Foundation; there were two newspapers, two book-stores, an art shop, a theater, a lecture hall and an orchestra.

Shawnee was reached from Memphis only by the badly managed Choctaw, Oklahoma & Gulf Railroad, which used obsolete equipment, made no effort to maintain a schedule and carried no Pullman cars. The three-hundred-mile trip required nearly twenty hours of travel in dirty coaches lighted with kerosene lamps. At night one slept fully dressed in a reclining seat not unlike a barber's chair. There was no dining car, and except for breakfast in Little Rock at the railroad station the only food available was stale sandwiches, oranges, bananas, crackerjack and popcorn, sold by the candy butcher. The windows were immovable; soot and cinders filled the coaches; and most of the passengers threw their orange and banana peels and other leavings from their lunch into the aisles. Snores mingled with the wails of babies through the night, and the variety of human smells, mingled with the pungent odors of orange peels, gave all of us violent headaches. It was a vast relief to debark at noon at the depot in Shawnee, and it was a gratifying thrill also to see blanketed Indians squatting on the floor of the waiting room in the station.

Building operations had not kept pace with the increase in population. It had been difficult for an agent to find a house for us, and on first seeing the place we were to live in temporarily my mother developed an antipathy to Oklahoma which increased rather than diminished throughout the twenty-two years she was to live in the state. The house was a damp, dismal and dirty one-story brick structure, with no electric lights, no running water; the kitchen was hideous with its torn, cracked and dirty wallpaper and its dilapidated coal-burning stove covered with grease and grime;

on the living-room floor there were a torn and ragged straw carpet and a few articles of nondescript furniture; in the bedroom there were no dressers or furniture of any kind except iron beds with sagging springs and filthy-looking mattresses. My mother had these mattresses moved into the barn at once and set to work scrubbing the house from front room to kitchen with lye soap and water. For the first several nights we slept on pallets, until new beds and bed clothing could be purchased and delivered.

To my mother the burden of living in such squalid surroundings was increased by the fact that it was almost impossible to hire servants at any wage. In Fulton, Mother had had a cook whom she paid a dollar and a half a week, a girl to help with the housework whom she paid a dollar a week, and the girl also did the washing and ironing. Servants in Shawnee were paid from eight to ten dollars a week when they could be had, which was rare. Mother thought this was too much to pay, so even when my father found and sent a Negro cook to the house my mother declined to employ her and added to her sense of martyrdom by doing all her work herself, including the laundry. The self-sacrifice involved in this was great, because all the water we used had to be drawn from a well.

Fortunately we were able to move out of this miserable place after three months and into a newly built story-and-a-half frame house, with space for a flower garden and for a vegetable garden, and with a small one-room servants' house in the rear. Here I had a room of my own, my two brothers had a room in the attic, and with a cook to help her my mother became more reconciled with her lot, for soon she took pride in the flowers she cultivated and the fresh vegetables she raised in her garden. We had no means of transportation, not even a horse and buggy, but since very few people had their own horse and carriage, not to have them was not an indication of poverty, such as it would have been in Fulton. For journeys out to the Indian reservations, picnics to the Mill Dam and drives into the country on Sundays my father would hire a horse and two-seater from a livery stable.

Indian camps within driving distance of the town included those of the Kickapoo, Sacs and Foxes, Seminole, and Pottawatomie tribes. The Kickapoos lived in tepees a few miles northwest of town and made silver ornaments, moccasins and beaded-leather articles which they sold on the streets in Shawnee or to visitors at the camp. The Indians were still wards of the government and had monthly allotments in cash as well as individual grants of land. Indian schools were maintained by the government at convenient points throughout the territory, and graduates of the schools were encouraged to complete their education at Haskell or Carlisle. It was rare, however, in those days for young Indian men and women to profit by the education they received at the two colleges for Indians. After graduation they would return to their people, the young men with American haircuts and dressed in blue serge suits, and the young women in their gray uniform dresses, and within a short time they would be wearing the dress, blankets and moccasins of their native tribes and pretending to white visitors that they could not speak English.

Aside from the Indians there was no trace of the wild and woolly West of which I had dreamed. There were cowhands, but no cowboys, and a cowhand was no more than a man of all work on a farm, who hoed potatoes, picked cotton, cut sugar cane, threshed wheat and did any and all kinds of chores as well as take care of the livestock. Shawnee was in an agricultural, not a cattle-raising, region; and in the bottom lands in the southern part of the county farms were producing record crops of potatoes, whereas the less fertile sections were producing bumper crops of cotton, alfalfa, sugar beets and broom corn. Alongside the railroad tracks were cotton gins and cotton compresses; there was a cottonseed-oil mill, a broom factory, a cannery and the beginnings of a railroad repair shop which was later to become one of the chief industrial supports of the city, bringing money into the local shops in the form of wages paid to mechanics. The town was bustling and cosmopolitan.

Development of the city was carried on with breath-taking rapidity, and with each new development there was a communal celebration. The Santa Fe Railroad erected a miniature Spanish castle for a passenger station and built a branch line through the town from north to south, intersecting the Choctaw, newly absorbed by the Rock Island, which ran east and west; and holidays were declared in the schools to greet the train of workmen while the mayor of the town drove the first spike in the first tie to be laid within the town's boundary line and made a speech. Five new large brick grade schools, equipped in the most modern manner with steam heat, sanitary toilets, washrooms and improved desks were erected. Twenty-one miles of streetcar tracks were laid, over which were to travel beautiful new yellow streetcars, of both the open and inclosed kinds. (Boys of my age contended for the privilege of turning the trolley at the end of the line, in pay for which we were permitted to ride the entire circuit as a passenger free of charge. Older boys, who could afford it, took their sweethearts for streetcar rides, and picnic parties were organized at the far ends of the line, largely for the thrill of riding there and back in the street cars.) And all the business streets, which had at first been soggy mud holes in which wagons sometimes sank up to the hubs in rainy weather, were paved with vitrified brick. Two candy and ice-cream soda shops, the Palace of Sweets and the Busy Bee, opened up and became the rendezvous of young lovers, especially on Saturday nights. Two nickelodeons showing Keystone comedies and Pathé dramas occupied two-story buildings which, with the coming of statehood and the passing of the saloon had been open gambling houses. Men's clothing shops displayed Society Brand, House of Kuppenheimer and Hart, Schaffner & Marx latest fashions in peg-top trousers, padded shoulders and pancake hats for which you might buy special bands from an assortment of color combinations.

Indeed the West became the East, by imitation, so rapidly that it was not until some years after the rapid transition that Oklahoma became conscious that it had lost its romantic frontier aspect. The development of the movies, with their thrilling "Westerns," was largely responsible for the late effort to perpetuate a tradition and a condition which was not liked or wanted when it existed. Farmhands who had never had to use a lariat in their lives ordered chaps and ten-gallon hats from Montgomery Ward, bought pistols and, when they were paid on Saturday nights, would dress up, get noisy on white mule and ride into the smaller towns like Tecumseh, Earlsboro and Seminole, firing into the air and yelling "Yippee!" Once in town, they would go to a nickelodeon and later swank around in the blue smoke of a poolroom, trying to learn how to roll cigarettes with one hand. My father used to say that it had got so that on Saturday nights there wasn't a well rope on any farm in the county; farm hands had them coiled around their saddle horns like cowboys in the movies.

The exploits of the Dalton brothers, of Jesse James and his crew of bandits, and of Al Jennings constituted a past which, by 1905, the anxious and responsible citizens of Oklahoma were happy to put behind them, that they might, in their timidity, pursue their own shrewd banditry under less sanguine auspices. There is not, and there never was, any glamor in being a poorly paid cashier of a small-town bank and in having your guts torn out with a double-barreled shotgun, aimed by a nervous-trigger moron under the coked-up guidance of a tin-pot hero such as Al Jennings.

In my boyhood, Al Jennings, after long pursuit by federal marshals who sought the reward offered because of his bank robberies, encamped north of Shawnee and sent in word to Cassius M. ("Cash") Cade, cashier of the First National Bank, that he was willing to give himself up to Mr Cade and let Mr Cade have the reward for his capture, but that he wanted safe conduct (that is, he did not want to be shot down) and a fair trial. This was given him; he was sentenced to the penitentiary; he emerged as a writer for the *Saturday Evening Post* and as a candidate for governor (in which candidacy he was defeated) and many years later, ironically enough, he was held up and robbed by a petty stick-up man in Brooklyn.

In those days, before I was fourteen, I could not associate myself with any of the more sanguine happenings of my time. I had read the stories of John Fox, Jr., *The Trail of the Lonesome Pine* and *Christmas Eve on Lonesome* and, in their descriptions of Kentucky woodlands, I would look back and picture the Kentucky I had known—except for rhododendrons, which I had never seen and which John Fox, Jr., mentioned frequently; and I was quickened to an exciting sense of the past by reading *The Hoosier Schoolmaster,* by Edward Eggleston, *The Conqueror,* by Gertrude Atherton, *Alice of Old Vincennes,* by Maurice Thompson, and *The Crossing* and *The Crisis* by Winston Churchill. And *Huckleberry Finn,* of course, gave all of us boys an escape from school routine and discipline at home; and at Mark Twain's inspiration we went camping, built rafts for the South Canadian River and lived a life of the imagination greatly at variance with the facts of our experience.

At first in Shawnee I felt as alien and deracinated as my mother. Years afterwards I was to sympathize with her plight and to understand why—under the handicaps of her temperament and conditioning and deep-seated provincialism she was to remain forever foreign and ill at ease in her new surroundings. She was spiritually a transient, never able, quite, to accept her new home as hers or her new sphere as embracing and absorbing her. Always, with each concession to the demands of keeping on, there had remained the *arrière pensée* of an ultimate, happy return to the elm trees, the gravel pavements, the brick sidewalks and the leisured inconveniences of Fulton.

This was a nostalgic illusion, for while Shawnee was progressing, Fulton was decaying; the hilltop on which had stood the Burton mansion from which she had been cast out had soon been cleared of trees and the barny old mansion by her acquisitive brother who had had no sentimental nonsense about him and had turned the site into a profitable real-estate venture by erecting as many cheap bungalows on the property as space would allow; tobacco was no longer a profitable crop for the farmers near by; the tobacco barns were torn down; the Illinois Central moved its division office away from Fulton and no longer routed its Memphis and New Orleans crack trains through the town for stop-over and crew change; the panic of 1903 had followed soon after our emigration to Shawnee and, although the effects of the panic were felt there, too, Shawnee was quick in recovering, whereas Fulton had settled down for years in a dull, apathetic, hopeless depression, for agriculture thereabouts had ceased to bring farmers into town with money to buy, traveling salesmen ceased to visit the town in numbers regularly and the resplendent Knight's Hotel fell into decay, its dining room was abandoned, the pretty trees in rows alongside it, untended and choked by soot and cinders from the I. C. tracks, withered and died; the shaded street on which she and her sister Janie and her brother Jim had lived with their families in houses her father had given them was soon to be bared of foliage, even the great elm cut down, the white picket fences would be gone, the grape arbors destroyed, the houses themselves which had been saved from fires would be ramshackle, unpainted and hideous, the lawns and gardens would be mud or arid clay, and this would be part of Nigger Town, with not only the four houses erected by my father behind the great barn and barnyard of our home for her servants and the servants of her sister and sister-in-law now mere shanties, but her home itself occupied by the gentle and kindly but poverty-stricken Negro who had been my father's restaurant porter; all would be ugly and pitiful rather than beautiful and enheartening.

Nor would the Fulton she knew ever return, for the past does not return; and moreover Fulton was an ingrown and unexpansive town where an unambitious and leisured close existence had bred, as in an old ladies' home, its factions, its gossip, its scandal, its false or fanciful legends of family heroics, its memory of sorrows and tragedies, its high degree of friendliness and neighborliness and hospitality bred in small groups of people who have communally met tribulations and trouble; and even with the coming of a degree of prosperity at the end of each seven lean years, the population would remain stable and the young newcomers, attracted there from farms or villages not far away, would merely replace the dribble of those who had gone, and they would have no knowledge of, or interest in, the curious, quaint history of that quiet, ghost-haunted border-state town, where for so long intermarried families were strangely divided by the old memory that the men of this branch of the family fought on the Union side and the men of that branch fought on the Confederate side, and that further divisions between families were made long ago because one member of this branch of the family had betrayed the family's class by marrying a member of the "poor whites" and still further family feuds arose sometimes when a Baptist married a Methodist or Presbyterian.

In Shawnee my mother wanted to return to all this, to leave an exciting, progressive, newly built town which in a few years had spread from a small settlement on the north bank of the South Canadian River up the hill and over to the Choctaw railroad tracks, around which the growing town clustered and began eagerly, hopefully to expand with the influx of each new train or wagonload of adventurous-minded, pioneer-spirited men and women from all parts of the country, democratic, individualistic and yet communally minded, seeking a new, inspiriting life, having left the stifling prejudices behind them.

In Fulton there had been other social divisions than those I have described, and snubs between neighbor and neighbor for reasons (as I was to learn many years afterwards) that were no longer clear to the participants themselves. They merely remembered, say, that the Snows did not speak to the Davises, for a reason both the Snows and Davises had forgotten: the Snows and Davises were on terms of economic equality—that is to say, that they were equally poor; the Snows and Davises had both fought on the Confederate side; the Snows and Davises both belonged to the Campbellite church. Yet they did not speak to each other. Why? They didn't know.

The reason may have had ramifications in the past history of Kentucky and Tennessee, as I discovered it in one case to be; and these ramifications are enough to baffle any strict logician. In one instance some kind of feud had started as far back as 1830. A New England lawyer and spellbinder had been sent to Kentucky by Massachusetts Whigs in the interest of Henry Clay's campaign for the presidency and had settled there when Jackson was elected. He had gained land and property and, although a campaigner for and a spoilsman of a man who had been swept into the presidency on an anti-gentry, aggressively democratic issue, was one of the first to create the notion of a "gentry" in Kentucky and constitute himself a member of it. He had had some sort of quarrel with another man of property who was a descendant of a man who had worked out his indenture and had acquired land in fee simple in Virginia, thus enabling his sons and sons' sons to become members of the landed "gentry" until this queer sprout came along, migrated from Virginia as a wholly convinced and converted adherent to the essential principles of Jacksonian democracy. There you have a pre-Civil War carpetbagger with aristocratic pretensions at war with a renegade but genuine member of the First Families of Virginia; and the feud had continued among the descendants of the two families just as a matter of form—with no open hostilities, as in the Powers-Goebel and other famous feuds—even in the utter poverty of the descendants of both families.

There was no logic in her nostalgia; but then there is no logic in

[65]

emotions at any time. Mother's spirit began to droop in Shawnee, and a fierce, grim resentment against her fate began to unsweeten her character and resolve itself into a prodigious effort and air of martyrdom—a martyrdom which became intensified when my father's first partner skipped town with all the money that had been accumulating for months as surplus and profit in the little iron safe beneath the bar of their saloon, leaving us penniless and my father embarrassed for capital to continue in business.

Mother did not like these new, strange faces in Shawnee; and she was hostile to them because she imagined they were hostile to her because she was the wife of a saloonkeeper. She did not cultivate her neighbors or encourage them to cultivate her. We were in Shawnee three years before she made friends with the wives in the houses in one block on our side of the street. A regular churchgoer in Fulton, she went to church once in Shawnee, reported that the congregation was too "mixed" and gave up attendance with the audible reflection that one can serve God faithfully without making a show of it on Sunday mornings.

My father applauded this platitude, but not too vehemently. His must have been a mute, secret, though heartfelt prayer and petition to God to sustain my mother's logic; for he feared a hearty concurrence might cause her to change her mind. He had no taste for sermons and had a great antipathy for wearing starched shirts and pressed, uncomfortable clothes. He liked Oklahoma; it seemed energetic and progressive to him in contrast to Fulton. But he was deeply conscious of mother's distaste for the raw, crude and energetic town, and he loved her enough to wish to mitigate her suffering. Servants were difficult to be had in those early days of the century in Shawnee, so Father sent her railroad fare back to Fulton and brought on our old cook. This faithful family servant lost no time in familiarizing herself with the wages paid servants in Shawnee and left us flat for an $8-a-week wage instead of the old $1.50-a-week wage we had been paying her, with a small house of her own in the back yard, found, and cast-off clothing. I was glad enough that she was gone, because she cooked those delicious Southern dishes fried in deep fat and served hot biscuits which augmented Mother's liver trouble and subjected me to frequent attacks of acute dispepsia. My father cut the grease of this rich Southern cooking with liberal potations of bourbon and so retained his magnificent exuberance.

Yes, as I have said, I at first felt in Shawnee as alien and as deracinated as my mother. I did not want to go back to Fulton; for within myself lay a dim apprehension of the necessity of enacting a long-cherished role as Daniel Boone, the pioneer in a strange wilderness. But a child is cautious, afraid, suspicious, like an animal, in new and strange surroundings. Almost at once I had to meet and get pummeled by the red-headed boy in the next block from where I lived, who overlorded the neighborhood and had twice issued tentative challenges by shying a clod at me and making ribald comments, audible to me, to his satellites about my appearance as I passed by on my way to school. I knew that I had to fight this boy at once, otherwise the situation would grow worse; so I sailed into him, licked from the start; and we lunged at each other, wrestled, pinched, bit, gouged and pulled hair, and finally he was on top of me, hitting me and crying " 'Nough?" until I said, " 'Nough" and he let me up and we shook hands; he asked me my name, and I asked him his; and we became friends, presently to be partners at turning trolley poles for street-car rides and in swimming jaunts to the South Canadian and on camping trips for the day out near the Choctaw trestle, where we pitched our tent of sewed gunny sacks, fried strips of bacon over a kindling-wood fire and ate it with bread and bananas we had stuffed in our rucksack.

But I had to proceed cautiously and timidly before I got used to my surroundings. In grade school, for instance, they used the vertical method of penmanship, whereas I had been taught the Spencerian; and I had to try to write vertically or get bad marks in penmanship. The teacher in the sixth grade, Miss Rogers, who was from a Northern state, thought I pronounced words badly and so endeavored to correct my southwestern Kentucky accent.

All this strangeness helped to turn me, I think (although there may have been other factors), from the normal, healthy, extraverted boy I had been in Fulton into a lonely boy who sought solitude consciously and found a world more interesting to me and better to my liking in books. I began to read avidly, shutting myself up for whole afternoons at a time in a "den" I had made in the attic of the house and reading. It became a habit with me that I have never been able to break, nor have I wished to break it.

Yet gradually did I begin to identify my surroundings as part of myself and to join as heartily as anyone in whatever was the popular thing to do—roller skating at the rink on Saturday nights; writing notes to girls in school and picking out a special sweetheart, Mary Belle Watts, whom I was expected to bring to every party to which I was asked; going on moonlight hay rides and furtively stealing kisses from Mary Belle while the other girls giggled if they caught us; learning to dance from a professional teacher; playing one-ole-cat at recess and baseball and football in season on Saturdays; and attending all the mass and community entertainments.

Mass and community amusements in Shawnee were varied. There was Chatauqua in the spring or summer; the circus in July or August; revival meetings; the green-corn and stomp dances of the Pottawatomie and Kickapoo Indians; the street carnival; excursions to the 101 Ranch for the Annual Rodeo and Wild West Show; Sunday band concerts in Central Park; barbecues and picnics.

Before most of the prairies to the east and northeast of the town were subdivided into farms and fenced in, the sports event was a jack-rabbit hunt. Greyhounds, whippets and Siberian wolfhounds were used in the chase. Men and women gathered for the event in horse-drawn vehicles and on horseback. There was always at least one contraption called a tally-ho; it was an omnibus coach drawn by six horses, driven by a cockarouse in dandified get-up, with a pearl-gray topper, yellow gloves and a yellow chrysanthemum in his buttonhole. Behind him on the perilous seats were women in starched finery, carrying parasols. This rig was the pride of a local livery stable, not privately owned. Other vehicles were buggies, buckboards, traps and surreys. The costumes were miscellaneous.

The whippets were kept in leash until after the greyhounds and wolfhounds had scared up a rabbit and given chase; they were not released until after the chase had been in progress for some time and the first hounds showed signs of exhaustion. The rabbits had a marvelous trick: when a dog got close upon him, a rabbit would stop dead in his tracks. The hound's momentum would be so great that he couldn't stop, but in going over the rabbit he would dip his head to snap the rabbit. Nine times out of ten he would miss and, because he had dipped his head, he would be carried over in a complete somersault. By the time he recovered his feet the rabbit would be off in another direction with good advantage in the start. I have seen one jack rabbit make monkeys out of a whole pack of greyhounds, only to lose out when the shorter and swifter whippets were released for the quick chase and kill. The long ears of the jack rabbits were scalped off as trophies. On the trophies there was a state bounty of a quarter a pair, because jack rabbits are destructive to crops. Their flesh was considered inedible except by the lower-grade Indians, so their carcasses were left on the field for the buzzards.

Another social event was attendance at the Indian stomp dances and green-corn dances. The Pottawatomie, Kickapoo and Seminole stomp dances were monotonous, dull and rather disgusting affairs. The beauty of Indian maidens is a myth as far as my experience goes: I have never seen a passably pretty Indian girl over sixteen years of age, unless she was half or quarter white; and the full-bloods usually get fat and lumpy shortly after twenty. Indian men, on the other hand, unless they are cross-bred, are almost universally handsome. The reason is obvious: the women do all the heavy labor. The stomp dances of that region were disgusting to me, because of the food the Indians brought to these ceremonies and ate. It consisted solely of uncleaned cow and pig guts, piled in tubs, and stank to high heaven. When a Kickapoo was hungry he went to a tub, cut himself a length of entrail, squeezed it out and ate it, without troubling even to wash it.

The Sacs and Foxes, on the other hand, were a clean and artistic race. I witnessed a ceremony of the induction of a new chief at the Sacs and Foxes agency north of Aydelotte, a few miles north of Shawnee, when I was a lad and was so impressed by the dignity and beauty of it that I set down in my diary upon my return eight pages of minute detail concerning the ceremony. The new chief, a handsome young brave, was as agile and as graceful as Nijinsky. I watched him dance for hours, executing leaps and cuts in the broiling sun while the thermometer registered 112 degrees in the shade.

He had been dancing that way, I was told, for two days and two nights, pausing only to stand in solemn dignity when two ancients in feathered headdresses gave a signal and one of them broke into oratory, or to allow another brave to dance, or to snatch a bite of food and some chewing tobacco.

PART II

Adolescence

CHAPTER VI

I Seek to Explore the Periphery of a Universe

Paul Corley. I Am Bewildered by Paul's Death. Three Men Who Were My Guides, Friends and Tutors. More Reading. Milt, Gus and Harry Pappathakos.

WHILE I WAS IN THE SEVENTH GRADE I made a friend of a boy whose example, and whose death three years later, were to make a profound impression upon me. This boy was Paul Corley and he was, in truth, a young Hercules who was aware of the enviable nature of his strength and who cultivated it with assiduity and intelligence. He did not smoke; he had never tasted either tea or coffee; he pursued a rigid diet; he rigged up a gymnasium in the basement of his house and, by suspending a lawn sprinkler from the roof, made for himself a cold shower under which he patted his chest and thighs after punching the bag and taking setting-up exercises every night for an hour before dinner. He was the best all-round athlete in school. In high school he was fullback on the football team, pitcher on the baseball team, center on the basketball team and shot putter and hammer-thrower on the track team. Paul was at first undecided between two strong ambitions; one to become an evangelist like Billy Sunday, whom he admired for his athleticism, and another to become the heavyweight boxing champion of the world.

Toward the realizations of these ambitions he read the Bible, Sunday School tracts, Spalding's sports manuals and every story, article or book he could lay hands on that had to do with boxing or with the careers of prize fighters. So great had become his prowess as an athlete, and so worshipful were his admirers among his fellows, that he had about made up his mind definitely in favor of prize fighting as a profession when he caught typhoid fever and died.

The death of Paul desolated most of us in high school. In many things I had aped Paul, excepting in his actual studies towards the professions of evangelism and prize fighting. Humility in the presence of Paul forbade me to enter into competitive ambitions with him. But casting about for a comparable future, I decided to become a banker and stockbroker.

To this end I learned by heart the section on stocks and bonds in Milne's Arithmetic; I made a large blackboard for market quotations which I set up, along with a ticker I had constructed by inverting a goldfish bowl on top of a jardiniere stand and putting under it a roll of wallpaper strippings which I filched from the waste can outside of a paint and varnish store; and I had followed the market quotations in the Saint Louis *Post-Dispatch* (three days late) as minutely as if they really conveyed any meaning to me. I read *Success* magazine from cover to cover and studied *System* more conscientiously than any textbook.

For the rest I followed the regimen and example of Paul Corley. I, too, selected a diet of cereals, milk, fruit and vegetables, with an occasional allowance of meat. I, too, resolved never to smoke or to take into my system any stimulant, including tea or coffee. I, too, had tried for and made the public-school, and later the high-school, baseball, football, basketball and track teams.

Two high-school teachers were in love with Paul, and their efforts to capture and dominate him gave me my first objective lesson in the disguises of love and of the intense egotism of its base. It was my first conscious realization of the disparity between actual and verbally asserted motives, between reality and ideality. Miss X was thirty, homely, tense, efficient, strong-willed, sharp-tongued and quick-tempered. She had a physically unattractive woman's capacity for pride-wounding epithets and clever verbal incisions of vanity which she cauterized with wit. Her eyes, which she knew how to flash with a nervous blinking, were so fiery and self-confident that by them alone she was able to sweep attention away from the severe angles of her body and the mottled texture of her skin, and to inspire in the average, unobserving younger male the conclusion that she was—in a way—beautiful. She had spirit, power and an enthusiasm for her subject surely—or so her male pupils assured themselves, with extensive corroboration from the prettier girls, who knew how to deal with competition—and she was by acclamation and by deeds of homage the most popular teacher in school.

In charge of the freshman and sophomore classes in Latin was a pink-and-blonde young woman, Miss Y, who was six years Miss X's junior, and who was gay, athletic, flirtatious, very pretty, merry-eyed and with a soft mouth which could not assume a look of severity even when Miss Y wanted to look severe. Unlike Miss X, she was lax in her discipline, lenient in her requirements of study and inclined to allow her sympathy for the dullest in her classes to outweigh her judgment in parceling out their grade marks. No one ever failed to graduate from her classes. She and Miss X did not approve of each other; or, more specifically speaking, Miss X expressed both an audible and visible disapproval of Miss Y, who smiled at her venomously and thought out ways of annoying her. She was clever at this. The easiest of these was playing the coquette to whatever man or boy Miss X was most interested in.

One day I was reading Shelley in the school library when Miss X came in and sat down beside me. I did not welcome the interruption, for I was deep in *The Revolt of Islam,* which fed some adolescent need within me for an impassioned revolt against some vague something. I observed, moreover, that Miss X talked incoherent nonsense about the poem and had her mind not on the poem nor on me but on Paul who sat at a table near by reading Owen Johnson's Lawrenceville stories in the *Saturday Evening Post.* Meanwhile Miss Y strode athletically into the room and went among the open shelves and began searching for some title. Paul had seen her enter. He arose from his seat abruptly and went up to Miss Y and began to talk to her. Miss X paled slightly and, neglecting to conclude a sentence with which she was interrupting my reading, she walked over in the direction of the two—who were by this time whispering obliviously with their heads close together—passed them, returned and, flouncing down into a seat beside me again, said in an exasperated tone, "Talk about not being wound around her little finger!"

Gumption warned me that this was an audible comment that required no rejoinder. Miss X had lost her interest in Shelley—such as it was—and was fingering a book desperately, the very title of which she was probably unaware. Mabel Newport, a roguish tomboy in a turtle-neck sweater and skirts so short they were the objects of critical comment by mothers in her neighborhood, poked her head around a pillar, engaged my attention and crooked her finger at me in a beckoning signal. I made my escape, but not before Miss X said, "I want to cross-examine you the first time I get a chance."

Mabel wanted me for a partner in tennis doubles. That evening Miss X called me on the telephone and asked me to come up to see her. I had gone with misgivings and had listened with nervous constraint when, after much beating about the bush, she said, "Paul has always stood out to me as being one of the strongest characters in school, and I have thought a great deal of him because he is somewhat like my younger brother; but after this afternoon I want to have nothing more to do with him. He has either lied, changed his mind or did not mean what he said when he told me that Miss Y did not have him wrapped around her little finger. I don't want him or you to think that I am jealous. What have I to be jealous of? I have the interest of you boys at heart and intend always to keep in touch with you; but Miss Y only wants Paul as an admirer. Paul is weak, and I did not think he was. Let Fred Higgins or Harry Hobson come along and pay her as much attention as Paul does, and she would drop him in a minute. Paul needs a few knocks like that to wake him up. He likes Miss Y and has always liked her. That is nothing to me, so I don't care. He likes her better than any other teacher in school."

"Please, Miss X, Paul has told me he likes you better than any other teacher in school," I lied. He hadn't said anything of the sort, and I don't know what misplaced gallantry caused me to say he did.

"Well, he didn't show that this afternoon. He was very much interested in his reading until Miss Y came in. He perked up mighty quick then."

"What do you want me to do? Speak to Paul about it?"

"By no means. He is old enough to know what he is doing. Don't

mention my name to him in connection with anything you have to
say to him about the library episode. Don't say anything about your
coming up here tonight."

"In that case I can't say anything at all to him." I had wanted to
add that I couldn't lie easily, but restrained myself. I felt sorry for
her. An idea came to me. A class party was being held within two
weeks. I surmised that Paul would be taking Miss Y. "I should like
to have the pleasure of taking you to the class party, Miss X," I
said, "if you are not already engaged." That meant I would have
to break a to me highly desirable date with Mabel Newport, but I
did not think Miss X would take me up.

"I should be delighted," she said, with a fervor that hinted of
vindictiveness. I was embarrassed.

"Let us make it this way," I said. "You leave the date open for a
week and if, before that time is up, Paul asks you, you accept him.
I would be awfully happy if you would." I deliberately put myself
in the soup for a week.

"I would never dream of such a thing! I'll go with you," said
Miss X. So I was her escort to the party, and this gave Mabel, whom
I wanted to take, a chance to kid me for weeks. Mabel was a darling
scalawag.

The death of Paul plunged me into a bewilderment of questionings and brought me for the first time into an examination of the
concepts of God, man and the universe—an examination which was
to lead me into a vast and disordered amount of reading. That the
healthiest boy I knew should be the first to die while the puniest
continued to live; that the kindest, most likable, most generous
and gentlest of all the fellows I knew should be taken by death,
seemed to me callously cruel of God. I said as much to my mother.

"You mustn't have such thoughts," she replied. "We are not on
earth to judge God's ways but to obey His commandments. 'God
moves in a mysterious way His mysteries to perform,'" she quoted
incorrectly.

This did not seem an adequate explanation or the height of good
sense on the part of God, so I resolved thereupon never to consult
my mother again upon problems of such nature.

In accordance with a hideous custom, I was one of the pallbearers at Paul's funeral and was told to wear a dark suit with a white tie and white cotton gloves. I stood near the bier in a suffocating room, which was pungent with the sickly odor of tuberoses. I had helped to carry the coffin to the hearse and from the hearse into the church and from the church to the hearse again and from the hearse to the grave. There had been more banks and wreaths of tuberoses and calla lilies in the church, and these were strewn upon the grave when the shovelers had done their work. The preacher had said solemn, untrue things in a perfunctorily lugubrious manner and at one point had so incensed me that I wanted to cry out, "He didn't! No such a thing! He wanted to be a prize fighter! He used to want to be an evangelist, but he changed his mind and wanted to be a prize fighter! And if he had lived he would have been the champion of the world!" And then, because of the oppressive heat, the thought died in my mind, to be succeeded by a terrifying intimation that maybe God had taken Paul's life because he had chosen between religion and prize fighting in favor of the latter.

The two episodes just recounted marked my passing from childhood into adolescence, that unhappy introspective period in the life of a sentient man, during which he ceases to live wholly in the present and seeks to explore the periphery of a universe of which he is the center, lives vicariously a thousand lives, identifies himself with a thousand heroes, and gathers unto himself an unreconcilable mass of sentiments, ideals and opinions which color his understanding of the biological processes of nature and insulate him from contact with an unbearable reality. It is a state in which poets remain as long as they are poets, and it is the period which gives the world its myths and religions, or at least that spirit of myth and religion which is not codified into laws and taboos. It is the period wherein man seeks to gather from the experience of others a residuum of wisdom which will facilitate his adjustment to a plan of life, but which, by that token, makes life for him thenceforward a constant discarding of theory and a constant sloughing off of illusions.

At the beginning I came under the influence of three men, all of whom took a paternal interest in me and became my guides, friends and tutors.

One of them was a fat and erudite dipsomaniac; another was a cultivated Catholic priest who was more devoted to learning perhaps than to piety; and the other was a ne'er-do-well newspaper man who had studied at Amherst in a vain search for a suitable profession among law, medicine, chemistry and pedagogy and had been a camp cook for cowhands on a ranch in the Southwest and had drifted into the newspaper profession through a natural gift for writing and because it was the easiest job handy.

The fat dipsomaniac was an editorial writer on a newspaper where I had taken employment in a manner to be set forth later. His name was Shannon Mountjoy; he had studied for the ministry; had abandoned theology for medicine and surgery; and had once taught anatomy at an Eastern university. He had written little essays, which had appeared in the back pages of the *Atlantic Monthly,* a few popular treatises on medical subjects which had appeared in the Boston *Transcript,* and had become an editorial writer after a protracted spree which had left him without funds and at the mercy of a newspaper editor who knew him and advanced him money for food and lodging.

He and the priest were drawn together by their interest in Latin literature, over which they had irreconcilable differences of opinion not only as to the merits of its various masterpieces, but also as to its pronunciation. Father Gregory had been instructed in the Italian method with its soft *g* and *c* and its Italianated diphthongs, whereas Mr Mountjoy pronounced Cicero *Kikero,* Caesar *Kaisar,* and made the *g* in Virgil hard and pronounced the *v* as *w.*

Since both of them professed to find ineffable beauty in Latin verse and both of them had committed to memory whole odes, epodes and cantos of Virgil, Horace and Catullus, their definitions of this ineffable beauty were based upon individual perceptions which were unlike in almost every particular. I listened to these Latin enthusiasts with something like awe and rapture, but I was at the same time being instructed by demonstration in the axiom that beauty exists only in the mind of the auditor or beholder, and that the individual mind has a capacity for creating an illusion of beauty where, to another eye or to another ear, beauty does not exist.

To Father Gregory, Horace's "Eheu fugaces" was an abomina-

tion of gutturals, a harsh and cacophonous piece of gibberish, as
Mr Mountjoy declaimed it. To Mr Mountjoy, the same poem was
an insipid and effeminate composition without music, majesty or
grandeur, as Father Gregory recited it. They were in agreement,
however, about the sentiment of the poem, which they declared
noble.

Both the music and sentiment of that poem escaped me, who was
thrilled no less by this fervor over the things of the mind and spirit,
and who was at an age more able to appreciate:

> *O matre pulchra filia pulchrior*
> *Quem criminosis cumque voles modum*
> *Pones iambis sive flamma*
> *Sive mari libet Hadriano.*

Jerry Rand, the third adult of this triumvirate, which was to encourage in me a love for learning, a taste for poetry and a curiosity
concerning the constituents of matter and man's relation to the
universe, had an admiration for Greek and a disdain for Latin,
which language he was fond of saying was a crude and barbarous
dialect fit only for traders and bargainers. "Latin found its highest
expression in the Roman laws," he would olympiate. "Law is a rule
of trade, and lawyers and auctioneers are bargain makers. Cicero
was a shyster."

Father Gregory and Mr Mountjoy, who thought well of Cicero,
particularly of his *De Senectute,* were at a disadvantage in this
assault upon a language and literature they cherished; for their
knowledge of Greek, while it was passable, was unequal to the
challenge of comparisons in syntax, prosody and vocabulary hurled
at them by Jerry, who also had a knowledge of Latin comparable
to their own.

When Jerry was drunk (which was often, though he drank because he liked to and not, like Mr Mountjoy, because he could not
help himself) he recited Homer, Theocritus and Anacreon. He delighted to tease Father Gregory and Mr Mountjoy by reciting a
passage from Greek and asking them, when he had concluded, "Do
you know what that is?" and waiting for them to answer.

Timidly Mr Mountjoy would sometimes make a bluff at recognition and would attribute a poem in Ionic Greek to a Doric poet.

Jerry would set him right elaborately, by showing certain modifications which separated the two poets by time and place.

When Father Gregory and Mr Mountjoy both confessed ignorance of the poem, Jerry would answer his own question by saying, "That contains at once the most perfect and the most poetic iambic hexameter ever written," or, "That is an exceptionally fine example of the mixolydian mode invented by Sappho."

Mr Mountjoy and Father Gregory tolerated Jerry's badgering because Jerry had a talent for listening when he did not have an urge to air his knowledge, and his fantastic life in many places had given him a fund of anecdote which they could both comprehend and appreciate.

Their sessions to which I was an enraptured auditor were held over a table in a Greek restaurant on late evenings in the fore part of the week when Father Gregory did not have to hear confessions or say the Mass. Occasionally Jerry, who knew modern as well as classical Greek, drew into the circle the Greek waiter and co-proprietor whose name was Miltiades Pappathakos (shortened to Milt Pappas), and who had graduated from the *gymnasion* in Sparta. They would dispute the scansion of a line from the *Iliad* to the discomfiture of Mr Mountjoy and Father Gregory, who were obliged to suspend their arguments and assume the role of auditors to a debate they did not comprehend.

I, unlike Father Gregory and Mr Mountjoy, enjoyed Jerry's Greek recitations and disputes without comprehending them; and they instilled in me a desire to acquire Greek as well as Latin that I might have the distinction of communing with the minds of Homer and Sappho. I was being taught Latin in school, and I acquired a Greek grammar and a Greek lexicon and devoted evenings of dogged industry to them. Impatient at my progress, I made my approach to the mind of ancient Athens through translations, in the Bohn Library, of Aeschylus, Sophocles, Euripides, Homer and Aristophanes. I found "Prometheus Bound" so much to my liking that I read three different translations of it and finally learned the whole of it by heart in the metrical version by Elizabeth Barrett Browning. Then I planned and began a poetic drama to be called, "Prometheus Unbound," only to find, when I had almost finished it, that Shelley had anticipated me, and such was the development of my self-critical faculty that I was able to perceive that Shelley had written a much better one than I had.

Courtesy forbade the intrusion of theological discussions in the circle; but since the three of them felt a responsibility toward my character and mind, they did not omit from their impromptu curricula a haphazard course in moral instruction, in *éducation* as the French use the term. The three of them urged upon me the idea of chastity in youth, each for quite different reasons. Father Gregory taught that chastity was commendable to God and a duty to a boy's future wife, if he should live to have one. Mr Mountjoy said that sexual indulgence drained away from the brain the fluids on which the cortices were nourished and should, therefore, be postponed until the brain had reached its full development. And Jerry warned against numerous entanglements as the shackles of freedom and against casual carnality as full of the danger of venereal infection.

Concerning alcoholic indulgence Mr Mountjoy and Jerry were unanimous in warning me against it. Mr Mountjoy, who swigged all day from a bottle, was a vehement Prohibitionist. "Drinking destroys the mind, the body and the character," he said, with the humility of one who is offering himself as a horrible example. "It is a curse. The country will be better off when it is dry. When I can afford it, I shall take the cure. If that is not soon, it will get me someday, stop my heart, and I'll keel over in the street." Jerry, who drank only whisky, was an advocate of the restriction of the sale of alcoholic beverages to light wines and beer, with the proviso that legislation should forbid the sale of alcohol in aqueous solutions of any sort to minors. "My authority for this is my own experience," he said, "but Plato ordained, in his Second Book of Laws, that boys should not taste wine at all, that up to the age of thirty men should drink wine sparingly, but that after forty men should drink wine at banquets to temper their austerity and make them human. For myself, whom I offer neither as a lesson in iniquity nor in piety, I employ alcohol as a substitute for love and as a consolation in adversity. There is this one thing I would impress upon you: The love of the imagination is more satisfying than the love of the flesh. Helen and Andromache are more real to me than any love of my own past."

[82]

I failed to understand how this could be; but as my thirst for learning at that period was more insistent than my sexual curiosity, Jerry's suggestions did not pique my interest. It had flattered me to be drawn into this company, and my docility and enthusiasm had been so eager that each took me as an irregular pupil and undertook to instruct me individually. Mr Mountjoy came to my house once a week to drill me in the pronunciation of French by causing me to read pages from Renan, Mérimée, Daudet and George Sand. When the drill was concluded he would talk to me about the Palatine anthology and what is known of the lives of Aeschylus, Sophocles, Euripides, Sappho, Anacreon and Theocritus. He presented to me the Bohn translation of one of the oddest and most fascinating works in literature, a book which I was thereafter to read in snatches when other books palled—*The Deipnosophists* of Athenaeus. "That book," said Mr Mountjoy, "will give you an idea of Greek life and manners that is probably closer to reality than any other book that has been handed down to us. That is because it is a work of compilation and not a work of imagination. The author was a prosaic and worldly fellow who cared nothing about literature as such. He was a voluptuary whose chief pleasure in life was to fill his belly with good food and wine. Whether he had the money to gratify his gluttony we cannot be sure. He may have had the appetite without having any means of satisfying it except through his imagination; and it might be that this great catalogue of wines and dishes is the work of a starving man. But though he may have been undernourished and emaciated, you may be sure he was a voluptuary. To him the book was a compilation of recipes. To make his cookbook readable he introduced gossip and conversation on learned subjects. By this means he managed to include fragments of verse by poets whose work would otherwise be entirely lost, including Sappho and most of the poets of the Greek anthology. Athenaeus is also the source of much of our information about the private lives of the great poets, and he enlivened his prosy book with legends concerning the famous courtesans. It is from him, for instance, that we learn that the gossip was that Aeschylus wrote his tragedies while he was drunk and that Euripides was a debauchee who hated women. All these scraps of gossip may be untrue, but they are entertaining."

Father Gregory was solicitous about my education in painting and architecture and loaned me illustrated books on art from the parish library. "You will do well, my son," said Father Gregory, "not to fill your head with the speculations of philosophers. I saw you carrying about a volume by Schopenhauer the other day. And you have begun to bother your mind too much with questions which can only result in confusion. I do not urge you to give up such reading as vexatious to the soul, for happily I believe you will shortly come to some such conclusion yourself. I have here all the books that are on the Index Expurgatorius and you are welcome to them at any time you choose to read them; but the Church is wise in these matters, and I suggest that you read poetry and acquaint yourself with the masterpieces of painting and let the philosophers alone."

Instead of profiting from this sensible advice, I crammed my head with an enormous amount of lumber, so eager was I in the vain pursuit of the answer to the riddle of life.

One day I had gone to see Father Gregory's paintings (for which he was later to become famous)—portraits of the pope and cardinals, interpretations of episodes in the lives of the saints and landscapes. Father Gregory was being remiss in his compact with Mr Mountjoy that there should be no proselytizing. But Father Gregory's slight sin was to be condoned, for I was plaguing him with questions. "No theology, Father," Mr Mountjoy had said, "for you must remember that I studied for the Protestant ministry and my mind is a thesaurus of divine exegesis. We should quarrel inevitably, and the nature of our quarrel would be much more serious than our squabbles over the pronunciation of Latin; for the soul is a rag bag filled with relics and mementos of our early life and of the lives of those who begot us, relics and mementos of no intrinsic value, probably, but for which we have an irrational attachment as to a lock of hair, a tintype portrait, or a seared flower which we cannot remember how we come by. My affection is equal to my admiration for you, and I should hate to see that affection cankered by the acrimony of our separate prejudices. Of the literary merits and of the character of any and all of the writing saints we may speak; but this boy's soul is budding, and we must let it seek the sun as it will. No theology, Father."

[84]

In the library of the vicarage I was listening to Father Gregory expound the genius of Giotto by reference to the symbols, composition, light, color and movement in reproductions in a large color-process folio. My attention was arrested by the detail of a fresco showing Jesus insulted by the Jews, and my mind switched from the contemplation of beauty to the framing of a question of dogma.

"Father," I began, "in the South I knew some people who were Baptists and some who were Christians, that is, they call their church the Christian Church, though the Baptists call them Campbellites. The Christian Church and the Baptist Church, my mother told me once, are just alike, except that the Baptists believe in close communion and the Christians do not. I don't know what close communion is, really, but the Baptists believe that only those who hold close communion will get into heaven, and Christians believe that baptism must be by total immersion, like the Baptists, but that the Baptists are excluded from heaven because of their close communion. Does the Catholic Church teach that nobody will get to heaven except Catholics?"

Father Gregory, remembering Mr Mountjoy's injunction, hesitated for a moment and moistened his lips before answering.

"My Mother, Holy Church, my son, is tolerant of all men and of all religions, creeds and denominations. The Mass is offered for the saints in heaven in thanksgiving to God for their salvation; for the living on earth, both the just and the unjust, the pure in heart and the sinful, heretics and schismatics, infidels and Jews; and for the souls in Purgatory for the prompt release of their sufferings. The Mass is the perpetual witness of the sacrifice that Jesus Christ, Our Lord, offered on Calvary for the redemption of all men."

"You use the Jewish Old Testament, Father. The Jews believe they are the chosen people. If the Old Testament is the inspired word of God, how can you accept it without believing also that the Jews are the chosen people?"

"The prophet Malachi foretold God's repudiation of the Jews and His refusal to accept their sacrifices that the clean and perfect oblation of the death of Christ would be substituted for the sacrifices of the Old Law. . . . But these are matters which should not be troubling you. Consider now how sublime is Giotto's use of color. Unfortunately the formula the old masters used for their pigments is lost."

That night I read, in Malachi, the passage wherein Christian theologians found their warrant for God's repudiation of the Jews in favor of the Gentiles: "I have no pleasure in you, saith the Lord of hosts: and I will not receive a gift of your hand. For from the rising of the sun even to the going down, my name is great among the gentiles, and in every place there is sacrifice, and there is offered to my name a clean oblation: for my name is great among the gentiles, saith the Lord of hosts."

This put a great burden of questions upon my mind, questions so abstruse I could find no answers for them, questions as big as those about the beginning of things before life was created or any consciousness existed, and as big as the question as to what there will be when the earth has ceased to exist; for was not this Malachi himself a Jew, and was not the Book of Malachi the last book of the Old Testament, placed in the Bible just before the beginning of the New Testament which begins, "The Book of the generation of Jesus Christ, the son of David, the son of Abraham," and were not David and Abraham Jews?

I had been talking to Mr Mountjoy about Oliver Wendell Holmes's *The Autocrat of the Breakfast Table,* and Mr Mountjoy recommended my reading Emerson's Phi Beta Kappa address. Thus it was that I tumbled upon the most tantalizingly allusive of essayists; and, out of sheer curiosity in following Emerson's allusions, within two years I had devoured Kant's *Critique of Pure Reason,* Schopenhauer's *World as Will and Idea,* Carlyle's *Sartor Resartus,* Plato's *Dialogues,* Sir Thomas Browne, Novalis, Ruysbroeck, Plotinus, Lucretius, Swedenborg, Diogenes Laertius, Plutarch, Locke, Hegel, Hume, Comte Fichte, the *Analects* of Confucius, *The Book of the Dead,* parts of the Koran, the Zend-Avesta, Thomas à Kempis, the Bhagavad-Gita, Juvenal, Persius, Hesiod, Homer, Marcus Aurelius, Epictetus, Plutarch, and Xenophon's *Memorabilia* somewhat in the disorder named. I thought I had found in Emerson the emancipator of my intelligence, and I paid the American iconoclast the homage of reading everything by and about him that I found available, including Emerson's *Journals,*

Charles Eliot Norton's *Letters,* and the works of Hawthorne, Holmes and Lowell, who might teach me better to understand my master by reason of the fact of their having known him.

I had not observed that extensive learning and classical scholarship had not been of great advantage to Mr Mountjoy and to Jerry in increasing their ability to earn a living. One day Jerry was discharged; for things had been going badly with the newspaper, and it was found necessary to curtail expenses. He joined the weekly gathering at the Greek café and announced that he had found a job in Okmulgee. "I was going to leave tonight," he said, "but I shall have to wait until morning. I went down to the yards to get aboard my private car and somebody was putting hogs in it."

The imminence of Jerry's departure affected me as in the nature of a bereavement; and Father Gregory and Mr Mountjoy showed by their demeanor that relief from Jerry's flings at their inadequacies in Greek would not be a complete solace in losing him as a companion in their rather pathetic retention of an interest in the things of the mind and spirit.

Jerry became a columnist on the Okmulgee *Times,* and a clever and witty one at that, exercising considerable influence in state politics. He reformed in his habits of dress as well as in habits in alcoholic consumption. He settled down, married and, when I saw him in New York twelve years later, he actually looked younger than I had ever seen him—neat and spruce as a pin.

On the occasion when I saw Jerry in 1923, I had just been asked by Ernest Gruening; then editor of the *Nation,* to write the article on Oklahoma in a series Gruening was running under the title, *These United States* (later published in book form in two volumes). The intent of the series was critically expository, muck-raking. I already had a great deal of material gathered during a stay of eight months in Oklahoma in 1920. Jerry supplied me with more data on political corruption in the state—during a long luncheon session at the close of which I told Jerry that, as editor of the *Times,* he would in patriotic honor be bound to denounce me and my article when it appeared. He said, "Of course!"

The article was a sensation in Oklahoma. The circulation of the *Nation* in Oklahoma hitherto had been limited to libraries and a handful of regular subscribers. But Gruening saw to it that editors of all the Oklahoma newspapers got marked copies of my Oklahoma article. A deluge of news stories, editorials and letters to the newspapers, denouncing and defending the article and me, filled the press of Oklahoma. Bitter fights arose between correspondents. I got a gunny-sackful of clippings, and letters came to me promising me a horsewhipping if I ever stepped across the border of the state. But of all the bawlings-out I got from the Oklahoma newspapers, the most magnificent, the most eloquent one was written by Jerry in the Okmulgee *Times.* It rose to Miltonic heights of invective and abuse. It was a journalistic masterpiece. Jerry could approach his subject with a purely impersonal, dispassionate, artistic purpose. Having no conviction about the matter except the one he shared with me, he could let pure art have complete expression. Some of the other editorial writers let emotions sway them, so their denunciations were weaker. (Jerry, as I write this, is on the copy desk of the New York *Sun.*)

The City Café at which we gathered after the newspaper had been put to press for the night was, as I have mentioned, run by the three brothers Pappathakos (shortened by the immigration authorities to Pappas—which means, of course, that the immigration authorities destroyed their real name, Thakos, and kept the modifier, Pappa, which in modern Greek is an addition to a family name indicating there has been a bishop of the Greek Orthodox priesthood in the family). The brothers were Miltiades (Milt), Konstantinos (Gus) and 'Erakles or Hercules (Harry).

Milt and Gus were graduates of the *gymnasium* (or secondary school) in Sparta, and Milt had gone to the university there. Both were learned in ancient as well as modern Greek and were able to read Homer and Plato with greater facility than most American college graduates are able to read Chaucer. Moreover, they pronounced ancient Greek in a manner vastly different from the Germanic way we are taught to pronounce it. Their way of pronouncing ancient Greek was a much more sonorous and agreeable way than the German-English-American academic way—a matter upon which I meditated with results to be found on pages 48 and 49 of *Titans of Literature.* (This unorthodox argument that the Greeks know better than German pedants how to pronounce their own language has seemed so reasonable and logical that I have received many letters from academic scholars congratulating me upon my point in scholarship and many letters from modern Greek scholars thanking me for what they had felt but dared not express.)

The general cultivation of Milt in arts and letters was surprising until I learned some years later from a book on modern Greece that the Greek laws making education through the high schools compulsory had resulted in such a crisis of unemployment that it had had to be repealed. Athens and Sparta swarmed with cultivated Greeks—lawyers, doctors, teachers: there were no native citizens to do the manual labor or sweep the streets—a fact which brought in hordes of Turks, Armenians, etc., who thus crowded out young men like Milt, Gus and Harry. Such young men came to America, if they could, and entered trade, setting up in the restaurant, fruit-store, candy or florist business, generally.

The way they got to America was by a complicated system of indenture. A young man who wanted to go to America would go to a labor entrepreneur who furnished him steerage fare, train fare and incidental expenses to whatever town in America—New York, Spokane, Dallas, Shawnee, or wherever there was need for a bootblack or kitchen helper. He signed a paper agreeing to work a certain term of months or years, depending upon the money advanced, and the employer was under contract to pay the entrepreneur the bulk of the young man's wages until the original amount plus interest (usually amounting to about three times the amount advanced) was repaid. While he was working out his indenture the bootblack usually slept on the benches in the bootblack booth or in the kitchen if he was a restaurant employee. His net wages were about a dollar and a half a week. He was under surveillance and dared not run away because he could be returned at any time to Greece since his entry under a labor contract was in violation of the immigration laws. When he had worked out his indenture the young Greek was free to enter the competitive employment field as a waiter, dishwasher, cook, peddler, bootblack with full wages, or employer of imported indentured labor. These Greeks were ordinarily thrifty, and they usually prospered.

Harry Pappas married the daughter of Jost Zweifel, a Swiss who ran the dairy farm which supplied most of the town with milk. Zweifel, too, was a product of Continental education. He spoke and read French, German and Italian, and, being well read in the German classics and in French literature, a musician who played several instruments, including the accordion and harmonica, he delighted to talk to me of Goethe, Schiller, Voltaire and Renan. Jost was a particular friend of my father's, and one day, when I was visiting my parents and he was spending the day with them and was quite drunk on homemade beer he had brought my father, he saw in my hand a copy of Hugo's *Les Misérables*. He exclaimed, like a tragedian of Bayreuth, "Le misérable, c'est moi!"

I took this maudlinity with greater seriousness than it needed to be taken: for the rest of the day I tramped the woods pondering those words, wondering what tragic fate it was which included Jost Zweifel, the healthy, happy harmonica player and dairyman, among the miserable. His children and his grandchildren would not have known what the words meant. They all made haste to make themselves as American and as unforeign as possible, stubbornly declining to speak or to learn the language of their parents—and perhaps, seeing that education and cultivation had profited their parents little, declining to absorb any more knowledge than they had to to pass the elementary-grade examinations.

As I write this it depresses me to record that Milt—that Miltiades who came to America with the classical Greek words for *honor, courage, economy* stenciled on his rucksack, who told me the legend of Ephialtes and who was patient in drilling me in the recitation of Sappho—that Milt is dead, a suicide victim of the American economic depression, and that Gus—that Gus who gave me free cups of coffee of cold mornings when I was carrying my newspaper route and let me read *Faust* at the counter by the hour before dawn had come up over the prairies—that Gus has long since returned to die a consumptive among the wine-grape vines of the Lacedaemonian hills where he grew up as a boy. Jost Zweifel, too, is dead, and one of his sons (I believe) lies in France, where he went to war with and against other posterity of his father's beloved Goethe and Schiller. And from Hercules' loins there are strange, sturdy children, mixtures of Greek and Swiss, to work out their destinies far from Marathon or the Jungfrau.

CHAPTER VII

I Take Stock of My Fifteenth Year

A Pantheistic View of Life. I Have No Firmer Belief in Philosophy Than in Religion. Quarterback on the High-School Football Team. Favorite Authors. Plutarch's Alcibiades My Favorite Character. I Dislike Marcus Cato. I Should Like to Be Like My Father. Emerson Becomes My Guide and Proctor. I Like Aristophanes. Shelley My Favorite Poet. Favorite Nineteenth-Century Authors. I Box with Fred Stevens. More Reading. On Right and Wrong.

(An exact transcription from my diary)

IT IS MONDAY MORNING. The Christmas holidays have begun and school is closed. I am sitting alone in my room, surrounded by my books and pictures and my scientific instruments, including a compound microscope which my father bought for me last spring and which I so much wanted. I amuse myself for hours studying the great world hidden to the normal eye under the lenses of that microscope. More than anything else it has given me a pantheistic view of life. My favorite saint is Saint Francis Assisi because he claimed kinship with the sun, the moon, the flowers, the wind, the water, beasts and insects. I hope I may sometime have a telescope that I may

at midnight hour
Be seen in some high lonely tower
Where I may oft outwatch the Bear,
With thrice great Hermes, or unsphere

BEFORE I FORGET

The spirit of Plato, to unfold
What worlds or what vast regions hold
The immortal mind that hath forsook
Her mansions in this fleshly nook;
And of those demons that are found
In fire, air, flood, or underground
Whose power hath a true consent
With planet or with element.

I have read more and thought more this last year than any year previously. Socrates bids us "Know thyself," and I have sought not only to know myself but to know Man's relation to the Universe. I am going to try to take stock of some of the things I have learned. We are not very religious in our house, and since we left Kentucky Mama has not made me go to Sunday School, for which I am glad, because the only preacher I have ever heard worth listening to is Bishop Quayle. I remember several things from his sermon, called "If Any Man Lack Wisdom, Let Him Ask of God": they are, "We are all born ignoramuses, and the most of us retain our birthrights"; "The question mark is the key to the door of knowledge"; and "The best way to know God is to know God's folks." I admire Father Gregory and I have a great affection for him. He is a good and kind and learned man. But I could not be a Catholic. I like the Catholic services, and I have gone several times to the Easter service and Christmas masses, which are very beautiful and moving. But I cannot believe that God has revealed Himself only to Jews and Christians. The story of the Crucifixion and of the Resurrection is probably the most powerful drama ever conceived, for it brings hope to the lowly and oppressed, and the lowly and oppressed are as of the sands of the sea; but I am inclined to agree with the old Vedic hymn that "All is a manifestation of Vishnu; the earth and sky are but transient paintings and heaven itself a decoy."

I have no firmer belief in philosophy than in religion. What are precepts? Men advise as befits themselves. And the natures of men are dissimilar. I have nothing in common with this or that philosopher; my inheritance, physical and psychic, is not the same as his, nor is my environment. Bacon and Locke differ in opinions, Aristotle, though a pupil of Plato, taught at variance with his tutor's doctrines. Man's instruction, I have concluded, is usually his own opposite. He realizes what he is himself, dislikes that self, and teaches by the rule of "Do not as I do but as I say."

All is opinion, a perfect delirium of opinion—Schopenhauer quoting Calderon, "Pues et delito mayor del hombres es haber nacido"; Thomas à Kempis quoting Ecclesiastes, "Vanitas, vanitorum"; Jeremy Taylor emulating Ezekiel; Mahomet promising a realm of houris; the Bhagavad-Gita foretelling Naraka; Tolstoi giving up riches and turning his back upon his former life to till the soil and preach humility; Pater becoming his own Marius; Whitman philosophizing from the top of an omnibus. With Schopenhauer I aver, "The world is my idea"; with Descartes I agree, "Cogito; ergo sum"; I nod to Ecclesiastes in agreement that all is vanity; I assert with Sir Thomas Browne that "A man's reason is his best Edipus"; Emerson is right: "The education of the will is the object of existence"; I believe with Omar that I am myself heaven and hell; but I accept the teachings of all men "cum grano salis."

I am quarterback on the high-school football team. Football is excellent exercise for both body and mind. It develops quickness of intellect, an ability to grasp a situation at a glance, and strategy. The quarterback must be somewhat of a general. He must pick the weak places in the opponents' line, use judgment so that he does not overwork his backfield, and devise tricks to outwit the other team. Concentration is developed, and every muscle of the body is called into play. Courage is gained and determination.

My favorite authors so far are Plutarch, Aeschylus, Emerson, Plato, Aristophanes, Goethe and Marlowe. I don't like Euripides much because he is a woman hater and shows women up in an evil light; and Sophocles, at least in translation, does not seem as great a soul as Aeschylus. I have read "The Iliad" and "The Odyssey" in Chapman's and in Butcher and Lang's translations; and I don't care so much for "The Iliad," except for the passages about Hector and Andromache and where Helen comes in. I don't approve of the morals of the gods in Homer; for they were jealous and capricious, spiteful and unjust. But neither do I approve of the morals of the God of the Old Testament. Those Jews were a verminous race, treacherous, cruel and deceitful, and yet the God that Jews and Christians believe in was supposed to favor them and to look upon them as His chosen people. If there is a viler and more revolting story of treachery and revenge anywhere in the world than that related in the Book of Esther I have not read it, unless it happens to be the story of how the sons of Jacob, with God's approval, treated Shechem, the honorable young prince who sought to marry Dinah.

Because I think that good manners and tolerance and kindness are the most valuable virtues in the world, my favorite character in history is Alcibiades, as his life is related by Plutarch. "The renown which he earned by these public services was equalled by the admiration he attracted to his private life; he captivated and won over everybody by his conformity to Spartan habits. People who saw him wearing his hair close cut, bathing in cold water, eating coarse meal, and dining on black broth, doubted, or rather could not believe, that he had ever had a cook in his house, or had ever seen a perfumer, or had worn a mantle of Milesian purple. For he had, as it was observed, this peculiar talent and artifice for gaining men's affections, that he could at once comply with and really embrace and enter into their habits and ways of life, and change faster than a chameleon. . . . Not that his natural disposition changed so easily, nor that his real character was so variable, but, whenever he was sensible that by pursuing his own inclinations he might give offense to those with whom he had occasion to converse, he transformed himself into any shape and adopted any fashion, that he observed to be most agreeable to them."

I want to be like that. I cannot think that any man is so endowed with truth or virtue that he may rightfully impose his own views and beliefs upon others and make himself offensive in that way. I have no desire to conquer the world like Alexander or Caesar. I wish merely to live my life as it seems good to me. My inward thoughts on things now differ so greatly from the thoughts of people about me that if I should speak out I should offend or horrify them. I love these people, and I want to learn from them, so I keep my peace, which is, I think, good manners.

Paul was right when he said that all men are liars. All humane men are liars. When one has a true regard for the feelings of others, has mutinous riots in his soul, and yet continues to appear genial, he is deceiving, but I call him blessed. Through courtesy and out of knowledge that no man is perfect, we should withhold our unfavorable opinion of others. This would be a strange and impossible world if it were inhabited by truth-telling men, men who always spoke out just what was in their minds. And what is truth? And how is one to know but that the plain-speaking mind is not warped and envious and narrow and greedy and coarse?

Having just written that, I may seem to be contradictory by saying that the character I dislike the most in Plutarch is Marcus Cato, and I am glad that Plutarch, who is the greatest of all moralists, disapproves of him also: "He reckoned nothing a good bargain, which was superfluous; but whatever price it was, though sold for a farthing, he would think a great price, if you had no need of it; and was for the purchase of lands for sowing and feeding, rather than grounds for sweeping and watering. Some imputed these things to petty avarice, but others approved of him, as if he had only the more strictly denied himself for the rectifying and amending of others. Yet, certainly, in my judgment, it marks an over-rigid temper, for a man to take the work out of his servants as out of a brute beast, turning them off and selling them in their old age, and thinking there ought to be no further commerce between man and man, than while there arises some profit by it."

Besides being an unjust and heartless man as who should sell his slaves and domestic animals when they were grown decrepit instead of showing mercy and gratitude for their long service, Cato was also a despicable and hypocritical man, an interferer and busybody regulating other people's affairs while his own conduct was blameworthy as lecherous. He was appointed censor, and at one time he threw out of the senate, Manilius, who would have been the next consul, "because," as Plutarch relates, "in the presence of his daughter, and in open day, he had kissed his wife." And yet "he would often, even in his old age, address himself to women, and when he was past a lover's age, married a young woman upon the following pretenses," and Plutarch goes on to relate a shady transaction, Cato being forced to marry by his son's censuring of his conduct.

[95]

BEFORE I FORGET

I should like to be as much like my father as I can, for he is the wisest and kindest and most tolerant man in the world, I do believe. It is strange that he partakes of those qualities that are so commendable in the character of Cato in that his plan of living is austere and frugal, nor does he care for luxuries, and at the same time he has those virtues that I admire in Alcibiades and none of Alcibiades' faults of licentiousness and effeminacy. Both men and women love my father, for he has a great wit and humor and he can keep a whole room roaring with laughter at his sallies, and I have never heard him speak ill of a woman ever; nor does he speak ill of men either except to ridicule to their faces those who are tight-fisted and mean-spirited and whom he has caught in some hypocrisy or meanness like usury or taking advantage of the poor and helpless, whereat he is courageous and his tongue is so sharp and stinging that the man is humiliated, while others who have reason to hate that man laugh at his discomfiture, and the man slinks away like a coward and is afraid to answer my father, for he knows that my father is right, and a little later on he will try to placate my father, being afraid of him, and attempt a sort of bribery, but my father will tell him what he thinks of him, and the man is more scared of him than ever. If my father were susceptible to bribery he would be rich, for that politicians, knowing how much influence he has with voters because all those who know him consult him as an oracle, because he is wise and just and all his many friends vote like him, the crooked politicians would pay him in coin or position for his influence. They have sought him, but my father always gives them a tongue lashing and never allows them to get nearer to his house than the front porch, saying to them that since they are not worthy of his friendship, they may not pass his threshold, and on one occasion when a pompous politician came into our yard without being asked while my father was watering the lawn and sought my father's support, my father called to him as he was entering the gate, "I am not in the market for any Peruna today," and when the fellow came on after that rebuff my father turned the hose on him, and the fellow fled. They are afraid of my father, too, because he is six feet tall and as straight and strong as an Indian runner.

I TAKE STOCK OF MY FIFTEENTH YEAR

Poor Mother thinks that Father should not make so many friends and that he should be more saving and industrious, and she plagues him with censure and questionings, and because he does not answer her back, as he used to do, but sits silent, with his head in his hands, or puts on his hat and goes out of the house to walk by himself, she gets frantic and hysterical and ends up with a headache. And so now when company comes there is always a strange transformation in him in that while people are there he keeps them merry with jokes and stories and comments, but as soon as they are gone he becomes morose because Mother always tells him he should not say this or that, because it is not respectable but in bad taste.

I hate to see company leave on that account. Mother thinks all Northern and Western people are vulgar and common, and she shuts herself away from people on that account and so makes enemies who think she is uppish. I feel sorry for her, because I don't think she is contented away from her people and she works and worries too much and seems never to have any real pleasure in life. And yet I remember when she was pretty as a young girl and gay and had a ringing laughter. I wonder what can be the trouble. I can't talk with Mother about any of the things I think, because she thinks I should not have any thoughts she has not first given me and makes me keep silent by saying that it is sinful not to believe in heaven and hell or to doubt the divine inspiration of the Bible. She says these things by rote because she is not religious; she does not go to church any more, and she does not read the Bible.

Emerson freed me from Christian dogma. His most profound utterance I believe is his prophecy concerning the New Generalization. Our beliefs, creeds, hopes and customs are at the mercy of the new generalization, he said, but "fear not this new generalization—it is always but an influx of divinity into the soul." Superstition, fear, untruth, mental and physical slavery, and corruption under the new generalization will yield to knowledge, moral and physical courage, freedom of thought and action, and spiritual beauty. The orthodox will cry out, in the words of Euripides, "All to wreck has gone the homage due to God"; but it will be an ignorant and unthinking cry. God will increase in grandeur before our eyes.

The Greeks tell us that Prometheus destroyed the fear of death by giving man Hope. Hesiod has it that Zeus gave Epimetheus a vessel and that inquisitive Pandora opened its lid and let loose all the evils of mankind, and only Hope remained. With hope urging us onward, we strive to do good deeds and to live the good life, which Plato says is a life of fullness but without extremes. We cannot be wise and worship an anthropomorphic deity; we cannot have happiness and be in constant fear of displeasing that deity. Victor Hugo has wisely said, "Religions do a useful thing: they narrow God to the limits of man. Philosophy does a necessary thing: it elevates man to the plane of God." But philosophy, if it is true, is a confession of ignorance and a constant seeking. I am like Wagner in Goethe's *Faust:* "Most zealously I seek for erudition, much I know—but to know all is my ambition."

Having read philosophy and found Plato and Emerson most pleasing and most instructive in the good life, I turned to biography, wherein each man finds traits to remind him of himself. I love unimportant, human little bits of biography and of autobiography. If Plutarch tells us that Pericles had an elongated head; if Diogenes Laertius tells us that Zeno's head was bent to one side; if Suetonius tells us that Caesar was sensitive about his bald head; if Cellini tells us that Torrigiani broke the nose of Michaelangelo; if Zenophon tells us that Socrates married a vixen to test his placidity; if Boswell tells us that Johnson counted the lamp posts that he passed and that Goldsmith wore gaudy clothes; if Franklin tells us that he walked the streets of Philadelphia with loaves in his pockets; if Carlyle tells us that Frederick the Great knew nothing of Shakespeare, Milton, Dante or Homer and adored Voltaire; if Holmes tells us that Emerson was particularly fond of pie; if Howells tells us that Whitman liked beer; we should commend them for these homely and intimate details.

All writing is more or less autobiographical, but autobiographies are unfaithful portraits; they are usually Cromwell's face without the warts. Marius is Hugo, but Hugo is not Marius. Every male character in *The Vicar of Wakefield* is Goldsmith, but Goldsmith is not even George. Rousseau is the Rousseau of the *Confessions,* but anyone can detect the lies in Cellini. Shakespeare is both Hamlet and Falstaff; but I believe he wanted to be Coriolanus.*

When I am in the mood for humor, Aristophanes is the writer who pleases me most. I like his *Clouds* the best, for although it makes great fun of Socrates whom I love, it is a masterpiece of fooling. The scene where Socrates is discovered suspended from a basket is extremely ludicrous, and the comedy of the scene that follows is eternal. When Socrates attempts to explain to Strepsiades that it is not Jupiter who gives us rain and causes thunder, but the collision of clouds caused by the ethereal vortex, Strepsiades says:

> *What is he?*
> *I've never heard of him; is he not Jove?*
> *Or is Jove put aside and Vortex crowned*
> *King of Olympus in his state and place?*

I am inclined to believe that Socrates and Aristophanes were good friends, and I detect an underlying vein of praise for Socrates. At all events Plato represents Aristophanes and Socrates dining together and showing great respect for each other. Aristophanes was almost a universal genius; for he was a scientist, a common-sense philosopher, a dramatist, poet, politician and humorist. He knew the world was round nearly two thousand years before Columbus demonstrated the earth's rotundity. He was a scientist with a comprehensive knowledge of physical forces. He was an iconoclast who assailed the polytheistic superstitions of the Athenians and the degenerate democracy of Cleon. One might say that he predicted aerial navigation in his description of Socrates treading the air in a suspended basket.

Shelley is my favorite poet, and next come Blake and Whitman. Wordsworth writes rhymed essays; Byron is too licentious and superficial for me; I have tried to read Longfellow's translation of the *Divine Comedy,* but it does not interest me; Coleridge is a mechanic without inspiration, and Dryden is like him that way; Keats is too feline for me; and Browning too puzzling. Milton's *Paradise Lost* contains some fine things, but his shorter poems

*This is, I think, the profoundest observation I have made in my critical career. It annoys me to reflect that I made it in a private diary at the age of fifteen and never developed it into a thesis which would have given me a Ph. D.

please me most, and I agree with Poe, who is our only lyric poet of any value, that a poem should be short. When I say this I except Goethe's *Faust* which I read in Bayard Taylor's translation and believe to hold almost all that poetry or drama can give me in varieties and depth of emotion.

Rabelais is coarse, vulgar and almost repulsive at times, but he is a learned philosopher, a Socrates plus Plutarch and Pliny. His obscenities carry an important meaning in the scheme of his book. As Byron said of Burton's *Anatomy of Melancholy,* Rabelais "prepares one for literary conversation more than any book I know of."

For Mother's last birthday I bought her a copy of Thomas à Kempis' *The Imitation of Christ.* I hope she appreciates it more than I did.

The learned English writer of the nineteenth century was not Macaulay (I used to like Macaulay and read nearly all of his essays, but he disgusts me at times, he seems such a great bag of wind, like Hugo)—it was De Quincey. De Quincey and Gibbon increase my desire for learning. The ease with which De Quincey propounds a metaphysical doctrine of his own by algebraic calculus, discusses the comparative values of Anacreon and Theocritus, judges Kant, Lessing, Herder and Pascal, cites Latin and Greek authors in the original and writes on history, religion, philosophy, poetry, mathematics, art, music, architecture and biography makes me feel abysmally ignorant and unread, but also makes me want to emulate him in his acquisition of knowledge. [Diary entry ends.]

I studied the prose style of Swift, Milton, Dryden, Defoe and Hazlitt. I passed through a period of intent imitation of Carlyle's volcanic vocables; of Stevenson's two long sentences followed by a short one; of Sir Thomas Browne's measured orotundity; of delight in archaisms and polysyllables; of Hugo's wordy antitheses.

On the other hand, I studied the verse forms of Herrick, Donne, Swinburne, Austin Dobson, Patmore, Suckling, Heine, Marlowe, Spenser and Francis Thompson—without any effect upon my meager talent for verse.

I built up a prodigious vocabulary of polysyllabic words and then began to discard it systematically. I laboriously wrote a prose composition of one thousand words of which all but twenty-one words were of pure Anglo-Saxon origin; and in which there was not one word above three syllables in length: my English teacher wrote on the back of the theme: "This is a hasty piece of work. You must give more attention to your studies."

I wrote a theme on Carlyle scrupulously parodying Carlyle: my English teacher wrote on the back of the theme: "You have used words! words! words! You must learn to write simpler and to use simpler words."

I wrote a theme tracing Stevenson's unacknowledged borrowings from Poe's "William Watson" and "The Gold Bug" and pointing out that in his essay on "The Books That Have Influenced Me" Stevenson had failed to mention any one of the books to which he was most indebted: my English teacher wrote on the back of the theme: "I wanted a theme on Stevenson's life—where he was born, when, etc. Besides, I think you have been unfair to Stevenson."

I began to entertain a disrespect for the brains of my English teacher.

FURTHER EXTRACTS FROM MY DIARY
(*The names only being changed*)

I went to a dance last night with Chloe Goodhue, and I did not get to finish my summing up of what I feel and know about life. When I came downstairs to dinner yesterday Mama wanted to know what I had been doing up in my room all morning, and I told her I had been thinking; but when she asked me what I had been thinking, I said I had been thinking so many things I couldn't tell her.

She said, "It is a pretty come-off if you can't tell your own mother your thoughts. Are they as bad as that?" I told her they weren't bad at all and that they were good thoughts, because I was trying to figure out what was the best way to serve God and my fellow man. This seemed to solace her.

In the afternoon I wrote some more, and about four o'clock I went over to Fred Stevens' house to box for a while. Fred is my best friend. He is moody and melancholy most of the time because

[101]

he is in love with Mary Courtland, a very pretty girl but not loyal; for Fred has been deeply devoted to her for two years, and she has thrown him over and goes out boating and buggy riding with Harry Minton, who is a senior and a very good football player but not up to Fred in goodness and loyalty.

I don't see what Fred sees in Mary anyhow. As for me, I like one girl as well as the other and no better. When I am melancholy it is not because of any girl but because of my lack of knowledge and my inability to make up my mind exactly what I want to do— go in for law, medicine, theology, business or science.

Fred likes to box with me because I whipped Harry Minton, although Harry is older than I am and weighs eight or ten pounds more than I do. Fred wants to whip Harry too; but I don't think he can do it because he is afraid of Harry; and about nine tenths of good boxing is not being afraid of the other fellow and doing your best right from the start to make him afraid of you.

Nat Morris nearly beat the stuffing out of me one time because I was afraid of him before we put on the gloves, on account of his having such a confident smile. Our school has a Students' Control Board of Activities, and one of the rules is that if any two male students have a quarrel or any difference of opinion that can't be arbitrated before the Student Court they must fight it out in the ring.

It is a very good plan, I think, and tends to inculcate good sportsmanship, for the one that gets a licking is thought just as much of as the victor, and he has had his chance to work off his animosity toward the other fellow. Fred and Harry haven't any real grounds to fight; because a fickle girl is nothing to fight about, unless Harry otherwise insults or injures Fred or vice versa.

I had a good time at the dance last night, but Chloe annoyed me by being so frivolous. I run, swim, ride, dance, go to parties and dances, play football, basketball, baseball and tennis, but these are trivial enjoyments. My deeper enjoyment comes from reading and from increasing in knowledge and virtue. I despair, upon reading Emerson's Journals, at ever reading as much as Emerson read.

In his sixteenth year he had read such books as I have read, like Homer, Plato, Aeschylus, Sophocles, Euripides, Aristophanes, Milton, Bacon, Montaigne, Shakespeare, Burke, Gibbon, Hume,

I TAKE STOCK OF MY FIFTEENTH YEAR

Byron, Lamb and Scott, but he had also read such things as *The Life of Sir Isaac Newton*, Mather's *Magnalia*, Adams' *Antiquities*, Symmons' *Life of Milton*, Madame de Staël's *Germany*, Humboldt's work on America, *The History of Philip II*, Holinshed's Chronicles, Camden's *Annales Elizabethae*, Bishop Hall's *Meditation on Conscience*, Congreve, Drake's essays, Hallam's *Middle Ages*, Ben Jonson's plays, Godwin's *Letters and Social Aims* and so on.

I have kept a "Common-place Book" also for nearly two years now, and it is filled with quotations and entries. Emerson never read any novels except *The Bride of Lammermoor* and does not quote much poetry, whereas I have read a great many novels by Dickens, Thackeray, Jane Austen, George Eliot, Victor Hugo, Hawthorne, Irving, Cooper, Hamlin Garland, Winston Churchill, George Barr McCutcheon, John Fox, Junior, David Graham Phillips, Robert Herrick, Alexander Dumas, Guy de Maupassant, Octave Feuillet, George Sand, Prosper Mérimée, Alphonse Daudet, Mary Johnstone, Boccaccio, and so on, besides a great deal of poetry.

I was entranced by Victor Hugo's *Les Misérables* when I read it and by *Notre Dame de Paris, Bug-Jargal, The Man Who Laughs* and all the other works of Hugo I could find in translation, including his "Postscriptum de ma vie;" but when I had finished reading him I changed around from profound admiration to something like repugnance, for he seemed to be a great windbag. Little Cosette I will always remember, and Monsieur Bienvenu, the magnanimous priest, and Quasimodo and Ursus; but these latter two because they are so grotesque.

But to get back to my ideas on life. In every man there is an inborn instinct to determine right from wrong. No matter what degree of civilization a man reaches, the instinct is the same as that of the barbarian. But each man differs from his neighbor in his conception of right and wrong. The difference between them lies in the ideals that each cherishes.

I once heard a physician say that if man lived up to his knowledge of hygiene the average length of life would be doubled. That statement is undoubtedly true. Everyone knows certain laws of physiology which he ignores every day and cultivates habits which, though injurious, he never breaks off. The same may be said of our knowledge of good and evil. We have our ideals of goodness and keep them in advance of our actions; for none of us do always what we know to be right.

Our ideas of good and evil are governed by the prevailing conceptions of right and wrong in whatever society we find ourselves. The Spartans allowed their youths and maidens to exercise naked together in the street, and the Spartan marriage bond was sealed when a maiden had a child by a youth. Among the Esquimaux the scarcity of women makes polyandry a recognized custom. In India, the mother throws her first-born to the holy alligators of the Ganges—this is infanticide to us but religious sacrifice to the Indians. Devotees in Calcutta throw themselves before the Juggernaut—this is suicide to us, but to the Indians it is the supreme self-sacrifice that earns eternal felicity. The Inquisition burned heretics—this was murder, but to the Catholics of the day it was the sacred duty of the Church militant. Witches were put to death by the Puritans of Salem—this was murder, but to the Puritans it was a Christian obligation. In the United States criminals are put to death—this is a form of murder, but our society holds that such murder is necessary and right. What men in general believe to be right, that is the only recognized right, and what they believe to be wrong, that is the only recognized wrong.

Marlowe's *Dr Faustus,* Goethe's *Faust,* and Carlyle's *Sartor Resartus,* all three describe the spiritual drama of everyone who thirsts for knowledge and who seeks among the multiplicity of creeds and precepts for some spar to cling to, as Pater says, "amid the perpetual flux." My observation, the Bible and biology teach me that man returns to dust. My heart tells me that Jesus was a good, merciful and tolerant man. Those are the only two articles of my present credo. [Diary entry ends.]

CHAPTER VIII

Lillian and Chloe

I Meet Lillian Avery, and Life for Me Becomes a Species of Somnambulism. Her Uncle Mistakes My Noble and Selfless Devotion to Her. I Write and Read Poems to Her. She Leaves Shawnee and I Never See Her Again. Chloe Goodhue, Frank Little Animal, Reduces Some of My Adolescent Difficulties to Zero. An Apostrophe to Her.

ONE OCTOBER MORNING in my sixteenth year I awoke from immersion in books to find myself suffused with an emotion that was an extraordinary novelty to me. A new pupil had enrolled in my class. I became aware of her for the first time as she accosted me in the hall and asked me to direct her to the principal's office. She wore a small felt cap like Rosalind's in the Forest of Arden, an Eton collar, a yellow-and-orange Windsor tie, a brown jacket and a Scotch plaid skirt. Her eyes were brown and liquid and watchful, like a doe's, her mouth full and indolent, her teeth too prominent, quite, for beauty, and her hair a coil of high-lighted, chestnut strands drawn into a severe knot behind, revealing the ears completely.

I answered her question without hearing what I said. I felt a stifling sensation in the region of the heart, as if the aorta had suddenly been filled too full. I wanted to touch her. I didn't want her to get away from me. I didn't want to lose sight of her.

"Please, may I ask your name?" I asked.

"Surely. My name is Lillian Avery. And yours?"

"My name is, my name is—my name is Burton, Burton Rascoe."

"Rascoe? Burton?"

"Yes. Burton Rascoe. I've got another name, but I'm called Burton mostly."

"Another name besides Rascoe?"

"No. Another name besides Burton."

"Is your other name as nice as Burton?"

"No. . . . That is, I don't think so; it's all according to the way you feel about it. It's Arthur. First name. I don't like it. Parents and people have always called me Burton. Anyhow, it is not nearly so nice, so beautiful, it is not wonderful like the name Lillian Avery."

"Oh!"

"Or like you. There is nothing so beautiful as you."

"Oh!"

She looked up at me with an unrepressed and confiding expression that almost paralyzed me with the surcharge of tenderness it generated. I walked with her toward the principal's office and waited until she had disappeared behind the door. I watched for her to reappear in different classes, at chapel exercises, at noon recess. I waited for her when school was out and walked as far as the corner of the block in which she lived. I had gone through the day oblivious of everything but her.

That night the image of her kept me awake for hours after I had gone to bed. The next morning I left the house early and waited at the corner until she came along on her way to school. She said nothing. I said nothing. We merely smiled. I took her books. We walked in silence. In the classrooms, the letters in my books were blurred; they conveyed no meaning; the voices of the teachers were but a hollow droning; the voices of the students were but a distant babbling.

This sort of thing went on for weeks.

Life suddenly became a species of somnambulism with me, from which I was awakened into a semiconscious state only when in Lillian's presence. My daily program was arranged with but one object in view—that of drinking in the sight of this girl. Looking at her satisfied an actual physiological craving curiously analogous to that of slaking a feverish thirst at a spring where there is no cup and one must bury nose and lips in the water and take repeated breaths between sips. During those first two weeks I had no further desire concerning her: I did not wish to kiss her or touch her; I wished merely to look at her and to serve her, wait on her, in order to win this ineffable privilege.

Had I been of a reflective mind, I might have mitigated the misery of absence from the sight of her by deducing that because she was a newcomer in school I had become so infatuated with her. The first girl for whom I had felt a violent longing, at the age of six, had been Dulcie Murphy, who was the only girl in the first grade with whom I was not familiar. Dulcie had been sent into Fulton from the country. The other girls I knew were like sisters, with whom I had played as long as I could remember. And so it had always been. Florence Meek, who lived in the same block I lived in, was undoubtedly a pretty girl, but she was my chum's sister, and about her there was no mystery. In the fifth, sixth and seventh grades, my sweethearts had invariably been girls from other schools or, in one or two instances, girls from other classes. Until Lillian came to high school, she was the only girl in my class with whom I had not, in a sense, grown as familiar as with a girl cousin or sister.

I became morose, melancholy and irritable. At night I would leave the dinner table before finishing my meal and go to my room, lock myself up and give myself over to fancies in which I pictured myself as her protector, who would build for her a house, win fame and money for her and sit with her on wintry evenings before a warm fireplace and hold her hands. I wrote to her and about her a mass of abominable doggerel in which she was apostrophized as "little soul," "animula," "Blümchen," "Röselein," and "carissima mea."

She was spending the school year at the house of an uncle, owing to some domestic difficulties and unhappiness (so I vaguely learned) between her parents in western Oklahoma. I discovered that Lillian's uncle was a man of evil mind who mistook the nature of my noble and selfless devotion to his niece. He humiliated me on one occasion so deeply as to plunge me deeper into love and to make me resolve to free Lillian, at the earliest opportunity, from what I imagined to be an intolerable bondage.

I had spent an entire Saturday washing and polishing the family buggy and harness and currying the driving mare. And on Sunday afternoon, after I had spent the morning dusting and pressing my suit, polishing my shoes and preparing my toilet with finicky care, I had called at the Avery residence at the hour Lillian and I had agreed upon. I had tied the hitching rein to the ring in the cement block at the curb and had approached the front door of the house in considerable trepidation, hat in hand. Lillian's uncle answered the doorbell himself.

"Well! What is it that *you* want?" The terrible man was in an incredibly bad temper.

"Is Lillian home?" I asked with a violent effort at self-assurance, and in a cold terror which the man's voice had induced in me.

"Yes! My niece is here! But you can't see her! She tells me that you intend to take her out driving. You have another guess a-coming. Get that nag and buggy away from in front of my house as fast as you can. And if I catch you on these premises again I'll give you a thrashing you will never forget." He slammed the door in emphasis.

I walked away with a deliberate, if pitiable, effort at dignity, slowly, but trembling all over, full of grief, anger and humiliation. So deeply wounded was my pride that I drove into the country alone, so that my parents might not question me in regard to the change in my plans for the afternoon. I meditated revenge upon Lillian's uncle and, finding no satisfactory one, I commended the miscreant to God, secure in the faith that God would exact a stern retribution for such an outrage to the finer sentiments.

The next morning I waited for Lillian as usual, but not without keeping a lookout lest her uncle see us. The only mention of the awful catastrophe of the afternoon before was when she began, "I am awfully sorry——" and I answered, "Never mind."

Day after day I was further humiliated in class by my teachers for my failure to prepare my lessons in geometry, Latin, history and German. I was abused by the football coach, whose constant command was, "Snap out of it!" My parents thought I was ill.

Crowning humiliation. The Oklahoma City High right half-back had broken through the line and had a clear field, except for me, to the goal posts. I had dived forward with the intention of catching the player just above the knees on my left shoulder. The tackle would compensate for all my recent failures. Just as I left the ground in this flying tackle, the runner swerved in his course and caught me square on the top of the head with his knee. My effort had stopped the player and had prevented his scoring; but I was not to know this until more than an hour later, when I was finally brought to consciousness in the school gymnasium. And for two weeks my neck was so stiff that I could not turn my head, and it pained me so badly that even in Lillian's presence I was not altogether happy.

Alone in my room at night I would listen to the wind whistle under the eaves; I would stare blankly at the pages of my textbooks without perceiving two words in relation to each other; I would get up and go to the window and watch the leaves swirl over the lawn, and the limbs of the trees dip and bend in futile and inane gestures, like the arms of a drunken man; the opening lines, "Ich weiss nicht was soll es bedeuten, Dass ich so traurig bin," of Heine's "Die Lorelei," would run through my head, and I would recite the whole poem inwardly, following it with "Du Bist Wie Eine Blume," and Goethe's "Heidenröselein." Then I would burst into a fit of sobbing and throw myself across my bed, burying my head in the pillow.

From this I achieved a sort of catharsis and would reproach myself for weakness. I thought crying was unmanly, and I had not cried since I was a child. I had felt shame at my inability to weep at the funerals of my grandparents; and I had been too frozen with wonder to shed tears when boys I had known had died. These new tears came seemingly without cause, and after a flood of them I thought myself dishonored until I told myself that in Homer the Greek heroes wept frequently from joy as well as from sorrow, that Jesus wept and that grown men in Shakespeare shed tears without shame.

While thus rationalizing, I could see the Trojan women uttering their ululations before the walls of Troy more plainly than I could see the trees on the lawn; I saw Jesus weeping with a heart bowed down with the sorrows of the world; and I saw Hector and Achilles go to their magnificent duel with their eyes still red with weeping. Lillian's face would dance before my eyes; and I would see the young Goethe in short pants and starched linen waist callously breaking the stem of a little rose near a hedgerow; and then I would see the lovely siren, naked on a smooth, sun-dried rock, combing golden hair with a golden comb, Circe in her glittering cavern surrounded by swine, Paola and Francesca embracing in midair on their flight to hell, Faust vouchsafed his vision of Helen whose kiss would make him immortal, and Leander, looking like Byron, using the Australian crawl in desperate seas toward a flickering light on a cliff as darkly sinister as a Boecklin painting. I would fall asleep with my clothes on, and perhaps an hour later I would wake with a violent start and then undress and go to bed.

I strapped *Leaves of Grass* and Palgrave's *Golden Treasury* among my books one warm October morning, and at noon I said to Lillian: "You cut classes this afternoon and I'll cut classes and football practice and we'll go out to the end of the streetcar line and walk around together."

She nodded. I had observed that since the first day I had met her, when she had been forward enough in her speech, she rarely uttered a syllable. She would nod or shake her head, smile or look toward the ground. I wrote poems to her; but out of humility in respect to my talents and out of fear of offending her taste, I practised a form of deception, the outcome of which spurred me to further efforts at versifying.

While reading Poe, Patmore, Keats, Shelley or Donne to her, I would insert between the pages of the book a bit of verse of my own composition. After reading the others, I would look for the response aroused in her by what I myself had written. It was always the same, whatever the poem: she would look at me with soft eyes, tighten her grasp upon my arm, and say, "That's lovely!"

I took this to be unprejudiced criticism in my favor. Some of the more meritorious of these compositions I was later on to alter slightly in their descriptive lines and address to other girls. But before time bleached the color of them, I held them to be too deep a revelation of my soul to acknowledge them.

We rode to the end of the streetcar line, got out and walked far from any paths or roads. On our walk I talked of myself and of what I intended to do in the world. As I talked I grew more intense. I was going to be a great biologist and get at the secret of life, and if biology did not yield up the secret I was going to be a great chemist, for (I thought) all animate and inanimate nature might be resolved into a small number of elements. I talked of the fall-tinted woods in terms of osmosis, carbonization, capillary attraction and solar energy.

"Do you know what the soul is?" I asked.

She shook her head.

I struck a match and pointed to the flame.

"It is also that power in the magnet and in amber," I said. (I had plagiarized this from one of Maeterlinck's essays.)

"Do you know what Schopenhauer says it means when we look at each other the way we do sometimes?" I asked.

An almost inaudible "No."

I pulled a notebook from my pocket and read: " 'The searching and penetrating glances with which two young persons of the opposite sex, who see each other for the first time, regard each other, is the meditation of the genius of the species on the individual which is possible through these two and the combination of its qualities. In this way the genius of the species meditates concerning the coming race in all who are capable of reproduction.' "

I slurred the last clause with some confusion.

When I had recovered my composure, I read again: " 'The vehement or intense longing directed to a particular woman is an immediate pledge of the indestructibility of the kernel of our being, and of its continued existence in the species.'

"Would you like to hear what sums up my religion?" I asked.

She nodded.

"It is this from Pater"; and I read: " 'The kingship of the mind over its own conditions, its real inherent liberty—"It is in thy power to think as thou wilt"—The essence of things is in thy thoughts about them:—All is opinion—conception—: No man can be hindred by another:—What is outside the circle of thought is nothing at all to it; hold to this and you are safe.' "

(What had really attracted me about that paragraph was Pater's punctuatory resourcefulness, which had enabled him to use dashes *before* some colons and dashes *after* others. To this day I haven't the slightest idea what he was talking about.)

"I want to learn sculpture," I continued, "and to model something as inspiring as George Grey Barnard's *Je sens deux hommes en moi* or as impressive as Michelangelo's *Moses*. I feel two natures struggling within me, my better and my lower nature; but I think my better nature will come out victorious. Victor Hugo supplied Barnard with the text. Hugo has one word he uses all the time, *abîme,* the abyss—the abyss and the stars, rather; because he is always putting extremes together—antithesis. He has a fine description of an election to the French Academy in *Choses Vues*— Things Seen—about how none of the members really pay any attention when a candidate is being voted on, some of them snoring away, and some of them talking, and some of them scribbling on pieces of paper. Then he's got another marvelous piece about when Talleyrand's body was lying out in the undertaker's; they'd taken out his brain from the skull—trepanning—and put it on a table to examine and preserve it, and an undertaker's assistant came along and thought it was part of the part to be thrown away and threw Talleyrand's brain down a sewer. That's the way things happen in life, I guess—not much reverence or just because people don't know or haven't been told. I want to cultivate my taste for music. Mother took me to Memphis to hear Kubelik, and I've heard Madame Bloomfield-Ziegler. Mother plays the piano fairly well. She used to want me to learn and hired a teacher for me, but I was too young then and thought it was for girls, and I cut my finger a couple of times so I couldn't go through my lessons, and Mother thought it was throwing money away, so she gave up. My favorite pieces are Liszt's 'Second Hungarian Rhapsody,' Handel's 'Largo,' some Minuet—I forget which—by Mozart, and some parts of Beethoven's symphonies I've heard at orchestra concerts and on the phonograph. Chopin's 'C Sharp Minor' nocturne is very lovely. I don't care for Ries's 'Moto Perpetuo.' Would you mind hearing something I have written?"

She nodded her head.

I read: " 'There is some sublimity in the soul of every man that neither he, nor we, are ever wholly aware of. It may be discovered only in some divine intoxication of lonely self-communion or is seen in some unconscious effort where the tender sympathies of the soul are laid bare. When all seems black; when the present and the future are enshrouded in dark doubt; when one's heart is surcharged with memories of misery and injustice: then a word, a noble thought crowned with human sympathy, expressed by word of mouth or on the printed page, breaks down the barriers to our own inner self, our true ideal being, and lets us perceive that we are really children of God. In that impassioned hour when, with the surge of divinity within our being, we become conscious of the true loftiness and beauty—the full meaning of life; when we speak to the spirit of our own silent selves and learn our quiet yearnings: —that hour is the crucial moment in our lives wherein we either grasp or reject the greatest offerings of our destiny; wherein we bid for happiness or destruction; wherein we choose between two profound alternatives, the abyss or the stars. Despite all jest, we are more serious than we seem.'"

"That is lovely," she said.

I took off my coat and spread it on the ground and asked her to sit on it. I lay prone beside her with *The Golden Treasury* spread open before my eyes. I read aloud, in a singsong voice, gesturing awkwardly with my right hand, without taking my eyes off the book, and while holding the book open with my left hand. I read Marlowe's "The Passionate Shepherd to His Love," T. Lodge's "Rosaline," the anonymous "In Lacrimas," Campion's "Sic Transit," and Coleridge's "Love." My left arm became cramped, and I got up to stretch. I swung my arms around, windmill fashion, and sat down, picking up *Leaves of Grass* this time. The book fell open at "A Woman Waits for Me":

> A woman waits for me, she contains all, nothing is lacking,
>   Yet all were lacking if sex were lacking, or if the moisture
>   of the right man were lacking.

I turned the leaves hurriedly and started to read "Scented Herbage of My Breast" and thought better of it. I read "Whoever You Are Holding Me Now in Hand," omitting the two lines:

> Or, if you will, thrusting me beneath your clothing, Where I may
>   feel the throbs of your heart or rest upon your hip.

[113]

I sought for others, but found that the poems that were really among my favorites, poems I had hitherto never thought of as indelicate, were hardly the sort that I wished to read aloud to her. I read "A Glimpse" and began to read "Salut au Monde," when my throat became dry and I noticed that a tear had fallen on the page. I turned my head quickly toward her, and she was dabbing her eyes with a handkerchief. I put my arm around her and kissed her hair. She leaned toward me and lay her head on my shoulder. She began to sob violently. I was frightened. I did not know what to make of it. I patted her shoulder awkwardly. I raised her head, brushed back her hair and kissed her on the mouth. The warmth and eagerness of her lips surprised and excited me, and in a moment it filled me with a mixture of wonder, ecstasy and terror.

I rose quickly and lifted her to her feet, put my arm around her and started toward the car line. Then, suddenly, tears flooded my eyes. I did not know why. I tried to stem them and get them out of my eyes before she saw them. I stopped short twice and took her tightly in my arms, before we got in sight of a road.

"I am going to—to—to—to work and study and live for you, and I will love you always," I said.

"No," she said. "This is the last time we will ever see each other."

I caught my breath in horror and self-accusation. "I am sorry—so sorry—it's awful—I didn't mean—— Oh, God, don't say that!"

"It's not what you think," she said. "I love you. I will always love you. But I go back home tomorrow. Mother sent for me. Uncle wrote her about you, and I get poor grades in school. I am leaving on the ten-o'clock train tonight. I couldn't bear to tell you."

The shock of this made me calm. She would write, and I could write to her? No; her parents would not permit it. They were both very strict.

I strained as if to absorb her in an embrace. We walked with numb precision to the car line and boarded a car. There was no one in the car except ourselves and the conductor for nearly a mile. I held her hand, but we both stared out of the window in opposite directions. She asked me not to get off the car with her.

I was submissive to this under protest, for there was anxiety in her insistence.

I never saw her again.

For three weeks my brain was a sponge, except on the football field. I cherished a feeling of extreme misanthropy. I read *Timon of Athens* with profound sympathy.

One evening, when I could no longer bear my grief alone, I called up Chloe Goodhue and asked if I might come over to see her.

She received me in the living room. She had closed the sliding doors which separated the living room from the dining room. A good fire was burning in the grate. When she had closed the remaining door to the room, she sat down upon the couch and beckoned to me, saying, "I know all about it. Come, put your head down on my lap and have a cry and you'll feel better."

She kept rubbing her hand smoothly over my head while I cried. Presently I ceased to cry. I sat up and put my arms around her and kissed her, with the sort of kiss that started out to be brotherly and sisterly and ended by being something else.

"You will get over it," said Chloe. "I love you, too, you know."

Chloe thought better of me as an athlete than as a poet and showed more appreciation of my talents when I made a flying tackle, knocked a home run, tossed a basket, breasted the tape, or cleared the bar at nine feet in the pole vault than when I strode about the room, book in hand, gesturing and declaiming. Chloe could swim better than I could; she could run as fast; she could ride as well; and she liked to wrestle with me; and she made pulp of my pruderies.

While we were riding horseback in the country one summer day we came to a stream that was shaded from the road by a clump of trees and shrubbery. Chloe swung off her horse, knotted the halter rein to a sapling and said, "Come on; let's go swimming." With that she ran behind the clump of trees. By the time I reached her she was half undressed. I blushed and gaped.

"Come on, you silly goose. Get off your clothes," she commanded, pulling off her stockings.

Doubts assailed me, and the blood pounded in my temples. I untied my tie nervously. Chloe had stripped before I had unbuttoned my shirt. I hardly dared look up. She ran to the bank, poised a moment to judge the depth of the water and dived. She dipped and somersaulted and splashed about like a porpoise, calling to me to hurry. My hand trembled violently as I dropped the left sock to the ground and made my way to the bank. She looked up at me with a frank and merry scrutiny, and I got into the water as quickly as my agitation would permit me. When I had finished the swim Chloe spied a patch of grass, stretched herself out on it and asked me to come and lie down beside her to get dry. But I was embarrassed, and I dressed as hastily as possible. Chloe did not stir.

"Don't you think you had better get dressed?" I called to her from where I was sitting, my heart pounding like a donkey engine.

"Why?" she asked.

"Somebody is likely to come along, and we might get arrested."

"Wouldn't that be a lark?" she teased.

Safe in my clothes again, I had conquered some of my shyness. I watched her get dressed, and the sight of her breasts and thighs made me dizzy with a strange delight.

"Sister will have to teach you something," she said abruptly as we were trotting slowly along the road again. "I can't."

"What do you mean?" I asked.

She declined to answer.

This frank little animal by her very naturalness scared the Puritan in me back to my books and presently I was reading poems and making calf eyes at a high-school teacher ten years my senior. This passion for Miss Thorsen (I never addressed her by any other appellation) was of a most spiritual nature, never, until its anticlimax, descending below the shoulders. There were afternoons and evenings throughout a summer of Mozart, Beethoven, Handel, Bach and Haydn. There were buggy rides into the country, handholding, kissing and weeping. And there were readings aloud of Marlowe, of Shakespeare's *Venus and Adonis,* of Milton's briefer poems, of Racine's *Phèdre,* of Petrarch, of Browning and of Poe. And there were poems in imitation of Poe, with Miss

Thorsen celebrated as an ethereal being, nebulous as to flesh, bone and sinew. I read the *Vita Nuova* and Petrarch's sonnets. There were reveries in which she and I walked, clad in white tulle like the serpentine dancers of the circus, over sunlit fields. Our kisses were passionate, but, to me, cerebral. I have rarely experienced the ache of longing more poignantly than was my ache for Miss Thorsen when I was away from her; and she reciprocated this adoration with a love that, from the look in her eyes, was distressed and painful. Then one Sunday she wept as I was about to leave the room in which we had been reading poetry all afternoon, and when I kissed her I was seized with such gross physical impulses that I became painfully and terrifiedly aware that physiology had intruded into our spiritual association. I broke away from her, my head hot and my heart thumping, and ran, in unmitigated fright and bewilderment, out of the house and up the street to the streetcar line. My head was turbulent and distressed, and that night I had fantasies of a character that had never occurred to me in connection with Miss Thorsen. I found the "Sankhya-Yog" of the *Bhavagad-Gita* a comfort as well as an admonition at this point, and copied this quotation from it down in my diary:

> That man alone is wise
> Who keeps the mastery of himself! If one
> Ponders on objects of the sense, there springs
> Attraction; from attraction grows desire,
> Desire flames to fierce passion, passion breeds
> Recklessness; then the memory—all betrayed—
> Lets noble purpose go, and saps the mind,
> Till purpose, mind and man are all undone.
> But if one deals with the objects of the sense,
> Not loving and not hating, making them
> Serve his free soul, which rests serenely, Lord,
> Lo! such a man comes to tranquillity;
> And out of tranquillity shall arise
> The end and healing of his earthly pains
> Since the will governed sets the soul at peace.

Presently I became intensely aware of Chloe again during rehearsals for the junior-class play. We began to go together just as if our romance had suffered no interruption; but Chloe set about definitely to make me jealous and succeeded in a distressing degree. When she had me thoroughly chastened and not in the least sure of her, she acknowledged this, at the same time letting me know that she would turn to Bert Loy or Carl Witte, who pestered her for dates, if my heart strayed.

"Let's go swimming, Chloe," I said one summer day as we trotted up the road near the stream where Chloe had once been impetuous.

"I can't. But I will stay on the bank and watch you."

"Why can't you?"

"If you were a girl you would know."

"I won't go in if you don't."

"Well, you can sit on the bank here and hold me and kiss me. I feel blue and miserable today. . . . But I'll be all right day after tomorrow. . . . Your pulse is beating so, and you're all hot. Now get off your clothes and take a swim and cool off. I'll watch you. I like to look at you. Such a fine, firm body. And you hold your head so straight, chin forward, and back like an arrow. Go on now! No fooling! Here, let me untie your tie! Such a pretty color! Did you select it? I'm going to make you up some ties sometime soon. There you are, now, sir! But let me unbutton your shirt, too! What makes you have that funny expression? And you're as red as a beet! You big baby! Let me feel your muscle. Oo-oo! What a hard muskle! Did you ever feel the muscle of my thigh?"

Chloe pulled her dress back toward her middle and exposed two thighs like mother-of-pearl. She flexed the muscle of her right leg, and a mound of sinew curved above the knee. She gripped it and then took my hand and placed it on it.

"Like steel," I said, "and yet so pink and beautiful." My fingers tingled.

"Isn't it, just!" Chloe said and flipped her skirt back below her knee. "Hurry, now. Let's see you dive. Can you do a back flip-flop?"

With my hand as a fig leaf, I made my way to the bank and dived in.

She laughed a merry peal of laughter when I began showing off my overhand stroke very conscientiously.

When I climbed upon the bank my hand served as a fig leaf
more adequately and more reassuringly than before, for Chloe
turned her head negligently while I grabbed for some covering.

"What makes you ashamed of your body?" she asked when I
was seated near her with my shirt thrown across my groins. "Now,
if you had a body like Dad's—he's got a potbelly and legs like
sticks, poor dear—or if I had a body like Miss Elison's, all scrawny
like a skeleton—that would be different. More clothes the better.
. . . But, still, I don't know as I would want Louise or May to
see you all naked. And then again it might shock them so they'd
keep away from you."

"I don't want anyone, anyone at all, but me to see you undressed.
Don't ever ask anybody else to feel the muscle of your thigh, like
you did me. Now, will you?"

"Of course not, silly. Not if you don't want me to. I wouldn't
want to do anything you didn't want me to. . . . Oh, yes, I would!
I'll do anything I want to do, and you can't command me! So, there,
sir! If I want to I'll ask Mr Hall to feel my thigh right out in
geometry class. Wouldn't he be surprised! And wouldn't May and
Louise make long faces! 'Disgusting!'—can't you just hear 'em?"

"I don't care about Mr Hall. But not Harry Lorber. You
wouldn't let him, now, would you?"

"That lummox! You know what's the matter with him? He
thinks he is a lady-killer. Ever notice that smirk on his face?
Don't you ever get a smirk on your face. I'll smash it off with a
claw hammer."

I had admired to a point of envy that "smirk" on Harry Lorber's
face. I did not think of it as a smirk at all. It was the same knowing
expression, I thought, as that about the mouth of the Mona Lisa.
It suggested to me an enormous self-assurance together with a
knowledge of the feminine heart which had not been disclosed to
me. I was glad that Chloe thought otherwise, and yet . . .

"He seems to have some right to think himself a lady-killer," I
found myself saying in Harry's defense. "He has killed quite a
number of ladies hereabouts."

Tales were told of Harry Lorber. Most of them Harry told himself, in language not at all delicate, but naming no names; they
involved leaving by back doors hurriedly, being disturbed by the

park policeman, going away without his socks, three abed with two awake, and subaqueous experiments in the bathing pool below a river dam. They were comical adventures to him, and all the more so when he could embroider the ridiculous aspects of his discomfitures. He was to me a character out of a Restoration comedy; but I felt that I myself would not be at all at home in a Restoration comedy and that hiding in a clothes closet to escape a wrathful husband would give me more fright than fun, and so I halfheartedly disapproved of Harry Lorber. Harry was a roué at eighteen, which, I thought, was a deplorable precocity. I did not want Chloe to fall into the hands of so expert and unscrupulous an amorist. Then, too, Harry and Chloe had been brought up in adjoining yards.

"You used to like Harry."

"I used to shoot dinks with him and play I-spy and one-ole-cat when he was in short pants. But he has gone girl crazy and isn't any good. He'll be a bum, you wait and see. He's really getting too aughecky [such was the retching sound she made into a sort of word that had vivid explicitness]. Let's not think about him. . . . I love you. . . . That is, I think I love you maybe."

"What makes you *think maybe?*"

"Because I don't know. It's the first time I ever felt just like this toward anyone. I've felt like it for a long time, long before you ever took any notice of me, long before you were blubbering to me about Lillian Avery, long back to the time you lifted me off the hayrick at that picnic in the fifth grade and kissed me lightly as you set me on the ground."

"I've loved you since that time, too, I think." That was a lie: I hadn't thought of her one way or the other until we were in second year of high school.

Chloe was a hoyden. She wore her skirts tighter and shorter than anyone else. She was gay and full of laughter. Her conduct was disapproved of by mothers with pensive-eyed, well-conducted, highly chaperoned daughters—and by the daughters. But there was no activity, mental or physical, which she did not do just a little bit better than any other girl. She baked prize cakes in the domestic-science class; she always tossed the winning baskets in basketball games; her Latin and German lessons were always perfect; she was the hit without being the star in class plays; she was the only girl in high school who was known to have *voice;* and she played the piano at commencement exercises.

Chloe, too, reduced some of my adolescent difficulties to zero by a natural magic and a superior wisdom which enthralled me; her family accepted it as a foregone conclusion that my troth was pledged to Chloe inviolably; she had accepted it presumably, and I had accepted it: we were bound by a general assumption that when Chloe and I came of age we were to go through the necessary formula of identifying Chloe as my wife and not merely my sweetheart.

But Chloe was more mature than I, as most girls are than boys, and she had definite forebodings that things would not turn out as, on the surface, it looked as though they might. It was prevision I never contemplated, and it was a foreboding I could not understand even while she was conveying it to me.

Toward the end of the senior year we were sitting in the wooden swing in Central Park in the late shadows of an April evening. We had kissed to satiety, and my arms were about her. A vague melancholy filled my mind. I asked:

"Will you still love me when I am an old man?"

Chloe laughed mischievously. "Yes, silly. What a question! Will you love me when I'm toothless?"

And she laughed mischievously again. Then she braced herself suddenly, as if hit by an idea—which she had been—and said:

"Now listen here, young man——"

"Don't call me 'young man.'"

"All right, touchy. How's this? Now listen here, dear," (and there was matter-of-factness, not tenderness, in that *dear*), "I love you. They all think you and I are going to marry someday. And I have thought it, too."

"But we are, aren't we?"

"I am not at all sure about that. In fact, I am beginning to doubt it very strongly."

"But don't you love me? I love you and nobody else but you."

"Of course I love you. And I have eyes to see that you love me. But that is not the point. You can't stay in this town all your life and wind up as a bank cashier or the proprietor of a butcher's shop. It isn't in you. You have got something else. I don't know just what it is, but you are going toward something. You haven't finished your schooling yet. You are going away to college. You really are going this fall, aren't you?"

"Yes. That is, I hope so."

"You are going all right, all right. You are going if I have to scrub floors to send you there."

The excessive sentiment of this struck her after she had said it, and she made a joke out of it immediately to counteract the effect: "See these lily-white, dimpled hands that are going to scrub floors so that a big lummox like you can sit on his bum-ta-ratum in college and spark around with dish-faced co-eds?"

"Great goodness, Chloe, what are you talking about! Haven't I been earning my way right along in high school? Have I ever asked a cent of my dad or anybody else? When have I ever depended upon anybody, let alone on a girl? Gee, that makes me mad, talking about scrubbing floors."

Chloe became suddenly tender: "That's just it, darling. You wouldn't let me scrub floors for you; you wouldn't let anybody do anything for you. Your own mother, I bet, is just crying her eyes out because you won't let her do things for you. She would probably be awfully pleased if you took her some socks to darn or asked her to sew some buttons on your clothes. But you won't let her."

"But why on earth should I? I can sew on buttons, and the laundry darns my socks for a few cents extra. Why in the world should I ask my mother to do it? Great goodness! She has got enough to attend to, managing the house and taking care of Dad and nursing her sick headaches."

Chloe elevated her arms in a graphic gesture of despair, heaved a sigh and said: "It's no use. Absolutely no use. Not with dynamite could I get anything through that damned brain of yours."

"What are you trying to get through this damned brain of mine? And since when have you taken up swearing?"

"Anybody would have to swear to make a dint in that thick skull."

"I thought we were having an argument—although the Lord

knows what it is about—not a name-calling contest. This damned skull is not so damned thick as you think it is, you damned——"

Chloe stopped whatever I was about to say with a terrified look and a startled exclamation, "Don't say that!"

"Don't say what?"

"Don't say whatever it was you were going to say. I couldn't stand it."

"I wasn't going to say anything. But I wasn't going to let you keep on saying my skull is thick."

And I paused to conjecture what it was I *was* going to say. I concluded that I was not going to say anything and that her interjection had saved me leaving the sentence suspended while my mind fuddled around trying to end it with some appropriate sentiment, at least some sentiment appropriate to my emotions.

"You weren't going to call me that?" asked Chloe with a sudden sadness and tranquillity of tone that touched me. I hadn't the slightest notion what she was driving at.

"I wasn't going to call you what?"

"What you were going to call me."

"What was I going to call you?"

"Whatever it was that you were going to call me."

"But I wasn't going to call you anything. I was just mad."

"Not anything? Really? Not a bad name?"

"Bad name? Bad name? What sort of a bad name would I be calling you? You are the sweetest darling I know of."

We embraced with tenderness, and Chloe drew back, straightened up and said: "You are going away to college this fall, aren't you?"

"Yes, I guess so."

"Of course you are. And nothing is going to stop you. And you are going on and on, further and further away from me, and the worst is that I can't see any way to stop it and wouldn't want to stop it if I could. That is, I would and I wouldn't."

"What do you mean, you would and you wouldn't?"

"I mean I wouldn't want to stop it for my own sake or for yours, because if I stopped it I wouldn't be I, and you wouldn't be you; and still if I didn't try to stop it I wouldn't be I and you wouldn't be you. It's all mixed up."

"It certainly is."

"But don't you see? Of course you don't see. But don't you understand that if you don't go away to college and go on to whatever work you are going to do in this world, you would not be the boy I love, and that if you do I will certainly lose you?"

"But you won't."

"But I will."

"No, you won't. You can't lose me. As soon as I get started in life you are coming right up and join me, wherever it is, and we will be married."

"And who is going to take care of you all that time, the way I have taken care of you?"

"I won't need to have anybody take care of me."

"You won't? You don't know yourself. Somebody will take care of you all right. All I hope is that she is a sleazy slut and that you sicken of her quick enough. Trouble is, she won't be: she will be the right sort. That would be just your luck. Maybe you will even marry her. Great God!"

Chloe burst suddenly into a violent fit of weeping. I was intensely moved and put my arms about her and drew her tightly to me; but I was also vastly puzzled: I did not know why Chloe was crying, or what she had been trying to convey to me, or what I should say. Anything I said, I conjectured, would be the wrong thing. I could not conceive of this disloyalty Chloe had suggested. I loathed in advance this girl that Chloe had conjured up who, Chloe thought, would take her place in my life. That person for a moment became in my mind an actual human being with real outlines and definite character. She was a girl compounded of all the elements I did not like (or thought I didn't), and as a result she was very much like Theresa Boleyn.

Theresa Boleyn was an oval-faced, pretty girl, with black hair and eyes and a velvety olive skin, and my best friend, Harry Thorpe, had been in love with her, was in love with her still, in fact, to his great misery. And Theresa had treated Harry shabbily, to my thinking, and had given her heart to George Andrews, a beau bachelor assistant bank cashier and member of the Elks Club, who already had half a dozen women on the string and also made no secret of "going down the line." I could imagine no boy more worthy of a girl's love than Harry and, in consequence, no girl less worthy of the love Harry bestowed upon Theresa, now that Theresa had been going around to Elks Club dances and to the theater with Andrews. So this girl that Chloe thought would supplant her became in my eyes like Theresa Boleyn and I had no trouble at all in disclaiming her.

"Do you think I would marry a girl like that?" I asked suddenly.

Chloe had already ceased sobbing, but with this question, she sat up quickly and displayed keen animation.

"Do I think you would marry a girl like what?"

"Like that."

"Like what?"

"Like what you said."

"What kind of a girl did I say you were going to marry?"

"You didn't say I was going to marry any kind of a girl. You said I was going to marry somebody else besides you, and that isn't true. Besides that, I wouldn't marry that sort of a girl."

"What sort of a girl?"

"Gee! You are trying to get me all mixed up. The sort of girl I wouldn't marry if I wasn't going to marry you."

"And what sort of a girl is that, for instance?"

"Well, like Theresa Boleyn, for instance."

"For the love of Pete! Since when have you gotten the itch for her?" Chloe shoved me away from her with some violence and without waiting for an answer to her question went on: "Very well, son, run right along and peddle your *War Cries*. If I have been nursing along the notion that you have something to you, I've been sadly mistaken. Especially if you have fallen for that empty-headed, doll-faced chippy. You know, of course, all that sweetness is all put on?"

Chloe's logic had my mind in a whirl. There was simply not one girl living I had ever met that I did not like except Theresa Boleyn, and I disliked her solely and exclusively on Harry's account. How Chloe could assume that I had thought of Theresa for one minute except in a sort of hatred, passed my comprehension. But I had taken Theresa literally at her face value.

There shot through me a sensation of intense anguish. "Who in the world ever said anything about my being in love with Theresa

Boleyn?" I asked. "I loathe her. She is the meanest, most heartless person I know. I could choke her the way she has treated Harry."

"Ah, so you want to choke her, do you?" Chloe said this with a tone of cynicism that implied that I wanted to do something else to Theresa besides choke her. She had me fuddled.

"No. I don't want to choke her."

"What do you want to do with her, diddle her?"

I was shocked, and my honor was impugned at the same time. "Chloe," I said, "I think that is a terrible thing for you to say."

"Oh, is it? And just why is it? Everybody else in town except you and your friend Harry has diddled her, and if Harry had diddled her instead of just holding her hand he might have kept her. But the Lord knows why he would want to. She has skinny legs and a fat behind."

All this erotic information was incredible, and it was in language I was prudish enough to resent in Chloe. I was on the point of saying, "I don't believe you," and yet it had somehow aroused in me a modified interest and curiosity in Theresa Boleyn. That this angel-faced, demure-looking girl should be enacting a clandestine role as the town's Messalina gave her an interest in my eyes I had not entertained before. Still I found it expedient to stifle that curiosity. I was even ashamed of the low impulses giving rise to it. Besides I didn't believe Chloe.

"I don't like for you to use that word *diddle*," I said with a certain very sincere but fatuous solemnity.

"All right." She laughed. "Hereafter I will use another word. Shall it be a five-letter word or a four-letter one?"

"I'd rather it wouldn't be either. Can't we just assume that such and such things exist without naming them? . . . What were we arguing about when we got into this mess, anyway?"

"We weren't arguing about anything. I was just telling you that you are going away to college and from college you are going on to something else and all the time you will be going away from me, and I can't help it and wouldn't want to help it if I could, because I love you."

Chloe became tender, and I was mush already.

"No, I am not, dear. I love you."

"I know you love me, you dear goose, and I love you. But when

I kiss you good-by, I am going to kiss you good-by and try mighty hard to find somebody soon like you. Because it won't be your own fault, but it is just the way things are. And meantime I am going to have as much of you as I can. Kiss me."

We kissed, got up from the swing and walked along a path, crossed a Japanese footbridge and entered a small island which was thickly covered with trees and shrubbery. It was past midnight. No moon was out, and the stars came through the straggling clouds weakly. We found a place, tufted with thick grass, near the water's edge and sat down upon it. Both of us were in melancholy mood: sat closely huddled, saying nothing; we did not even kiss.

While we sat thus, each plagued by a separate, unfathomable misery, a flashlight was thrown upon us.

"Come on!" a gruff voice called in the darkness. "Get out of there."

The flashlight was switched off; the outlines of two policemen were silhouetted beyond the hedge. Fright seized me, and the thought of arrest and disgrace to Chloe sent terror through my heart. But the policemen said not another word and walked away.

Once beloved, *still* beloved, Chloe, how infinitely, mercifully wise you were, how much more sentient and percipient than was the innocent, troubled, foolish and sentimental young colt who sat beside you, silently, that night, who loved you dearly, more dearly, at the time, than anybody or anything, quite sincerely and wholeheartedly! He did not even know that the quarrel you picked with him was out of your deep intimations while he had no such intimations at all; such is the difference between the natural understanding of a sentient girl under twenty and the complete lack of understanding of anything by a boy of the same age. He— that is, I—did not know what you were talking about, or what our quarrel was about that evening, although now, nearly thirty years afterwards, I recall the words so vividly. And now I know what you meant and what the quarrel was about.

Every lad under twenty is a compound of eager foolishness, hope and fear, a craving for affection and an inner gratitude when it is shown him—however he may pose as self-reliant—and of a courage within himself that is at troubling war with doubts of himself. For myself, I knew I was going away to Chicago, though at that time I had no sure knowledge of the means whereby I would get there; and even that night we talked I had pretty clear intimations of the major things I would *do* ten, even fifteen, years thence in my work; and these things I have done, with more tribulations and sorrow than I anticipated, but also with forms and moments of happiness I could not foresee or imagine.

You were brave-spirited, gallant and joyous mostly, a sprite like Fanchon (or was it Fanchette?) the Cricket in that novel by George Sand we read aloud together? And, although we lost each other and haven't seen each other in a quarter of a century and I don't know where you are and you may never read this, this is a salute in homage and in gratitude and in love to that Chloe you once were when I was a lad so remote from myself now that I can regard him as a boy I once knew and smile indulgently and compassionately upon his seriousness, his eagerness, his valiant if pathetic attempts to learn something; for you, the Chloe that once was, were a major factor in that lad's slow, unending progress toward education.

CHAPTER IX

Earning a Living

I Dig Potatoes and Earn Thirty Dollars. I Get a Job Carrying Papers. I Drift by Accident into Newspaper Work. The Technique of Earning a Living a Solved Problem.

As EARLY AS THE AGE OF THIRTEEN I had conceived my position in my father's household as a form of parasitism. I had not arrived at this view of myself through any precocious talent for analyzing the logic of a situation, independently and in the abstract, but because of the chance arising wherein I found myself in need of a new pair of moleskin pants, sweater with leather shoulder pads, shoes with leather cleats, and a real Spalding leather helmet if I was to aspire on the freshman high-school team to the captaincy and quarterbackship, which positions I had held on the eighth-grade team which had won the championship of all the grade schools.

That I should be elected to the captaincy and quarterbackship of the freshman high-school team, made up of the best players among all the graduates of the grade schools, I had accepted as a foregone conclusion, and in anticipation of this honor I had felt that my torn and shabby canvas knickers, my raveling sweater into which I had sewn leather pads, and shoes onto which I had tacked bits of leather to form cleats, did not make up quite the proper costume for receiving the honor about to be bestowed upon me. I had wanted to look the part, and this vanity, when I had shopped around and had added up the cost, had proved to be very expensive. The total cost, including jock strap, belt, stockings and rubber nose guard, would be more than eighteen dollars.

This had been, to me, an almost incomprehensible sum of actual money. I had doubted whether even the cashier of the First National Bank could afford to spend all that money in a lump. Hitherto I had gone to my father when I wanted a quarter for a baseball mitt, a nickel for a bowl of chile, a dime for a motion-picture show; and I had found it easy to swindle my mother out of any incredible amount, even up to as much as seventy-five cents, on no plausible pretext. If she had that much in her little glass jar that sat in the lower drawer of her dresser, I could have it by the simple expedient of saying, "Mama, can you *lend* me fifty cents?" The actual definition of the world *lend* had never occurred either to me or to my mother, or, if it had occurred to her, she had merely accepted it as a polite euphemism.

The ease, however, with which it was possible to extract any absurd amount of money (up to fifty cents and more) out of my mother, had begun to trouble my conscience, at about the same time my calculations told me that there was nowhere near anything like eighteen dollars in that little glass jar kept in the lower drawer of my mother's dresser. The question of getting together eighteen dollars had then become a problem of major importance.

So, meditating upon the possible chances of acquiring eighteen dollars and, at the same time, reflecting upon the slender amount in the glass jar and upon my father's hardships as a boy, it had occurred to me that for the few chores I had been doing about the house I was being paid an absurdly large salary: I was getting board, lodging, clothes and spending money for a total amount of labor amounting to less than ten hours a week—and my father, when he was a "bound" boy, had worked twelve hours a day for less. And that last suit my mother had bought had cost fourteen dollars.

I had learned in the classroom what a "parasite" was: it was like a lichen or mistletoe or vermin; it drew its nourishment from other organisms, and it wasn't in good repute, either biologically or as a mere word. And I, I had concluded, was just that—a parasite—and had set about altering my status.

The whole eighteen dollars would not be needed for nearly

three months yet. Fred Higgins had told me he was going to get a job digging potatoes that summer on a farm where he could get two cents a bushel and could earn fifty or sixty cents a day, while the crop held out, besides "keep," which meant food and lodging. So that summer I dug potatoes with such fanatical energy that I had made as much as seventy-eight cents a day, and in two months saved up over thirty dollars. I should have worked longer and quite as fanatically, except that the farmer had no more potatoes to be dug up.

That thirty dollars had been so far beyond my needs that it had given me a new character in my eyes. I had spent just a trifle more than eighteen dollars on my football outfit and had kept nearly a dollar to dissipate on chile and hokey-pokey ice cream and had opened up a savings' account at the First National Bank with an initial deposit of ten dollars.

That amount I found it easy to augment, if one had the proper stuff in oneself. I got a job, on my return from the farm, carrying papers. By prodigious luck I had got Route 1, which was in the business district and covered less than a mile. It was an easy route: you set your alarm clock for 3:30 A.M., built a fire (in cold weather) in the base burner for the family, went to the office, had your papers counted out to you, slid papers under doors, chased up several flights of stairs, got a cup of coffee and a doughnut given you by Gus Pappas at the City Café, got home for a breakfast of beef-steak, potatoes, biscuits and coffee at 7:30 and then went to school. On Saturday mornings you collected from your customers and later got paid by the circulation manager. You got $1.50 a week for carrying the papers and 10 per cent of the collections, making in all about $1.80. And you practised or played football Saturday afternoons.

I had not been long at the job before I discovered that, besides the "deadheads" (advertisers who received the papers free) on my route, there were a certain number of subscribers who could not be counted on to pay their ten cents every week, or, indeed, any week, and these subscribers were to all outward appearances solvent and of good repute—lawyers, doctors, farm-loan brokers and real-estate dealers. The people of shadier reputation—saloon keepers, gambling-house keepers, and the two benignant women who were chatelaines of second-floor sets of dubious lodgings—paid promptly and very often gave you a quarter and told you to keep the change; but money could not be extracted out of these others even by repeated visits.

So I had asked for and had got Route 7 on the plea that I had a horse and could carry Route 1 on foot and Route 7 on horseback. The former carrier of Route 7 had decided he did not want the job any longer and had taught me the route. It was a route in a remote residential district, with subscribers often living an eighth of a mile apart. And while carrying Route 7 and Route 1, I concocted a scheme which had been enthusiastically accepted by the business office of the newspaper; for the business office was in a quandary as to how to meet the very problem I proposed to solve.

I proposed to take over all eight routes, hire and pay the carriers, deliver "deadhead" copies and pay the newspaper one cent apiece for every newspaper, excluding "deadheads," which I and my carriers took out of the office. That had meant that I was to pay the newspaper six cents a week for every newspaper taken out of the office and, out of the four cents difference in the amount of subscription, was to pay all the other carriers and, in fact, take over all of the responsibility of the local circulation end. This proposal had come as a boon even to the circulation manager himself, though it relieved him of a $16-a-week job; for he was a pressman by trade, and as a pressman he could count out the papers delivered to me, feed the press on the same work shift and, in consideration of this extra labor, demand and receive eighteen dollars a week.

My first act had been to call my carriers together, tell them that I was now their boss and offer them 20 per cent on collections instead of 10. But I had also instructed them to cease delivering papers to any subscriber who owed more than thirty cents, which meant three weeks in arrears, unless the carrier had good reason to believe the account was collectible.

This meant that during the first week of my being boss of circulation, the circulation of the newspaper was cut down about 10 per cent; but that dead-weight 10 per cent I had not had to pay for, because I had contracted to pay one cent for each copy I took out and not one cent for each copy that heretofore had been delivered to subscribers. Subscribers who were in arrears had telephoned the newspaper that their copies had not been delivered, which was just what I had expected; and they had been told that the carrying concession was in private hands and that it would be necessary to consult the carrier of the route.

These carriers lost no time in telling everybody they encountered the names of the people they refused to deliver papers to because they would not pay; and this speedily came to the knowledge of all the delinquent subscribers, who immediately paid up their arrears and saw to it that there was a dime ready when the ragamuffin carrier came to the door every Saturday morning. (The most obstreperous of my carriers was a runt named Charley Higgins who always rough-housing. I had to paddle him several times to keep him from wrecking the type cases. He grew up to be six feet four inches tall, a University of Chicago football hero and Olympics champion.)

My net profit, including that from my own route, had been only $3.85 the first week, but the second week it had been $8.20, and the third week, $9.45. It had become stabilized around that amount when I sold my concession for $45 cash to the circulation manager I had supplanted. This circulation manager, then reverted to pressman, had conceived the idea that he could feed the press, count out the papers and run my business all at the same time.

I had accepted the cash offer for the scheme I had created, because another, and more congenial, job had just been offered me. One morning in January 1908, after my own route had been delivered and all the carriers were gone, I had sat down at an office typewriter, an old Oliver machine at which I had been practising, and had written what sounded to me like an editorial. It was, though I did not know it, one of the oldest stand-bys of editorial writers and the sturdiest perennial of editorial-column flora. It was an editorial on the relationship between consumption and genius (see Appendix I). Had I known, this was also one of the perennially debatable subjects, expression of an opinion on which was sure to get publicity for any harried and obscure biologist, neurologist or psychiatrist who was being nagged by his wife to get out and do something instead of fiddling along with charts and case notes that nobody ever hears of.

[133]

Blissfully unaware of this situation, I had read a newspaper dispatch in which some noodle, a physician and professor of pathology in an Eastern university, had said that genius, and in especial literary genius, was dependent upon one's having tubercular germs in the blood; and the author had cited the case of Robert Louis Stevenson and had mentioned offhandedly Goethe, Balzac, Thomas Babbington Macaulay, Ralph Waldo Emerson and Thomas Carlyle.

Tapping out on the typewriter, I wrote what I thought would sound like an editorial. I was genuinely aroused over the subject, but I was much more aroused over the proper cadence and punctuation of the sentences. I looked up several polysyllabic words in the big dictionary to make sure they meant what I thought they meant and that they were spelled the way I had spelled them.

I showed this effusion to Ulysses S. Russell, the editor, who, upon reading it, displayed an incredible enthusiasm. To be sure, this editor had just taken a very hefty swig from a brown bottle in his desk, in my presence, before reading the bit, but that did not quite account for his antics.

"My boy," he said, clapping me upon the back, "this is a masterpiece! I salute you as my new chief editorial writer. . . . Hey! Cecil, come here. . . . See this editorial? Young Rascoe here just wrote it. I want it to lead the editorial columns tomorrow morning, regular editorial measure, with boldface head, but double leaded. Sign his name to it. Get that? . . . [Turning to me] Got any more ideas?"

I had none whatever. I could not account for such enthusiasm over a plain statement of facts.

"You are carrying papers or something of the sort here, aren't you? How much are you getting?" he asked.

"I made $9.60 last week, sir."

"Nine dollars and sixty cents! Carrying papers? How much are you holding out on us? A newsboy isn't paid such salaries around here. Ask the business manager. Every time I ask for a dollar he talks about bankruptcy."

"But, sir, it isn't just that I am carrying a route. I am taking care of the whole circulation end, and I am hiring and paying the boys. And the business manager is very well satisfied with the arrangement, for he is getting more cash money weekly than he used to."

"What's this? What's this? You mean to tell me he is *satisfied* with any arrangement involving money? All right! I will make him dissatisfied. You go to work, right now, as my editorial assistant, at ten dollars a week. How does that suit you? And you can keep on going to school. You are to write at least one editorial a day on your own hook and any I suggest to you. Tomorrow is the anniversary of Poe's birth. Sit down and write an editorial on Poe, and write an editorial on the need for more sprinklers for the city streets."

Thus I drifted quite by accident and quite precociously into newspaper work, and thus early I accepted the fact, without thinking much about it one way or the other, that I was salaried and independent, in a job less physically arduous than that of carrying newspapers and bossing newsboys, and certainly more congenial. Within less than a month after I had become a daily contributor to the editorial page, writing my stuff in the evenings on an office typewriter and later to hie myself home to study my high-school lessons, I had also been drafted for reporting work after school hours and was assigned to "cover" school-board meetings, aldermanic-council sessions and political gatherings.

The fact that I knew nothing of the issues involved in these meetings and that the speakers agitatedly spoke sentences which had no meaning for me did not seem to matter to the editor or to the readers of the newspaper or the performers themselves; my reports were duly printed on the first page, just as I wrote them from my memory of what had been said and what had taken place. And on reading accounts of the same affairs in the rival paper, I saw no reason for censuring myself on the score of taking money under false pretenses; and so I had accepted the fact that I was now a reporter as well as an editorial writer.

Within a month, then, I had become a seasoned newspaperman, and when the editor who had hired me was succeeded by Mr Mountjoy, I had been astounded but pleased to find that Mr Mountjoy accepted me as an equal, without any condescension whatever and for all the world as though I were an experienced newspaperman, and that when Jerry Rand had been hired as a reporter he, too, had accepted me as a fellow reporter.

[135]

Earning a living, then, had early become for me a natural habit in my daily routine of study, recitation in class, theme work, athletics, learning and playing roles in high-school dramatic productions, performing my duties as class president, as editor-in-chief of the student monthly and as associate editor of the student annual.

And so, too, I had accepted it as part of the nature of things that when I needed money I should take any job that came to hand and not consider it, any more than newspaper work, my life's career or as something to be contemptuous of; for even in the work of selling shoes, as an extra salesman, on Saturdays during one period while the newspaper I worked for had temporarily suspended publication through proceedings in bankruptcy, I had been initiated into the trade secrets whereby an elaborate code system conceals the size of a shoe because most women are ignorant, and are kept ignorant, of the actual size of their feet, believing they wear size three when they are shod in size five, and refusing to accept a shoe as too large if the salesman even so much as hints that the shoe he is offering is size three and a half.

The technique of earning a living, then, had early become for me a solved problem; for you simply took any job from washing windows, sweeping out offices, acting as cashier in a barber's shop, to selling shoes and haberdashery or acting as a ticket taker in a nickelodeon, when you needed money. And if your income dropped considerably through some unfortunate circumstance over which you had no control, you modified your scale of living: you moved out of the elegant furnished room with private bath and breakfast in a private residence and took up lodgings in a cheap rooming house, reduced your expenses for pleasurables and luxuries, wore your winter suit through the summer and made your light topcoat serve in winter if your heavy coat was worn threadbare. You asked Gus or Harry Pappas to extend you credit temporarily so that you could eat one full meal a day, at the City Café, of soup, roast beef, mashed potatoes, vegetable salad, ice cream and coffee for two bits, and for the other two meals you boiled your own breakfast coffee and made your own breakfast toast on the top of the gas heater in your room and ate a ten-cent bowl of chile for lunch.

[136]

You also occasionally paid your parents a visit on the farm and ate enormous amounts of chicken and dumplings, Hubbard squash, candied sweet potatoes, corn bread and biscuits and other delicacies you were not used to eating. And when your fortunes changed, you paid up your bill at the City Café, ordered an elaborate meal for Chloe and yourself, took Chloe out to the amusement park, moved back into your room with private bath at Mrs Replogle's and bought yourself, in time, new clothes.

Adversity I had come to accept, not as a calamity, but as a temporary inconvenience in no way affecting my happiness or hindering my career; for I had no career except to live and breathe, read books, go to school, be in love and play on the high-school teams. And such a career I found just as easy to pursue in one circumstance as in another.

CHAPTER X

Seventeen

My Diaries for 1909 and 1910. The Execution of Francesco Ferrer Moves Me. I Write Eulogies of Men of Science and Record Quotations from a Host of Authors. More Reading. I Take Private Lessons in Greek and French from a Greek Waiter. Emotionally the Most Crucial Period of My Life.

In my diaries for 1909 and 1910, I discover:

1. That I recorded the deaths of Swinburne, George Meredith, Edward Everett Hale, Coquelin, Modjeska and Frederic Remington, and commented on the work of each of these.

2. That I was greatly moved by the newspaper accounts of the execution in Barcelona of Francesco Ferrer, the Spanish revolutionist who was found guilty of treason. I wrote a rhetorical account of the event, prefacing my grandiloquence with these quotations:

Qui cogit mori
Nolentem, in aequo est, quique properantem impedit.—Seneca.
Nihil cogor, nihil patior invitus. Nec servio Deo, sed assentior.— Seneca.
Mors est non esse.—Seneca.
Lice destroyed Democritus, and other lice killed Socrates.—Marcus Aurelius.

At the conclusion of this reaction to Ferrer's execution, I wrote: "His last words were 'Long live the modern school!' The modern school shall live. It is an outcrop of the Carbonari, an offspring of the French Revolution, an echo of the 'Young Italy,' a reappearance of the Spirit of '76. It has before it the culmination of a great reorganization; it is smoothing the road for a better posterity; it is breaking the final chains forged about humanity. The Desmoulins affair, the meetings of the charcoal burners, the Boston Tea Party, the work of Rosseau and Voltaire, the publication of Mazzini, the uprising of the Jena students, the work of Daniel O'Connell—all have their counterpart in Spain today. Spain is to be a republic. Humanity demands it. Oppression cannot exist at this stage of the world's development." (Note of comment, 1936: Oh, sweet faith and optimism of youth! Spain had to wait twenty-two years to become a republic. And after she did she was practically razed to the ground in dreadful civil war.)

3. That I was convinced that the men of science would liberate the world and, therefore, wrote eulogies of Ernst Haeckel, Thomas A. Edison, Luther Burbank and Maurice Maeterlinck; and that I read Maeterlinck's *The Life of the Bee, The Intelligence of the Flowers,* Jost's *Plant Physiology,* Parker and Haswell's *Textbook on Zoölogy,* Haeckel's *Riddle of the Universe* and Tyndall's *Sound.*

4. That I recorded quotations from William Blake, Horace, Walt Whitman, Emerson, Dante, Hadrian, Cicero, Max Sterner, Schopenhauer, Aristotle, Arthur Symons, Victor Hugo, the Mahabharata, the Bhagavad-Gita, Walter Pater, Friedrich Nietzsche, Virgil, Bernard Shaw, Southey, Heine, Oscar Wilde, Anatole France, Aeschylus, Ibsen, Seneca, Robert Burton, Diogenes, Laertius, Athenaeus, Goethe, Gray's poems, six dialogues of Plato, the complete letters of Charles Eliot Norton, the Koran, Schiller, Lafcadio Hearn, Carlyle, Sir Thomas Browne, the Upanishads.

5. That besides these authors I also read some or all of: the first volume of Emerson's *Journals* (just published) and all of Emerson's *Essays* and *Addresses;* all of Lowell's essays and the *Biglow Papers,* Oliver Wendell Holmes's *Autocrat of the Breakfast Table, The Poet at the Breakfast Table, The Professor at the Breakfast Table* and *Elsie Venner,* parts of Boswell's *Life of Dr Samuel Johnson,* Hugo's *Les Misérables, Bug-Jargal, Notre Dame de Paris, The Toilers of the Sea, The Man Who Laughs,* and *Things Seen,* Bryant's translation of the Odyssey, several of Plutarch's *Parallel Lives,* Cicero's *Tusculan Disputations* and *Letters to Atticus,*

BEFORE I FORGET

Juvenal's *Satires* and Perseus' *Satires* in the Bohn translation series,
Boccaccio's *Vito di Dante,* Vasari's *Life of Michelangelo,* Voltaire's
Philosophical Dictionary, his epic the *Henriade,* his tragedies
Edipe, Zaïre and *Mahomet,* Poe's *Tales of the Grotesque and
Arabesque* and his poems, the *Meditations of Marcus Aurelius,* the
Discourses of Epictetus, most of Burton's *Anatomy of Melancholy,*
the *Oedipus Rex* of Sophocles, the *Knights, Clouds,* and *Birds* of
Aristophanes, the Bible, Shelley's complete poems and his *Necessity of Atheism,* selected poems of Keats, selected poems of Byron,
Hesiod's *Works and Days,* translations from the Greek Anthology,
Milton's *Paradise Lost,* parts of Kant's *Critique of Pure Reason,*
Schopenhauer's *Essays,* Selected Essays of Montaigne, Diogenes
Laertius' *Lives of the Philosophers,* the *Deipnosophists* of
Athenaeus, the *Journal* of John Woolman, the Vedic hymns in
translation, Tolstoi's *Confessions* and *What is Art?,* Turgenieff's
Fathers and Sons and *A Sportsman's Diary,* Edward Scribner
Ames's *Psychology of Religious Experience,* Hall's *Adolescence,*
William James's *Habit* and *Varieties of Religious Experience,*
Ben Jonson's *Volpone,* the *Gargantua* of Rabelais, Swift's *Gulliver's
Travels* and *The Tale of the Tub,* the selected poems of S. T.
Coleridge and his *Biographia Literaria,* De Quincey's *Confessions
of an English Opium Eater,* Bryce's *American Commonwealth,*
Taine's *History of English Literature,* Cellini's *Autobiography,*
Smollett's *Life of an Atom,* Heine's *Travels in Italy,* Alfred de
Musset's *Confessions of a Young Man,* Stevenson's *Pulvis et Umbra,
Virginibus Puerisque, William Watson,* and *Familiar Studies, The
Imitation of Christ* by Thomas à Kempis, *The Causeries du lundi*
of Sainte-Beuve, *Père Goriot* by Balzac, Christopher Marlowe's
Tamburlaine, The Jew of Malta, Dr. Faustus and *Hero and
Leander,* the *Germania* of Tacitus, Dean F. W. Farrar's *Life of
Christ* and *Lives of the Fathers,* Renan's *Life of Christ,* Ibsen's
Peter Pan, A Doll's House and *Peer Gynt,* James Huneker's
Egoists: A Book of Supermen, Visionaries, Melomaniacs, and
Promenades of an Impressionist, H. L. Mencken's *Philosophy of
Friedrich Nietzsche,* Nietzsche's *Human All-Too-Human* and *The
Birth of Tragedy,* Bernard Shaw's *Plays Pleasant and Unpleasant,
Plays for Puritans, The Quintessence of Ibsenism* and *Man and
Superman,* G. K. Chesterton's *Orthodoxy, Tremendous Trifles* and

[140]

The Man Who Was Thursday, and Hazlitt's *Essays on the Fine Arts.*

In addition to these were the texts used in English, German and Latin classes in high school. I also read the *Bookman, Current Opinion,* the *Saturday Evening Post,* and *Collier's* fairly regularly at the library.

6. That I wrote seven poems and one tragedy in blank verse—all very bad indeed.

7. That I took private lessons in ancient Greek, modern Greek and French from a graduate of the University of Athens who was a waiter in a restaurant.

8. That there was a period through the latter part of my sixteenth and throughout my seventeenth year when I did not write as well (or anything like as well) as I wrote when I was fifteen and sixteen. Since these were periods of extensive and gluttonous reading in nearly all fields of literature, especially of the classics, it would be easy for me to reflect that much reading does not enable one to write better; but the explanation is not as simple as that. I could hazard guesses in explanation, but I honestly do not know the reason.

What I think is the explanation lies in this second discovery I made on rereading these diaries closely, and that is that, although my diary is volubly concerned with the things of the mind and spirit, it records nothing (or very elliptically) of my emotional experience. And this was, emotionally, perhaps the most crucial period of my life. Certainly it was one of the most intense and exciting. It was a period of moments of great joy and intense, almost unbearable unhappiness. It is a period of sensitive pride in youth; and the turn of events subjected my parents and me to acute humiliations and me to periods of terror, fear, dejection and shame.

CHAPTER XI

A Leonardo I Would Be!

I Acquire Some Pressroom Technique. Hero Worship of Leonardo da Vinci and of Goethe. Reporter, Editorial Writer, Colyumist and Assistant Librarian. Business Manager, Editor and Ad Writer for the *Tatler*. I Invent a Retired Professor and Record His Sayings. Ghost Writer for Clubwomen. A Vacation Visit to Chicago. Preoccupation with the Contemporary European Literary Show.

During the first year of my work as a newspaper carrier I learned to feed a job press, a drumhead press and the folder, to set headline type by hand, to operate a linotype machine, an addressing machine and to use a typewriter—all by eager curiosity and earnest practice in the early-morning hours between the time when I arrived at the *Herald* office at four o'clock and the papers were ready for the carriers, which they sometimes would not be until nearly six o'clock.

The printers and pressmen were patiently instructive to their voluntary apprentice and, taking pride in their own abilities, were eager to impart such points of technique as I was curious to learn —such as how to flip a newsprint sheet so a current of air would separate its full length and breadth from the sheets below, and thus make it easy to slip the sheet into the automatic slots which would carry it around the drumhead and over the flat bed of type; how to ink the rollers properly and disentangle an imperfect sheet which had caught in the web; how to read type as it lay in forms on the stone and how to use the agate rule; how to lock up a form, cut boiler plate and tack it onto lead blocks; how to use printer's jargon and the names of the type fonts. The pressman who taught me how to feed the flatbed press used to go to sleep, on a pile of fresh newsprint, with his eyes wide open (the only person I ever saw who could sleep that way), and I would feed the run until Bert Cecil had run several hundred papers through the folder and had counted out my route allotment.

I was prompted to acquire mechanical efficiency in all branches of the printing trade just as I was later to learn the art of making picture frames, because my hero worship at the time was centered upon Leonardo da Vinci, whose ability to do so many manual things well, from bridge building and contriving new engines of war to sculpture and painting, excited me to emulate him in the humble means at my command. I read everything about Leonardo in encyclopedia articles, essays and in Vasari's *Lives of Eminent Painters* and conceived it as my obligation to myself to be dexterous at many trades and to be able to make things with my hands, not with a definite aim to earn a living at any particular trade but thus to increase my appreciation of the manual arts and crafts and to make myself into something of the full man I considered Leonardo to be.

Smile, if you wish (as I do), dear reader, but do not laugh at this boy I once was, who aspired so high and whose reach and stature have been so slight, who has built no bridges, designed no engines, painted no masterpieces, hewn no stone and has progressed even in the use of the tools of his trade—words—not much beyond Leonardo's casual use of them in his *Notebooks* and his letters to princes applying for jobs.

Nor smile at that boy's wishing to be like, in manners, to the young Alcibiades, as those manners were attested to by Plutarch and the Platonic dialogues; nor at his having resolved not to make the mistakes which led Alcibiades into voluptuousness, disintegration and banishment. Nor smile at his taking the student, Goethe, as hero and resolving also to so study the visible universe of living things as to approach the secret of life.

For my heroes might have been Jesse James, Al Jennings or the Dalton boys, or I might have had, but for aspirations like these to keep me out of mischief, one of several fates I shudder now to think of. Three boys I used to play with and who, even in high school, were as fine, as likable, as intelligent and ethical as any of their fellows, later went to prison, one for attempted bank robbery, one for shooting a man in a hold-up, and another for embezzlement.

So, on those clear, silent mornings when at the far end of my newspaper route I would watch the breath-takingly beautiful sunrises which occur on the prairies and, thinking of Leonardo, dream of painting one such sunset, I was happy in a way an adult rarely finds to be happy. The Shawnee schools did not have the manual-training shops then that they were soon to have, or the instruction in drawing; and, out on these prairies, I would indulge myself in meditations of mild self-pity to dampen my sheer joy in living in such a beautiful world, and my meditations would have to do with the ways I would educate my children and provide for them so they would not have to get up at three-thirty in the morning to deliver papers, and work on Saturday morning collecting until noon, and work as cashier in a barbershop from one in the afternoon until midnight, while other boys and girls were going to the movies or dances or taking trolley rides to Benson Park, and boating on the river and gayly drinking ice-cream sodas in Gleason's Drugstore or the Busy Bee.

These dream children of mine, when I was but a child myself, devising intricate new ways in which to fold newspapers so they could be hurled from the sidewalk to front porches, would be educated in gymnastics and music like the Greeks; they would have the tools and the means to learn the manual arts; they would learn to speak clearly and forcibly without stammering as I did; they would be free and well-rounded in physique and interests and talents.

Parenthetically, I must say that by the time I achieved children I had no very definite notions about how they should be educated at all, and my circumstances were such that I could not have put these ideas into effect if I still entertained them.

In my junior year in high school I held two regular jobs simultaneously. I was a reporter, editorial writer and conductor of an occasional feature column in the *Herald*, entitled "Séances with the Mental Medium." And I was assistant librarian at the Carnegie Public Library. In addition to this I was editor of the high-school annual, secretary of the student council, and when the time came along to produce the junior-class play I acted in this.

Moreover, I fell in with a scheme of a young society woman, Aloysius (sic) Larchmiller, to issue a monthly magazine called the *Tatler,* which was to be to Shawnee what *Town Topics* was to New York. Miss Larchmiller had no money to put up, nothing, indeed, to contribute except the notion for the magazine and some gossip of the town she wanted to air in print. She proposed that I be business manager and editor, because even in my freshman year I had been elected business manager of the high-school paper, an unusual honor accorded a freshman, because I knew something about printing.

I had to get estimates from printers on the cost of printing the fourteen-page slick paper magazine we planned; and, after getting the estimates, I had to figure out a price rate for advertisements, get up a dummy, and get enough guarantees, in the form of contracts, for advertising to indemnify the printer against loss. I also had to write all the advertisements. This was fun. Elbert Hubbard, with his *Philistine* and the *Fra,* was just then attempting a revolution in advertising by writing advertisements which were snappy and "literary," and, in doing this, Hubbard had won the enthusiastic support of Thomas A. Edison, Harvey Firestone, the Armour Packing Company and other national advertisers. So I imitated the Hubbard ads, wrote my copy before soliciting the advertising and thus landed six pages of display advertising in the first issue. Herewith are some samples of these effusions:

From the *Tatler,* Shawnee, Oklahoma, December, 1910. Volume 1, Number 1:

SHOWS MAY COME AND SHOWS MAY GO, BUT THE ODEON FOREVER

W	Because people demand the best. For several moons we have been catering to the Elect, teaching them at times with scenic
H	films, reproductions of the classic dramas, and scientific pictures, appealing to their better natures with picture stories,
Y	and obliterating the blues with the merry jollity of our comics. We provided mental recreation and stimulate thought
?	at five cents per copy. THE ODEON.

BEFORE I FORGET

From the *Tatler,* Shawnee, Oklahoma, December, 1910. Volume 1, Number 1:

Laughter is the supreme anodyne, the antidote for grouch, grumps, glum and goo-goo. Every laugh lengthens your life. We are medical specialists and always prescribe the haw-haw. We tickle your mental palate and send you away in a whistling mood of jollity. Classy vaudeville with a change of an excellent bill of motion pictures three times a week.

Matinee Sundays　　　　　THE FOLLY　　　　　East Main Street

From the *Tatler,* Shawnee, Oklahoma, December, 1910. Volume 1, Number 1:

HAVE YOU AN OLD SUIT, WEARABLE YET OUT OF COMMISSION BECAUSE OF WRINKLES AND GREASE SPOTS?

Have you a new serge or tweed that you hesitate to send to the cleaners for fear of shrinkage, or the destruction wrought in boiling and washing? French Dry Cleaning is the only sane way. That suit of your neighbor's is not a new one—it has only made the pilgrimage to Congdon's. The longevity of cloth depends upon the exclusion of dirt and the care taken in cleansing. The most delicate fabrics are safe in our hands: We have the most complete French Dry Cleaning Establishment south of Kansas City.

The Spots Do　　　　　　　　　　127–129–131 N. Beard
Not Come Back　　　　　　　　　　　　Phone 223
　　　　　　　　CONGDON'S LAUNDRY
　　　　　　Launderer's To His Majesty The People

We had omitted to stipulate a per-copy price on the first issue and so decided to issue the magazine free, available on the counters of all advertisers in the number of copies desired by the advertiser. The magazine was a monthly, and it ran for two issues, when Miss Larchmiller exhausted her supply of quips at the expense of beaux and belles of the Elks Club society, and I got bored with the job just as a new and more interesting source of income developed unexpectedly, of which more anon. Meanwhile I had cleared forty-two dollars on the first issue and thirty-eight dollars on the second

[146]

for myself, over and above all expenses, including Miss Larch-miller's one-third split in the profits.

I did not care for the *Tatler,* principally because I considered Miss Larchmiller a shallow woman and because I gagged at such items she wrote as these:

By a recent wedding Shawnee was bereft of the town beau and also the visiting girls' delight. Of course, we know that there are just as good fish in the sea as the one just caught, but we really do not believe it of the sea in which we fish.

Chafing dish parties are becoming quite the fad this winter, but one of our most popular bachelors was unkind enough to remark that they were only "fishing" parties.

Mr. D. P. Sparks, Jr.—The darling of the gods and girls. His wife is sure to love him to distraction and will never have any cause for complaint except non-support. Has made too many "home runs" to be caught easily.

Not liking the magazine, I contributed to it only my overset from "Séances with the Mental Medium." This overset matter contained an obituary on Tolstoi, a comment on the announcement of a complete translation into English of Nietzsche's work (four volumes of which—*Beyond Good and Evil, The Joyful Wisdom, The Birth of Tragedy,* and Part I of *Human, All-Too-Human*—I had already read in the T. N. Foulis editions in translations by W. A. Haussman, Thomas Common and Helen Zimmern), a notice on the death of William Vaughn Moody, a comment on Maeterlinck, an announcement of the forthcoming translation of *Jean Christophe* by a new musician-writer, Romain Rolland, and this blast after having read G. K. Chesterton's *What's Wrong With the World,* which is expressed in language I should not use now but which still discharges my unchanged sentiments:

From the *Tatler,* Shawnee, Oklahoma, December, 1910. Volume 1, Number 1:

WHAT'S WRONG WITH THE WORLD?

Gilbert K. Chesterton, a clever mountebank, who by reason of his prodigious array of words and his ability to execute with it some

astonishing maneuvers, has drawn the attention of the world to his
efforts has once more disturbed our sensibilities by attempting to tell
us "what's wrong with the world." As all things have some worth,
this effusion has its worth: it is a direct attack upon the faddist. It
calls a halt upon this blind adherence to new quasi-culture; it hurls a
bolt at unreasoning idolatry by the wee-thinkers who boast of freedom
from dogma. Men often mean when they say, "Come, let us reason
together," "Come, let me steep your intellect with mire." Investigation
eliminates many things: the seemingly profound is often found to be
in reality a well-dressed lie or a pompous commonplace. "Truisms
pass current, etc., etc.," said Rouget, haberdasher to small minds
and secretary to forgetting great ones, and begot a thesaurus that
brought him much monies. The credulous with receptive minds,
strong imaginations, and unbounded enthusiasm break away from
the mass to form a class of greater asses, who pay obeisance to some
charlatan and pour lucrative libations at his shrine.

Chesterton is stupid. His perhaps once fine perception has been
blunted in a rush after we-all-know-not-what and, failing in his quest,
misconceives the value of those who have pushed further than himself.
Becoming disgusted with his own incapacity, he turns cynic, and
urges an abolition of progress, a return to classicism, polytheism,
superstition, despotism, militarism, and what-not of the past. He
assumes man to be too free without his bonds and wishes to re-
incarcerate him. He overestimates the value of the papal bull and the
tumbrill. He vaunts that all things are better as they are or were and
desires the progress of society to be retro-grade. He is stupid; else he
does not believe that which he asserts.

"Séances with the Mental Medium" gave me exercise in composition, permitted me to work off in print the ideas and impressions
I got from reading and afforded me a lot of fun. When I started
the department everybody knew me as a mere lad of sixteen, and
I, knowing this, knew they would take no stock in what I had to
say if I signed my name to the stuff. So I invented a retired professor whom I alleged I occasionally went to see and recorded his
sayings. I pretended that he was modest and wanted no publicity,
so I should not have to give him a name. The column carried a
subtitle, "Reports of visits made by Burton Rascoe," and the pieces
were in the form of quoted discourses to me (See Appendix I).

These pieces aroused curiosity and discussion in the town. The mayor called upon me at the *Herald* office, asking me to introduce him to the professor who had so honored Shawnee with his residence; my teachers in high school plagued me for information about the old savant; and various guesses were made that white-haired old Mr Search, the bank president who had a good library and who conducted a Bible class, was the source of my reports—and all this I enjoyed hugely because I became a personage in the town by the simple fact of knowing the savant's identity, and I could listen without embarrassment to encomiums on my own learning and wisdom from people who did not know they were praising me and who would not believe me if I told them I invented the character and wrote the stuff.

Both by accident and by stealth I stumbled upon my most considerable free-lance income. It was during the early fall months of my junior year in high school, which was also the beginning of the season for the weekly meetings of the women's clubs, among which were the Entre Nous Club, the New Century Club, the Waukahoma Club, the Monday Bridge Club, the Thursday Bridge Club, the East Side Club, the Wednesday Thimble Club, the Sew-a-Bit Club, the Priscilla Club, the Harmony Club and two literary clubs—the Hawthorne and the Round Table.

The small-town culture clubs of those days were accustomed each spring to write to various professors in the state university, asking them to outline programs for their next season's efforts in self-improvement. The professor who was approached by the Hawthorne Club, say, would draw up a list of titles of papers to be read before the club by its members during the club season, each member of the club to be assigned a subject seriatim. These professors must have had a malicious and sardonic sense of humor; for (as I was to discover) the subjects they assigned these poor women were nutcrackers of the weightiest magnitude, each one calling for enough research and careful treatment to win a Ph. D., if properly treated.

As assistant librarian at the Carnegie Public Library my duties were to arise at six-thirty in the morning in order to have my breakfast and be at the library early enough to shake down the furnace, sweep the floor, dust the shelves and reading tables, open the mail, distribute the newspapers and magazines to their proper places and open the library for Mrs Parker's (later Mrs Funk's) arrival at eight; after attending classes from eight-fifteen until twelve-fifteen I was to return to the library and stamp incoming and outgoing books for one hour while Mrs Parker was at lunch. In the afternoons I attended to my work as a newspaper reporter from my last class at two-thirty until six or six-thirty, snatching my dinner meanwhile and returning to the library as sole attendant until ten. After ten I would return to the *Herald* office until twelve or one to do my newspaper writing, and talk with the men at the office or over steaks and coffee at the City Café.

One evening a woman approached my desk with a look of great anxiety on her face. She demanded to know if we had any book with all of Shakespeare's works condensed. I told her that Lamb's *Tales from Shakespeare* gave the stories of some of the plays in brief story form and that in Warner's Classical Library the more notable plays were skeletonized; and I produced them for her. The Warner Library volumes were bulky and formidable-looking and, after she had glanced at the Lamb book, I gathered that I was not being very helpful to my patron.

She asked me if I knew in what play of Shakespeare's the character Mephistopheles was to be found. I told her I could not recall any such character in Shakespeare, and after looking through the variorum index I could find none. I told her that Christopher Marlowe had a character in *Dr Faustus* called Mephistophilis (Marlowe's spelling) and that the play was based upon the same legend used by Goethe in the drama, *Faust,* in which the devil appears as Mephistopheles (Goethe's spelling); and I drew down from the shelves the huge volume in fine print of Bayard Taylor's translation, with which I was familiar, having just recently completed three months of reading it.

She asked me if I had read it. I said I had. She asked me if I had read Shakespeare's *Richard III*. I said I had. Then she came to the secret of her anxiety. Among the subjects suggested by some professor for members of the club, the low comedian had given one to be entitled "A Comparison Between the Characters of Mephistopheles and Richard III," and she had drawn this stunner. Moreover, it was Tuesday and she had to have the paper ready for the club meeting on Friday afternoon. I told her that apparently either the Marlowe Mephistophilis or the Goethe Mephistopheles was meant.

When she asked me if I had read the books I knew what she was driving at and so, without making the point too obvious, I suggested that I might "help her out." She bit, eagerly. She asked me point-blank if I would write the paper for her, adding that she would be glad to pay me for doing so. I told her I would. She cautioned me that no one must ever know, and I agreed that no one ever would know.

That night, armed with Taylor's translation of *Faust* and a copy of *Richard III,* I started to work on the paper in the *Herald* office after I had written a few sticks of stuff for the morning edition and, fortified with a pitcher of black coffee which I brought over from the City Café, I finished the paper by four o'clock in the morning, went home to sleep for three hours and resolved to notify the woman her paper would be ready for her if she would come to the library while I was on duty at noon. She came for the paper and took it away with her surreptitiously; but she returned with it that evening. There were some allusions in the paper which she did not understand, and some words of which she was not sure of the pronunciation. I made notes for her on the allusions and drilled her in the pronunciation of the words.

On Friday evening, just when I was going on duty at six-thirty, the woman came into the library in an even more distracted frame of mind than she had been on Tuesday evening. There were quite a number of students and adults in the library, at the reading tables and among the shelves, so she asked me if I would step into the librarian's office for a moment. It turned out that her paper had been such a vast success that she had been overwhelmed with praise. She was afraid it would leak out that she had not written the paper. She made me promise over and over again not to betray her. She asked me how much she owed me, and I, not having thought of a rate of payment up until that moment, hazarded three dollars as a suggestion, with a reservation to take two if she objected. But she was so obviously gratified that I knew I had made a mistake and should have asked for at least five.

From that day on I began to scan the faces of the clubwomen who came to the library desk, looking for signs of worry over the papers they were required to prepare and read. One by one I got as clients every member of the Hawthorne Club except a former school teacher, and every member except one of the Round Table Club. I wrote two papers a week, one for each club, varying the price for each from three to ten dollars in accordance with my knowledge of the women's ability to pay. Some of the papers were printed in full in my own newspaper, and excerpts were printed from others. Each woman bore the guilty conscience that she was the only one who was achieving local glory under false pretenses; and, as far as I could learn, not one of them ever suspected the others.

In preparing these papers I got the best exercise in writing that I ever had, for I had to vary the tone and the vocabulary of every paper. Stendhal always read the Code Napoléon before he sat down to write, so that no "literary" influences would creep into his style: I read Sir Thomas Browne, Carlyle, Macaulay, Stevenson, Hazlitt, Southey, Lowell, Pater, Dryden, Swift and Dekker for precisely the contrary reason—in an effort to catch and imitate their rhythm and their diction.

This income from ghost writing, added to my salary as a reporter and my salary as library assistant, enabled me not only to buy books I wanted for my private library (at the library discount; for I had stocked the public library with classics I wanted to read, with Mrs Parker's and Mrs Funk's consent, to the exhaustion of a budget which some members of the library board wished expended largely on novels by Harold Bell Wright, Amelia Barr, George Barr McCutcheon, Hall Caine and Harold McGrath), and to purchase the most collegiate-looking outfit in town (it consisted of a House of Kuppenheimer suit in brown checks, with padded shoulders, a pinched waist, a coat with flaring skirts and slantwise pockets, peg-topped pants, pressed both sidewise and down the front to preserve the peg and ending with narrow cuffs two inches wide; tan oxfords with fancy brass buckles instead of laces, a pancake hat with a narrow brim and a detachable sweatband in the junior-class colors, and a white stock—for all the world like a Blumenthal cartoon of rah-rah boys in the *Saturday Evening Post*), and to treat Chloe and Mabel and Lucille to full-course dinners at the City Café, trips to Benson Park, trolley rides, buggy rides and movies—but

through the tall mullioned windows of the library became murky with the close of day and chandeliers as well as table lights had to be turned on.

I walked across the University of Chicago campus, out onto the Midway Plaisance and across to Cottage Grove Avenue, where I caught a streetcar home, and resolved that, somehow, in the fall of next year I would enter this university.

A few days later I was to acquaint myself with the open shelves of the Chicago Public Library and with a quaint bookshop on Adams Street, between Wabash and Michigan, called Kroch's, largely stocked with books in French, German, Polish, Spanish and Italian, and with A. C. McClurg's, known as the largest bookstore in the world.

Thus it was, also, when I visited in Lansing, that although I learned to drive a car there and went through the Reo factory and danced evening after evening at an amusement park where my cousins were members of the orchestra, and fell quite sentimentally in love with a soft-eyed brunette, and spooned much with still another girl, forgetting utterly for the time being the girls in Shawnee —despite all this I spent a considerable time in the public library of Lansing and in the library of the Agricultural and Mechanical College, reading magazines we did not get in Shawnee, and Ibsen's *Brand* and Shaw's *Quintessence of Ibsenism,* and a book which was to open a whole new world to me, *Masks and Mistrels of New Germany,* by Percival Pollard, a fascinating book about the Über-brettl movement wherein such poets and dramatists as Schnitzler, Wedekind and Dehmel were taking art out of the custody of pedants and bringing it to the people in beer halls and vaudeville theaters.

And so, when I returned to Shawnee at the close of August, to complete my final year at high school, to ghost-write papers for clubwomen, to write for the *Herald* and to pursue my duties as assistant librarian (which afforded so much time and materials for reading), I was already turning away from a preoccupation with the classics to the dazzling contemporary literary show provided by contemporary Europeans, and thus I read my classroom texts in German—Goethe's *Egmont,* Heine's poems and Storm's *Immensee*—with profound avidity that I might read more readily

Hauptmann's *Die versunkene Glocke*, Wedekind's *Frühlingser-wachen*, Dehmel's lyrics and Schnitzler's *Anatol, Marionetten* and *Der grüne Kakadu.*

Anatole France, Bernard Shaw, Gerhart Hauptmann, George Moore, James Stephens, W. B. Yeats, Gabriele d'Annunzio, Chekhov, Andreyeff, Gogol, Kuprin, H. G. Wells, Arnold Bennett, Joseph Conrad, Rémy de Gourmont, Jules Laforge, Tristan Corbière, Paul Fort, Verhaeren, Barrès, Bourget, J. K. Huysmans, Marcel Schwob, Stendhal (new to me), Flaubert (only a name to me), J. M. Synge, Ford Maddox Hueffer, Galsworthy—all these were to open my eyes to a colorful, exotic, fascinating contemporary world, and the inciters of my curiosity about these intoxicating writers were the critics, James Gibbons Huneker, Arthur Symons, Percival Pollard, Vance Thompson and George Moore.

Here were men to whom I am indebted and toward whom I am grateful for letting me know that there was a varied and lively literature of my own time, quite other than the dull warmed-over Victorianism of Henry Van Dyke, Julian Hawthorne, Hamilton Wright Mabie, William Dean Howells, Brander Matthews and the smug writers nourished by Richard Watson Gilder on the *Century,* Henry Mills Alden on *Harper's,* Ellery Sedgwick on the *Atlantic Monthly,* W. C. Brownell on *Scribner's* and Paul Elmer More on the *Nation*—all rigid, ruthless tyrants acting as Catoesque censors and arbiters of public taste and morals.

CHAPTER XII

Ambitions

Some Already Realized, Others Still to Be. I Return from My Vacation Broke. I Sell an Article to the Oklahoma City *Times* and Become a Newspaper Correspondent in Shawnee. Farm Work in Seminole.

THE IRONIC ESSENCE OF Sinclair Lewis' *Babbitt* is in the unhappy hero's reflection upon his past, "I have never done a single thing in my life that I really wanted to do."

But I wonder if that can be true of any man or woman. It would seem, from all the evidence Lewis gives concerning the inner and outer life of his hero, Babbitt achieved every concrete ambition he ever had. He wanted to be a successful realtor, the envied owner of an imposing house and of other appurtenances which would label him a success in the eyes of the citizens of Zenith. And he achieved these things.

If, in achieving them, he was prevented from doing other things he wanted to do, that is an earnest that he did not want to do these things as passionately as he wanted to do the things he did. If what he wanted to do turned out, upon achievement, to please and satisfy him less than he had expected, that is only the inevitable irony which makes the illusion more attractive than the reality. If, late in life, Babbitt discovered that he had wanted the wrong things and had put too much energy into the getting of them, that is not to say he did not want these things in the first place.

For myself I can say that I have realized every concrete ambition I ever had and that I feel certain that I shall realize those concrete ambitions I have now. These yet-to-be-attained accomplishments or realizations of desires are things I feel in my mind, my heart, my insides, my whole being, will come about.

What is more, I *know,* without being able to tell why or how, precisely, they will come about, that such and such things will happen pretty much as I now expect, and I anticipate (from long experience in illusion and reality) that I shall take less pleasure in the *fait accompli* than in the pursuit of it. In this, perhaps, I have a middle-aged resignation to life's perpetual anticlimaxes while at the same time, happily, I am propelled ordinarily by a young man's curiosity and capacity for illusion.

I do not wish to sound mystical about this; for I believe it is a rational and natural fact that everyone accomplishes whatever he or she most ardently and most continually wishes to accomplish, and that the failure to do so is a measure of the weakness of one's will and desire. Maybe. . . . I am not *sure* about this.

Thus I have known two, three, five, and even ten years in advance what, concretely, I would become or, concretely, I would do. I would not know the steps, the means, the accidents, the slip-ups leading up to these activities and beings; and for that reason I never forced them or consciously worked to bring their realization, for I am without aggressiveness, almost without personal initiative.

Excepting the time I presented myself at the employment office as a student ready for any and all work to maintain myself, I have asked for only two jobs in my life, and those jobs I did not get. I have created jobs or they have come to me. I have never even written a book I was not asked to write, and I have been urged to write several which I never got around to writing.

And yet, in this seemingly lackadaisical manner, I have never doubted that, whatever I felt, I knew it would occur; and it always has occurred.

When I was fourteen or fifteen years old I wanted to live in Chicago sometime and I *knew* I would; the university I wished to go to was the University of Chicago and I *knew* I would; there was only one newspaper in the world I ardently wished to work on— the Chicago *Tribune*—and I *knew* five years in advance that I would someday work there; when I was a reporter I *knew* I would someday be literary editor.

When I was literary editor of the Chicago *Tribune* I *knew* I would someday live in New York and be literary editor of the New York *Tribune*.

When I was on the New York *Tribune* I *knew* I would someday have a daily syndicated column of observations and impressions not concerned with literature.

When I was writing a daily syndicated column I *knew* I would someday have a try at editing a magazine.

When I was editing a magazine I *knew* I would publish my first considerable book at the age of forty. (*Titans of Literature* was published in my fortieth year.)

In 1927 I wanted $50,000 and *knew* I would get it: within less than a year I had over $100,000, almost without any effort on my part.

And I knew about this book twelve years before I started writing it.

As you will see, my ambitions have been modest, and in some instances they have been petty; but they have always been within the realms of the possible, considering my limitations and my abilities. I have not been grandiose in my desires or megalomaniacal in my ambitions, although I believe (citing Hitler, Mussolini, Lord Northcliffe, W. R. Hearst, Jesse Livermore, J. P. Morgan, Otto Kahn) that those who have such desires and such ambitions and who are ardently and single-mindedly devoted to achieving them always succeed in their aims, even if the success is only brief, transitory and a sell.

My ambitions, I say, have been modest. I have never desired to be President of the United States or dictator of a people, or a political orator or a husband of Peggy Joyce or a millionaire or owner of a yacht or an immortal of the American Academy of Arts and Letters or one known to headwaiters of fashionable restaurants. In certain aims I am wholly lacking in ambition.

Experience has taught me discrimination by the very ease of anyone's accomplishing that which he or she resolutely sets the heart upon doing; and it has taught me, too, that accomplishment is usually not half so gratifying as one thinks it might be. But to have vaguely but determinedly before one the consciousness of a goal which one *knows* somehow, not rationally or explicably or in detail beforehand, will be achieved—that is the sweet illusion which keeps life from being a bore.

I have even known two men who wanted to die, like Tiresias, more than they wanted to do anything else, but they wanted to die "naturally" and not by suicide; and they were dead within a year, naturally.

So in the autumn of 1910 I *knew* that in twelve months I would enter the University of Chicago. Then a series of calamities began to befall me. It seemed as if Fate had begun to stack the cards as heavily as possible against my going.

I had returned from my vacation broke. School opened, and I resumed my studies, my work at the library and my work on the newspapers. But the newspaper did not resume its salary payments to me. It eventually went into bankruptcy, owing all of the employees thirty days' salary, only a small per cent of which we were able to collect after weeks of liquidation.

With the coming of statehood to Oklahoma, my father's saloon business had been wiped out without redress to him of any kind, because Oklahoma was admitted as a state only on condition that prohibition be state-wide as a protection for the Indians in Indian Territory, a half-section of the state which had been dry. And my father had been put to various new ways to make a living—running a restaurant, trading horses, getting up barbecues, and dealing in real estate, in none of which he was conspicuously successful.

In the autumn of 1910 the family income had been so reduced and so precarious that Mother was forced to take in roomers, do all of her own work, including the washing and ironing. I had to contribute to the family resources until my father traded the town home for some land in Seminole, Seminole County, only a small part of which was under cultivation, and Mother, Dad and my two younger brothers went there to live in a three-room log cabin with dirt floors.

My ghost writing had not begun, and my salary as assistant librarian was inadequate to my needs; my once splendid blue-serge suit became shabby, my shoes had holes in them which I covered with cardboard cut to the shape of my foot, and I had to go without breakfast except the coffee I made in my room, eat a ten-cent bowl of chile con carne at lunch, and a twenty-five-cent dinner.

I found an old man, who was a veteran of the Crimean War and of the Sepoy mutiny, acting as a porter in the Saddle-Rock Hotel, then a déclassé place, half hotel, half bawdyhouse. I wrote an article about him which I sold to the Sunday editor of the Oklahoma City *Times*.

This was the first bit of writing I had had printed in other than a local publication. The old man was almost inarticulate, and his memory was nearly gone; he had been at the siege of Sebastopol but could tell me nothing about it; so I had to read up on Balaklava and fill out the article with stuff cribbed from a history of the siege.

But my story gave me entree to a metropolitan newspaper, and presently I was appointed the Associated Press correspondent in Shawnee, Shawnee correspondent for the Kansas City *Star* and Shawnee correspondent for the Oklahoma City *Times*. I was assigned to cover professional boxing matches, lacrosse games between Indian teams, football games, Indian festivals and stomp dances, and murder and manslaughter trials in Tecumseh, the county seat.

Thus by the beginning of 1911 I was in funds again; for the *Herald* had been reorganized with Victor Harlow as editor and publisher, and the huge new Hoe rotary press, payment for which had bankrupted the paper, resumed its work, and I was rehired as part-time reporter and editorial writer.

How I managed to survive without a breakdown during that final year in high school I can account for only on the grounds that I have always been slight in weight and stature but have always had a strong constitution, much nervous energy, a good digestion and an ability to sleep any time and at any place soundly and without dreams.

But during that final year I never averaged more than four hours' sleep a night and often worked three days and nights at a stretch without any sleep whatever. For, in addition to the various remunerative jobs I had, I was also editor-in-chief of the high-school annual, business manager of the high-school paper, secretary and treasurer of the senior class, captain and quarterback on the football team, captain and catcher on the baseball team, organizer of the senior prom and actor in the senior play. I had also flunked mathematics in my junior year and had to carry it as an additional subject in my senior year.

During my sophomore and junior years my grades had been poor, so I decided to go out in a burst of glory and, therefore, studied to such an effect that I got the highest possible mark in each study.

Shortly after school was ended I resigned my job at the *Herald* against Mr Harlow's protest and my job at the library, and went down to my father's farm to rebuild my nerve force and physique by two months of labor at farm work before going to Chicago. I had to cover a murder trial in Tecumseh before going to the farm, and each evening when I came into the *Herald* office to write up the progress of the trial Mr Harlow sought to dissuade me from going to Chicago.

He finally offered me the editorship at eighteen dollars a week to start immediately and twenty dollars at the close of the summer; he said I could write anything I wanted to and make of the paper whatever I wished; he said a college education was worthless and he knew, because he had one; but, in the end, I thanked him and said "Eppur si muove," at which he smiled and shook my hand; I cleared out my desk, handed in my last "take" and caught the Rock Island train to Seminole. My books and belongings had already been packed and shipped from my rooming house.

Farm work I like, and if one could only make a living at it farming would be my vocation, I think, with writing as an avocation, a hobby with which to amuse myself. I like everything about farming except the acts of God in excess rain or droughts and the prices paid the farmer for farm products. Plowing and harrowing and weeding are the most nerve-resting and invigorating of all forms of exercise; harvesting wheat, corn, cotton, alfalfa and potatoes is hot work, usually, but it is a leisured work, soon accomplished, for the harvest season is short; growing a vegetable garden is fun, and with sun, soil and water and a few cents for seed one can grow a profusion of delicacies; hens and chickens are very little care (although turkeys are a nuisance); pigs must be fed, but they do not require much attention until the slaughtering season; cows must be fed and milked in season, and their young calves must be weaned, but for the most part the animals on a farm live their own lives; and the combined working hours of the farmer (as a city man knows hours of labor) amount only to about three months out of the year. The rest is but a piddling about, sawing wood, repairing the barn, building fences, hunting, fishing, whittling, loafing and inviting one's soul—and wrangling with the bank, trying to stave off foreclosure, and cussing whatever political party happens to be in office.

But the spread between what the farmer gets for his product and the price at which it is sold to the ultimate consumer, after it has passed through the middleman, is so great that only a man with an outside income can afford to live on a farm and maintain living standards prevailing even among the lower middle classes in the city. In 1911 and again in 1921, when I was on the farm in Seminole County, a strong farmer could not carry across the street on his back enough tanned cowhides to pay for a pair of shoes, so low was the price for hides and so high the price for shoes. He could not afford to hire harvesters for his corn because the price obtaining in town would not pay for the labor, but if he needed corn shorts for his cattle out of harvesting season he would have to pay a whopping price. He requires but little cash for his year's needs and that principally at harvest to pay harvesters, but if he hasn't cash in the bank he must pay usurious rates of interest (often as high as 40 per cent) for the use of it—in discounts from the face value of his promissory note to evade the maximum legal rate charge for interest.

I spent two months on the farm cutting sugar cane, harvesting wheat, stacking hay, slopping pigs, hoeing cotton, riding horseback through the countryside and rounding up grazing horses and driving them into a corral at night, chopping wood, hunting rabbits, swimming, lying for hours on a rock in the sun, making friends with gypsy cotton pickers and trying to learn the secret of a gypsy lad my own age, who would build a fire on the ground, take red-hot embers and put them in his mouth, walk slowly across the fire in his bare feet and charm snakes, as well as perform ordinary feats of magic.

[163]

Rattlesnakes, water moccasins and copperheads were numerous in that part of the country and greatly dreaded. Of these the cotton-mouth water moccasin is dreaded the most, for its venom is reputed to be the most quickly fatal: the poison of the rattlesnake works more slowly, and the rattlesnake, moreover, gives warning of its strike; you can step on a drowsy rattlesnake unwittingly in the fields, as I have often done, and if you get away in a hurry (which you usually do) the rattler won't even bother to coil. But a cottonmouth is quick and dangerous, and he will pursue you if aroused.

I saw a large cottonmouth on the edge of the creek in the ravine below our barn and corn crib, and I ran toward the house, shouting, as I went, for Dad and my brothers to bring a shotgun and hoe. Dad and George got very excited and came running, but the gypsy boy came running with them, telling them not to kill the snake. When we got near the spot the snake saw us and started to weave slowly toward us instead of away. Dad lifted the shotgun, but the gypsy boy asked him please not to shoot: he regarded the snake for a few seconds, walked slowly toward him, reached down, grasped the snake by the back of the neck, lifted him up and let the snake coil about him. He never released his hold on the snake's neck; but the snake seemed quiet and not angered. We walked with the gypsy boy and the snake back to the house, but at a safe distance away. He asked my father if he could keep the snake, and my father said he could, if he would keep him far enough away from the house. The only explanation the gypsy boy would give me was that he was not afraid of snakes: he made friends with them.

I read no books that summer, but contented myself with hardening my muscles, resting, loafing and storing up energy. My father said I was peaked and that I ought to spend a whole year on the farm. Further he said that if I would do so, he would somehow finance my first year in college; although he could advance me no money now, not even five dollars, until the crops were harvested, which meant in late October, for his principal money crop was cotton. His advice about my health was doubtless good; but I was eager to start my adventure.

So when the time came when I had figured on leaving, I bade a sobbing mother good-by and watched, with tearful amusement, the queer antics of my father who was flinging his arms about, stomping and acting as if he were angry and impatient with the delay. He kept saying, "If we are going to go, let's get going." He was doing this to keep from crying; and he did not altogether succeed. George and Henry, who had been silent and moody the night before and had finally picked a quarrel among themselves to relieve their tension, had got up early in the morning and gone off into the woods because they had not wanted to say good-by.

I went to Shawnee on the local, bought my coach ticket all the way to Chicago, via Holdenville and Kansas City for the night trains, and spent the day saying good-by to friends in Sam Yunt's bookshop, Victor Harlow, Bert Cecil, "Old Man" Cecil, Ulysses S. Russell, Shannon Mountjoy, the cashier, the printers and Miss Lemon at the *Herald*, to Joe of the Chile Parlor, to D. P. Sparks at the Gents' Furnishings Shop, to Mrs Funk at the library, to the Pappas brothers at the City Café, to the barbers in the barbershop where I had worked as cashier, to Ed Beeson at Beeson's Drugstore and lastly to the home of "Miss Lizzie" (Elizabeth Gerhardt), my teacher and principal in the eighth grade, a strong, brilliant, realistic woman my mother's age, who ever since I was graduated from her class had been my friend, confidante, consoler in adversity, counselor and proctor and vicaress for my mother in my mother's absence. Of "Miss Lizzie" I find I cannot write much, for I was one of her "boys"—i.e., one of her special pets, among whom were Calhoun and D. P. Sparks (men much older than I), Leslie Hagener and men who had graduated from her classes and had married and begot children. She was a fiery, hot-tempered, brilliantly articulate and just woman who had a German contempt for inefficiency and a Scotch Calvinist refusal to hold her tongue when she saw what she took to be evil, dissimulation or hypocrisy; so she made enemies as well as friends. After she had been grade-school principal for many years, politicians on the school board of whose petty trickeries she had been openly contemptuous and censorious got a regulation passed requiring all grade-school principals to have a college degree, which Miss Gerhardt did not have. Valiantly she determined to use her sturdy and incisive mind, even at her age, to get a college degree in less than a third of the time ordinarily required, and to this end she enrolled at the University of Chicago and emerged triumphantly with her degree; but she had so taxed her strength that she had a paralytic stroke and from this had been an invalid for years, her mind still functioning incisively but confined to a chair and unable to use her hands. . . . A noble spirit. . . . And that night I left for Chicago, there was no expressed sentiment in her about my going. She was strong, grim, almost masculine then; and she was sternly admonitory, like a hard-boiled drill sergeant giving both advice and orders to a recruit.

There was a small group at the station to bid me good-by, all cheerful and jolly and encouraging. Chloe was there, kidding me almost constantly with her delightful chuckle. When the conductor called "All Aboard!" and I ran from the station portico where we had been standing because it was raining, Chloe ran to the steps of the train with me, threw her arms about me, and we kissed once. She broke away, pushed me, laughed and said, "Good-by, you big lummox!" Then turned with a muffled "Oooh!" that wrenched my heart and made me stumble when I climbed the steps as the train pulled out of the station. . . . Six years later, I wired her that I was on a trip and would be laid over for two hours in the town she was living in and would like to meet her husband, see their baby and her. The three of them were at the station, the husband so much taller and better-looking than I that I had a momentary twinge of jealousy; the baby fat, cuddly, friendly and obviously nursed properly; and Chloe more radiant than I had known her, still merry-eyed, still with a quip at me and a chuckle—one destined to meet life on its own terms, somewhat merrily.

I found a place in the nearly empty coach, with its black leather seats and its archaic swinging dim gas lights. I inspected the sandwiches Mother had fixed up for me because I could not afford to spend money, en route, except for coffee at the railway restaurants.

And as I stretched back, my melancholy mood went away suddenly and I experienced a strange, unexpected but quite exhilarating sense of relief. Relief from what, to this day I don't exactly know.

PART III

College

CHAPTER XIII

On My Own at Chicago

I Arrive in Chicago with $1.85. Errand Boy. A Job as a Waiter
in a Boarding House. Campus Correspondent for the *Inter-
Ocean*. Usher at a Motion-Picture Theater at Night. Waiter
and Night Clerk at the Harvard Hotel. I Matriculate at the
University of Chicago. A Fertile Source of News Stories. A
Scoop that Got Me a Job on the Chicago *Tribune*. Will Cuppy.
Isabel Paterson. A Brush with James Rowland Angell. Tif-
fany Blake Recants.

I ARRIVED AT THE La Salle Street station in Chicago with the blue-
serge suit I had on, a black broad-brimmed hat which Tito Lannom
had given me, and, in a rattan suitcase, a curious black broadcloth
evening topcoat which somebody else had given me against the
rigors of Chicago winters.

(This hat and topcoat later gave me an entirely unwanted reputation for eccentricity in the matter of clothes. It was assumed, of
course, that the broad-brimmed black hat was typical Western
headgear; but my classmates in college thought it was odd of me
that with it I did not also wear high-heeled cowboy boots. And
they could not figure out the topcoat. It was a double-breasted,
form-fitting affair, tailored around the waist, with flaring skirts. It
also had a button concealed under the collar in the back on which
to button a cape, like the one worn by the Leyendecker dandy
who for so many years figured on the cover of *Town Topics*. I
never wore the cape.

But, since that swanky evening topcoat was the only overcoat I possessed, I had to wear it all winter. They thought it was strange that I should wear the coat at all; but they thought it was stranger still that I should wear it in freezing weather. Chilled to the marrow, I put on a prideful false front and said that I had been inured to the cold on the Western prairies and could not bear a heavyweight overcoat.

Having told that lie, I had to live up to it. Before the winter was over I was in funds and could afford an overcoat, but I had to keep on wearing the topcoat. And that winter of 1911–12 in Chicago was the weather man's delight—new "coldest day" records were established week after week.)

In the suitcase I had changes of underwear, both summer and winter weight, socks, shirts, ties, collars, nightshirts, a sweater, a pair of overshoes, a fountain pen, a notebook, comb and brush, toothbrush and an old-fashioned razor with a leather honing strap. In my pocket I had $1.85. I successfully resisted the importunities of the porter to carry my bag and went across Van Buren Street to a Thompson restaurant for coffee and doughnuts. Then I called up my aunt, saying I was in town, and she invited me to come right out.

I had not notified her or my uncle that I was coming because it was not in my plans to camp myself upon them, generous and hospitable as they were, even if they should invite me to do so. I went out on the South Side elevated to my uncle's apartment, where I was greeted warmly by my uncle, aunt, my two girl cousins and the Negro cook they had brought up from the South. I wanted to go right out to the University, but my aunt insisted that I stay for lunch and ordered her cook to prepare a meal of fried chicken, cream gravy, hot biscuits, candied sweet potatoes and coffee.

Soon after eating and an exchange of family news I took the Cottage Grove Avenue streetcar to the University campus and went over to Cobb Hall, in which was located the faculty post office, the information bureau and free employment agency—all in charge of one of the finest-spirited, kindest and best-natured gentlemen I ever met, a plump, rosy-cheeked Irishman named Kelly. I scanned the cards on the bulletin board advertising board and room to students in payment for service as waiters. I picked the one closest to the campus and told Kelly I wanted the job. But I also told him frankly my situation.

It was August 4. School opened on October 1. I not only had to earn my board and room during those two months, but also had to earn and save up forty dollars for tuition, ten dollars for matriculation fee, ten dollars for laboratory breakage and about eight dollars for books. Kelly said he could employ me during those two months as messenger boy around the campus, and between the campus and the downtown business office of the University, at twenty cents an hour. I told him I would report for work in the morning.

In addition I secured through Kelly a job as a waiter in a boarding house on Fifty-fifth Street. My duties were to arise at six o'clock in the morning, bathe, dress, don my apron and jacket, set my table, eat my breakfast and serve at table from a quarter of seven until eight o'clock; luncheon was not served, but I was to return at five, have my dinner and wait on table from six until eight. I checked in and was shown to a gabled room in an attic which I shared with another student waiter, a Finn who was working for a doctorate in theology and who read and spoke eleven languages and dialects and had a reading knowledge of Hebrew and Sanskrit. (He told me he wished to be ordained in the Baptist Church and to preach the Baptist Gospel in Finland. I thought he was joking at first, but since he was an inordinately serious chap I later came to believe that he had accepted that as his mission in life.)

After dinner at my uncle's home that evening I went down to the Chicago *Tribune* editorial offices and saw Guy Lee, with whom I had worked on the Shawnee *Herald*. He introduced me to Walter Howey, the city editor, who answered my request for the job as campus correspondent pretty much as I was prepared to hear him answer it.

He said he already had a man at the University. But when Lee explained to him that I was a trained newspaper reporter, Howey told me that if I should dig up any scoops or news out of the regular routine, he would pay me space rates.

That neither saddened nor gladdened my heart. I was prepared for it. I walked right over to the *Inter-Ocean* office and applied there for the job as campus correspondent. I was hired—to be paid at space rates at six dollars a column, not including headlines. I knew this would not mean much at first; only summer students and faculty were at the University; the campus was quiet; there would be little news to be had.

I told my uncle and his family about the work I had found and left their house that evening. Next morning I performed my duties as a waiter and ran all the way to Cobb Hall to check in as early as possible. I told Kelly about my *Inter-Ocean* job and asked him to tip me off to any news. Calling me "Ras" affectionately, he told me he had another job for me—in the evening, if I could make it. It was that of being an usher in a motion-picture theater from eight until eleven at fifty cents an evening.

I told him I would take it and went on my first errand for him, which was that of carrying some important-looking papers to the University business office on La Salle Street and returning with other important-looking papers, after signing and getting receipts at both ends. By a show of great industry, tact and agreeableness, I induced the landlady to let me off at five minutes of eight. I ran all the way to the theater to report in at the time Kelly said I should. For nearly two months I did this, running to and from Cobb Hall every morning and evening five days of the week, and to the theater seven nights a week. On Saturdays and Sundays I was matinee usher at the theater also.

At the approach of the school term I had to drop my errand-boy and usher jobs and take another job at the Harvard Hotel as waiter and night clerk. When school opened I did not have enough money saved up to pay all of my tuition and other fees, but I signed a note to the University bursar to pay the required balance within sixty days.

I was matriculated by James Weber ("Teddy") Linn, a dean of the junior colleges. Teddy asked me what degree I was going in for. I answered, in all seriousness and with no attempt to be funny or smart, "I didn't come to this university for a degree; I came for an education."

Teddy was quick-tempered, a ruddy, round-faced, sandy-haired professor of English, who smoked cigarettes, drank with alumni and collegians at a saloon on Stony Island Avenue in celebration of football victories and looked anything but the conventional idea of a professor.

He bristled, looked at me in angry astonishment and seemed ready to take me down a peg; then, seeing I was quite serious, changed his mind and said to me, in a tone that was friendly, confidential and as man to man, "A lot of 'em get out of here with degrees but damn few with educations, including, I might say, deans and professors."

Having said this, he held a pen poised over an interrogation blank, and in sharp, barking tones asked me what courses I intended to take. I rattled off the list of them, including psychology, philosophy, French, German, Greek and Latin. When he heard the last two, he said, "That means you go down for an A. B. No Greek or Latin in the science or philosophy courses."

When I specified the courses I *wished* to take during the first semester, he told me the ones I *could* take, and further told me I should have to take a so-called science course which I had not specified. He mentioned botany, zoölogy, trigonometry, political economy, mineralogy and commercial geography. I told him I had had excellent courses in all these in high school, except trigonometry, and that I knew how to use a compound microscope and knew more about minerals and plant and vegetable life than I ever expected to retain, and that I had had enough of math. He persisted that I should have to take one of these, anyway: the rules required it.

I asked, "Well, what is the easiest course you've got among these I have to take? Remember, I have to earn my living while I am here."

"Commercial geography has a reputation of being a snap. Most of the football players go in for it."

"Put me down for that, then."

He did, and I cursed him for months after that, although he really thought he was helping me out.

It *had* been a snap course, but a new instructor, a woman brought on from Vassar, had been put in charge of the freshman class in commercial geography and apparently had been told to tighten it up.

The class was the largest I ever saw at the University. Square-faced plug-uglies, with huge shoulders and sleepy heads, who had been recruited as football material or because they were hammer and discus throwers, filled the room. There were one Hindu and one Japanese in the class, and they were the only ones who ultimately passed the course with anything above C minus. (About fifty of us failed utterly.)

The daily required amount of collateral reading with written reports would have meant an average of two hours a day in the library. And in addition we had to answer such questions as, "How much timber was exported from Vladivostok in 1910?" and, "What is the annual export of hemp from India?" No one in the class except the Hindu and the Japanese could ever answer any of these questions.

Either one of them, I might add, could always answer any of them. That was their métier. Both of them had registered for theology, because that meant lower tuition and lower dormitory rates, and they duly took courses in Biblical exegesis and New Testament doctrine, although one was an orthodox Hindu and the other a Shintoist, and they both loaded up on all the science courses they could take—and elected tennis for physical culture. In which, by the way, they both were also uncannily expert.

Just before school opened I got a scoop on the other papers on the suicide of a student, and the sports editor of the *Inter-Ocean* not only ran my preseason football stuff but also began giving me assignments to cover minor sports events on the South Side. One week, however, I did not get my check for the string I had turned in, and when the city editor tried to give me an argument about it instead of paying me what he had obligated himself to do and what I had earned, I quit the paper without his ever knowing I had quit until I began scooping his paper right and left as campus correspondent for the *Tribune*.

I had discovered a fertile source of news stories, hitherto untapped, and not since my time properly exploited by campus correspondents. The University of Chicago Press, like those of Yale, Cornell, Harvard and Columbia, publishes a number of learned journals, such as the *Journal of Sociology*, the *Biblical World*, *Journal of Archaeology*, the *Journal of Philology*, the *Classical*

Journal, the *English Journal* and the *Journal of Semitic Languages.*

Contributors to these are usually research students and professors who, under the absurd system of promotion requirements of American academic institutions, have to do a continuous amount of research work and "publishing."

Publishing, in this sense, means embodying the results of these researches in articles, with scads of footnotes and bibliographical references, and publishing them in these journals, which are read only by their fellow specialists in the same field.

Nevertheless, these theses quite frequently contain something not only news but downright startling and of interest to the ordinary newspaper reader.

The authors, however, have no sense of the news value of their discoveries and, although (as I found out) they are avid enough for and jealous of publicity within their own circle, they have no notion of the general interest in what they find.

I made it my business to read these stodgy journals with close attention. I often got first-page news stories out of them.

Perhaps I would discover that Professor Breasted had translated a new batch of hieroglyphics, revealing the divorce laws under Hammurabi, or some Greek professor would have something new to say about Helen of Troy, or there would be dug up a new ancient account of the flood mentioned in Genesis, or there would be an article by a psychologist showing that, by the invention of electric buttons and appliances and by the introduction of such foolproof instructions as "Cut along this line," people were gradually finding it unnecessary to use their minds at all and so were becoming morons.

It was easy enough to turn a highly technical article on the University's experiments at Yerkes Observatory on the rigidity of the earth into a news story anyone could understand. For instance, the experiment proved, at least to the physicist's satisfaction, that the core of the earth is solid, and not a molten mass, as some of them had supposed.

It was easy for me, therefore, to say in the "lead" of my story that the ancient superstition that hell was within the bowels of the earth was finally laid, and that, contrary to the usual scientific hypothesis, the center of the earth is not the pit of a great number of potential volcanoes but a substance more solid than steel.

The story which got me a job on the Chicago *Tribune* was a scoop out of the *American Journal of Sociology*. A member of the faculty of the University High School had carefully accumulated a vast amount of data on the percentage of students in high schools who use ponies, violate the honor system, cheat in examinations and steal hotel and Pullman-car towels and bars of soap, and had written an article about his findings.

The contention of his article was that a great number of high-school students cheat and steal. And that, of course, was my news story. It wasn't news in the strict sense to anyone with an elementary observation of human life, but it appeared to be news to the professor, and it was treated as news by my city editor, who played it on the front page after saying to me, as soon as he read it, "You are hired! And you will get a bonus for this." The bonus, it appears, was justified, because it gave editorial writers all over the country something to write about for nearly a week to come.

Parenthetically I may say that editorial writers never need anything to write about to fill their space and rarely hit upon such a burning topic as my story from the *Journal of Sociology*.

When I entered the University the "dean" of campus correspondents was Will Cuppy, representative of the *Herald*. Cuppy had been an infant prodigy at the University, graduating at eighteen, and had stayed on until he had become the oldest infant prodigy in the history of active American student life.

He had been there eight years when I got there, and he stayed on four years after I left. In his first year he had written, and the University of Chicago Press had published, a book of short stories called *Maroon Tales*. It had been an assignment by the editor of the University Press.

The University of Chicago was a very young university, having only recently evolved, through the financial genius of President William Rainey Harper and John D. Rockefeller's money, from a one-building Baptist college into one of the most liberally endowed and up-and-coming American universities.

The University authorities were painfully aware that the school had not yet had time to develop traditions, especially such traditions as were associated with the old Yale fence, the Harvard elms, and the beer-bust at Princeton. They thought that tales about Chicago students would do the trick, and they hit upon Cuppy, the extremely bright lad in freshman composition, to create Chicago's myths and legends.

He did it very satisfactorily to all concerned, except that even now the University of Chicago hasn't any traditions except the one about Walter Eckersall's eighty-five-yard drop kick which defeated Michigan and made Coach Yost so mad he wouldn't play any more with the University of Chicago. Cuppy later told me that he wrote two versions of *Maroon Tales*. After he had written the first version he took the manuscript and a book of synonyms out to a bench on the Midway Plaisance and, wherever he could, changed little words into big ones. The polysyllabic version is the one posterity may inspect.

Cuppy's unofficial deanship enabled him, as I was soon to discover, to enjoy a life of indolence and leisure as a result of the leg work and industry of the other correspondents, including myself. He would give out assignments to us, like a city editor, and ask us to meet him at four o'clock in the library of the Reynolds Club and share with him the news we had dug up. His contributions consisted only of five-minute interviews on athletic matters with "the old man" (Coach Amos Alonzo Stagg) or Assistant Coach Pat Page. After these conferences we would go to our separate offices and write up the campus news of the day for our newspapers.

Cuppy lived at the Phi Gamma Delta Fraternity House. He spent most of his time in the English library, reading English dramas from *Gammer Gurton's Needle* to Shaw and Pinero. He was a plumpish, fair-haired, droll young man with a constant air of fatigue and boredom, lightened only by the occasional chuckles which followed his own observations on comic manifestations of human nature, including his own.

When I first met him, he was obviously afraid of the great world outside of the University, reluctant to enter the competition it demanded and antipathetic to it. That was why he stayed at the University so long, a second home wherein he had been flattered and coddled because of his unusual brilliance as a young student.

But I was on my own and, unlike him, without any remittances from home. Out of necessity I was showing enterprise and resourcefulness apart from the routine of campus correspondence. I did not mind interviewing deans or professors on some item of general news and sharing the results with Cuppy and the other correspondents in return for Stagg's or Page's daily lugubrious statement that varsity athletic prospects were discouraging.

It was part of the Old Man's system to disparage his athletic teams, no matter how good he thought they were. I could have written daily interviews with Stagg or Page all the time I was at the University, without ever seeing either of them and without drawing from either of them a protest or denial, simply by variations on their formula of pessimism. I think maybe Cuppy often gave us the results of interviews he had not had but had merely anticipated. What I did object to was turning over to Cuppy the other scoops which I had dug up after hours of research among the technical journals published by the University of Chicago Press.

In time I revolted and began scooping Cuppy. I scouted around for feature stories to sell to the Sunday magazine section. One of these features, for instance, was about the Swiss lens grinder, Lepelletière, who ground the optical parts of the instruments used by Michelson which enabled him to carry on the monumental experiments which, among other distinctions, made him the first American Nobel prize winner in science. I also began to get important assignments from my city editor to cover news events on the South Side not connected with the University. My string sometimes ran above sixty dollars a week. In other words, I was making as a free lance about twice as much as regular staff reporters were getting.

Whether the pressure of competition I imposed upon Cuppy caused him to resign his job and go to New York to enter a stiffer field of literary competition, or whether the example of his fraternity brother, Roderick Peattie, who had made some minor success in New York as a playwright, inspired him, I do not know; but at all events he did go East with the announced resolution to write "the Great American Drama."

How far Cuppy has got along with that Great American Drama, nobody except him knows. The only visible evidence I ever had of it was the sight of hundreds of small library catalogue cards penned haphazardly on the walls of the old fisherman's shack he lived in for so long at Jones's Beach, and in which he wrote those famous and unique books of humor, *How to Be a Hermit,* and *How to Tell Your Friends from the Apes.*

The first I heard of Cuppy after he left Chicago was when I got a letter from him after I became literary editor of the New York *Tribune.* It was a very droll letter, largely concerned with Aldous Huxley's *Crome Yellow.* I printed it and wrote urging him to do some book reviews for me. It took a great deal of urging to get him started and a really terrific amount of urging to keep him going once he got started. He has to be pampered and encouraged and told he is good every minute or he will think you consider his stuff is too rotten to print.

He used to bring in his copy sometimes when I was very busy and lay it on my desk. Usually I would grab it eagerly and begin reading it as a welcome relief from whatever else I was doing, sure of some chuckles of amusement. He always expected me to read his stuff immediately, to chuckle appreciatively, pat him on the back and tell him it was fine. Occasionally I was too rushed to do this. Then (as I learned later) he would go out into the other room where Isabel Paterson was and sink into a chair utterly dejected. He would say to her, "Burton doesn't like my reviews any more. I don't think he is going to print any more of them. Is my stuff that bad?"

Mrs Paterson would reassure him, compliment him on his last printed piece, spur him on. The job of encouraging Cuppy got to be too much for me. Mrs Paterson and Florence Brobeck took it on. Miss Brobeck got him to write some cookery articles and, by working with Mrs Paterson might and main to keep him going, there was finally evolved the series which largely go to make up *How to Be a Hermit.* Mrs Paterson certainly deserves having *How to Tell Your Friends from the Apes* dedicated to her: she had to give up writing her own books to see that the pieces composing it finally got written.

I don't believe for an instant that Cuppy thinks his stuff is bad. I believe he knows that he is what he is, one of the wittiest of contemporary writers, a humorist who uses none of the stock laugh-provoking devices but says funny and illuminating things in an unexpected manner. It is not that he needs encouragement, really:

[179]

he is just lazy. By reducing his material needs to a minimum, he has to work very little to make enough to live on. If he gets mass encouragement through his books' becoming very popular, he may alter his mode of living and so make it necessary to do more writing, or he may go back to writing the Great American Drama.

I had only one unfortunate brush with the University authorities while I was campus correspondent. In fact, only one man in authority caused me difficulties—James Rowland Angell, now president of Yale, then dean of the faculties at Chicago. It was an embittering experience, and I regret to say that I have not yet cleansed my soul of the iron that sank into it, for Dean Angell, even when he was proved to be clearly in the wrong, did not deign to apologize to me for the embarrassment he had put me to—an embarrassment which might well have not only brought my academic career to a close more quickly than I myself terminated it but also might have cost me my job and made it difficult for me to secure another one.

I attended the lecture courses in Kent Hall, not to earn University credits but to find news material. During one of these lectures, a Professor Hoxie, of the Department of Sociology, made some statements so different from the usual noncommittal academic reiterations that I got nearly a column story out of what he had to say. Professor Hoxie's point of view apparently was deemed too radical and subversive for the University authorities, who hitherto had shown an unprecedented liberalism in the freedom allowed members of the faculty.

I do not know whether Professor Hoxie had denied to Dean Angell that he had made the statements I had attributed to him, or whether Dean Angell took it upon himself to deny them in Professor Hoxie's behalf. At all events, on the following morning an editorial appeared in my own newspaper, apologizing for the news story I had written, denying its substance on the authority of Dean Angell and explaining that it was not the policy of the *Tribune* to keep on its staff irresponsible reporters who faked interviews and doctored facts.

The author of the editorial was Tiffany Blake, chief editorial writer. Although I afterward became friendly enough with Mr

Blake, I never quite forgave him for not observing the elementary ethics of a newspaperman, which is to get at the truth of a situation and not to present one possibly prejudiced piece of testimony out of several which might contradict it. Dean Angell had telephoned Mr Blake, denying that Professor Hoxie had said what I had quoted him as saying. He wrote and published his editorial of retraction without even telephoning me to ask if I had any justification for myself.

I did not see the editorial before I went to class the next morning, and it was not until I returned to my fraternity house for lunch that I heard about it from my city editor, Walter Howey, who assumed at once that I was in the right, for he had confidence in the reliability of the men he hired as reporters. He asked me to try to get hold of some others who had attended the lecture and bring them down to testify in my behalf.

At first I was almost paralyzed with anxiety, for I had not noticed who had attended the lecture, and it might take me a day or two to find out who had been present. Meanwhile it would be the word of an obscure freshman reporter against the dean of the faculties of the University of Chicago, and the word also perhaps of the man I had made responsible for the statements.

I thought of going to Howey and telling him that I had no proof for what I had written and that if he couldn't take my word I was of no value to him anyway, and that, therefore, it would be up to him to fire me or not, as he saw fit.

I rarely read the *Daily Maroon,* the student daily newspaper, because I did not consider it a good source of news, since I was always scooping the campus paper on matters of campus interest. However, I hastened over to the *Daily Maroon* office and looked into the current file. There I found on an inside page a story by Leon Stolz, in which the direct quotations from Professor Hoxie were, almost word for word, those I had given in the *Tribune.*

The *Maroon* heading was not eye-and-attention-attracting as the *Tribune's* had been: it was something like "Professor Hoxie Talks in Kent." I took a copy of the paper and reached the *Tribune* office as soon as I could. I handed the *Maroon* to Howey, saying, "Here is a story in the campus paper almost word for word the same as mine, written by a reporter I did not even know was there."

Howey read the story, clapped me on the shoulder and said, "Good! Now we will go in and see Mr Biffany Fake. He is going to apologize to you."

The tone in which he said this was both venomous and exulting. The contempt which newsmen have for editorial writers is rather general; it is based on the newsman's assumption that it requires neither brains nor enterprise to express an opinion, whereas it requires both to present a readable and accurate account of something that has happened; it is also based upon the newsman's unhappy knowledge that editorial writers are ordinarily better paid than reporters. Howey's antipathy was violent. Too often bright men from his staff had been "elevated" into editorial positions and thus, as he thought, lost to the newspaper profession forever.

He took me into Mr Blake's office and in cold, almost snarling terms said, "Mr Blake, this is Mr Burton Rascoe, our correspondent at the University of Chicago. You have maligned Mr Rascoe; he has actual grounds for a suit against the paper; after you have heard his story I want you to write a retraction. But right here and now, I want you to apologize to Mr Rascoe personally, and hereafter I don't want you to be denying anything in the news columns unless you have proof that one of my reporters has lied."

Mr Blake reddened but kept his temper and his silence under this humiliating accusation and demand. He said that Dean Angell had phoned him denial of the story and that it had not occurred to him to doubt the word of a man of his position and prestige. When he had read the corroboration of my story, he did apologize handsomely to me and told Howey, before we left, that he was very sorry and that he would write an editorial clearing the news desk and me of the stain he had caused.

The editorial appeared, but I heard nothing from Dean Angell. At the time I thought it was highly discreditable for any man to take advantage of his power or prestige to jeopardize another man's job, damage his reputation or inflict an injury thus carelessly and without any reasonable effort to learn the truth. Nor, indeed, have I deflected from that opinion. Even if what I had written had given the University an evil reputation and had resulted in staggering withdrawals of endowments (which it did not), if it was the truth or a true report legitimately acquired by a reporter, it should have been admitted, at least tacitly, and not denied to the injury or possible injury of someone who was not responsible for the event but only responsible for reporting the event. It puzzled and saddened me not long after that to read in a morning paper that Professor Hoxie had committed suicide.

CHAPTER XIV

Blessed Damozel

Aunt Ada and Uncle J. T. My Father Regretfully Discharges a Piano Player. Shyster Lawyers and Drunken Indians. I Meet and Fall in Love with Hazel Luke. I Play the Part of a Pittsburgh Playboy for the Chicago *Tribune*. The Ways of Martin D. Stevers.

Occasionally, on saturday or sunday, I paid a visit to my aunt Ada, for whom I had a great, almost filial affection. It was she whom I went to see, rather than my blood uncle, J. T., or their daughters, Pearl and Mary; for J. T. was a man whose interests were so dedicated to schemes for making money—he was landlord of an apartment building and several office buildings, a motion-picture theater owner, a dealer in livestock and the organizer of one of the first intercity motor bus lines—and to the pursuit of women (he had a succession of mistresses of the heavy, blondined type romanticized by Miss Mae West) that he was rarely home except for meals, and when home he was usually silent and morose; and Pearl, although sweet and pretty, was lifeless and incapable of conversation, while Mary was still a baby.

Aunt Ada was wholesome, beautiful and full of fun and sentiment. She delighted to tell bawdy stories, and she kept newspaper clippings of sentimental verses: her favorite piece of music, which she loved to sing and to hear played over and over again, was "Honeymoon," with the catch line "If all the moons were honeymoons." She condoned her husband's flagrant infidelities without rancor or reproach; and often invited to her house for dinner the women with whom he took no trouble to conceal his intimacy.

Perhaps she did this in a vain effort to allay gossip and to en-
lighten her humiliation in the minds of neighbors, because J. T.
would take his mistresses to the theater or drive with them in his
Stanley Steamer in the very street and neighborhood in which he
lived; but I believe her motives were more unselfish than this. She
adored J. T., and her entire life was given over to humoring him,
making him comfortable, anticipating his wishes, forgetting pride
and self and children in contributing to his welfare.

J. T. was a well-built man, well over six feet in height, with the
kind of handsomeness common in American men at the beginning
of the century—the kind that was only slightly idealized by Charles
Dana Gibson—men with square jaws, high cheekbones, sharply
chiseled brows. Gibson himself looked like that in his younger
years, and so did Richard Harding Davis and thousands of typical
American men of the day, as one will discover by looking at photograph albums of the period.

But J. T. I did not like. I did not hate him; but there was nothing about him that could command my respect, not even his ac-
quisitiveness and his ability to get along in the world. For he was
chinchy and actuated by a meanness of spirit which was incredibly
base to me. I had known several examples of this. His own brothers
and sisters had told me how he had done them out of their share
of their father's (my grandfather Burton's) inheritance. He was
the eldest son, and my grandfather had trained him in business,
paying him a salary, staking him in ventures of his own and
sharing with him in the profits of their joint enterprises.

After my grandfather's death, J. T. had contested the will and
had had it thrown out, by adducing jointly signed contracts to
establish that he was an equal partner in all my grandfather's enterprises, hence legally heir to one half of the entire estate, plus
his equal share with his five brothers and sisters and one adopted
son. He had got all there was, and promptly he had razed the
"ancestral" home and had converted the entire property into a
site filled with hideous, cheap, four-room bungalows, all alike,
and had made a good thing, financially, out of it.

And once he had foreclosed on a jeweler in Chicago to whom
he had loaned money and, after he had sold off the items of value,

he shipped to my father in Shawnee a box of junk—cheap rings, bracelets, watches, necklaces, etc.—without warning and asked my father to try to sell them for him or trade them for Indian land on commission. Both requests were impossible, for my father knew nobody in Shawnee would buy the stuff, and Oklahoma Indians were not of the sort who would trade valuable land for shoddy trinkets, even if they were allowed to do so then by the government, which they were not. My father shipped the stuff back to him, whereupon my uncle claimed the box had been broken into and five hundred dollars' worth of jewelry taken, for which he held my father responsible. There had been no inventory, but a Shawnee jeweler had told my father the entire lot was not worth a hundred dollars. Nevertheless my father paid this absurd claim because he "did not want to have hard feelings."

My father's magnanimity did not prevent me from having hard feelings toward J. T.

My love for Aunt Ada, however, outweighed whatever ill regard I had toward J. T., and so, in visiting her, I took pains to be courteous and respectful to him. Nor should I bother to recall him now, except for the reason that contact with him made me puzzle much over the questions of love and marriage and, indirectly, it was responsible for the most momentous event in my life —my marriage and my assumption of the full responsibilities of married life when I was not yet twenty-one.

My mother's elopement with my father was, obviously, a love match, and a love affair it continued to be until his death at sixty-nine, a love affair that was passionate and violent, with outbreaks of jealousy and recriminations and reconciliations throughout the long years of their marriage.

My mother was the more provocative in these quarrels, which I found so distressing as a boy, and my father, naturally gentle, amiable and pacific, used to try to avoid them by silence, refusal to talk back or by putting on his hat and leaving the house; but I have seen him jealous, too, and on the least justifiable of pretexts; for, accustomed as he was to having her whole thought and energy centered upon him and her immediate family, his jealousy was provoked and his suspicions fantastically aroused when she spoke in admiration of some man.

She knew this, I believe, and from time to time consciously played upon it whenever their life seemed to be running in too placid a tempo. It brought excitement into their relationship for the two of them to act as insanely as young creatures tormented by love; but as a child I did not perceive this psycho-philosophical point: all I saw was the visible actions of two people in anger, and all I heard was the cruel words they hurled at each other; and they were persons I loved more deeply than anyone or anything else— at the time.

Once I remember that my anguish was most intense at the very moment I realized (with the preternatural acuteness of childhood which senses very accurately the comedy adults engage in even when the adults are playing, so they think, tragic roles) that the catastrophe I was called upon to witness had no more reality for the actors than has a sanguine tragedy on the stage, after which the actors cream off the grease paint, don ordinary clothes and, over beer or coffee, talk about their next jump, grumble about the management, boast about their talents or enact petty tragicomedies among themselves.

It happened during the depression year of 1908, which followed upon the panic precipitated by the failure of the Knickerbocker Trust Company in New York City, reverberations of which were felt all over the country. The nerves of all adults, I imagine, were frayed through that importance money assumes when it suddenly almost ceases to circulate.

People can get along without money in a community of barter or in a community of exchange of services where there is a medium of exchange; but whenever there is an almost immediate and complete cessation of currency in a community used to currency, people are put to desperate means to get it. Fear and anxiety encompass them, and in fear and anxiety people cling most desperately to those that love them or upon whose love they feel they have a claim. And in this clinging they are most hysterical when their imaginations betray them into suspicions that they are alone, deserted or betrayed.

My father had somehow managed credit to open the first motion-picture house in Holdenville, a coal-mining town some thirty miles from Shawnee. Shawnee had two motion-picture houses, and they had been prosperous. My father had canvassed the towns near Shawnee which had no motion-picture houses and had lighted upon Holdenville as offering the best prospects. He had leased the one-story "opera house" in which road-company repertory shows had been given and, in the normal routine of opening a motion-picture theater—a nickelodeon it was called in the West and Middle West, or a nickelette, as it was called in the East—he had employed a piano player who would play music appropriate to the stuff that was being shown on the screen.

Mother had not seen this piano player. I had. She was a sad-countenanced, prim and angular woman of forty or thereabouts, with a defeated aspect, who was kind to me when I, a lad in knee pants, went down to Holdenville with my father to see his theater and the movies he exhibited. I liked her.

Mother hated her without seeing her, for her imagination had led her to believe that my father had opened a motion-picture theater with no other purpose in mind than to enter into a liaison with this woman. She accused him of this and, having no answer to such a preposterous accusation and being frantically concerned as to how he was going to get his investment back, he was driven to extremes of desperation when my mother demanded that he fire the woman.

In vain he had pleaded that the only person who had answered his advertisement in the local paper for a piano player was this woman, and that if he fired her he might as well close down the theater, for people would not sit through the hopping pictures without musical accompaniment.

I was sleeping in my attic room, that sanctuary against these bickerings which I had fitted out for myself, with a padded window seat, a bookshelf, a writing table and a frieze of Murad and Egyptian Deity cigarette boxes I had gathered (I did not smoke). There were loud words and screams and then Mother's voice calling me. I had come down in my nightshirt to behold my father in a comic role: he was brandishing an ancient horse pistol (which I knew, he knew, and Mother too must have known, required a bullet, the kind of which had not been made since the Civil War, and which I knew, he knew and Mother must have known had no bullets in it) and saying he was going to kill us all—me, Mother and himself. After contemplating me for a moment, he burst into tears, took me in his arms, tossed the horse pistol into the coal bucket and allowed me to lead him to Mother, who embraced him hysterically.

My mother achieved, somehow, that night, her point; for the next day our house was quiet and peaceful, and my father went down to Holdenville to discharge the piano player. That trip must have been like that of a man who signs the warrant for his own arrest, for he took me down with him as if to assure Mother that everything would be quite on the up-and-up and there would be no finagling and he would give the hussy the proper come-uppance for interfering with the domestic life of a properly constituted, if renegade, Baptist.

I am sorry, but I don't remember what happened. I like to think, and I am inclined to think, that my father was generous when he discharged this piano player. I hope he was considerate as well as tactful, that he improvised reasons which made it necessary to dispense with her music and that he made these reasons plausible and that, in stating his fictitious regrets, he made no mention of the real circumstances and that, knowing there would not for a long time be a similar opportunity for a piano player to earn a salary in Holdenville, he had beggared his own pocket to give this poor woman (who had been a struggling teacher of piano in a town where piano lessons were rare) temporary hope against the claims of adversity.

Without knowing the truth of the matter, that I am sure he did; for, as already mentioned, I have known him not only to give my uncle, J. T., five hundred dollars in settlement of a claim for an alleged loss in transit of some jewelry junk, but I was also to come to see him hand over, without a murmur, more than fifty thousand dollars in settlement of phony claims of title to the land to which he already had title and had bought in good faith under deed approved by the county court and under federal Indian approval.

When oil was found in Oklahoma fields title-clouders kept digging up Indians who, if drunk, for as low as fifty dollars a head would swear that they were illegitimate descendants (and so not in the federal records) of original allottees of land from the government, and let lawyers use them as instruments in suits to mulct the guileless and bewildered farmer who was unfortunate enough to have oil found on his land. Lawyers made millions in this legalized larceny, but there is no record of an Indian's having profited by being a lawyer's client.

I have seen my father allow many unscrupulous men to get the best of him and build Lucullan estates on the prairies of Oklahoma on money rightfully his and know they were swindling him and still be friendly with them and rejoice in the reflection: "Yep. But I didn't work for this money. I've got calluses on my hands, but not from digging oil wells. Them calluses and that bone felon's from slopping pigs on a parcel of land I didn't think was worth anything until one of them witch doctors come along and I paid him twenty-five dollars to find me a water well. He found me a water well finally, right on the top of that knoll, and it cost me sixty, maybe seventy-five, dollars to sink it; and I already made out of it a lot more money than I knew was in this world; because that witch doctor also told me there was oil all around my place, because his hazelwood stick bobbed around like a float when a sucker is nibbling the bait. But, you know, I never took any stock in them witch doctors, but this witch doctor—he was a funny, preacherlike fellow with a sorrel complexion and didn't look like his liver was any too good—well, he found there was some water un'neath the very highest spot on my land; he couldn't find no water down there in the gulleys where 'twasn't so far to dig, so I tried to find out if he was in the water-well drilling business and besides my twenty-five dollars wanted more money to dig me a well too in the remotest spot there was on my land for any well. You can't tell about them preacher fellows. Sometimes they are on the square. This fellow sure was. I wish I knowed where he was; I'd like to give him a little token of my appreciation for telling me to hang onto my land, because there was the best pool of oil in Oklahoma floating under it. . . . All right, all right: Jim, he beat me out of about a million dollars, but Jim's my friend; he's just an old Tennessee country boy trying to get along, and you would go a long way trying to find nicer folks than Jim and his wife is. Jim's one of the decentest fellows you ever saw: you remember when he had the general store and he and his wife lived up in the back? Well, when there was a rush on Saturdays, with all the farmers coming in for hundred-pound sacks of flour, Jim got to thinking it wasn't right for his wife to be wheeling them flour sacks out and lifting them to the wagons while he was just mis-adding up the bills in his own favor, so he hires himself a nigger boy on Saturdays to help his wife in her work, and he pays this nigger boy in credit checks, so that this nigger boy could go out and sell a dollar credit check for fifty cents, and the fellow that took the credit check could get forty-eight cents' worth of goods in Jim's place at the advertised retail price. And Jim's considerate in many things an ordinary fellow wouldn't think of. All the days of their poverty Jim's wife had to run downstairs and out into the yard and pump up enough water to make 'em coffee for breakfast. Well, you know what Jim did? He'd no sooner got one or two million dollars than he ups and gets a water main fixed up so's his wife can have the water come right out in the sink and she don't have to go down that ladder and out into the yard for it. The whole shebang must have cost him eighteen dollars at the lowest estimate. You can't hold me to no judgment of a fellow as free-handed and generous as that."

No. I hope and think that my father did not discharge his piano player without an advance payment of unearned salary whereby she might look around for other work.

But, whether he did or not, his future as a Loew, Laemmle, Lasky or Goldwyn plopped; for even the hand-holders among the swains of Holdenville ceased to identify themselves with King Baggot and Maurice Costello when there was no piano music to sustain their illusion. My father's entry into the Fifth Estate had been blocked by my mother's jealousy of a piano player she had never seen.

My father returned to Shawnee, and he put me to work sawing creosote-soaked crossties, with him at the other end of a crosscut saw, in mid-August to make sure we would be kept warm for the winter. My four-year-old brother Henry brought in from the back alley a rolled packet containing six five-dollar bills; and my troubled mother gave Henry ten cents to buy hokey-pokey ice cream and did not inquire who had lost the money, for we needed it very badly.

I remember that I was afraid it might have been lost by the

butcher's boy or the grocer's boy out of collections and that, because of this loss, one of them would lose his job; but Mother
reminded me that the butcher's boy was the butcher's own son and
the grocer boy was the grocer's own son, and the probabilities were
that word of the loss would be bruited about, in which case there
would be ample time to make restoration.

These things I thought of, too, twenty-five years later, when I
visited Shawnee and strolled into the butcher's son's fine butcher
shop and watched him whack a saddle of lamb neatly with a
cleaver and extend to me a firm, pleasant hand of greeting. He
recognized me and did not obviously take note of the fact that,
whereas he had grown firm, solid and immense, I had remained
a 130-pound bantam. I asked him if he knew anything about that
matter of the thirty dollars found by my kid brother twenty-five
years before. He didn't.

Marriage, as I had seen it function, seemed to me a bondage
vigorously to be avoided that April afternoon in 1913 when I went
to see Aunt Ada. Only a day or so before there had been an informal symposium around the dinner table at the fraternity house,
and I had said I did not think a man should marry until he was
thirty and had at least ten thousand dollars in the bank.

Aunt Ada, J. T., and Mary were not at home when I arrived.
Pearl answered the doorbell and led me into the living room, where
she introduced me to a girl whose name I did not catch. The
girl was slim and dark. Her hair was dark brown, abundant and
wavy, parted in the middle and done up in a knot in the back.
Her skin was satin-smooth and the tint of faintly colored meer-
schaum. Her lips were full and curved to an ample mouth, and
her smile revealed white-pinkish even teeth. Her eyes were liquid
and the color of the stain of ripe walnut hulls.

She had on a black satin dress with tight sleeves to the wrist,
and about the wrists were ruffles of starched white lace. The V
at the neck was starched white lace also. She was quiet, but I
heard the music of supernal carillons emanating from that exquisite
small body. She regarded me with a mingled look of piqued curiosity, tentative rapprochement and disenchantment, and made
me stammer and feel frightfully ill at ease—until I sat down, which

I did awkwardly, because I tried so consciously to sit down with nonchalance and grace.

I remember that I hoped my eyes did not bug with the whole force of the emotions my first comprehensive glance at this incredible creature engendered within me. Apprehensively I tugged to my rescue all the scraps of man-of-the-worldness I could think of, so that this quiet girl, whose whole being orchestrated all the sad, sweet music of the spheres, should not see too early that I was a lad of impulse. I yanked the pressed seam of my right trouser leg and folded the right leg across my left. I lolled with the most self-conscious negligence, and then I forgot, suddenly, my poor, pitiful remembrance of stage business in drawing-room comedies by ham actors and sprang actively to my natural self; for this dark girl sent a signal through her eyes that I might dispense with unnecessary antics because she found me agreeable in spite of them. . . .

Bale, Erasmus, Hospinian, Vives, Kemnisius explode as a vast ocean of obs and sols. . . . Sanguine thence are soon caught, young folks most apt to love and by their good wills, saith Lucian, would have a bout with everyone they see: the colt's evil is common to all complexions. . . . And St Chrysostom said, "For how shall I know thee to be a man when thou kickest like an ass, neighest like a horse after women, ravest in lust like a bull, ravenest like a bear, stingeth like a scorpion, rakest like a wolf, as subtle as a fox, as impudent as a dog? Shall I say thou art a man, that has all the symptoms of a beast?" . . . The blessed damozel leaned out, leaned out, leaned out, leaned out from the silver, ivory, golden bar of Heaven . . . leaned out, leaned out . . .

"Do you dance?" I asked.

"Yes." (This was the nth degree of understatement, as I afterwards learned; for she had been a professional dancer, had been taught special routines by Harry Pilcer when he was teaming with Gaby Deslys, and she had been a solo dancer in vaudeville at the age of nine; she had only recently left the cast of the musical comedy, *The Goddess of Liberty,* because of a nervous breakdown, and in that show she was understudy to the soubrette and a member of the chorus.)

"Pearl, will you play something?"

[193]

"But, Burton, dear, I play so amateurish. Plink-plink, plonk-plonk. My right hand never knoweth what my left hand doeth. Isn't it sad?"

"Pearl," I said, "you are of great price, ah-wah, too rich for carnal swine, and if at random strung you'd change the pebbles of my puddly thought or, ah-wah, words to that effect. Et cetera. But do you, please, I exhort you, ah-wah, play something."

"You like her already, do you?" Pearl asked pertly.

I was tongue-tied.

"Will 'Honeymoon' do?" Pearl asked and started to play it in her precise, metronome manner.

I bowed low before the girl and took her hand to assist her to arise, and her hand was warm and quiveringly alive. Touching her, holding her in my arms, was ecstasy, and quickly I steered her out of the living room into the long hall, and when we reached the end of it I kissed her—at first tentatively, inquiringly, supplicatingly, and then as I wished to kiss her, protractedly.

All was settled then and at that moment between this girl and me, not more than five minutes after we had met, without words spoken or open commitments, and as a consequence of that then-and-there settlement by a kiss I sit here, this July afternoon, in Larchmont, a suburb of New York, writing out these memoirs in a sunroom, while Miss Schmieg, my secretary, types what I have written, and a tall lad named Burton, Junior, comes in from the Art Students League and says his work is going well, and my daughter, Ruth, has, somehow inexplicably, in her hands a button-hook, a can of Three-in-One shoe polish and a wire-haired brush, to add to the impedimenta she is to take with her when she enters Northwestern University in the fall; to my right there is the rock terrace I built by digging out with pick and shovel the hypotenuse of a right-angled triangle which constitutes the up-and-down dimensions of my small demesne; "Rookie," the puppy police dog, barks on his runway into, at least, sergeantcy, and the fatted squirrels I fed to repletion with cracked cocoanuts outside my window have hidden themselves and no longer scold me for not feeding them.

This small demesne, even with its mortgage, is more to me than the property I own outright in inherited lots and my small equity in six oil wells in the Seminole Pool in Oklahoma; for here I move and have my temporary breathing. Those two tall white ash trees and their aggressive, angular black ash companion are, whether they know it or not, my friends: their healed-over, staunch, troubled knots ask me to consider the beautiful canopy their upper-spreading limbs display, and they ask me also to forget these lobed branches.

While we were still dancing I made a date with this girl to take her to the indoor track meet which I had to cover for the *Tribune* at the University that night and, rushing matters precipitously, I told her that I also wanted to see her the next afternoon.

She said that would be nice and so, as soon as Pearl had finished playing a second piece of dance music, I led her back into the room, and as soon as I decently could I told Pearl that I had to be getting on to the office and left. Pearl followed me to the door and at my whispered request gave me the girl's name, address and telephone number.

I went to the office and wrote some routine stuff, ate a sandwich that had been brought in by the office boy, and took the elevated to Indiana Avenue for my first visit at Hazel Luke's house. She and her mother and father lived in a small flat on Calumet Avenue.

The mother I liked immediately; she had an olive complexion like her daughter, coal-black hair and eyes of very dark brown, larger in build than her daughter, plumpish but well proportioned. She was gracious and kindly and bore no outward signs of the illness from which she was within a few months to die or of the strain under which she was trying to make ends meet as a dressmaker while her husband was beginning work in Montana as a dining-car supervisor after a long period of unemployment.

I recall very little of the events of that evening, so enraptured was I in a newly found ecstasy, but I remember that I persuaded Hazel to go to the office with me after the meet and sit on a bench in a corridor outside while I wrote the story of the sports event, whose bare results I had already telephoned to the office.

Nor do I remember much about the events of the next day, except that in the fog of young love's befuddlement I took her for a stroll in the Field Museum and afterwards for a long walk along the lake, at the conclusion of which I told her that I was in love with her and wanted to marry her. She said she was in love with me, too, but that she did not want to give her consent to an engagement without telling her mother about it.

I told her that I would do the talking to her mother, which I did with great fervor that night, and so before I left at one o'clock in the morning Hazel Luke and I were engaged. It was clear, of course, that a marriage could not take place immediately, because I was still in school and had no money beyond the weekly space payments for the work I did in the sports and news departments of the *Tribune*.

Our love affair, thus begun, was continued under the peculiar handicaps and the strange hours of a morning-newspaperman who was at the same time pursuing regular courses of study in college. But the courtship was also carried on in the grand style by a most fortunate assignment at the time. Several nights a week, at least, I could sustain the illusion of being able to entertain my beloved in an opulent and even extravagant fashion.

The *Tribune* at that time had some sort of feud with Al Tierney, the proprietor of the gaudiest and most expensive night club in Chicago and a power in the underworld of the South Side. Tierney's café was called the Cadillac and was at the corner of Calumet Avenue and Thirty-ninth Street. There was an excellent floor show, two orchestras and an atmosphere of swank. The food was the best to be had in town, and the stock of wines was excelled only by Schlogl's and the Bismarck.

The *Tribune* had pulled many wires to get the restaurant closed down and had campaigned against it as a public nuisance, the hangout of gamblers, racketeers and gunmen. But this only succeeded in advertising the place. Even when the *Tribune* attempted to give a list of Tierney's clientele, Tierney's trade increased rather than diminished. The *Tribune* sent two reporters, John Williams and George Morris, to take down the license numbers of the cars parked in the vicinity of the café each night and the next morning published the names of the owners of the cars.

The *Tribune* also sent its star reporter, John Lawson, to the café for several nights to report any indecency, disorder or indecorous aspects of the goings-on; but Lawson was a conscientious man and on each of these occasions reported back that there was no story because the café was as quickly and decently run as any in town.

Howey, the city editor, had an idea when all these other attempts against Tierney failed. Chicago had a one-o'clock curfew law, after which time it was illegal to serve drinks in any saloon or restaurant. He called me in and instructed me in my assignment.

This assignment was repugnant to me at first, because I had an ingrained dislike for snoopers and informers, and throughout the time I was cast in this role my conscience was so disturbed that I had to be argued into keeping up with the work by Howey's and Lawson's pointing out to me if I was to be as thin-skinned as that I would never get far in newspaper work, wherein spying and violations of privacy were an essential part of a newspaperman's function.

I was to pose as a rich playboy from Pittsburgh. I was to carry constantly at least a hundred and fifty dollars and to spend that much in a single night if necessary. I was to go to the Cadillac in full evening dress, top hat and all, and have two or three companions, including at least one female, in my party. I was to tip liberally, order champagne and champagne cups and at the midnight supper to order the most expensive items on the bill of fare.

I chose Stevers as my regular companion, and on our first visit to the Cadillac we took Imogen Frizell, the daughter of the woman who ran a boarding house for co-eds next door to the fraternity house. The other fellows who lived at the fraternity house I would take with me in turn.

I had to make this a rigid schedule of alternation, because after Stevers' first glowing account of our food, drink and entertainment four of the fellows got into arguments, which nearly ended in fist fights, as to which would be our companion of the next excursion. Lots were drawn, and because our food at the fraternity house was ordinarily tasteless and uninspired, a fraternity brother whose lot it was to go to Tierney's with me three nights hence would begin starving himself for the ordeal so that his appetite would be adequate.

My spending was so ostentatious and my tipping so liberal

that after the first few nights of my visits to Tierney's the head-waiters and waiters would quarrel for the right to serve me, and, no matter how crowded the place was, space was somehow magically cleared close to the stage and a special table set up for me and my guests.

Night after night I would pretend to forget the closing hour and attempt to procure drinks after one o'clock, but I was never successful in getting the evidence I sought. In fact, I breathed a sigh of relief each time my attempt failed.

The waiters would always tell me, as they told the other patrons, of the approach of the closing hour and warned me that no drinks could be served after one o'clock.

Even when I pretended to be drunk and summoned the head-waiter to tell him that I had not been notified of the closing hour and gave him a ten-dollar bill, he returned the bill, saying that he did not know what detectives might be in the room and that Tierney's could not afford to violate the law.

My third successive evening with Hazel almost ended our affair as quickly as it had begun, on account of this Tierney assignment. It was a tragicomedy of misapprehensions, and it was to be followed on Wednesday night by one even more ridiculous.

I told Hazel I would call for her at seven-thirty and asked her to dress, saying that we would go to a place to dine and dance where other people would be in evening clothes, and not explaining the nature of my assignment.

For the first time, actually, I enjoyed the prospect of going to Tierney's, putting on the dog and splurging like an imbecile son of the idle rich. It had not only galled me to be acting the role of a snooper; it had made me vaguely angry that I was being urged to spend in a single night four and five times what I was earning in a week to secure a silly bit of technical evidence for the *Tribune's* or somebody on the *Tribune's* private grudge against Al Tierney.

I knew that the one-o'clock closing law was a farce in the first place and that Tierney was probably one of the few saloon and restaurant keepers in town who was obeying it and that he was staying within the law on that unimportant little point the more flagrantly to violate laws in the hearts of decent men.

But with the opportunity to take Hazel with me, the prospect of going to Tierney's assumed a romantic and glamorous aspect. I could dazzle her with this glimpse of me as a reckless and debonair man of the world. However brief would be our excursion into the *high life* (the "eeg leef" as the Parisians, adopting the American expression, pronounced it), it would be thorough and something we could look back upon with pleasure when we settled down into two rooms to make a frantic go of it on my pitiable little salary as a reporter. . . . Or so I thought.

I wanted to be alone with Hazel that first night and so disappointed Stevers and the rest by telling them so. Resplendent in tails and top hat, white silk gloves, opera coat with white cape and Stevers' father's black ebony stick with a silver top, I went to the elevated station on Sixty-third Street and took a train to Forty-third Street, picking up a taxicab there for the remaining three blocks to Hazel's house that I might arrive in the style in which I was dressed. I kept the cab waiting, and we drove to Tierney's, where the headwaiter bowed and scraped, as usual, clapped his hands smartly and produced for us, like a conjuror, a table in the most desirable spot on the crowded floor.

When we were seated, Hazel looked at me with an expression of mingled trust and expectant curiosity. I learned afterwards that, knowing little about me, she thought for a moment that she had been seriously misled and that, instead of the hard-working young student reporter she had been led to believe I was, I was a rich young ne'er-do-well intent upon seducing and betraying her.

This reluctant suspicion deepened the more gaily and realistically I began to enact my role as a Pittsburgh playboy for the benefit of the waiters, by ordering champagne cocktails and choosing the vintage with a fake show of connoisseurship, selecting an elaborate dinner with much colloquy with the waiter about the various items, ordering a small bottle of Liebfraumilch to go with the sole and a still Burgundy to go with the steak.

A damper was put upon the proceedings when the champagne cocktails were served and Hazel declined to drink hers. She said she did not drink. I tried to pass the matter off nonchalantly, drinking my cocktail easily as I had once seen a tenor in a musical comedy do it while he sang of his remembered loves; but the waiter complicated matters by noticing that Hazel had not touched her cocktail whereas I had drained my glass. He thought there was something wrong with the cocktail and was anxious to make amends, asking if it was too sweet or too sour or too cold or not cold enough and suggesting another cocktail or the same kind more carefully made.

After we had had our soup and were dancing between courses, I told Hazel the whole story of why I was there. This was a great relief to her, and she fell in with the plan, saying she would sip her wine when it was served and that when the waiter was not looking we could exchange my empty glass for her partially full one and keep the duplicity up throughout the evening. In this manner the evening passed off gaily.

My sordid little job suddenly became the instrument of ineluctable romance: we were in the Vienna of Schnitzler and Bahr and Dehmel, everything was quite heavenly and as it should be.

The next morning I was trying, as usual, to snatch some cereal and coffee and at the same time finish dressing in order to make an eight-fifteen class when the telephone rang. It was Hazel. Her voice was miserable. She said, "Mother says I can't see you any more." I asked her why, and she said that her mother had smelled liquor on her breath when she went in to kiss her good night last night.

I told her I would fix that; I would be there within an hour to talk to her mother. I cut class, hurried to the Luke flat and, leading Mrs Luke by the hand into the front room, not only frankly and fully told her the whole story, but told her that Howey expected me to take a girl with me whenever I went to Tierney's, preferably a girl who would drink and act up to the part I was playing; that I did not want to be with any other girl except her daughter; and that if she had any real regard for the happiness of both of us she would not only trust me to take proper care of her daughter but would encourage her to play the part she had started to play the night before.

Mrs Luke smiled sympathetically and indulgently after this plea, put her arms around me, kissed me and, drawing Hazel and me together, left the room.

But the experience of the night and the lurid stories the newspapers had been running about white slavers and kidnapers had implanted a touch of fear in Hazel's mind which, on Wednesday night, Stevers was to be the innocent means of augmenting.

Wednesday night was Stevers' night to go along with me to Tierney's, and it was also the evening on which Mrs D. Harry Hammer, the only society-minded mother of the boys at the fraternity house, was giving a large dinner dance at the Lexington Hotel for her awkward, loud-mouthed hooligan of a son. All of us at the fraternity house were in duty obliged to attend this formal shindig. It was a ghastly affair, with large-bosomed dowagers gushing and gurgling over the fluttering debutantes and ill-at-ease youngsters, and with men with paunches and an air of importance trying to renew their youth by flirtations with girls young enough to be their granddaughters.

Stevers is, and always was, a card, a Chaplinesque character, born with the instincts in behavior of a grand seigneur and condemned to exercise them in unappreciative and slightly ribald surroundings, careful cultivator of all the formal graces of a Chesterfield and all the accomplishments of a gentleman out of Meredithian comedy. He was a youth whom Henry James would have taken with gravity and admiration.

Even now few things delight him as much as the careful mixing of a salad dressing; he can talk of wines with an air of authority, although his tipple is usually gin and ginger ale or whisky and soda; he is in his element when he is carving a turkey, entering the opera on an opening night (even if his seat is in the gallery) or ordering an expensive meal with an epicure's regard for the proper rotation of viands and liquids.

Steve's front, I regret to report, was in curious contrast with his private concerns. Immaculate always on the street, he was the sloppiest, the messiest roommate I ever encountered, always doing things in the exact reverse of what you would normally expect. He had, for instance, the inveterate, curious habit of carefully putting trees in his shoes and arranging them with soiled socks neatly folded in the top drawer of the bureau and throwing his shirt and suits in a heap on the floor of the closet.

He never hung up a towel, washed out his tub, put his soiled linen in a laundry bag, fastened the top on a tube of shaving cream or emptied an ash tray: not having a valet, he acted always as

[201]

though he were for the moment deprived of one and therefore helpless to perform the functions performed by a valet.

Yet mysteriously his linen always seemed to be clean and his trousers pressed when he emerged for inspection, although as his roommate I never saw how this could be possible, for his bureau drawers were always a jumble of used shirts and his suits were always in a pile on the closet floor. His shoes and his top hat were the only items of dress he handled with solicitude; and I never could figure out why he put his shoes away in a top drawer.

When there were teas at the fraternity house, it was Steve's custom not to put in an appearance until the tea had been in progress a full hour. Then he would come down the back stairs, walk around the block and in through the front door. He would have on a cutaway coat, pin-striped trousers, high collar, Ascot tie, patent-leather shoes and would be carrying yellow gloves and shiny black topper in his hand when he entered the door. He would be shaved and powdered and wearing a grave, mysterious air.

With great formal dignity he would go from one girl in the room to another, bowing and greeting them all until he had completed the rounds, engage the chaperon for a few minutes with a throaty-voiced monologue and then, consulting his watch with a meditative frown as though he had suddenly remembered an important engagement, he would bow, kiss the hand of the chaperon, explain that he was desolated that he had to be leaving and, with salutes to those near him, he would make his way to the door, bowing and smiling and, taking his topper, gloves and cane, would be gone.

His destination, invariably, was either the Greek restaurant on Fifty-seventh Street, where he would order a sandwich and a cup of coffee, or the bar on Stony Island Avenue, where he would order a glass of beer and linger over it until the tea guests had safely departed.

Stevers avoided the Hammer party on the far-fetched excuse to Mrs Hammer that on that evening he had an important business conference; but he showed up at ten-thirty, paid his respects to the hostess, gravely bowed and shook hands all around and, drawing me aside, ostentatiously put the back of his hand to his mouth as though he were conveying to me an important secret message but actually saying, "If you are ready to go now, I'll tell the old gal Howey sent me to get you for an important news story that has just broken."

He didn't even know Howey. But tell the old gal he most impressively did: the party stopped with silent, ominous expectancy and watched while Stevers made a mighty mystery out of it, and before we reached the corridor I could hear the buzz of curiosity over the importance to which Stevers, in his grand manner, had lifted me.

But by this same manner he had nearly scared the wits out of Hazel. She had never met him before, and when I introduced them he acted so formal, cool, sinister and mysterious; he was so sleek and spick-and-span in his black tails, white shirt, white tie, white (powdered) face and curled yellow-white hair, that jumbled headlines about white slavers went spinning through her head.

When we got into a taxicab, Stevers sat facing us on one of the collapsible extra seats, his arm resting on his stick, his air preoccupied, his demeanor distant and his lips silent.

Afterwards Hazel told me that she kept saying "Hail Marys" and telling herself that, whatever Stevers might be, I was much too innocent and guileless-looking to be in cahoots with him on any nefarious enterprise. She was relieved when the cab drove up in front of the Cadillac restaurant and the footman and attendants began to treat her as though she were Cinderella stepping out of the pumpkin coach.

Stevers was magnificent that night. I have no doubt, from my experience with him, that most of the poor, unimaginative folk who find themselves in exalted positions would have no means of sustaining the looks, the appearance of their positions if they did not have models set before them by men of imagination. Anatole France was right when he said that the obscure, sometimes illegitimate, daughters of scrubwomen who made their way upon the stage of Paris taught duchesses how to act like duchesses and thus gave duchesses a way of life so difficult to follow that the more independent members of the breed reverted to the natural sluttishness of their bent and appeared like the hags Proust describes, with black fingernails and very soiled satin dresses. Peddlers' daughters knew how duchesses *should* act and speak; and so did Meredith, a tailor's son, and Henry James, the son of a Syracuse, N. Y., manufacturer, and so also did Michael Arlen, the son of an Armenian rug peddler in London.

Stevers had a high sense of all the grander gestures, and on that night he was at his best. For, although he deferred to me as host and as keeper of the privy purse, he showed Hazel and me how such an evening as we had before us should be ordered. He chose our wine with a maximum of meditation, consultation with the waiter, colloquies with the sommelier, and well-timed hemming and hawing. Our table came alive under Stevers' creative touch, and the waiter was obviously happy to do his part in making an evening perfect for a connoisseur and a gourmet.

As we left the place that night there was a fanfare of salaams from the waiters, bus boys, the orchestra, the checkroom attendants, and my cab was waiting for me, the door opened and held in hand by the bowing footman.

But Stevers was not going with us; he was going home. Gentleman that he was, he did not presume to intrude upon my privacy.

After Hazel had settled herself in the seat of the taxicab and I was about to get in, I heard Stevers coughing with a deep "a-hem" from the curb.

I knew what this meant. He did not even have a nickel for carfare to the fraternity house.

Hastily I reached into my trouser pocket, extracted a bill, rolled it in the palm of my hand and walked over to Stevers, saying, as I clasped his hand in a formal greeting, "Good night, old fellow," and walked back to the cab.

He had grasped the bill deftly, so no servant could see the transaction, and holding it firmly he did not even put it into his pocket.

Instead, he twirled his walking stick in a beautiful, meditative manner and walked away from the curb and down the street with the lightness and bravado any grand duke might have envied.

CHAPTER XV

Friends, Fraternity Brothers—and Disillusionment

Bohemian Social Life at the Harvard Annex. I Join Sigma Nu. I Get Drunk at a Political Convention. T. R. Roars, "I Feel Like a Bull Moose!" My Youthful Notion of a University as a Seat of Learning Suffers a Disillusionment. Steps in Sentimental Education.

THE COMPARATIVE AFFLUENCE I attained through my work on the *Tribune* did not set in until February 1912, six months after I had come to Chicago to enter the University. When I had to give up the errand-boy and the theater-usher job and take the job as waiter and night clerk in the Harvard Hotel, my wages were paid in board and room and laundry at the hotel and in tips from those I served. A classmate of mine named Allsop and I were the only student waiters. There were three waitresses, all of them professional servants, and it was their duty to clear and reset the tables after Allsop and I had finished our service.

The clients of the hotel were young instructors at the University, two or three students, two young women who were enrolled at the Art Institute, a young woman who was studying music in the vain hope of becoming a concert singer or an opera star, a young lawyer, a young doctor, and a young German who was secretary to Harold McCormick, the reaper scion and opera patron.

Allsop and I were on terms of social equality with these guests, always invited to their parties—and, unhappily in consequence, never (or rarely) reminded by any of them of our menial positions by the tokens of tips. Among those I regularly served there were two elderly couples who were apparently living out their days at the hotel. Regularly on Saturday nights they would each leave me a tip of a quarter, discreetly hidden under their napkins. (The napkins, by the way, were not removed at each meal: each had his own napkin and a napkin ring in which the napkin was kept rolled for three days running before being sent to the laundry.) My cash income, therefore, was rarely more than a dollar a week. This was my recompense for the general acknowledgment that I was not of the servant class, even though I regarded myself as a servant and strove to maintain a definite pride in the obligations of my servitude: I rinsed my glasses under hot and cold water and polished them; I was, in all ways, I think, as good in my work as the Polish lads and lassies who competed with me and were tipped lavishly.

I had my indebtedness to the University to pay off, and I had some slight expenses for suburban train fare and streetcar fare on my trips to the Loop to turn in copy at the *Inter-Ocean*. The bottoms of my shoes gave out, and I could not mass enough cash to purchase new ones. I cut strips of cardboard to cover the holes. Like the Charlie Chaplin of the films, however, I was all the more meticulous in the care of my clothes by my consciousness that I was threadbare. I shined my shoes every morning, cleaned and pressed my ties, kept a razor-edge crease in my trousers, shaved regularly and in other ways kept myself well groomed like a down-at-the-heel dandy. With Allsop I even worked out an arrangement whereby we would both be fairly well barbered. I would borrow a pair of shears from "Primy" (as we called her: she hoped to be a prima donna), and Allsop and I would trim each other's hair around the ears and shave each other down the sides of the neck.

Needless to say that during those early months at the University I could not participate in any of the social activities of the campus. I could not even afford the nominal dues of the Reynolds Club, the democratic student club in the quadrangle which was endowed by a philanthropist specifically to provide billiards, bowling, a dance hall, reading room and other appurtenances of club life for students as poor as I.

I could not even afford to eat lunch at the student mess hall where food was served at cost. I should have liked to have my noon meal of coffee and rolls in that magnificent dining room (where the waiters were all students like myself), but I had been in there once, and all the other students around me were eating two- or three-course lunches, and I was embarrassed by my poverty. Thereafter I walked all the way up to a counter restaurant on Fifty-fifth Street.

Nevertheless I was not saddened by my condition. I indulged in no self-pity. I had no desire to participate in the social life of the University as it was manifested in what I had seen of it. There were, as I could see, a great number of students, both girls and boys, for whom the University was a four-year residence in a country club. I was neither envious of them nor contemptuous of them: their parents could afford the indulgence, and the boys and girls seemed, in the main, likable enough, but, to me, peculiarly vapid and uninteresting.

There were snobs among them, of course, and a few of them were self-consciously superior in manner; but inasmuch as the student body was recruited largely from middle-class homes and from homes in which sacrifice had been made to educate the children, the spirit I encountered was remarkably free from snobbery. The collegiate heroes, Davenport, the track star, and Nelson Norgren, the football captain and all-round athlete, were poor boys, lionized and loaded with student honors.

In spite of my very obvious poverty I was rushed by several fraternities and invited to join two, before I began to refuse invitations to fraternity lunches and dinners with the candid statement that I was opposed to fraternities in the first place and could not afford to join in the second. Even these declarations did not prevent me from being invited to the fraternity houses as the guests of students with whom I had become friendly in the classroom.

There were many older students of prominence in collegiate affairs, such as Leroy C. Baldridge (later to become famous as an illustrator), who had my democratic convictions against fraternities as hotbeds for snobbery; and, moreover, the bohemian social life of those who lived at the Harvard Annex was more to my liking than the formalized social life of the campus.

At the Harvard Annex we lived a Trilby-like existence with no Svengali. We would have chafing-dish suppers in "Primy's" room to which we all would contribute something—ingredients for Welsh rarebit, wine, cakes, sandwiches, beer and kümmel, and there would be talk of art, music, literature and life, charades, impromptu entertainments, music and singing. The two girl students at the Institute would invite me to the dances and parties of the students and models. We would club together, paying Dutch, for concerts and the opera (gallery seats), excursions to the Field Museum and to Polish dances in Halstead Street on the invitation of the porter of the hotel and his two sisters, one of them very pretty, who were chambermaids. We were all young; we were sentimental; we were romantic; we dreamed of accomplishments in the arts, and even if we never attained them we knew we had the good comradeship, the glamor, the excitement of our illusions and the plain reality that we were having a mighty good time.

"Primy" got a job in the chorus of the opera. She took lessons in voice and in French and Italian and would practise her scales for hours at a time. Her dark eyes glowed with fervor—and, unfortunately, with undernourishment and overwork. She had a small allowance from her parents in Ohio, so small that, with her lessons and her carfare, she could not afford to eat at the hotel. She had a small gas burner and tube which she fastened to a jet in her room and would make coffee and toast for herself in the morning, clear away and hide her cooking utensils from the eyes of the proprietress of the hotel, do without lunch and sneak canned vegetables and soups to warm up in her chafing dish for her supper.

We all loved "Primy," and we would take turns, on wintry nights, of waiting for her at the stage entrance of the Auditorium until after the opera was over, piloting her through the sleet and snow and biting winds of Michigan Avenue to the suburban station of the Illinois Central and from the Fifty-fifth Street station to the top floor of the hotel annex.

[208]

None of us could afford to bring "Primy" home in a taxi, even from the station, and we would arrive home with her covered with sleet and snow after having plowed through the drifts all the way from the station. She would be shivering and soaking wet to the knees from the melting snow. And the gang would be there with a gas fire going, hot coffee, maybe some brandy, cheese and ham, crackers and cakes. She would kiss us all, tearfully happy, take off her shoes, hang up her wet stockings to dry or duck behind a screen to take off her dripping skirt and return wrapped in a quilted bathrobe.

Harms, perhaps, would be there—a huge, beetle-browed, square-headed student of sociology who liked to talk philosophy with Leroy Baldridge (a tall, serious lad with soft voice, timid manner and an almost feminine beauty of facial features and curly blond hair), and Harms imposed upon himself the hazards of dressing like a bum and mingling with the down-and-outers of South Clark Street, sleeping in ten-cent flophouses or on the floors of saloons and eating the coffee and stew hand-outs provided by the political lords of the underworld such as "Bathhouse" John Coughlin and "Hinky Dink" Michael Kenna.

Harms acquired lice and barber's itch in his search for sociological information; but that did not deter him. . . . Fritz Gross, a graduate of Heidelberg with a duelling-saber cut on his cheek, an excellent command of English and French and a sound general culture to show for it, would sing German *lieder* or recite Heine and never refer to his job as secretary to the president of the International Harvester Company.

Henry Blackman Sell, then in the picture-frame department of Marshall Field & Co., and later literary editor of the Chicago *Daily News,* editor of *Harper's Bazaar* and head of an advertising agency in New York, might be there with Arthur Knapp, a student of painting at the Art Institute; and Walker, a young law-school graduate, preparing briefs in a law office in the hope of being a real lawyer sometime; and a medico and Allsop. . . . And on occasions of a party, the girls to whom we were each temporarily attached. . . . The stiff regimen "Primy" imposed upon herself, the long hours of work, the exposure and undernourishment in time broke her health; she returned to her home in a small town

[209]

under doctor's orders, her dreams of an operatic career shattered.

These people all meant much to me; but somehow almost nobody I knew at the University, except Stevers and Adelaide Rosman, did, including the professors. I was restricted by my undergraduate status to taking instruction from instructors, rarely from full professors or from men of the rank of Herrick, Moulton, Breasted, Tufts, Millikan, Michelson, Allen, Manly; or even Lovett, Linn and Boynton (the triumvirate of white-haired boys from Harvard brought West, along with the older William Vaughn Moody and Robert Herrick, by the indefatigable Harper, who dangled before them glittering pennies from the Rockefeller endowment and made promises that "a city gray"—the University—would arise from the ashes of "the city white"—the World's Columbian Exposition—on the site of which the University was founded and, with endowments, began to spread).

Linn, Lovett and Boynton taught English composition. I took no English composition at the University. When I entered the school, all of us freshmen, on the first day of class, including certified entrants, were required to write a composition overnight telling why we had come to the University. I entered into the spirit of the thing with great gusto, great seriousness, great candor and great irreverence.

I was informed two days later that I had been given credit for English I. I was informed also that I was one of two in the large class of freshmen who would not be required to take English I. Passing grade marks in English I and English II were primary requirements of the University in the matter of obtaining a bachelor's degree.

That first composition we were required to write was imposed to determine the degree of illiteracy among high-school and secondary-school graduates with which the faculty would have to cope. The degree of illiteracy in that freshman class of which I was a member must have been appalling: 90 per cent of the class were not allowed to take English I; they had to spend a semester at the University High School to learn how to spell common words, use sentences with subject and predicate and know the difference between a full stop and a comma. After that they were permitted to re-enter the class of English I and hope to pass it and English II in order to enroll as students of medicine, law, theology or pedagogy or to go out into the great world as customers' men in brokerage houses, advertising solicitors, bond salesmen, Ford agents, real-estate operators or whatever, certified with a sheepskin as being "bachelors of arts," "bachelors of science" or "bachelors of philosophy."

The tragic thing in this to me was not the occupations they intended to follow (for, as a matter of fact, few of them had any idea about what they wanted to do after they left college except vaguely to rely upon the fact that their fathers or uncles or fiancées' fathers or uncles would find them work of some sort); nor was it in what so many of them found themselves later swirled or pushed into (for some of them—as I know now—rose rapidly from customers' men in brokerage houses to positions of local financial and social esteem as such authorities on market trends that when they were swept into and under the whirlpool of 1929 none of them suffered any loss of "face" or prestige—they merely sank plumb-like with others in the same boat; and there were bond salesmen among the English I illiterates who later did exceedingly well with "war babies" and owned yachts and knick-knacks and even feathered their nests in the 1919 panic perhaps only to blow out their brains in 1929 or sit wistfully by when the "market" began to swerve upward in 1927).

No, there was nothing tragic to me in the occupations they intended to follow or in the quite especial aimlessness of their lives. What was tragic to me was that, once having acquired the degree of bachelor of arts, or of science, or of philosophy they should take no interest whatever in any of these; that they should forever after regard art as an affectation, science an imposture (unless it was manifested in some invention which made quick dividends) and philosophy a complete tedium.

And yet, as I looked about me, I could not blame any of them. They were having a "good time," and no doubt a certain anxiety was pervading even the most supercilious of them.

When I came into ample funds as campus correspondent for the *Tribune,* I yielded to the importunities of one of the fraternities which had rushed me—Sigma Nu. I still had a prejudice against fraternities, and I should not have joined Sigma Nu but for a combination of circumstances: (1) I liked and admired three Sigma Nus—Martin D. Stevers,* an editor of the *Daily Maroon;* Count Rochambeau Lovellette (he was a pre-medico who, in spite of his fancy name, spoke no French and couldn't even learn it, an American of several generations of French descent, who joined up at the beginning of the war and died of typhoid in camp at New Orleans, after having been chosen by the famous Chicago surgeon, Dr Murphy, inventor of the "Murphy button" in surgery, as his special protégé and probable successor); and Parke Watkins, a postgraduate student in chemistry, who was later to show a pepsin reaction to Wrigley's chewing gum and thus save the company millions (although the Wrigley Company used barrels and tuns of pepsin in the preparation of their chewing gum, the pepsin did not show in any of the known chemical tests of the product, so the federal government, under the Food and Drug Act, enjoined the company from using the word *pepsin* in labeling and advertising the gum: Watkins finally devised a test which gave the pepsin reaction); (2) Sigma Nu had a "literary," as against a social or athletic, tradition in that among its members there had been editors of *Cap and Gown,* of the *Daily Maroon,* and of the student monthly literary magazine; and (3) the fraternity house was, in effect, an agreeable and reasonable boarding place.

Stevers became, and remains, one of the three closest personal friends I have ever had. Although when one joins a fraternity one takes oath to regard all fellow members as brothers, Stevers is the only one for whom I can be said to entertain that sort of feeling and relationship, except in its loosest sense. For a quarter of a century now this friendship has endured in mutual affection and respect and mutual tolerance for vagaries and missteps.

I don't remember that either of us has ever reproached the other for anything or wounded one another with those attacks upon the ego which so shatter self-confidence and which are so common among two persons who account themselves friends. This has been possible, I believe, because each of us regards the essential nature of the other as inviolate, something not to be questioned

---

*Stevers subsequently became an encyclopedist, and he is the author of *Steel Trails: The Epic of the Railroads,* and *Sea Lanes, A History of Marine Transportation.*

but accepted even in any disquieting revelation of an aspect of it, and certainly not to be criticized in a dogmatic or superior manner. We have each, at times, regarded the other as comic, even fantastically preposterous, figures, headed straight for jams of the most distressing kind, and neither of us has been foolish enough to try to forfend the other against a chastening experience or has sought the puny complaisance of "I told you so."

Stevers, Hiram Kennicott and Ronald Peattie got me into the honorary literary society, the Quill, but the only meeting of the society I ever attended was one in which we were called together to have our pictures taken. Stevers was also responsible, I think, for getting me on the board of the student magazine, but the only thing I ever read in the magazine I thought was any good was a troubling story of a pogrom in Russia written by Janet Flanner,* an intense and fiery black-haired girl who evoked my profound admiration by the skill and emotion with which she did everything—whether it was rehearsing a play, playing basketball or tennis or leading the cheering at a football game or making notes in the library.

The fraternity was a noisy and boisterous microcosm housed in an old red-brick residence owned by the University. It was a communal enterprise with officers elected from among the upper classmen—a steward, who hired the cook and housekeeper, budgeted the cook in the matter of food, collected dues from all members and board fees from residents, and kept all fraternity accounts; a proctor, whose job it was to preside at table, preserve decorum and see that ill-bred freshmen learned correct table manners; and an alumnus counselor.

There were disciplinary meetings one evening in every fortnight, whereat each member of the fraternity was expected to voice whatever criticism he had to make of any other member in the presence of that member and the rest of the fraternity. The idea was that no member was supposed to voice any criticism of a brother behind that brother's back or to cherish any distaste for that brother's actions, except in that brother's presence and before his fellows. Nor was any member to nurse resentment against his

*Miss Flanner has been Paris correspondent of the *New Yorker* since its founding.

critic, for the criticism was designed to improve the conduct of the member and thus to reflect credit upon the standards of the fraternity.

These meetings were, I believe, salutary, for they often acquainted members with faults they were not aware they had, such as boisterousness and braggadocio, bad manners, negligence in toilet and dress, pruriency, obscenity and idleness; and, once criticized, a lad would trouble to overcome his faults to escape further criticism.

Nor can I remember that these criticisms aroused enmities, even though the aim of them was sometimes lost in recriminations which were, in themselves, salutary in that they let off steam. Expulsion was a rare and grave matter, attended by national officers and conducted by a court-martial, with a fellow member, a law student, acting as counsel of defense: I witnessed only one, and that was concerning an alumnus of the chapter against whom charges were made by alumni.

Formal initiation into the fraternity was an elaborate ritual very like, I imagine, the mumbo-jumbo of all fraternal-order initiations. And there was a mock initiation, comprising various ancient hazing tricks played upon a blindfolded victim. Members of our chapter of the fraternity were notably abstemious, as were the members of all the fraternities, with, I think, two exceptions, and these were fraternities in which sons of the rich predominated. Our drinking was confined largely to beer on the occasions of celebrating a football victory. Only one of our members was accustomed to get drunk regularly, and his was a very special neurotic case; for he was an extremely puritanical and idealistic youth, sensitive, talented and grave, who had the misfortune to fall violently in love with a beautiful whore who danced and solicited in Freiberg's Dance Hall on Twenty-second Street.

Until the red-light district in Chicago was closed down in 1912 in a reform movement instigated by the Illinois Vice Commission (whose published report on prostitution was declared, by a curious irony, to be too obscene to be sold, distributed or sent through the mails), a rather barbarous custom prevailed among the fraternities at the University of Chicago. Older members of the fraternity were delegated to initiate freshmen, particularly those from small towns and farms, into the mysteries of the red-light district, instruct them in prophylactic and answer any question an inexperienced adolescent was likely to ask. This was called "taking the froshes down the line," and, whereas the initiation was not obligatory, I knew of no freshmen who declined to go along at least as sightseers, which, indeed, most of them were.

The aim of the initiation was to prevent pruriency, the infectional dangers encountered by students picked up by streetwalkers, and also to prevent young students from getting so "girl crazy" they could not progress in their studies. That was the theory, and the initiation was in charge of medical students, most of whom had a precociously hard-boiled view of physical functions.

Freiberg's Dance Hall was a notorious place on Twenty-second Street under the elevated between State Street and Wabash Avenue. Around the corner was the high-priced restaurant of "Big Jim" Colosimo, vice overlord of the South Side, one of whose gunmen was a young punk named Al Capone from the Four Corners in New York. And three blocks down on Dearborn Street, just off Twenty-second, was the Everleigh Club, the ornate and luxurious resort run by the Everleigh sisters, Minna and Ada, patronized by the so-called *jeune dorée* of Chicago's Gold Coast and by the wealthier class generally. On Dearborn Street, and on Archer and Armour avenues, there were vice resorts of every kind, price and nationality, and whereas the major profits of the region were reaped by impresarios like Colosimo and the First Ward alliance of politicians, crooks and police, the income from the exorbitant rentals on the properties provided heavy incomes to some of the wealthiest and most unassailably respectable of Chicago's aristocracy—many of the males of which were patrons of the Everleigh sisters, who served only vintage wines and caused their girls to behave with alluring modesty in the receiving parlors —the grand ballroom, the Japanese parlor, and the buffet room— and to appear in correct evening dress.

Freiberg's was an immense dance hall whereat two orchestras played continuously, with tables on both sides of the dance floor and in a balcony. Hostesses were on hand in bevies from whom the patron chose a partner for drinking and for dancing. The hostess was given an aluminum check for every dance and for every drink she induced a patron to buy. The hostesses always drank an expensive drink with a fancy name which was only sugar, grenadine, lemon juice and water. And, after one o'clock, a hostess was permitted to leave with whatever patron she had snared for the night.

This most puritanical of our fraternity brothers fell in love with one of the Freiberg girls the first time he went there. She was a beautiful, delicate, sad-eyed young woman with a pleasing air of taste and refinement about her. She was quiet, soft-spoken and somewhat embittered, and she stood out in contrast with most of the other hostesses, who were brazen or boisterous or coldly meretricious. It was required of the hostesses of Freiberg's that they be modestly dressed and that they dance in a formal fashion —as in distinction from the vulgar and cheaper dance halls where the hostesses danced in silk underwear to expedite the swift turnover of lust.

My fraternity brother fell hopelessly, sentimentally, insanely in love with the harlot, and every time he would get his allowance check from home he would cash it and ask me to go along with him to Freiberg's to see the girl. There he would dance with her once or twice, but for the rest of the night he would keep her at the table, holding her hand and slipping bills to her whenever she showed signs of impatience or fear of losing custom for the night. He did not want to bed with her, and usually he would give her the last batch of bills he had left, on the promise that she would sleep alone that night.

Meanwhile he would get maudlin drunk, and after I got him home he would go into paroxysms of grief and rage, tearing up bedsheets and breaking up furniture and at last falling asleep with his clothes on. I often danced with the girl at his suggestion (because he did not like to dance with her himself and did not want her to be subjected to the embraces of the casual patrons of the place), and she frankly found him a puzzle she pitied but did not love or even especially care for.

She was, she told me, the mother of a child of five, with whom she had been abandoned by a husband when she was eighteen; she said she could never love anyone else and that the child's security and education were all she lived for. She was pious, conventional to an extreme in her ideas of respectability and thoroughly convinced that she was irretrievably damned. How much of her story was true and how much she was merely acting I don't know, for with harlots it is one of the stocks in trade to have an appealing story ready to satisfy the sentimental male's almost inevitable nosy question, "How did you ever fall into this evil way of living?"

Within a year my fraternity brother had so immersed himself in research work that he was cured of his neurosis, and in time he married, had children and entered upon a normal successful life.

We had one Casanova in the fraternity and he was, strangely enough, a brilliant advanced student in philosophy who saw nothing incongruous in spouting Hegelian dialectic by the hour and retailing with relish some rakish amorous exploit immediately afterward. His ideas of good and evil in the abstract were on the loftiest plane, and he was very dogmatic about them; but his behavior was that of a monkey in a zoo, involving copulation without sentiment, romance, affection or even liking. In philosophy he was a Hegelian logician of absolute idealism, in whose behavior, in association with his ideas, there was no logic. After graduation he rose rapidly to a full professorship of philosophy in an Eastern college, for his learning was great and his dialectic flawless.

There was a comedian in the fraternity—Ed Sickle. He was a fat boy, nephew of A. J. Lichstern, the wheat-pit gambler. Ed was a generous, amiable loafer who went to the most ludicrous extremes to get himself noticed by his fraternity brothers. He was without any talent or purpose except unconsciously to amuse, and he would tell utterly fantastic lies about his exploits in an effort to impress us. One night he staggered into the fraternity house, where several of us were sitting around reading, and collapsed on the floor, his hair disheveled, his vest jerked open, his tie awry and dirt obviously smeared on his face (obviously, because no other dust or dirt was on him). He gasped that he had been held up and robbed at the corner, slugged with a blackjack and left for dead. With that he appeared to swoon into unconsciousness. But he had omitted to transfer his watch from his vest to his trouser pocket where it could not be seen. No one paid the slightest attention to him; we scarcely looked up from our books. He arose after a while and went to his room to think up something else.

BEFORE I FORGET

As a reporter I was given a police card and a nickel-plated fire badge used to pass the fire lines. The badge wasn't necessary as long as one had a police card, so I let Ed have my badge. There was no present I could have given him which would have delighted him half so much. He would flip his lapel, showing the badge on any or no occasion, and at the faintest sound of a fire alarm he would cut class or drop anything he was doing and waddle away as fast as his fat legs would carry him for the thrill of showing his badge to a policeman so he could get inside the fire cordon.

After he got inside there was nothing for him to do, so he took to carrying a pencil and notebook so he could pretend to take notes, thus to impress police and onlookers with the idea that he was a reporter. He invented the fiction, for the benefit of the others in the fraternity, that he was my confidential undercover man and that his work involved secret investigations in the underworld needed by me in my work as a reporter.

He carried the fiction to the extent of believing it himself and thus contrived to make acquaintance with precinct captains and desk sergeants at the police stations in the neighborhood of the University, and actually brought to me information which occasionally developed into news stories. But he lived in such a dream world of his own creation that I always checked on any information he gave me.

Once he was a great help. On a terrifically cold day a fire broke out in a twelve-story apartment building near the Midway, and scores were trapped, many suffocating and one or two burned to death. It was a miserable tragedy, with the firemen helpless in face of the high wind and extreme cold, the fire having gained such headway that the building was a furnace, and most of the acts of heroism had been performed before the firemen arrived.

I was the first reporter on the scene because the fire was only a few blocks from the fraternity house. Ed tagged with me. He had the good sense to buy en route two quarts of brandy, which he meant as a bribe to the police, but which not only proved a warm stimulant against the cold but also put the police, the fire chief and ambulance attendants in a mood to supply me with names and facts no other paper got.

Twelve years later I encountered Ed in an elevator in Marshall

Field's in Chicago. He was the same Ed—important and mysterious. He looked suspiciously around, then invited me to take a peek inside his coat. On his vest was the gold-and-silver badge of a special deputy policeman, and under his arm was a pistol in a holster. More—his face beamed; his eyes twinkled; with a look of unutterable satisfaction he drew from his pocket a tin box. He was engaged in the manufacture and sale of a new brand of shoe polish. Man of business and special deputy: he was a personage at last.

With the exception noted above, I know of no one who, during the time I was there, came to the fraternity house drunk (gay, talkative, in high spirits, yes; but not drunk) except myself—on one lamentable occasion when I awoke to find myself trussed up under a bed, my hair gobbed with axle grease, my belly painted with black ink and my bottom with red ink in punishment by my playful brothers for my moral delinquencies and for rousing them out of bed to let me in at five o'clock in the morning.

I had been got in that deplorable condition by my unfamiliarity with the potencies of liquor and through the insistence of the governor of a Western state, who was attending the Republican National Convention and who subsequently (as a Roosevelt adherent) attended the Progressive or Bull Moose Convention in 1912. He was cockeyed when I met him, and he fell upon me like a leech, insisting that I was the spittin' image of his son who was in a military academy, so he said. Because of this resemblance, by a strange process of reasoning he plagued me to drink drink for drink with him, and I think he tried every concoction known to the versatile savant of the Congress Hotel bar, including mint juleps and what was called—extempore, I imagine—a pile driver, made of equal parts of champagne, beer and gin.

At the close of the spring term at college I had been put on the *Tribune* staff as regular reporter on general assignment work, and I stayed on at the fraternity house with a few of the students who had got jobs for the summer. The principal events of the convention were covered by the *Tribune's* circus of able political writers, John Callan O'Laughlin, Arthur Sears Henning, Parke Brown and, on special assignment, Samuel G. Blythe. My assignment was to attend sessions at the Coliseum and hang around the bars and lobbies of the Auditorium and the Congress in search of feature stories, sidelights and humorous items.

The whole thing—the juvenile imbecility of the delegates with their parades, tooting horns; the hick demagogues with their ancient meaningless oratory; the faction fights and the orgy of emotionalism—all seemed a ribald and distressing spectacle of democracy in action; and the only accounts of the show I read with genuine instruction and enjoyment were the superbly written and devastatingly ironical daily articles written by Arthur Brisbane, who was in fine sardonic form, for the Hearst papers were at the moment Democratic.

On the afternoon of the day Theodore Roosevelt bolted from the Republican party I was stationed with other reporters in the anteroom of his suite, my ears alert to catch any items of human and humorous interest; and I got a batch of them, including one which was sent out over the Associated Press wires and later reprinted in the *Saturday Evening Post* and which was about how T. R.'s secretary evaded a persistent and importunate Texas delegate who wanted to see the colonel: He always said the colonel was taking a bath, which led to some amusing complications when the same delegate was given the same answer three times in one day.

Coming from the anteroom into the corridor, I ran into an *Inter-Ocean* reporter, who introduced me to this spifflicated governor of a Western state. At their insistence I stopped at the bar for a couple of drinks, and when I insisted that I had to get back to my office to write up my day's chore, the amiable governor insisted on going over to the office with me and sitting outside until I had turned in my copy.

Then he took me back to the Congress bar, where we drank dinner. At about nine-thirty I got word that Roosevelt was going to make a speech from the balcony of the Elizabethan Room shortly, announcing the formation of a new party and setting forth his policies and program. I dragged Governor ———— along with me to the Elizabethan Room upstairs, stumbling over drunks sprawled or squatting asleep on the floors, and awaited the stubby, intense, pugnacious, vital little fighter (I say "little" because his height was only average and he gave the impression of being a large man, which he was not) who made his way in gleeful dudgeon, his teeth bared in his familiar smile but his eyes mad as hell, through the mob of silly people who wanted to experience the foolish vanity of shaking his hand, up the stairs to the edge of the small balcony, waited for the applause to die and roared, "I feel like a bull moose!" whereat he emitted a sound which I took to be an imitation of the fighting roar of the animal. I broke away from my incubus the governor, got to a telephone and gave the city desk the first words and a description of the appearance of Roosevelt and said I would stick around awhile and then call it a day, unless something happened, for I knew that the speech and all formal events concerned with it would be adequately covered in both the routine and the special ways.

I had not got rid of my incubus, and I was fatigued. I followed him to the bar, en route to which he gathered up another newspaperman and a political crony, and we lined up at the bar to test the bartender's powers of endurance and invention, the while I listened to the maudlin eulogies of the governor about my striking likeness to his son. At around midnight the governor suddenly bethought himself that the one thing he had particularly wanted to see in Chicago, aside from the Masonic Temple and the House of All Nations, was the Everleigh Club.

I knew where the place was but had never been there, but the *Inter-Ocean* reporter elected himself guide and cicerone, and presently we were sitting at an inlaid teakwood table in the Japanese Room of the most ornate bordello in Christendom and drinking champagne, while three quiet, decorous, good-looking, well-dressed young women drank their wine and listened with suppressed boredom to the dark, amiable and drunk little fellow's apostrophes to his state, his family and his capital city.

The musk of the room, the dim lights and the wine on top of all the mixtures began to fuzz my wits until I had to keep shaking my head to avoid falling asleep. Also I was ill at ease, tongue-tied and wondering how I was going to escape, and when one of the girls whispered to ask if I was going to spend the night with her, I got so nervous that I felt the warning of impending nausea and, making incoherent excuses, I hurried out into the street. After violent retching I sat down on the curb to await the passing of the

[221]

buzz saws through my skull and finally caught a Cottage Grove Avenue car in the general direction of the fraternity house. I went sound asleep and did not wake up until the conductor roused me at the end of the line in South Chicago, whereupon I had to pay another nickel and ride back to Fifty-seventh Street.

That whole generation of college men from 1911 to the beginning of wartime prohibition was, in comparison with a later generation, extraordinarily temperate. An older generation at the University had not been, and there were even on the faculty and holding full professorships three men whom I occasionally saw (to my vast, provincial surprise as a freshman, for even the smoking of cigarettes by respectable adults was new to me and unheard-of among educators) visibly, unmistakably drunk even in the morning, or so shaken with hang-overs that they had to dismiss their classes. It was a relief and an education in tolerance to me that the students took no particular notice of such things and the faculty did not act, so far as I knew, in any highhanded disciplinary manner; and besides, the three men concerned were about the most brilliant and valuable adornments of the faculty.

Among the newspapermen, too, in Chicago temperance was the rule, except in the sports department, where the tradition of hard drinking survived. On the local staff there was for a time one habitual drunk, two or three, including Howey himself, who went on periodical benders, and one or two who would occasionally, after a banquet or after a Polish wedding or a May-wine celebration by the Germans or a Bastille Day celebration by the French or a festival by the Italians or Greeks, be so befuddled that Durkin would have to ply them with black coffee and even make them dictate their stuff to a rewrite man; but for the most part the drinking was convivial and after hours, with perhaps a cocktail and wine at dinner at Stillson's bar, across the street from the *Tribune* on Dearborn and Madison streets. With the approach of prohibition, however, ordinarily sane persons were seized with a sort of terror that presently there would be no alcoholic beverages of any kind obtainable anywhere and began to drink frantically and to hoard and store liquors against the long drought.

It will be seen from the above that even in my first year at the University I had suffered from the first disillusionment of my youthful notion of the University as a seat of learning, wherein under the inspiration and guidance of men of scholarship and magnanimity I should breathe in and absorb fruitful things of the mind and spirit. With the exception of Dr Beeson, who taught me Livy, Catullus, Horace, Terence and Plautus, and his young and brilliant substitute, Keith Preston, who encouraged my interest in all the Latin poets, including Martial, Juvenal and Persius, Propertius and Lucretius, I remember but three teachers—Linn in English, whom I had just two days, Phillipson in German, and Clarke in public speaking—with anything but anger, disappointment or distaste.

Those others spoke their set, threadbare daily speeches in a negligent and routine way for the twentieth or fiftieth time without troubling to revise their feeble witticisms, which they had thrown in long ago to give a faint, human touch of levity in a pathetic effort to appear knowing men of the world; they seemed to regard the class, not as a heterogeneous group of individuals with varying degrees of capacity and interest to learn, but as a jelly-like mass to be blown into some queer amorphous form by the droning winds across the human larynx, winds as articulate as a dulled phonograph record and as mechanical.

Years afterward, from Keith Preston, Carl Van Doren, Mark Van Doren and John Erskine, who had been teachers and who loved teaching and who have the special qualifications which make good teachers, I learned what was in fault there among those teachers from whom I expected to get so much and from whom I got so little. The fault, they severally pointed out, was in the whole scheme of American pedagogy and in the conditions which make for advancement in the teaching profession; a scheme and conditions which require the young teacher who aspires to the salary and position of a full professorship to give his best energies, not to teaching, but to laborious and continuous research and condemn him to petty politics among the members of the faculty and frown upon any departure from the strict routine of imparting information, giving out routine class assignments and grading papers in a mechanical, impersonal way.

I actually hated and (when I think of it) continue to hate my teacher of Greek at the University. There had been no Greek instruction available to me in high school; but I had learned to read

Greek passably by the laborious method of self-instruction and with the help of my Greek restaurant friends, Miltiades and Konstantinos Pappathakos (both of them graduates of the *gymnasium* in Sparta and familiar with ancient as well as modern Greek) and, although my pronunciation was faulty in that it did not adhere to the Germanic method, there could have been no youngster who had ever entered that sour-puss tyrant's class more eager than I to learn Greek well that I might read it with ease.

And he set me to learning pages of paradigms by heart—not the uses of inflections, mind you, but paradigms flat, useless and meaningless except as their several parts are arranged in a sentence. William Dean Howells once wrote that he could write, he knew, an English sentence passably correct, but that he could not recall the rules of grammar nor could he recite the inflections and declensions. I was in the same case: the *Anabasis* was old hat to me and dreary old hat at that, but I was not even permitted to show my skill in reading it. I was required to be able to answer correctly instanter such commands as these: "Give the second aorist middle of verbs ending in *mu,* subjunctive," or "What is the second plural optative of *eimi?*"

I struggled hard to meet the disagreeable, misplaced fellow's requirements. I got sheets of butcher's paper, covered them with these paradigms and hung them on the walls of my room, trying to photograph them in my memory; I drilled myself in the silly memorizing of them until three and four o'clock in the morning. But in class I would slip, hesitate or be in doubt; whereupon would come the swift, sarcastic, stinging lash, in an exaggerated ironical politeness, designed to pillory me before the class as an incompetent and hopeless moron. After enduring months of this I resigned myself to flunking the class as completely and as thoroughly as if I could not read the letters of the Greek alphabet, and began spending my evenings poring over Greek texts and comparing them with the versions on the opposite page of the Loeb Library series of translations.

And, at the end of my second year in college, I decided that mine was not the temperament which could profit much from academic instruction as it was available to me at the University of Chicago. I had learned something about life in association with my classmates and in observing my fellows, but, with the exception of what I got from the spirit and enthusiasm of Beeson, Preston, Phillipson and Clarke, I had got nothing commensurate with what I got by myself in the Harper and the departmental libraries of the University.

Even Dr Edward Scribner Ames, whose published work, *Psychology of Religious Experience,* had so fired my admiration for the man when I first read it in the Shawnee public library that I resolved someday to take instruction from him in class, gravely disappointed me, and I got nothing from his classroom exercises, in which he always seemed tired and bored to exasperation. I listened to his sermons on Sundays at the Church of the Disciples of Christ, and I found these sermons a solace, a joy, an inspiration or a provocation to meditation; but in his class I got only some familiar doses of Dewey's and Tufts's *Ethics* and such questions as, "If you were forced to make a choice between saving your mother or your fiancée from drowning, which would you save?"

It was not, I concluded, precisely the individual teacher's fault (with the exception of the hateful fellow who taught first-year Greek; and maybe even *he* was required by his superiors to teach Greek as he taught it); nor, I concluded, was it entirely my fault that I could gain so little from the University. It was partly the fault of my temperament, which was a mixture of enthusiasm and energy and a consuming curiosity in the Aristotelian sense—that curiosity which Aristotle says is the strongest of human passions and which was, at that time, the strongest and most persistent and most insistent passion I possessed.

I derived many incidental benefits from the University, including cut-rate student tickets to the opera, to violin and piano concerts and to the symphony-orchestra performances; and dutifully, eagerly, happily I went to the opera once or twice a week during the season, sitting in the gallery, and to the Chicago Symphony Orchestra concerts on Saturday nights; and from this and long-continued experience I developed an active and articulate distaste for that aesthetic hybrid, the opera, and an enduring love for the music of Bach, Brahms, Haydn, Mozart, Beethoven, César Franck, Wagner (some of it), Sibelius, Prokofieff and, particularly, worshipfully (among moderns), Szumanowski.

BEFORE I FORGET

My knowledge of the technical points of composition, counterpoint and harmony remains immeasurably superior to my knowledge of musical texts; nor can I read a page of simple composition with my inner ear, much less hum or play it; but this fact or these facts did not cause me to decline an invitation to be music critic for the Chicago *Tribune* for a season—for my knowledge of music is as technical, I believe, as was Bernard Shaw's when he began his journalistic career as a critic of music and painting. The reason the technically uneducated journalist can get away so easily with music criticism is that musicians are, by and large, the least articulate of human beings, except through the medium of their art, wherein most of them are not too articulate, either, and know it, and so remain embarrassed and resigned to interpretation, which is not, exactly, creative, although it may be and occasionally is.

Socially, too, by accident rather than by design, I spent more of my time with girl students at the Art Institute than with co-eds at the University; and so went rather to art-student parties and dances than to like affairs at the University. My sentimental attachments at the University had been consciously, cautiously, deliberately halfhearted and casual, because I wished to avoid emotional entanglements at that crucial stage in my adjustment to the severe requirements of competence in a profession in a highly competitive world. But these steps in sentimental education I did not avoid altogether, as is naturally the case with a boy of eighteen or nineteen or twenty, and so in succession I made murmurs to four girls and walked with them in the moonlight on the Midway or took them to the opera, to concerts, to dances and brought them to fraternity teas to find them dubbed, as was the facetious custom of the fraternity, "The Clinging Vine," "The Passion Flower," "The Modest Violet" and "The Quivering Aspen."

But the girls I knew at the Art Institute were more adult, more sophisticated (in the right sense), more intent upon the work they were doing than the girls at the University, most of the latter of whom appeared mainly to be biding their time against an appropriate and desirable marriage or reluctantly preparing themselves to teach (I except, among these, Ernestine Evans, Janet Flanner and Marie Armstrong, who later became good journalists).

From girls at the Art Institute I got more stimulation and emotional nourishment than from the girls I had known at the University, and theirs at the Art Institute was a freer spirit of camaraderie, mutual exchange and help and genuine, undemanding and unjealous companionship than at the University, where the social competition among the girls was rife, severe and, where men were concerned, petty, catty and vindictive. Perhaps this was because the students at the Art Institute were, on the average, poorer than students at the University, forced to get along on less, more conscious of the necessity of graduating quickly into the always precarious livelihood incident to their profession.

The normally candid who will divest themselves for a moment of their inherited and conditioning *préjugés nécessaires* will agree, I think, that the conditions of life, not only of life in a capitalistic society (as some would argue) but in a savage community or in any conceivable society, make for the most artificial relationship between the young of the two sexes and contribute to a consequent, continuous duplicity in courtship, for each, both male and female, want two separate, different and almost irreconcilable things at the same time and the two wants of the two persons, perforce, rarely coincide.

Both of them want separately and individually a continuous life, secure against hazards, the most dangerous of which is, potentially, the surrender of any part of oneself to any individual, the investing in another person a responsibility in one's own continuance. This throws up barriers between two persons, young, healthy creatures of the life force whose immediate desire, if they are normal and physically attracted toward each other, is that conjunction which discharges accumulated emotion, relaxes nerves but somehow, mystically, unites the two persons in a common responsibility of which the possibility of an ensuing child is only a remote and, for the moment at least, a negligible factor.

The more conscious each is of his or her individuality and the more conscious he or she is of a need to preserve it against a quick blight or slow disintegration, the stronger the barrier is between his and her immediate desire; and, conversely, the higher the urgency of the desire to overleap the barrier; for nature does somehow strive to preserve the finest, and by the finest we mean the most alive, the most sensitive, the most intense.

[227]

And nature's efforts are so often so frustrated, so abortive, and so completely a failure that we do not need to consider the spawn of the salmon but merely to recall the perfect loves, the ideal loves of our folklore and literature, and reflect how frequently these unitings ended only in quick death without issue.

For Rémy de Gourmont is wrong when he says: "La seule occupation de l'être est de renover, par l'acte sexuel, la forme dont il est revêtu. . . . Quel est le but de la vie? Le maintien de la vie. Mais l'idée du but est une illusion humaine."

That is a shortsighted and unobservant sensualist's conclusion; shortsighted in that one of the frequent visible aims of nature is the bringing of two people together for no other conceivable purpose than sterile sensual enjoyment; unobservant in that the aim of nature has been, patently, to so experiment and refine the species that we, as descendants of the men of the Stone Age, exist.

It is sheer frivolous sophistry and cynicism to avow that the human species has not progressed since men dwelt in caves; and it seems to me more than a human illusion to believe that our descendants, ten thousand years hence, will be unlike ourselves and somehow, in ways not to be foreseen, better.

That is why I cannot contemn any Utopian scheme wholly; for, whatever may be the scheme's patent defects and however unworkable and impermanent it proves in practice (as were, for instance, Brook Farm and the Oneida Community), it proves that human aspiration strives constantly toward a not clearly envisaged perfection; and thus the occupation of life is not, as Gourmont asserts, the renewal of life in the same form in which it is clothed, but a multiple, a variegated occupation, not the least of which is by combinations to evolve new mutations.

Even before I had completed my second year at the University of Chicago I had decided that at the completion of my spring semester I would check out. What I had been able to learn in the classroom had been very little; what I had been able to learn outside, in the Harper Library, Crerar Library and the Chicago Public Library under my own direction and of my own volition had really constituted whatever progress I had made in my education during my two years as a registered student. And I was egoist enough to consider this progress to have been considerable.

I was in revolt against the whole system of education as it was practised at the University. It was my opinion and still is that a university should be considered a seat of learning and not an educational institution; that it should be there for those who have a desire to learn and not be run as an "institution"—that is, like barracks training under compulsory military service, wherein a raw recruit is taken in, put through the paces, and turned out able to perform the manual of arms; or like an institution for the rehabilitation of wayward girls, where the regulations are gauged to the co-ordination and intelligence of the lowest common denominator among the entrants and after some months or years of routine, mechanically performed, the wayward girl is turned out, presumably now competent to take her place as a normally constituted and responsible unit in the social economy.

It was, and is, my opinion that by the time boys and girls reach the age when they are ready for college, they are, and should be considered, more or less adult; and if they are not, it is the fault of the primary and secondary systems of education; that to require boys and girls of university age to take certain courses that are repugnant and uninteresting to them "as a matter of discipline" is barbarous and idiotic, using up energy uselessly which they might employ profitably in subjects they are really interested in.

The educational process as I had seen it at that beautiful and wealthy university, insofar as it was represented by the so-called College of Liberal Arts, was largely a wasteful farce. Even the two years of it required of those who enter the colleges of law, medicine, chemistry or surgery—which are subjects requiring exact knowledge, exact technique and hence an exacting discipline—seemed to me designed to handicap or cripple future lawyers, doctors and chemists rather than benefit them; for so much of the curricular regulations and methods of classroom instruction is designed to give the student an active distaste for the very branches of general knowledge deemed necessary as a cultural base for a man in the professions, instead of inculcating them. It is no wonder that so many graduates with degrees cannot frame a decent letter, talk intelligently on general ideas, or that they rarely read a book except a sensational best-seller which in social self-defense they think they have to read.

[229]

So, at the conclusion of my second year at the University of Chicago, I bade university life good-by with no regrets whatever, even though in doing so I was voluntarily reducing my income by a third or by a half. I could no longer work on space rates, because I would have no "beat" or specified area of news sources exclusively as mine. I should have to accept a salary of $25 a week as a regular member of the *Tribune's* staff, whereas on space I could often make from $35 to $60.

But, even so, with no regrets, I bade good-by to university life. And besides, I knew I was soon to assume the responsibilities of a married man and could dawdle no more on a pretty campus under the pretense that I was acquiring an education there.

PART IV

Newspaperman

CHAPTER XVI

A Great Newspaper Staff

The Staff of the Chicago *Tribune*. Walter Howey, City Editor. James Keeley, Editor and General Manager. Joseph Medill Patterson. Howey Resigns and Gives Patterson the Jitters. Eleanor Patterson Buys the Washington *Herald*.

THE STAFF OF THE CHICAGO *Tribune*, when I joined it, was one to inspire the best efforts in any young recruit. The editor and general manager, James Keeley, was famous for having pursued the defaulting banker, Stensland, into the interior of Africa and brought him back for trial and punishment. He had also collaborated with Joseph Medill Patterson and Harriet Ford on the highly successful newspaper play, *The Fourth Estate*. Patterson, then a rich young Socialist heir to the newspaper, had startled his class (that of upper society) by his radical novels, *A Little Brother of the Rich* and *Rebellion*.

Bert Leston Taylor ("B. L. T.") was conducting his column, "A Line o' Type or Two"; Finley Peter Dunne was writing a Mr Dooley story every week for the Sunday *Tribune;* H. E. Keogh was conducting the column on the sports page, "In the Wake of the News," to which Ring Lardner, then a sports writer on the Chicago *American,* succeeded on Keogh's death in 1913; John T. McCutcheon was chief cartoonist; Clare Briggs was sports cartoonist; Lillian Russell was beauty adviser to the women readers; Marion Harland was conducting a department called "The Helping Hand"; Jane Eddington was cooking expert; Dr W. A. Evans was writing a daily article on health and hygiene; Percy Hammond was dramatic critic; Glen Dillard Gunn was music critic; Richard Henry Little, famous as a correspondent in the Spanish-American and Russo-Japanese wars, had free rein to write anything that came into his head on the feature page.

Writing for the Sunday magazine section were Courtney Riley Cooper, Thyra Samter Winslow, Edwin Balmer, William McHarg, Oney Fred Sweet, Mae Tinee, Guy Lee and Richard Matthews Hallet. On the sports staff under Harvey T. Woodruff were Hugh E. Fullerton (already well known as a magazine writer), Walter Eckersall (the famous Chicago quarterback and drop-kicker), and Reed Parker (the loudest-lunged and looniest cheer leader the University of Wisconsin ever had).

On the news staff were: Lucian Cary (now a fiction writer), George T. Bye (now a literary agent in New York), Mark Watson (later editor of the *Ladies' Home Journal* and now on the Baltimore *Sun*), Marquis James (Pulitzer Prize winner in history), Terry Ramsaye (historian of the motion pictures), Sunby Hanson, John Callan O'Loughlin, Paul Williams, John Holme, Parke Brown, George Morris and John Lawson (then Chicago's most celebrated news writer, a star reporter, who was killed in a plunge down an open elevator shaft in the Press Club).

Among those who joined the staff later were: Floyd Gibbons, James O'Donnell Bennett, Sheppard Butler and Edward J. Doherty. A young leg-man and police reporter stationed at the Maxwell Avenue station, who wrote no news but phoned it in, was Alfred ("Jake") Lingle, twenty, later to became so in cahoots with gangsters and racketeers that he was shot to death by one of them in the Randolph Street tunnel. The head office boy was Jimmie Durkin, then nearing forty, an uneducated product of the slums with a most remarkable memory for names, initials, streets and local information.

Durkin was more than office boy. He was an institution. He was also an unofficial assistant and counselor to the managing director, the managing editor and the city editor. Impish, bland, alert, obscene, he was afraid of no one, deferred to no one, talked back to anybody. He gave out assignments to rewrite men without instructions from the city editor whenever a story came in over the phone; he called "Thirty!" to reporters, dismissing them for the night; whenever the fire-alarm buzzer sounded he would sing out the location and perhaps add information such as, "There's a three-alarm over on Wells and South Water Street. Lot of shacks and granaries there. Come on there, Cary; shake a leg! Take them dogs off that desk and give 'em a workout. You ain't doin' nothin'." . . . As a stunt Keeley had sent Durkin, "The world's most famous office boy," to London as social ambassador of the *Tribune* at the coronation of King George V. It was reported of Durkin that when he was introduced to the new king, he put out his hand and said, "Hy'yah, George! How's the king business?"

In the obscurity of the art department were Dean Cornwell (later to become magazine illustrator and mural artist), Herbert Morton Stoops (later to become a magazine illustrator), Garrett Price (later comic artist for the *New Yorker,* etc.), Sidney Smith (later creator of "The Gumps"), Frank King (later creator of "Gasoline Alley"), Harold Gray (later creator of "Little Orphan Annie"), and Carl Ed (later creator of "Harold Teen").

In charge of the news was the perfect combination—E. S. Beck, managing editor, and Walter Howey, city editor. Beck was a man of education and natural refinement, a graduate of the University of Michigan, conservative, tactful, mild-mannered, conscientious; he took his job more seriously than any other man I have ever known. He was "married" to the *Tribune:* it was (and, as I write, still is) his life. He was on the job from eleven in the morning until five the next morning, rarely taking a day off, seldom going on vacation and hating a vacation when he did take one. He read, in proof, every word of news that went into the paper. He had only one phobia: misspelled names or its complement, wrong initials. And he appeared to know the initials and spelling of every name of even minor importance in Cook County. He acted as an excellent governor for that amazing engine of energy, Walter Howey.

Howey (now in charge of the news photo service of the Hearst organization and principal owner of the patents for telephonic transmission of photographs) was a journalistic genius of the kind which began to disappear with the advent of the World War. He insisted on news stories being written in a colorful, dramatic or humorous fashion; they had to be readable and entertaining first.

[235]

Their strict news value or relative news value was unimportant to him. The overthrow of a monarchy in Europe, a national election, an earthquake in Italy, he considered mere annoyances, occasioning fights with the telegraph editor (fights umpired by the managing editor) over space to be given other than local news.

Howey was, essentially, provincial and local, with a local, provincial point of view. And he was right in this from the angle of newspaper circulation. Residents of Chicago and the Middle West up until the war began were not interested in European or world affairs; they were not interested in what happened in New York; they were not very much interested in what happened in Washington. Their point of view, uninformed but full of common sense and mild cynicism, was reflected articulately in Finley Peter Dunne's colloquies, in Irish dialect, between "Hinnissy" and Mr Dooley.

Howey's character as a city editor was best reflected in one of his first admonitions to me, "Don't ever fake a story or anything in a story—that is, never let me catch you at it." He wanted good stories, well-written stories, stories that had some literary distinction of their own—and scoops, if possible. He himself was the best reporter and the best news writer on the staff. A silent, tight-lipped prowler in the underworld who had made himself familiar with the ward-heeling politicians, gangsters and crooks, he knew the best sources of news involving murderers, bandits, racketeers and their women. He had come to the *Tribune* after a series of exposés of corruption in the administration of Mayor Busse which he had dug up for the *Inter-Ocean:* his stories had driven the mayor out of office. And he had got his first job in Chicago by accident.

Coming up from a small town, he had applied for work in various newspaper offices and had been turned down until he was broke, hungry and footsore. One afternoon in Randolph Street he thought that he was suffering from hallucinations prompted by undernourishment. In front of him, out of the middle of the sidewalk there began to swarm a bevy of fairy children with colorful cobweb wings and brilliant costumes. He caught his breath and rubbed his eyes. The fairies still seemed real. Moreover, they were excited and screaming. He hit his head with his fists, and just then a fire truck swung past him. A clamor arose.

It was the beginning of the Iroquois Theater disaster on the afternoon of December 30, 1904, in which six hundred persons, mostly children, lost their lives. Howey was the first newspaper reporter on the scene: he phoned the city editor of the *Inter-Ocean,* who told him to go to work on the spot.

It was typical of Howey's method of writing a story that he should begin his "lead" on the Iroquois fire *lento,* with hushed, dramatic suspense, describing the queer sense of illusion experienced by a pedestrian on Randolph Street in the afternoon on seeing the fairy chorus from *Bluebeard* escaping from the cellar through an opening in the sidewalk, and developing his lead *crescendo* with the first paragraph ending on the number of lives lost. (It was Keeley's sensationally unprecedented stunt to carry no news story of the Iroquois fire on the first few pages of the *Tribune* at all, but to devote the entire space to an accurate list of the dead. This *was* a stroke of genius, because the morgues and hospitals were so full of victims that the one question in the minds of nearly all Chicagoans was: "Was anybody I know or am related to in the fire?" Thousands of families in the city were concerned.)

Howey's prose style was reminiscent of Victor Hugo's method of giving dramatic significance to small events and employing antithetical adjectives. He liked to picture a scene, briefly, just before an event happened and then tell what happened. A diamond merchant was murdered under peculiar circumstances in the McVicker's Theater building one afternoon. Howey in writing the lead of the story learned what act was on in the vaudeville theater at the time a shot was heard, and learned also what every tenant in the building was doing. He then pictured a wigmaker hearing a thud and, while adjusting a toupee, remarking to a customer that a new consignment of beer was being unloaded for the saloon on the main floor below; he pictured an adagio dancer nearly loosening his hold and thus almost causing his partner to sail out into the audience. Then he tacked into the story with information about the murdered eccentric and his habits, and lastly into a description of the gruesome and baffling find on the part of the police.

There was a frightful train wreck in Western Springs, a suburb of Chicago, and half a dozen reporters and photographers were dispatched to the scene by Captain Stott, day city editor (he was a real captain, having served as a cavalry officer in the Spanish-American War). Lucian Cary was delegated by Howey to write the front-page lead. When he had finished it, Howey read it over and told him how he wanted it written. Cary tried again. It wasn't what Howey wanted. He turned Cary's copy over to Mark Watson. Watson wrote a lead, and still it wasn't what Howey had in mind. He turned Cary's and Watson's copy over to me and told me how he wanted the lead to be built up. I tried. The deadline for the first edition was only a few minutes off. Howey read my lead and then sat down to a typewriter and, writing at incredible speed, tore off a news story that was a classic of newspaper writing.

Howey was only slightly exaggerated and caricatured by Charles G. MacArthur and Ben Hecht as the managing editor in the newspaper play, *The Front Page*. Howey was cynical and sentimental, bitter about marriage, objecting to his reporters' having any emotional interests outside of their newspaper work. He discouraged matrimony among his reporters even to the extent of threatening to cut their salaries or discharging them if they married. He paid his staff the lowest salaries in the city, proportionately, but he was such an inspiration to work for, so encouraging to his men when they had done good work, so lenient with them when they failed to get news they were sent after and so grateful for good writing that reporters would work for him for much less than they could get elsewhere.

And, of course, the *Tribune* was a great medium to write for: it was the principal newspaper not only in Chicago but in the Middle West and was not so far from living up to its boast (then) of being the World's Greatest Newspaper. Founded by Joseph Medill, William Bross and Alfred Cowles in 1855, the *Tribune* had fought slavery and had nominated Abraham Lincoln for the presidency in 1860, and, developing foursquare and relentlessly on a policy of independent and unfettered publication of the news and of service to the community, the newspaper was a magnificent institution, exceedingly prosperous (netting about $6,000,000 a year) and exceedingly powerful.

Howey had a corrective for all the literary flights he encouraged in his reporters. That corrective was a copyreader named Joe Pierson (later editor of the Army edition of the Chicago *Tribune* in

Paris, for a period before his recall). Pierson was a broad-faced, nearly bald, sullen fellow who looked like a Tory cartoonist's caricature of a Socialist. He wore a narrow collar about two sizes too big for him and a black string or black Windsor tie. His clothes hung loosely from him and were never pressed. All the reporters hated Pierson, or at least hated what he did to their copy. He liked flat, unadorned statements of fact; he abominated adjectives; and he did not like humorous or ironical sentences, epigrams or quips. When Howey thought one of his reporters was getting too literary, he would turn the reporter's copy over to Pierson to read. The result would be emasculation and murder: the truncated corpse would seem to leer obscenely at the reporter out of the news column next morning, often sending the reporter across the street to Stillson's bar to drown his sorrow and curse Pierson.

Keeley had the face and other unpleasant aspects of a particularly vicious bulldog. He was both pompous and tyrannical, with some of the symptoms of egomania so often present in those who by sheer aggressiveness and limited but concentrated resourcefulness have arisen rapidly from lowly origins to positions of power. He looked like Alfred Harmsworth, Lord Northcliffe, the paranoiac British newspaper baron; and, like Harmsworth, had been brought up in the slums of London. The appalling effects of the contemptible British caste system were rampant in his make-up. Even British servants are snobs; and once an Englishman lifts himself by his bootstraps, so to speak, into a position of power and authority, he is not only likely to have an enormous contempt for the class from which he sprang but to identify himself, by way of acute compensation, with omnipotence, and so become patronizing toward those whose boots in other circumstances he would have been happy to lick. The Greek sin of *hubris,* or arrogance, which, in Sophoclean tragedy, Nemesis punished with piteous exactions, is latent nearly always in the characters of such men.

Keeley I always regarded as a comic figure; but this was because I was never directly responsible to him. If I had been directly responsible to him I should have been so frightened and intimidated by him that I should never have worked more than a day or so under his direction. But Keeley did not speak to ordinary news reporters; he would stride through the city room entirely ignoring their existence. When he wished to question or give instructions to a reporter, he did not do it directly: he would summon Howey and the reporter and exercise the infantile caprice of ignoring the reporter's presence and speaking to the reporter through Howey in the third person, like an unlimited monarch.

When I was day city editor of the *Tribune* (reporting for work at eight o'clock in the morning and thus relieving the man on the dogwatch, whose duty it was to stay on, after the final edition had gone to press and reporters and editors had gone home, to get out extras in the event that a sensational news story should break over the City Press or Associated Press wires), it was Keeley's habit to telephone me (or rather the city desk; he never took cognizance of my name or existence except as a voice responsible directly for five minutes to him) at precisely ten o'clock.

He would always ask for the news. It was my duty to report to him anything of special interest which had come in over the Associated Press wires or through the pneumatic tubes from the City Press Bureau (a co-operative news-gathering association operating locally on much the same plan as the Associated Press operates nationally and internationally). He might also ask who had written a story which he wished later to complain about to the managing editor; and he might also give me some instructions for immediate execution. Mostly, however, this routine report to him was as humdrum as a reiterated "All quiet on the western front."

Nevertheless, at ten-ten each morning Beck would phone, often with a trace of agitation in his voice, asking me, "Keeley phoned? What did he say?" This anxiety from a man already twenty years in the employ of the newspaper and three years in the position of managing editor! If I had been so afraid of my job, I should not have been able to do any work at all; for by the time Keeley called, Beck could not have had more than four hours of sleep: he never left the office until five in the morning. And, although I do not think Beck was afraid of Joseph Medill Patterson as he had been of Keeley, so profoundly had Beck been conditioned to this anxiety about last night's newspaper by Keeley's bulldozing that when Patterson, following Keeley as editor, would call at ten, Beck would still call at ten-ten to know what Patterson had to say.

Patterson is immensely superior to anything Keeley ever was, either as editor, journalist or person. He has always had a social conscience; he is by nature, by action and by conviction democratic and equalitarian; he established the first American tabloid and made a huge success of it; and he is a writer of a clear, simple and vigorous prose. He is impulsive, erratic and impatient, unpredictable, a man who acts and works on hunches. He is devoid of all except the most elementary reasoning power; and his mistakes have been made through the initial errors of assuming that he was thinking when he was merely feeling, and of attempting to apply a logical process to matters of pure instinct and emotion. His most charming quality is that of trying to live up to his principles. And half the time he does not know what his real feelings are, so numerous are they, so complex and so checked and leashed by obligations to his conscience, to his employees, to the handful of heirs of the Chicago *Tribune* properties, to his belief in his mission in the world and to his innate, half-repressed, half-satisfied quest for a full, free life of admirable action and true *noblesse oblige*.

He has had a hard life, as the brainier and more highly talented sons of the rich always have in America; and he sensed this in those brave, ambitious days when he was not long out of Yale and undertook to write an indictment of his brother rich men's sons who did not assume the obligations of their fortune, in *A Little Brother of the Rich.* In his mind many of them had taken the handicap life had offered them lying down; they had gone in for silliness, snobbery, wastefulness and drunkenness. He has always been a hero worshiper, and it is probable that in this phase of his career his hero was the romantic Socialist, Jack London, who was also by way of being the current literary sensation, and at that time Patterson had literary ambitions. At all events it was, at that time, his conscientious whim to appear at the parental box at the opera wearing tan shoes, covered with muck, and a lumberman's shirt open at the neck. He compromised with social demands by wearing with these ensigns of revolt a badly pressed but well-fitting black tail coat and trousers.

Patterson's mother was the daughter of Joseph Medill, founder of the *Tribune;* his father was Robert W. Patterson, son-in-law of Joseph Medill, who became general manager of the Chicago *Tribune* during Medill's lifetime and editor of the paper after

Medill's death. Joseph Medill had another daughter who married a McCormick of the reaper clan. She had a son, Robert R. Mc-Cormick, who, at the time I first joined the newspaper, was connected with the *Tribune* law firm in a very junior capacity—his name was last in the law firm's name. Joseph Medill Patterson was a name sufficiently known to me as a writer—as well known as, and classified in my mind with, Reginald Wright Kauffmann and David Graham Phillips—but I did not even know he had any connection with the paper until nearly two years later, when he became mildly active in the Sunday department and then took over supervision of the Sunday department.

Mrs McCormick and Mrs Patterson, as heirs of Joseph Medill, had the last words in the management of the newspaper; and, as mothers will, even when their sons were approaching forty, they still thought of them as irresponsible boys and declined to give them any responsibility: that they left to Keeley.

Keeley, on his part, treated Patterson as a minor irritation in his job as editor. Whatever Patterson would suggest to him, no matter how bright the suggestion was, Keeley would dismiss with the impatience of a tetchy roughneck dealing with a moron. There was on Keeley's part jealousy there, and a deeply felt intimation that this clear-eyed, well-mannered, intelligent, unaggressive, eager-to-learn young man would one day supplant him if he gave him half a chance. In Patterson's efforts to succeed as a reporter, Harvey Woodruff told me the copy desk and news room had hazed Patterson mercilessly. Copyreaders took a delight in killing his copy or reducing a whole column he had written to a bare paragraph somewhere in an inside page, stripped naked of every phrase or modifier by which young Patterson might recognize it as the product of his brain.

But Patterson bided his time. There were some old people in Boston living on the fat of an ancestor's investment in a few shares of stock in Joseph Medill's original purchase of the bankrupt property of the original Chicago *Tribune*. In cahoots with his cousin, Robert R. McCormick, he engineered a *coup* to get the proxies of these stockholders, spring them at a meeting of the board of directors at which Keeley presided, and have themselves elected with Patterson as president and McCormick as chairman of the board of directors. Then when Keeley walked out on them for showing such initiative and encroaching on his power Patterson lost no time in moving into Keeley's hastily vacated office as editor-in-chief, however, with very definite misgivings about his ability to run a newspaper; McCormick left the law office for the more commodious sanctum on the editorial floor as general manager and co-publisher with Patterson. He, too, was shaking in his boots, for Keeley had told them he would buy the *Record-Herald* and run them out of business. Buy the *Record-Herald* Keeley did—with money put up by various backers—and soon ran it on the rocks and sold the hulk to Hearst.

Patterson's first and most serious (for him and the newspaper) brush was with Howey. Patterson's father, Robert W. Patterson, had adopted two shrewd editorial policies in active opposition to his father-in-law, Joseph Medill, founder of the paper. Those policies were: (1) every news story was to be free of editorial bias or opinion; (2) space was to be given on the editorial page to letters attacking the *Tribune,* or differing with its editorial expression of opinion. The elder Patterson had gone to bat with old Joseph Medill on the first of these policies and had won out. The World's Fair in 1893 was followed by crop failures and one of the great panics. Depression settled on the land; the Socialist party gained in strength, and Eugene V. Debs, perpetual Socialist candidate for the presidency, gained enormously in prestige and power. He was a threatening challenge to the Republican party. Old Joseph Medill one day ordered the city editor to use the word "Dictator" in front of Debs's name wherever it occurred. "Dictator Debs" spotted the paper. Patterson, as general manager, called the city editor on the carpet, reminding him that his orders had been that there was to be no editorial comments embodied in the news columns. The city editor said he was acting under orders from Joseph Medill. Patterson told him to disregard the order and omit the word "Dictator" before Debs's name. Next day Joseph Medill asked his city editor why his order to refer to "Dictator Debs" instead of "Mr Debs" had been disobeyed. He was referred to his son-in-law, who won with him the debate on the point.

The *Tribune* news columns *were* free of editorial bias when I went to work there. No propaganda, political or otherwise, was permitted to be expressed in the news columns. (News, however, factually reported, can be the most effective of all propaganda; and when the *Tribune* wanted to break or ruin a corrupt politician, it had only to report the plain facts about his operations and activities. At almost any time it could have broken or ruined the career of almost any politician it supported in its editorial columns by recording the plain facts about *his* operations and activities.) Reporters were fired merely for accepting presents from grateful persons who wished to express their gratitude for some good turn done them by an honest presentation of the news. John Lawson once gravely returned a five-dollar derby hat sent to him by a restaurateur whose restaurant he had mentioned.

Joseph Medill Patterson was zealous in maintaining this incorruptibility of the news columns fostered by his father. And zealotry is a dangerous attribute when it is not tempered by intelligence. Howey was making $8,000 a year in salary as city editor of the *Tribune*. And he was quite satisfied with it. Hearst had offered him $35,000 to come to him, and Howey had turned the offer down. The *Tribune* was a better paper, a better engine, a more respectable medium to work with. It had solidity, permanence, power and prestige. Howey loved the *Tribune*.

Along came David Wark Griffith, producer-director of *The Birth of a Nation,* the outstanding genius of the motion pictures. He met Howey, became fascinated with his mind and with his work; he thought Howey had something they might work out together in the new field of motion-picture development; he offered Howey a job at some flattering salary. Howey felt that his job was that of a newspaperman and that his future was with the *Tribune*. He declined the offer, but as a slight gesture of good will to Griffith he wrote a two- or three-paragraph legitimate news story about Griffith's being in town and about Griffith's production plans.

Patterson considered this press-agent stuff and not only called Howey on the carpet for it but apologized in the editorial columns for this slip-up in the news columns. Howey walked right out of an $8,000 a year job into a $35,000 one as managing editor of the Chicago *Examiner*. And he started, forthwith, to get revenge upon Patterson in so thoroughgoing fashion that there has been no let-up even to this day.

Into Howey's position there was elevated from the copy desk a gullible fellow whose new power went dizzily to his head, deluding him with notions of grandeur and mystifying all the realities of life about him. He had not been in office a week before Howey had planted a fake story on him. The Hearst newspapers were about to release a serial in their Sunday supplements simultaneously with the release through the motion-picture houses of a motion-picture serial adapted from the fiction serial.

It was to be called *The Ten Million Dollar Heiress*. Howey engaged an actress, rehearsed her role with her and installed her in the Blackstone Hotel. She was to be the sheltered, inexperienced daughter of a South Bend manufacturer, who had suddenly fallen heir to millions and had come to Chicago to learn how to spend it.

It was the custom of both papers, to avoid being scooped, to carry in the early editions, on page two or three, a coverage story on some event they meant to play up extensively in later editions. Thus, if the other morning newspaper should, by chance, spring the story to the full extent in an early edition, the newspaper would not be scooped on its own story.

The new city editor of the *Tribune* scanned the first and second pages of the *Examiner* with closest attention. One night he read a disparaging paragraph or so about a woman, who had registered late that evening at the Blackstone, claiming to be an heiress to South Bend millions and who had come to Chicago to learn how to spend her money. The *Examiner* story hinted that the woman might be a fake and that press-agentry might be at the bottom of the hotel publicity release.

The new *Tribune* city editor swallowed the bait. He allowed that there was a big story there; the woman was real; her story was true. He summoned his best available reporter and a photographer. He got an interview—an astonishing one, two columns long, leading from the first page and adjoining, on the second column, a two-column picture of the attractive young woman.

Howey yanked his "coverage" story for the later editions and next day announced the forthcoming motion-picture fiction release to be called *The Ten Million Dollar Heiress*. He also thanked the *Tribune* for press-agenting the Hearst fiction-movie property in its news columns.

Next week the *Examiner* was about to begin its serialization of the memoirs of the Monk Iliodor, comrade of Rasputin. Howey planted a cable in Helsingfors about the breath-taking escape of the Monk Iliodor, a member of the royal household in Russia, and how he had saved from destruction and confiscation his intimate record of life behind the throne in imperial Russia and of Rasputin's evil influence upon the royal family.

The *Tribune* ran the cable on the first page. And again Howey thanked the *Tribune* in an editorial box for press-agenting in its news columns a Hearst Sunday-supplement serial. He hoaxed the *Tribune* so thoroughly, scooped it so continuously that Patterson was full of the jitters, vexed and drastically destructive: he fired an old man who had been a faithful servant of the paper since boyhood and had been relegated to the dogwatch, because the one time, in the ten years he had been on the dogwatch, he had gone out for breakfast instead of having coffee and rolls brought in, and during the fifteen minutes he was gone, the Associated Press flash had come through announcing the death of Ex-President Theodore Roosevelt—and the *Tribune* had missed getting out an extra.

Howey continued to put bent pins in Patterson's chair for years. Patterson's sister, Eleanor, formerly Countess Gizycki, deriving a large income from the *Tribune* properties, wanted to buy a newspaper in Washington as an outlet for her great energies and for personal and social reasons. She was the author of a novel somewhat autobiographical, depicting her girlhood in Chicago, her presentation at the Czar's court in Russia and her unfortunate marriage into the Polish nobility.

She is articulate with the pen and has spirit and audacity. Howey persuaded her to write for the Hearst papers a series of exposés of the Gold Coast, or society life, in Chicago. He signed it "By Eleanor Patterson" and under the name, in italics, he explained, "Sister of Joseph Medill Patterson, editor of the Chicago *Tribune.*"

She tried to buy the Hearst newspaper in Washington, the *Herald*. Hearst will kill one of his newspaper properties, but he has been known to sell only one—his Fort Worth paper; they say he has regretted it ever since. He would not sell the *Herald*. But Howey had an idea; and he knew it would annoy Patterson. He offered Eleanor Patterson the editorship of the *Herald,* at a ridiculously small salary. She accepted it. Thus Heart's strongest competitors in Chicago and New York, the Chicago *Tribune* and the *Daily News,* supply the really mentionable income of one of the Hearst editors.

Eleanor Patterson's first act as editor of the Washington *Herald* was to write a short, front-page, boxed, signed editorial, ribbing Mrs Alice Roosevelt Longworth (with whom she had a long-standing social feud): for this she was willing to spend two or three million dollars to acquire a newspaper.

A sardonic, unforgiving fellow is Howey.

CHAPTER XVII

Joseph Medill Patterson

His Fecundity of Journalistic Ideas. His *Notebook of a Neutral*. A Disciple of Bernhardi. His Misreading of Darwin and Huxley. Tests His Opinions during the World War by Sailing on the *Cymric*. Branded as Pro-German. I Write an Article on the Leo Frank Case and Receive Hundreds of Threatening Letters. Robert R. McCormick. Strong-arm Circulation Methods. Max Annenberg. The New York *Daily News*.

Patterson was editorial supervisor of the Sunday *Tribune*, without title, when I first joined the news staff. The title of Sunday editor was borne by a succession of men and finally assumed by Miss Mary King, who had begun work on the *Tribune* as secretary to Medill McCormick, who, preceding Keeley, had for a short time been editor and publisher of the paper. Miss King had served as secretary and assistant to three Sunday editors. Patterson was Sunday editor in fact, and most of the innovations in the way of features, ideas for new departments and changes in make-up originated in Patterson and were given to Miss King in the form of orders which it was her business to execute. She had to find the proper person to write any feature story Patterson demanded or to conduct any department Patterson wished created.

She was a remarkably efficient executive, acting as a perfect subordinate medium through whom Patterson's ideas (usually expressed in the form of memoranda scrawled in large, nervous handwriting with a red crayon pencil and signed, "J. M. P.") were realized in print. She acted as a buffer between Patterson and members of the staff, fulfilling her function more adequately than most men could have done, for men have, as a rule, a feeling of individuality (often vain and petty) which revolts against their acting as uncreative intermediaries for the transference of dictatorial orders, whereas the perfect secretary (and, in this case, the perfect Sunday editor) is one who, through unqualified admiration and respect for her employer's abilities, does not jealously seek to oppose his ideas with her own but sees to it that his ideas are carried out promptly.

And, because Patterson was dictatorial, impatient and impetuous in his own field, a tyrant who had been subjected to the tyranny of his mother and of James Keeley during the period of his journalistic apprenticeship, Miss King not only saved much wear and tear on Patterson's nerves by removing all occasions of insubordination to Patterson by assuming the burden of giving the orders herself, but she also was able to keep a number of men in their jobs whom Patterson would have fired with ruthless impatience.

Patterson had gone to Groton and had been graduated at Yale, and he had married in his first year out of college only to find that his mother, who held the purse strings of his inheritance, tightened them all the more on his reaching man's estate and, moreover, made the way difficult for him to ascend from the lowest rungs as a reporter to the editorship of the paper which had been his father's. This money pinch, doubtless, had much to do with Patterson's becoming a Socialist, and the handicaps he encountered in a rapid rise to a position of authority on the newspaper he was destined one day partly to own, no doubt caused him to give up newspaper work for a while and engage in reform politics. He was eager and idealistic but impatient and inexperienced. He served out one year in the House of Representatives of the State of Illinois and then got himself into the chair of commissioner of public works in Chicago. Irritated by his inability to carry out his schemes for reform against the opposition of the ward machines which ran the city, he threw up his job in disgust after two months and thereby, incidentally, threw his entire staff (whom he had personally hired) out of jobs for a long time to come.

BEFORE I FORGET

As supervisor of the Sunday sections Patterson was fertile in thinking up new features which would add to circulation. He sought to broaden the appeal of the Sunday *Tribune* until it should become a comprehensive magazine embodying nearly every type of reading matter and picture appeal that individual magazines carried as their own specialty. He hoped to make the purchase of magazines redundant. He was the first to see the motion picture as an expanding industry in which the readers of newspapers would have a lively interest—in news and gossip about the stars; and, against the skepticism of the snobs on the paper, he established a motion-picture department (suggested by Mary King); he created such departments as "Bright Sayings of Children," in which proud parents were paid a dollar apiece for each bright saying that was printed; and he originated and supplied the "continuity" to the artist for one of the most successful of all comic strips, "Little Orphan Annie"; he saw the possibilities of the invention of the rotogravure press and ordered from Germany the first rotogravure press installed in America for the printing of a newspaper supplement (I was made first editor of this rotogravure section in addition to my other duties); mindful of his obligation as promoter of cultural interests among the masses, he chose famous pictures from the Art Institute of Chicago and had them reproduced in four-color on the front page of the Sunday supplement and inaugurated a page (which he turned over to me to edit) of essays and articles of the type that might be found in the better-class magazines and caused me to write, in my own handwriting, "In no magazine will you find better reading than there is on this page," and have the strip etched and run across the top of the page; he was mildly insane on the subject of maps and never let an edition of the Sunday paper appear without a map made according to one of his own suggestions; he authorized Miss King to buy short stories and fiction serials from the most popular writers of the time, such as George Barr McCutcheon, Harold MacGrath, Gouverneur Morris, Edwin Balmer, Booth Tarkington, Henry Kitchell Webster and Richard Matthews Hallet, and he was resolutely fair about the presentation of opinions in his paper, whether he shared or opposed those opinions.

I was always diffident in my relations with Patterson, less out of

[250]

self-distrust of my abilities (which he succeeded in taxing to the utmost) than out of deep admiration for the man and for his fecundity in journalistic ideas. I liked his ideas, for the most part, for they were based upon a hatred of snobbery and a genuine democracy of instinct and feeling; there was no pretentiousness or humbug in him, and his logic in general ideas was simple and fundamental.

I entertained a sort of hero worship toward him, for, in many respects, he seemed to me what a man, with the responsibilities he would inevitably assume as editor of a great newspaper, ought to be. This hero worship deepened in me with the publication of Patterson's *The Notebook of a Neutral,* printed first in the Chicago *Tribune* and published in 1916 as a small book; for this was the only book of the hysterical period before we entered the war which calmly, clearly, logically and with facts strove to offset the effect of British propaganda in this country and the pro-Ally attempts of the wealthy classes of America to drag us into the war.

In this book Patterson was wholly American and realistic, resolutely neither pro-Ally nor pro-German, although he was accused of being the latter after his exposure of the emotion-swaying means belligerent countries employed to recruit their soldiers and send them to the front with a will to fight. He pointed out that, by swallowing the British-propaganda notion that the submarine is an "immoral" weapon, America might later be brought to the difficult pass of attempting to defend its extensive Atlantic and Pacific coast lines without the use of submarines.

Into the welter of propaganda-fed sentimentality which was pushing us closer and closer into a declaration of war, Patterson tried to inject a dose of common sense. He was distinctly in favor of our entering the war on the side of the Allies, not for sentimental reasons but for enlightened selfish ones. He recalled briefly the history of wars during the past hundred years on the European continent:

England proclaims every power moral that is allied with England and every power immoral that is opposed to England. A hundred years ago the English described Germans, Austrians, and Russians as "our gallant allies," among whom, ironically enough, "the brave Prussians, under the dogged leadership of old Blücher," were singled

out for the most lavish praise. At the same time the British government officially described the French Emperor as "outside the pale
of social and civil relations," and having dethroned him, forced upon
the throne of France in his place the hopeless and detested Bourbons.

He continued to point out the alliances of England and observed:

Now the wheel has gone full circle. The former allies, Germany and
Austria, are Huns, and in particular "the brave Prussians under the
dogged leadership," etc., are "baby-killing Junkers," while the same
Hohenzollern family with which the English royal family has been
proudly exchanging daughters for the last century, since it fights
against England and France instead of with England against France,
has become the spume of hell.

Through all the permutations and combinations of international
politics the wonderful governing class of England has kept one beacon
light for guidance, and only one—the interest of the British empire.
Whatever nation could temporarily subserve that interest became
temporarily a moral nation, and whatever nation opposed that interest
became, during the continuance of its opposition, the vilest of the
vile.

Has this policy on the whole proved successful? If you are in doubt
about it look at the map of the world, where you will find one fifth
of the land and all the oceans painted British red.

Patterson then led up to his argument that we drive a bargain
with England and, if necessary, enter the war on the side of the
Allies—*but* with a definite idea of what we were going to get out
of it.

The points he proposed that America drive in the bargain were
these: (1) We could offer Great Britain more ammunition and war
material than we are now supplying at very much lower prices than
our thrifty manufacturers are now charging; or perhaps we could
furnish the ammunition free from our government arsenals. (2) If
Great Britain refused a naval alliance we could refuse to let her
have any ammunition on any terms whatever. (3) Next, after the
war we could increase our navy and make it more effective, so that
Great Britain could not feel that the major burden of our defense
was laid upon her. After a successful war, he laid down the things
which would be advantageous to us, as (1) Belgium to be under
the protectorate of France, with Antwerp a free port for British

ships; (2) the return, of Alsace-Lorraine to France; (3) the autonomy of Poland under a German protectorate as a constant German threat against Russia and vice versa; (4) the banishment of the Turk from Europe; and (5) the extension of our "protectorate" over Mexico.

All this, Patterson argued, would be to strengthen us for what he believed to be our inevitable war with Japan. Moreover, in the fifth of these steps, the extension of our "protectorate" over Mexico, Patterson threw out tentatively an idea which he was later to expound as a doctrine of Americanism: He argued in the editorial pages of the *Tribune* that we should annex Mexico and the Central American states, by conquest if necessary, and ultimately try to induce Canada to break off from England and join us in the United States of America, embracing the entire continent.

It was typical of Patterson's bland honesty and naïvety that he proposed this imperialistic program, not with moralistic hypocrisy, as England has always done when she wished to take over new territories for exploitation, or as Mussolini did in justifying the invasion of Ethiopia, saying that it was a duty of the civilized nation to carry the fruits of its own great progress into backward countries and among backward people, but as a measure for increasing the military and economic power of this country.

Patterson was by that time no longer a Socialist but an ardent disciple, not only of the more materialistic scientists, but of the more blatant philosophers who carried the materialistic view to its logical reaches and conclusion. He was a disciple of Bernhardi, who had been for a long time the articulate spokesman of the Prussian Junker spirit and of the Kaiser and Kaiserism; and Patterson dared quote Bernhardi approvingly in a nation and to a nation furthest away in sentiment and ideals from the spirit of Junkerism.

Patterson quoted General Bernhardi as saying that war is a biological necessity and that it makes for progress, and he commented upon this by saying:

I think he was right, by and large, and that is why I do not believe that the German idea can be beaten in this war.

He had in mind the methods of organization then existent in Germany and the state Socialism which prevailed in Germany, be-

[253]

fore the war, under a military-minded Emperor. Patterson said that England was Germanizing its social structure as fast as it could, and that only by doing so could the British and their allies hope to defeat the Central Powers. Patterson still retained enough vestiges of his early Socialism to have a vast admiration for the practical results of the sort of state Socialism which prevailed in Germany before the war. He knew that all German municipalities were run on a more modern and civilized basis than the municipalities of England and America. There were no slums in Germany, no housing conditions remotely resembling the horrible insanitary congested districts of London, Manchester, Edinburgh and Glasgow, and there was no political graft and corruption such as prevailed and prevails in every large city in America.

These bland pronouncements of Patterson's were greeted on every hand by horror and derision—by horror on the part of the liberals of the *New Republic* and the *Nation,* and by derision on the part of editorial writers who knew the temper of the sentimental people well enough to realize that, even if one entertained such notions, they must be sugar-coated or disguised with moralistic sophistries.

Patterson had the habit of signing his interoffice communications and letters to intimates with a large, scrawled, "J. M. P.," so Arthur Brisbane hung on him the sobriquet "Jomp, the Cave Man," in ridiculing him for what looked like megalomania, and certainly was, in essence at least, an imperialism which, as the war showed, was soon destined to be as archaic and out of date as petty kingships and czardoms.

When Patterson wrote, "The German idea will have world power after the war, because it has proved its fundamental strength in conflict with a hostile world," and, "Another reason why we should wish Germany to take Poland is because that would throw the apple of discord between the two great military empires of Europe. And nothing could be more disturbing to the peace of mind of western Europe and America than Germany's reversion to Bismarck's policy of 'reinsurance'—a personal understanding between the Kaiser and the Czar," he showed how limited his vision was.

And at the same time he showed how, with the sudden accession of inherited, unearned power, he could persuade himself that whatever he thought was true, or wanted to think was true, was of necessity true because he thought it. This is a psychological tick which is at the base of both the motive and the métier of a dictator; and the more benevolently disposed the dictator imagines himself to be, the broader the sweep of his social vision, the more tyrannical he is likely to be. There is no tyrant so exigent as one who imagines his motives are higher than purely selfish ones.

Patterson was, and is, void of broad humanitarian feelings and has repeatedly written editorials arguing that the ailing and unfit should be put to death so that they will not be handicaps to the strong, thus revising the notion of the survival of the fittest to mean that the physically unfit should not be permitted to survive.

Physically a strong man himself, with the means and leisure to enjoy change and exercise (in a way, for instance, a night city editor or a tubercular writer in his employ could not), he took a cosmic materialistic view in regard to the destiny of the race and of the country, which view is an absurd misreading of Darwin and Huxley.

When he was a young man, he used to prove to himself that being brought up in an atmosphere of wealth and comfort had not made him soft or effeminate—by going down to Hinky Dink's saloon in Chicago and picking a fight with one of the toughest-looking mugs he could find in the place. Usually he was ganged and bounced out on the sidewalk, but not until he had showed that he was the physical equal of a tough and that he could "take it."

His was a misreading of Darwin or Huxley at second or third hand; for it is not only absurd to contend that a prize fighter should survive whereas an ailing physical weakling like Darwin should not, it is also contrary to the facts that the strongest of prize fighters has the *virility* or *vitality* of a Darwin or even lives as long as a Darwin (for example, Darwin died at seventy-three; John L. Sullivan at sixty).

Far from the pre-war German idea's prevailing after the war (or having "world power"), as Patterson in 1915 so confidently declared it would, the German idea has disappeared altogether, and dictatorship and gangsterism have taken its place not only in Germany but all over Europe.

Even an Allied victory did not cause the German "idea" to per-

meate the British social structure as Patterson thought it already
had in 1915; in fact, it is safe to guess that if any attempt had been
made to Germanize the British social structure the empire would
have collapsed, for, although the British Tommy can be induced to
fight under the most transparent of hypocritical pretexts, centuries
of the British tradition (and illusion) of individual freedom would
not admit of the regimentation and the all-prevalent "Verboten"
sign of Germany before the war.

Patterson (then) was mentally and temperamentally incapable of
seeing, foreseeing or allowing for the imponderables of life—the
effect of sentiment (religious, ethical or traditional), of ideals
(however disregarded in private practice), of chance and accident.
And I dwell so much upon him because watching him in action
and observing the workings of his mind had much to do with the
intellectual concepts, the views of life I was necessarily forming in
my early twenties; for Patterson was by way of being a portent and
a power, or at least he had all the potentialities and the engine (in
the Chicago *Tribune*) for affecting the destinies not only of the
people in his employ but the American people as a whole.

And as, even with his limitations, he was still the honestest and
most intelligent *thinker* (with the possible exception of Theodore
Roosevelt) with whom I had come into contact, the only man I
knew in a position of importance who accepted personally and
literally the implications of his principles and the logic of those
principles, it was profoundly disturbing to me to realize how little
thought, as thought, figured in Patterson's mental processes, and
how much his thought was mere unsubtle, unpremeditated, simple
manifestations of sensitive but not very complex emotions.

His sense of humor or of the comic was so rudimentary that he
laughed unroariously every time he saw a new set of drawings of
the Katzenjammer Kids and sent jokes to B. L. T. which were so
bad that Taylor would not print them.

(Taylor used to show me some of these terrible specimens of
Patterson's humor; and I have little doubt that Taylor's consistent
refusal to lower the standard of his column by printing them had
something to do with the dislike Patterson entertained for Taylor,
a dislike which became tensely mutual when Patterson peremptorily
ordered Taylor to discontinue the fragments of autobiography in

the vein of *Pipesmoke Carry* which Taylor had begun to run occasionally in his column, and which Patterson continued to entertain after Taylor had died, causing him to make, on the occasion
of a memorial service to Taylor in the Majestic Theater, probably
the most ungracious obsequial speech ever uttered.)

Patterson's military preoccupations, his superficial reading of
Von Clausewitz, his delegating me to write a series of articles on
"If Germany Should Fight the United States," "If Japan Should
Fight the United States" and "If England Should Fight the United
States" (all based upon comparisons of the military and naval
strength of those countries with that of the United States and
drawn from dozens of books, now forgotten, on military and naval
strategy, on America's defenselessness, on the Navy Blue Book
and on the new weapons in warfare) and his acceptance of General
Friedrich von Bernhardi's *Germany and the Next War* as a book
of final truths were all disturbing to me.

I had reviewed the Bernhardi book in the *Tribune* in the early
stages of the war, when the German drive on the western front was
in its most ominous and relentless stage of progress. I had not "reviewed" it in the usual sense of that term—that is, I had not criticized or commented upon it: I had written a lead summarizing the
points made in the book and had quoted, directly, the most important or most sensational passages. I had gutted the book and
made a news review out of it, thus making it unnecessary for anyone to buy or read the whole thing.

It would appear, indeed, that Patterson himself never troubled to
read more than I had quoted of Bernhardi, for the Bernhardi
dogma I quoted was subsequently to constitute practically all of
Patterson's observations on war, defense and the destiny of nations
and was even to supply him with the notion that we should annex
Canada even if we had to rake up a pretext of a war on England
in order to do it.

The salient passages which I quoted from Bernhardi's book
were so obviously to be Patterson's intellectual ammunition (transferred, of course, to Americanism and American necessities) for a
long time to come, that I found it instructive to compare them with
The Notebook of a Neutral and Patterson's subsequent unsigned
editorials. Bernhardi wrote stuff like the subjoined, and Patterson

cribbed heavily from it later and in fact lived on it intellectually for many years:

War must regain its moral justification and its political significance in the eyes of the public. It is necessary that its high significance as a powerful promoter of civilization should become generally recognized. We must learn to understand that economic and individual interests alone must never be the decisive factor in a truly civilized state. We must recognize that the most valuable treasures of a nation are not material but moral; that it is necessary to make sacrifices and to suffer in the great cause; that sacrifice and suffering are more precious than enjoyment. In short, we must become convinced that a war fought for an ideal or fought with the intention of maintaining one's position in the world is not a barbaric act, but the highest expression of a true civilization; that war is a political necessity, and that it is fought in the interest of biological, social and moral progress.

Wars are ennobling because small-minded men are swamped in the greatness of the movement. The nations and states are at their greatest when fighting with their whole strength for liberty, independence and honor. Only in states which calculate with the possibility of war will the character of the nation possess that energy which enables them to develop their moral or mental forces to the highest degree.

War has its ideal side and peace has its blessings. At the same time peace is no blessing if it lasts too long, especially if its maintenance has to be paid for with the abandonment of the national ideals. Such peace dishonors a nation, and in such a peace small-mindedness and selfishness flourish, while idealism is destroyed by materialism and the simplicity of manners by luxury.

In such times money becomes all-powerful, and character is of little value. The more deeply we penetrate into history the more clearly we recognize that peace is a normal and desirable state but that wars are required from time to time in order to cleanse the moral atmosphere.

Charles Darwin proved that nature is ruled by an unceasing struggle for existence, by the right of the stronger, and that this struggle, in its apparent cruelty, brings about selection, eliminating the weak and unwholesome. That great naturalist has shown that only those types survive the struggle for existence which possess the most favorable conditions. The struggle for existence is ruled by biological laws.

The law of the struggle for existence applies also to men. While that struggle among animals and plants is a silent tragedy, men struggle consciously and have regulated their struggle by certain rules.

If men and states acted absolutely and unselfishly war would be avoidable. That is a condition which can neither be expected nor hoped for. Hence war is inevitable. It may, of course, happen that biologically weak nations combine, form a majority, and vanquish a nation of greater vitality. However, history teaches us that their success will be only temporary. Greater vitality will vindicate itself, and the united opponents will decline by abusing their victory. Hence a strong nation renews its strength after a temporary defeat, and thus secures an ultimate victory. German history illustrates the truth of this general rule.

In Bernhardi's welter of sophistries and pseudo-science there remained such a residuum of half-truths and apparent truths that it is not strange that Patterson, with his honesty and directness, accepted them as the basis of his thinking while rejecting the more subtle, involved lies, allegations and assumptions traded upon by the British war and foreign offices to justify England's entry into the war at a time when England might have prevented it by warning Germany that, in the case of aggression in France, England would enter the war on the side of its ally. The three principal instruments of British and American propaganda that were used to whip up American emotions which would lead us into war were: (1) violation of Belgian neutrality; (2) the allegations of German atrocities committed upon women and children in Belgium; and (3) the sinking of the *Lusitania*.

Patterson pointed out that: (1) it was not a surprise to the military authorities of England and France when the Germans thrust through Belgium, but that, in the great debate in the French parliament in 1912 and 1913 on the three-year law of compulsory military training, it was openly conceded that Germany would do so, and that this debate was not in camera but widely published in the newspapers, "in consequence of which the condition of the French forts on the Belgian frontier was investigated, quite a bit of graft was discovered and scandal resulted"; (2) it was highly inconsistent, to say the least, for the Allies to deplore the German violation of the treaty to respect the neutrality of Belgium and to rejoice when Italy violated her treaty with Austria and entered the war on the side of the Allies or when England herself violated the neutrality of Greece to seize Mytilene; (3) Patterson had been in Belgium on three separate occasions since the beginning of the war, with the Germans as far as Liège, from the north in Antwerp with the Belgians and from the west with French staff officers in the strip of Belgian territory near the sea, and that, although all armies "are armed to commit the atrocity of death on whosoever resisted them," there were no atrocities, even in kind, committed in Belgium by the Germans which differed from the atrocities committed by the Russians in East Prussia in August 1914; and (4) "By the way, it has never been printed or otherwise acknowledged in England to this day that the *Lusitania's* cargo consisted, in part, of ammunition."

Patterson had the magnificent integrity to test his opinions. Much was being made of the sinking of the *Lusitania,* which was carrying ammunition, and yet nothing was being made of the sinking of the *Arabic,* which was not carrying ammunition to England but gold to America, "presumably to pay for ammunition or other war material," and both the *Lusitania* and the *Arabic* had received the same degree of warning from the German government. Patterson made it a particular point to return to America on the *Cymric*—

one of the largest of the ammunition carriers, sister ship to the *Arabic,* in order to see if my opinion concerning the *Lusitania* was in any way modified by the fear, for a period of twenty-four hours, that a German submarine might kill me without further warning than I already had had. My opinion has not changed. The war is between England and Germany. Each is trying by intimidation and destruction on the sea to starve the other and so preserve itself. The grain of wheat that inserts itself between the millstones may expect to be crushed; the American passenger who chooses an English ship now takes the risk of the venture. Before sailing on this ship I left behind me a note, which would have been produced had occasion arisen, to state that I wanted to be the subject of no representations or inquiries whatever, as I had gone into the thing with my eyes open.

These gestures of Patterson were (to me) much more than mere gestures, indicating a consistent integrity in accepting personal responsibility for, and the consequences of, his opinions. They lifted him, in my estimation, miles above most of the men of his age, and presumably of his intelligence, who were articulate vocally and in print on the subject of the war.

Robert Herrick, a university professor, was writing a weekly article for the highbrow page I edited, in which he hysterically denounced America as a soulless country filled with speculators in war bonds and munitions and too pusillanimous to defend civilization by joining the Allies against the Huns. He had no sons to enlist in the war and, as I knew for a fair certainty, would not enlist for service himself; Percy Hammond, lazy, fat and sensual, was rabidly pro-Ally and venomous about Patterson's and the *Tribune's* neutral stand, although there was no chance of his endangering his life, and when we finally did enter the war he tried frantically to prevent his son from enlisting.

In all of the correct, genteel magazines of the country, members of the American Academy and Institute of Arts and Letters, too frail or old to join up themselves and without issue or with male issue under age for service, were plangently denouncing America for delay in entering the war "to save democracy" and "to save civilization."

Robert Morss Lovett, a sincere pacifist, was already almost a pariah among his fellows for advocating peace, and it was Lovett's tragedy to lose his son by death at the front shortly after we did enter the war, while his detractors lost nothing and, by virtue of being with the majority, found the way made easy for them to rise to the top of their professions and indulge in the luxuries of war profiteering and speculation.

Even Jane Addams, great humanitarian genius that she was, who had given her life to the education of slum children and the amelioration of the conditions of the immigrant poor of Chicago, was under a bitter cloud of derogation and slander for advocating peace.

Poor William Jennings Bryan, who was so sublimely right on many important issues and so foolishly wrong in the reasons he gave for his rightness, was the laughingstock of the "intellectuals" for his pleas to keep us out of war.

And I had seen that bewildered and dismayed former college professor, Woodrow Wilson, vainly trying to cope with popular sentiment, catch it, mold it and utilize it for something which would be at once a satisfaction of his curious ego and in consonance with his academic theories of "the New Freedom."

[261]

BEFORE I FORGET

For advocating that the United States enter into an alliance with England and go into war on the Allied side if necessary, but only with a definite understanding as to what America was to get out of it—specifically a defensive alliance against Japan or any other aggressor and a co-operative rule of the seas—not only Patterson, but the *Tribune* also, was branded as pro-German.*

It was stimulating to work under Patterson's flow of ideas; for even if he did not have me in mind to execute them when they occurred to him but were turned over to me by Miss King as being, in her opinion, the person most likely to do them to Patterson's satisfaction, and even if they involved research and writing I had no special stomach to engage in, the very research and the necessity to articulate the results of this research were to add to my knowledge of the world of affairs and to deepen my sense of values; and through him I was privileged to write many things I am distinctly proud of to this day.

For instance, he asked Mary King to assign someone, and Miss

*A flagrant example of this is to be found in a letter written by Stuart P. Sherman to Paul Elmer More on January 20, 1918, published in those two bulky volumes, *Life and Letters of Stuart P. Sherman,* piously, blindly, worshipfully edited by two of Sherman's former subordinates in the department of English at the University of Illinois, Jacob Zeitlin and Homer Woodbridge. Because I had reviewed Sherman's *On Contemporary Literature* adversely in the Chicago *Tribune,* Sherman described the *Tribune* in his letter to More as "the largest and vilest of the Chicago papers" and added, "That interesting paper, you may know, has the habit of retaining always one pro-German staff writer to counterpoise the work in the adjoining column of the pro-English writer." Sherman was living in Urbana, Illinois, when he wrote this; he saw the *Tribune* regularly. More was living in Princeton and very likely never saw the *Tribune*. We had been at war nine months, and not for one single minute after a state of war was declared on Germany did this hitherto justifiably neutral attitude of printing both pro-German and pro-Ally articles exist on the *Tribune.*

Sherman knew this, or else he was reprehensibly negligent in not checking upon his facts; for he was counting upon More's ignorance to spread a calumny branding the *Tribune* as traitorous *because that paper had printed an adverse review of one of his books.*

It was a calumny so outrageously improbable that only a self-centered academician could have perpetrated it. At the very moment Sherman was petulantly writing More about the untoward fate his complacently vicious little book of literary essays was meeting, and conveying the idea that the Chicago *Tribune* was traitorous, both editor-owners of the paper were in active service at the front.

Patterson, as a lieutenant of artillery, within a month or so was under fire in the Lorraine sector, and Robert R. McCormick was on his way to becoming a colonel rapidly, although not so close to actual danger. Sherman I considered to be an unscrupulously clever opportunist who had a faculty for convincing himself that his shifts of position to achieve a better income and larger prestige were in the interests of national honor and morality. I could respect a man like Patterson with whose

King chose me, to study the Leo Frank case and write an article about it. He offered me no suggestions whatever. He did not intimate whether he thought Frank was guilty or not guilty. He obviously intended me to give my closest attention to the matter and to present it in the most judicious and most conscientious manner. And he did not even tell me that: he merely told me to do the article.

Not until he wrote the eight-column streamer head to the article himself, "Will the State of Georgia Hang an Innocent Man?" did I have an inkling of what he thought was the justice of the trial of Leo Frank for the murder of one of the girls in the employ of Frank's pencil factory, and even in that headline there was a question, not an assertion.

I studied the transcripts of the evidence for weeks, the Burns Detective Agency reports, the newspaper accounts; I absorbed them in such a manner that I could have, at any moment, given you a witness's answer to any question at any point during the trial; I knew every physical detail of the factory and its location in Atlanta, the hour the tragedy probably occurred and how many people were normally on the near-by streets at that hour, the character of the witnesses, the character of the defendant (which was not, by the way, a savory one) and the sentiment in Atlanta.

I was so full of the whole case and so troubled by all the implications of it (its anti-Semitic phase and its contrary which led Jews to unite to defend Frank without inquiring into his guilt or innocence but merely because he was a Jew) that on the day of the deadline for the article I did not believe I could write it. I did not start to write it, in fact, until three-thirty in the afternoon.

I finished it by six o'clock—nearly seven thousand words in two hours and a half, written more rapidly than I can type ordinarily and without pause or reference to notes. It was all in my head and

expressed opinions I might disagree; I could not respect a man like Sherman even when I agreed with his literary evaluations.

I could—and did, in fact—respect Paul Elmer More thoroughly, while at the same time violently opposing More's primary assumption that property is more sacred than human life and all his subsidiary assumptions out of which flow the well-read, cultivated, urbane *Shelburne Essays;* for at least More had the character to stand by and take the consequences of his convictions; he never took a mean advantage, he never tried to play both ends against the middle. More himself saw this fault in Sherman and counseled him vainly against it, as the Zeitlin-Woodbridge volumes show and as the Messrs Zeitlin and Woodbridge were too stupid to see.

it all came out, neatly, symphonically, ending *de capo,* and when it was in type I changed not a word.

My conclusion was that Frank might have committed the murder, but that he ought not to be convicted *on the evidence produced;* that on the evidence, with the prosecution's principal reliance upon the testimony of a Negro porter who told two entirely different stories on the stand, the whole question of justice and of fair trial was at stake, with the presiding judge yielding to mob hysteria and the jury being intimidated by open threats from the mob outside the courtroom.

It seemed to me that it wasn't Leo Frank's life that was the issue but the whole principle of fair trial; and this feeling was complicated by the troubling fact that Jews were contributing to a defense fund and agitating against Georgia and Georgia prejudice with no other conviction than that Frank was an innocent Jew who was being unjustly accused; that the Jews were emotionally convinced that Frank was innocent because he was a Jew, wherein they were in the same case as the Atlanta anti-Semites who were convinced that he was guilty by the mere fact that he was a Jew, and both sides were fanning the flames of race hatred and prejudice with no reference to the case in point at all.

My own conclusion that Frank was not *proved* guilty was sufficient to get the *Tribune* denounced in newspaper editorials throughout the South and me (a Southerner born) to get hundreds of letters from persons in various remote parts of the South who could know nothing more about the case than what they read in the local newspapers, saying I would be shot on sight the moment I dared show my face below the Mason and Dixon line.

All this was troubling to my youthful belief in the rationality of human beings, for fear and prejudice were aflame in the breasts of Northern Jews and Southern anti-Semites, orderly review of evidence was estopped, and, as it turned out, a higher court's review of the case was killed by a mob's abducting the prisoner from jail and obscenely hanging him.

Among the assignments Miss King gave me as commands to her from Patterson were articles on the military history and character of the commanders of the belligerent forces—Kitchener, Ludendorff, Von Falkenhayn, Von Hindenburg and Von Kluck, Joffre and the Grand Duke Nicholas. Each of these articles I wrote was a digest of clippings in the *Tribune* "morgue," and in the first of these assignments I drew from a clipping of an article in the Baltimore *Sun* by Henry L. Mencken.

This clipping was of five years before, and in it the military genius of "Kitchener of Khartoum" was extolled by a young journalist who was at that time in an ardent stage of admiration of British jingoism and writing verses in slavish imitation of Rudyard Kipling. My coming upon this clipping opened up my first correspondence with Mencken. I wrote to him saying I had read and swiped from his article for a hack-work chore on the Chicago *Tribune,* and he wrote to repudiate his former belief in Kitchener's military genius. Mencken's admiration for the moment was for Ludendorff. Ludendorff was a stuffed-shirt military Junker who curled up and died when a house painter named Hitler snapped his fingers at him.

These patchwork rewritings of what had already been said in print about these military leaders led me into my first intimate experience with the way a fraudulent presumption of knowledge carries conviction with those who presumably have an exact knowledge in that very field. I knew nothing about military strategy, nothing about the theories and experiences of Joffre, Ludendorff, Kitchener and Nicholas and cared less.

I presumed nothing; I was neither dishonest nor disingenuous about my knowledge: I merely lifted from and rewrote a batch of clippings which others had lifted and rewritten; I did not sign my name to the stuff or make myself responsible for the information the articles contained. I was merely doing a hack job.

And yet Robert R. McCormick, already a major in the Illinois National Guard, a student of military campaigns and an intimate of the Grand Duke Nicholas, correspondent and accredited military observer on various war fronts, sought me out and talked to me gravely and importantly, as though he and I were privy to great issues of tactics and strategy which were quite outside the ken of ordinary men. He would come in, attired in whipcord breeches, English officer's jacket, boots, spurs, Sam Browne belt and officer's cap, a polo stick in one hand and three yelping German police dogs on a leash.

He would go up to the roof of the *Tribune* building, mount a mechanical horse and practice polo shots from the contraption, and while some hireling was busy taking care of those noisy dogs, he would discuss with me, as one man to another who knew a thing or two about military affairs, the plans of the German army. To me this was comical.

I think he got the idea I was especially deep and knowing in such matters from the fact that, not knowing the least thing about them and having already forgotten the tripe I had written (or rather rewritten), I never contributed anything to our dialogue except a cautious and noncommittal, "I imagine perhaps you are right."

I was interested, however, in the gossip he brought back from St. Petersburg about the Queen of Roumania, and I think that he, also, was more intellectually concerned with that than with the relative merits of Ludendorff and Von Mackensen.

I can say for Patterson that not once did he ask my opinion on something about which I could not conceivably have any experience or exact knowledge, although once, poor geometrician that I am, I helped him work out an artillerist's problem of range and angle of fire.

While the awkward giant, McCormick, was still playing "Soldier" like a rich boy in knee pants, and with as much sense of reality, and riding his mechanical horse on the roof of the *Tribune,* Patterson was going through his successive stages of hero worship of men actually alive and functioning.

In the very beginning of the war, and before it, I was keeping abreast of literary, polemical and political affairs in France, England and Germany by reading the *Mercure de France,* the *Nouvelle Revue Française,* the *Revue de Paris,* the *English Review,* the *Spectator,* the *Statesman,* the Frankfurter *Zeitung,* the *Manchester Guardian* and Maximilian Harden's *Die Zukunft* and, after the war had got under way, I not only followed Harden's fiery journalistic diatribes against the Kaiser and his functionaries but translated them into English, secured publication rights and used them on the highbrow page occasionally.

These Harden articles, vigorous and denunciatory and published without suppression or hindrance in Germany, pleased and fascinated Patterson, and when I ran a picture of Harden the likeness to Patterson was so great that Harden became one of his pet enthusiasms.

I had to run pictures of Harden regularly in the rotogravure section, as well as line drawings of Harden as initial pieces to the Harden articles, just as when Patterson discovered a likeness to himself in the pictures of Winston Churchill I had to use photographs of Churchill in the rotogravure section whether there was any special reason or not.

And then, long after the war, came Patterson's preoccupation with Lord Northcliffe's unique position of power as the power behind the throne in England, the maker and unmaker of premiers, cabinets and peers, the reputed creator of Kitchener as commander-in-chief and the reputed executioner of that creation. Northcliffe's power had been built solely upon the enormous circulation of his penny papers, first upon the boob-beguiler *Questions & Answers,* later upon the illustrated daily tabloids and the Northcliffe chain of newspapers.

Patterson had, I think, back in his mind the idea that by imitating Northcliffe he might rise to the same sort of power Northcliffe exercised in England. If so, it was a vain and unreflective hope, for Patterson had need only to open his eyes to what was happening with his own paper to become aware that the same conditions do not obtain in America as those which enabled Northcliffe to rise to power.

England is a small, tight little island; the United States is a heterogeneous wide expanse of land with interstate, intercity, and interregional jealousies and distrusts. Hearst, with all the circulation of his newspapers and with all the financial resources at his command, never has had any considerable influence even in New York City, much less in the nation as a whole.

And, as for the Chicago *Tribune,* the paper has had no political influence as long as I have been acquainted with it. The paper is unable to re-elect a chief justice of the municipal court, much less influence the election of a governor or a president. As long as I was on the *Tribune* (eight years) it was, in fact, political death almost for one's candidacy to be sponsored by the *Tribune* in any municipal or Cook County election.

There was, indeed, a stereotyper in the *Tribune* composing room who made a small fortune (large enough to buy an apartment house) over a period of years by the simple expedient of offering odds of two to one or five to three against any candidate or any project on which the *Tribune* set its pre-election approval.

He never lost a bet. "This paper," he used to tell me, "couldn't elect a dog catcher." It wasn't that he didn't like the *Tribune:* he did. It was simply that he had observed that the majority vote in state, county and municipal elections nearly went in direct opposition to the *Tribune's* editorial policy.

The reason or reasons for this are not altogether clear. But it probably has something to do with the average Middle Westerner's dislike and distrust of arrogance and self-righteousness, two qualities which quite perceptibly emanated from the editorial pages from the days of James Keeley, a tin-pot Mussolini.

Throughout the core of the Middle West, Illinois, Indiana, Michigan, Wisconsin, Iowa and parts of Missouri, the Chicago *Tribune* was *the* paper (and still is) taken by everybody who could afford a newspaper at all, read and cordially hated. It was regarded somewhat like an insufferable rich relative, tolerated but privately detested.

But only because of its editorial page.

The news service of the *Tribune* was, for many years, the best organized and best presented of any newspaper in the country; the features were multifarious and embraced everything from John T. McCutcheon's, Carey Orr's and Clare Briggs' cartoons and Sydney Smith's comic strips, Ring Lardner's sports features and B. L. T.'s column to various kinds of valuable free services—such as legal, medical and investment advice, each department of which maintained a large, conscientious staff which answered thousands of inquiries weekly by mail as well as the inquiries printed with answers daily.

And the strength of the paper in Chicago in sheer circulation "coverage," as the jargon of the advertising department calls it, was and is immense, for the *Tribune's* only competitor in the morning field was and is the *Herald-Examiner,* a Hearst paper, a heavy money loser annually, but, in local politics, a strong paper politically.

The *Tribune* has not only quietly eliminated other competition as a morning newspaper over a period of years, but has firmly squelched every attempt to invade the Chicago morning field. The late Cyrus H. K. Curtis once had the idea of starting a morning newspaper in Chicago, but the *Tribune* quickly dispelled the idea from his mind by making immediate preparations for throwing all of the Chicago *Tribune* and New York *Daily News* companies' resources behind a new newspaper in Philadelphia to compete there, on his own ground, with Curtis.

And in these matters of meeting competition the Chicago *Tribune* has not been squeamish. Not since 1910. That was the year the Chicago *Tribune* found it expedient, even if against its conscience, to hire away from the Hearst papers the man who had been responsible for a precipitous drop in the *Tribune's* circulation and a consequent rise in the circulation of Hearst's *Examiner*—Max Annenberg.

Those who were accustomed to purchase their morning *Tribune* at the corner newsstand on their way to work suddenly found that, morning after morning, the *Tribune* was "sold out." There would, however, be plentiful stacks of the *Examiner*. Grumbling, they would take an *Examiner* in lieu of a *Tribune*.

What had happened was that Andrew M. Lawrence, publisher in charge of the Hearst papers in Chicago, had hired Max and Moses Annenberg as circulation managers of the two papers, and the Annenbergs had in turn hired a crew of sluggers and gunmen. The gunmen would waylay *Tribune* delivery trucks, confiscate the newspapers and dump them into the river. The sluggers would visit the newsstands and intimidate the dealers into refusing to take an adequate supply of *Tribunes* and, by way of making their requests clear, would beat up those who protested, wreck the stands and destroy the *Tribunes*.

This was the beginning of gangsterism and racketeering in Chicago.

Under the Annenbergs, and acting as their lieutenants in charge of bruisers, bullies and "punks," were "Mossie" Enright, "Red" Conners, Bob Holbrook and other gunmen later to become notorious in gang warfare.

Acting upon the theory that what is sauce for the goose is necessarily sauce for the gander, Jim Keeley of the *Tribune* got Max Annenberg to break his contract with Lawrence and come to the *Tribune* with his sluggers on a $20,000-a-year guarantee and bonuses on a graduating scale for increases in the *Tribune's* circulation.

Annenberg guaranteed to Keeley that not only would he increase the *Tribune's* circulation but would *decrease* the *Examiner's*.

Lawrence sued Annenberg for breach of contract, and when the case came before the courts the contract was held invalid because it stipulated that Annenberg had been hired by the Hearst organization to commit unlawful acts.

Lawrence quickly assembled a gang of gunmen, including Gus, Dutch and Pete Gentleman, Vincent Altman, Eddie Barrett and Frankie McErlane. And the war was on. Gunmen rode alongside the drivers of the newspaper delivery trucks, and gunmen from both newspapers cruised the streets in limousines and automobile trucks, waylaying rival delivery trucks, and gun battles would ensue, terrifying pedestrians and even clipping them with stray bullets.

The gang bosses began to rub each other out. Dutch Gentleman, a Hearst gunman, was shot to death, while he was standing at the bar of a saloon, by Annenberg's lieutenant, "Mossie" Enright, who entered the saloon flanked by a V formation of other gunmen behind him, walked up to Gentleman, twirled him around and emptied his revolver into Gentleman's belly.

Vincent Altman, another Hearst gunman, was shot to death by "unknown assailants" while he was standing at the bar of the Briggs House.

Yet Annenberg triumphed; the *Tribune's* circulation went up by leaps and bounds, and the *Examiner's* correspondingly went down. Comparative peace reigned; Annenberg settled down to the less sanguine duties of a circulation manager and, when Patterson succeeded Keeley as editor, Patterson sought Annenberg's advice on the treatment of news. With the outbreak of the war, the *Tribune* began to use an eight-column streamer head in every issue (an Annenberg suggestion), and after the war it continued to use it whether news justified it or not. Patterson ordered Beck, the managing editor, to submit the eight-column streamer for the final edition to Annenberg every morning.

Meanwhile, with the reign of peace in the newspaper offices, the sluggers and gunmen were gradually eased out of jobs and forced to find new unlawful means of livelihood. They began to organize "protection" rackets, extending to various industries. Department-store owners were told they needed "protection" for their delivery trucks, just as the newspapers had had; and when the owners were not convinced, the racketeers proved that such was the case by beating up delivery boys, wrecking trucks and destroying merchandise.

Having thus proved that "protection" was needed against themselves, the assailants were hired, and gunmen sat alongside of drivers of every delivery truck in Chicago. "Protection" was extended to the cleaning and dyeing industry, to speakeasies, movie theaters, restaurants and even to hotels—the same sort of "protection" formerly offered by the corrupt politicians and the police to resort owners and dope peddlers.

Racketeers took over the whole extortion racket hitherto limited to ward bosses and the police department. When the politicians refused to join forces with the racketeers, their competition was eliminated by force. Thugs merely adopted the practices of the law enforcers. The law enforcers raided the illegal houses which did not pay for immunity against raids.

Thus, out of the Hearst publisher's hiring the Annenbergs and their gunmen and sluggers to cripple competition in newspaper sales, grew the worst reign of lawlessness in Chicago that any city has ever known. But the Annenbergs themselves, rich in bonuses and successful speculation, were soon to become eminently respectable, Max taking charge of the circulation of Patterson's experimental tabloid, the New York *Daily News,* and later of Patterson's disastrous experiment in running a magazine, *Liberty* (Patterson lost $14,000,000 of the Chicago *Tribune* company's money in that venture), and Moses Annenberg becoming a successful publisher himself, first with a chain of racing sheets and *Radio Guide* and more recently with the Philadelphia *Inquirer*.

When I first knew Max Annenberg, sometime in 1914, he was already a power and something of a pet in the *Tribune* offices—a burly barbarian, endeavoring with conspicuous success to live down his reputation as a roughneck and at the same time to enhance it.

If that seems impossibly contradictory, the explanation is easy. Max was a leader of thugs and gunmen at the outset of his career, an underworld character knowledgeable in the ways of the underworld, a powerfully built man who kept himself rigidly in training by abstemiousness in drink and diet and regular exercise in riding and boxing.

He was alert and alive, physically courageous, a believer in the discipline of the fist and blackjack and of revenge with the gun. He had no respect for the law, and therein, in Chicago at the time, he showed his intelligence; for the whole social and political organization of Chicago was so shot through with corruption, graft and thievery on the grand scale that there was scarcely a wealthy family in Chicago which was not deriving a considerable portion of its income from lawlessness of some sort—rents from gambling places and houses of prostitution, expropriation of public lands, profits from jerry-built slums or industrial highbindery.

It was precisely in physical courage that Annenberg differed from his gunmen hirelings and could keep his leadership over them; for most of them were such yellow rats at heart that they had to keep hopped up with cocaine all the time to avoid going to pieces in time of danger.

It was for Annenberg's great bruiser physical courage, his complete disregard of civilized conventions and farcical law enforcement, that Patterson was drawn to him in vast respect and admiration.

Annenberg was accepting the conditions of his time, his place, his inheritance and was intelligently making use of them to his own betterment and advantage, accepting the hazards, even the hazards of mutilation and sudden death.

As a Socialist and, in a brief excursion into practical politics, Patterson had wished to change these conditions to which Annenberg had so successfully adjusted himself, and, failing and sensing that all attempts to change such conditions would inevitably fail, he knew at the same time that he could not function like Max in the jungle law of Chicago. He was born to social respectability and to an inevitable hypocrisy: he was physically strong himself and courageous, as strong perhaps and as courageous as Max, and yet he could not himself defend his properties: he had to hire Max to do it for him.

Max, therefore, had to be a hero to him, for Max was his vicar and so, progressively, he had not only to accept the onus of Max's gangs' shootings and sluggings and condone them as his own acts, but argue them away as salutary in the promotion of the greater good.

It was but a step from Patterson's personal problem of guilt and innocence—from gang warfare to maintain and increase the *Tribune's* circulation—to his acceptance of the higher ratiocination of Bernhardi that war is a biological necessity, conducive to the higher good.

Meanwhile Max was anxious to put his bruiser past behind him and enjoy the benefits of cultured associations and social respectability. He was taking up golf and was riding mornings on the bridle path of Lincoln Park; he was looking forward to impressive church weddings for his children, country estates and all the recreations of American men of substance and "background"—to the very things, in fact, which Patterson, with an authentic background and growing substance, not only did not practise but condemned as sissified manifestations of Thorstein Veblen's indictments against the leisure class.

So Max was, when I first knew him, being busy with the dual role of forgetting his gangster activities and keeping the heroic or glamorous aspects of it alive. He wore, therefore, a turtle-neck sweater and a loud check cap set at a sinister, hard-boiled angle; he was loud, boisterous and hearty, excessively amiable and sociable, slapping the office girls he encountered so resoundingly on the back that they would wince and redden with impatience. He was friendly, likable, restless with nervous energy, boastful and full of braggadocio.

In 1928, Patterson's sister, Eleanor (formerly the Countess Gizycki, then Mrs Elmer Schlesinger) wanted to start a weekly magazine, and Patterson and Annenberg had both named me as their sole recommendation for the editorship, and, as Annenberg was acting as Mrs Patterson's business counselor in the proposed venture, I had several long talks with him, but mostly about Al

Capone and the Chicago gangsters and very little about the magazine.

(I had as much money as I needed at the time, was reluctant to take up editing a magazine again, and tried to dissuade Mrs Patterson from investing in the project by exacting a whopping salary with graduating bonuses and telling her she would have to be prepared to lose $300,000 a year for two or three years before the magazine would turn the corner and begin to make money. She told me she was prepared to do this. I was all the more eager to dissuade her when I derived from talks with her that her principal motive in owning a magazine was to have a department in it wherein she could stick pins into Alice Roosevelt Longworth and was willing to lose $300,000 a year for three years for this privilege. I had finally to call the whole thing off because I could not tolerate her husband, the late Elmer Schlesinger, who was once a brilliant trial lawyer but, when I knew him, an argumentative maniac, and, as a host, hysterically given to picking quarrels with his guests, badgering his wife's guests as if they were defendants under cross-examination.)

Max, on the occasions of those talks, recited in vivid detail several of the episodes in which he barely escaped assassination. On one occasion a gunman who had a grudge against him somehow got by the guards and into Max's office in the *Tribune*. There was a heavy carpet on the floor, and Max didn't know the man was there until he barked at Max, who was reading a paper on his desk, to put up his hands. The gunman then told Max that he was going to kill him, but not until he had told Max what he thought of him.

This he did at great length, at too great length, for he talked so long and so loud that he did not hear Max's son, Ivan, accidentally walk into the room. Ivan knocked the pistol out of the man's hand; but it was Max who demanded the pleasure of messing the fellow up. Max did not call the police or prefer charges against the would-be murderer. He knocked and kicked the man out of the room, across the hall and all the way down the four flights of stone stairs.

On another occasion Max told me Walter Howey had hired Dion O'Bannion, a gunman later notorious in the bootlegger wars and victim of another gangster's submachine gun, to kill him. (This, I think, was merely a supposition of Max's—that O'Bannion had been hired by Howey—and probably had no basis in fact.) Max said he and Mrs Annenberg were riding in Lincoln Park at seven o'clock one morning when he spied O'Bannion lurking behind some bushes waiting for him to come within range.

He maneuvered Mrs Annenberg between him and O'Bannion and, keeping behind her because he knew O'Bannion would not shoot her, they rode straight up to O'Bannion, whereupon Max dismounted, because O'Bannion had put his gun away, and asked him what he was doing.

"He had got himself all hopped up for the job," Max said, "but he had been waiting so long the effects were worn off. He had lost his nerve and was jittery. I frisked him, took his gun away from him and told him he oughtn't to be monkeying with that thing, because he was liable to get himself hurt. He never bothered me any more."

Max told me then (in 1928) that if he were chief of police he could clean up every gang in Chicago in less than a week, from Al Capone's on down. "I would throw Al in the can so quick," he said, "his pants would catch fire."

"On what charge?" I asked.

"Vagrancy. Technical, like they do in Georgia when a Negro hasn't got any money and they need another hand on the chain gang. Then, when his lawyer and a bondsman came to spring him, I'd jug them, too, and keep them there. There is always enough on every gangster's lawyer and bondsman in Chicago to hang them if the police want to use it—enough to disbar the lawyers and send the lawyers and bondsmen to the penitentiary. And so, all the way down the line. I would round up the trigger punks, give them a thorough shellacking and take their dope away from them. After three days they would be so crazy for a shot they would tell everything they know."

I asked Max how it was that Al Capone had never been killed by gunmen from rival gangs. "How are they going to get to him?" Max asked. "He is always protected by bodyguards. The only way to get him would be to buy off both bodyguards and hire one of them to do the job. The other would have to be in on it, so the killer could make his getaway.

[275]

"Another thing: If the police really wanted to get rid of Capone
. . . Capone doesn't carry a gun himself. It's against the law. But
his bodyguards do. Arrest the bodyguards for carrying concealed
weapons. And shoot Capone accidentally and for keeps in the
process. . . . Easy."

Contrary to a very generally accepted piece of gossip, the Chicago *Tribune* did not start the first New York tabloid newspaper,
the *Daily News,* in order to avoid paying high excess-profits tax.
As the story has frequently come to me, it was with the idea of
deliberately losing money that the *Tribune* started the tabloid,
and nobody could have been more surprised than the *Tribune*
owners when it began to make money hand over fist.

Now anybody with any reflective sense ought to know that if
the money is going to go anyway, one might as well pay it to the
government as sink it in a losing enterprise; for you know to the
cent how much you are going to have to pay the government, but
there is no way of telling how much money one is going to lose in
an unprofitable newspaper.

Patterson began working on the idea of a tabloid newspaper as
soon as he got out of the army after the war. He had got the idea
from Northcliffe's tremendously profitable *Daily Graphic* and
London *Illustrated News.* He had taken a direct hand in the Chicago *Tribune's* rotogravure section from the first run off its
presses. As rotogravure editor I saw the offerings of the news-
photograph agencies every day and bought what I considered the
best. From the batch of photographs I bought and the layouts I suggested, Patterson made the final selection and changed or okayed
my layouts. He studied the English tabloids and illustrated newspapers and the *Police Gazette.* On the Chicago *Tribune* we were
running our rotogravure section in tabloid form—in fact in exactly
the same tabloid form that was adopted for the *Daily News,* because it was an easy conversion of the size of the newsprint paper
rolls.

Patterson had definitely wanted to make a success of the *Daily
News,* and he neglected no angle in his calculations for two important personal reasons, which I shall explain in a moment. To
this end he meditated upon the factors which had made for large

circulation in the past, and the evidence before his eyes showed him that the things people were most interested in were, and in order, (1) Love or Sex, (2) Money, (3) Murder. They were especially interested in any situation which involved all three. There was a fourth item, Health, and this was closely related to the first, slightly related to the second, in that health gives one an advantage in making money, which in turn reduced the handicaps in love, and remotely related to the third, in that military drill strengthens the body and trains the muscles to reduce the hazards of death in the mass murder of war.

Patterson was, as a renegade Socialist, still an equalitarian, and he wished to reach and influence the lowest common denominator of literate American intelligence, i.e., the broad base of America's population, not the proletariat in the sense of the dumb, illiterate manual laborer, but the lower bourgeoisie, the file clerks, factory workers, salesmen, machinists, druggists, delicatessen owners, chain-grocery employees and managers, the small home owner and buyer on the installment plan, and, as his promotion genius, Leo MacGivena, who coined the phrase, "Sell it to Sweeney," would say, the Sweeneys and the Sheenies of America.

This was an honorable ambition if the associated motives were honorable, and, in Patterson's case, they were. He had, then, no desire, I think, to make more money for himself, for his irreducible income was already beyond his needs; and he had no desire to exploit the people, for his vision still was toward a better life for all, and it was palpably within his power, if he could appeal to enough people through giving them what they urgently wanted, to give them what they should have also; and what they should have, as Patterson conceived it, was Patterson's personal and individual convictions about life altogether and American communal national life specifically.

CHAPTER XVIII

Dramatic Critic and Pooh-Bah

Percy Hammond. Frederick Donaghey. I Substitute for Percy Hammond When He Goes Abroad to Report the Peace Conference. James O'Donnell Bennett. John Reed. Sheppard Butler. The Chicago Woman's Club Campaigns against Sex in Literature and the Hootchy-Kootchy Shows on South State Street. My Apologia for Taking Percy Hammond's Place as Dramatic Critic. Some Tongue-in-Cheek Japery. "The Theater Isn't What It Used to Be, and It Never Was." I Hold Six Full-Time Jobs Simultaneously on the *Tribune,* and the Fun of Being Dramatic Critic Wears Off. Why Some Shows Failed in Chicago. Nerves and Lack of Sleep Bring Me to the Verge of a Nervous Breakdown. The Gold Coasters Demand My Removal as Critic of the Drama.

I HAVE HEARD THAT WHEN Percy Hammond was a young man he was slim and that his hair was an aureole of golden curls. When I first knew him he was already fat and florid, and his light, thinning hair gave the impression of being pink because the faint ruddiness of his flesh was reflected in its sheen. His eyes were beady, and his lips were full and petulant, like those of a spoiled child. For years he lived under two absurd delusions: one that he was a victim of insomnia and the other that his appetite for food was gone.

He had groused to me one day that he had had only two hours of sleep for nights on end and that he had not been able to eat anything for a week. That same night I saw Mrs Hammond in the lobby of a theater during the intermission of a show. She told me a distressing experience she had gone through on the preceding day on account of her husband. It had been a Sunday, and she had invited some people in for a buffet luncheon. She had had two chickens roasted and put into the icebox, along with celery, olives, potato salad, ham, cheese, milk and other items suitable to a Sunday-afternoon lunch. She had given her cook a holiday and meant to serve the meal herself.

At two o'clock in the afternoon, just before the guests arrived, she went to the icebox to see if everything was in order. The two chickens were but picked skeletons—only the drumsticks and bits of stuffing were left; most of the vegetables had disappeared, and less than a pint of milk remained. Percy was still asleep, but she awakened him with reproaches. He had come in at one o'clock, this insomniac who had no appetite, and had cleaned out her icebox. Moreover, he had slept more than twelve hours at a stretch following this gorge. When guests arrived she had to make excuses and scurry up food from a delicatessen.

Percy was like a spoiled child in other ways. He was forever getting a mad on somebody—Joseph Medill Patterson or an office boy, it didn't matter which, if Percy took offense. The victims of his temperament rarely knew what they had done to cause Percy to quit speaking to them, which he always did if he felt affronted. The mad never lasted long as a rule; it ran its course in about three weeks. During this time, in conversation Percy would attribute to his erstwhile friend fantastic vices and acquaint you with an extensive list of imaginary petty crimes and misdemeanors which, Percy would inform you, he had personal knowledge his former friend had committed.

If you knew Percy at all well, of course, you let these accusations go into one ear and out the other, knowing full well that perhaps by four o'clock the next day Percy's mad would have run its course and he would again be a bosom friend to the man he had villified.

One night when I was assistant Sunday editor in charge of the make-up of the entire Sunday paper with the exception of the news section, I had to perform my routine duty of inquiring of Percy how soon he would have his copy ready. On Thursday nights he had to write his leading article for the Sunday paper and get up his news notes of the theatrical world. He was a procrastinator, and if I did not ask him how soon his copy would be ready, when it was already due to be in the compositor's hands, Percy would make no move to go about his elaborate preparations to write.

Although he had a desk of his own in the city room, he preferred to write at Clifford Raymond's desk. Raymond was an editorial writer and, as such, was usually gone for the day at five o'clock along with the other editorial writers. At that hour the city room of a morning newspaper is just beginning to get galvanized into activity. The editorial writers' rooms were just off the library, which was tomblike at night, and, removed as they were from the city room, they offered Percy silence and freedom from distraction.

In the large lower drawer of Raymond's roll-top desk Percy kept a coffee percolator, a heavy cup such as is found in all-night coffee stands and a pound or two of ground coffee. Percy's first movement toward writing his article was to brew a whole percolator full of excessively strong coffee. Meanwhile he would arrange around him, on the otherwise unoccupied space of the desk, on two chairs drawn up to the left and right and on a table behind him, a copy of Shakespeare's works complete in one volume, Roget's Thesaurus, Webster's Unabridged Dictionary and Bartlett's Familiar Quotations. Sometimes, if he found composition particularly difficult and coffee an inadequate stimulant, he added to his formidable paraphernalia a pint bottle of whisky.

He might consume the entire brew of coffee and the contents of the whisky bottle, keep the compositor who could read his writing idle for hours, and me in a state of nervous apprehension that at the last moment I would have to fill the space allotted to Percy with something else; but somehow, if he showed up at all, he would get his stuff in—and in time to go to press on schedule. And the stuff would be a delight to read.

The actual point of the article might be comprehensible only to Percy, myself, a few others—and to the person Percy had a mad on at the moment; but others, without detecting the point, would be charmed by Percy's iambic cadences and his dexterous use of an unusual vocabulary.

Percy said he liked to use polysyllables because it gave barbers and actors a vain sense of getting an education while reading him. He wrote sententiously for comic effect and because, in his hands, the sententious sentence became a neat weapon of irony.

He liked to employ false humility in writing about an actor or an event in the theater and to make his point so ambiguous that it would confuse the mind of the person he was writing about (or he so intended), so that the person would not be able quite to figure out whether he was being praised or made malicious fun of.

In all cases where there was any doubt about the interpretation, Percy's intention was the latter.

I have known Percy to write a whole article built around one phrase, and the rest of the article would have only a factitious relationship to the phrase, although this factitiousness would be concealed and not readily apparent to the casual reader. He might, for instance, wish to say something wittily malicious about Bert Leston Taylor: the epithet or image of characterization would be inlaid in an intricate mosaic of parodied lines from Shakespeare and quotations from Bartlett amusingly tampered with, and the ostensible point of the whole article might be something else entirely, such as random animadversions on a current Ziegfeld show. And he loved to get letters from actors thanking him for what they took to be warm praise when Percy had actually submitted them to a merciless ribbing. Writing was often a game Percy played with himself to work off his grudges.

On the night I spoke of some paragraphs above, Percy was sitting at Bert Leston Taylor's desk in the local room (i.e., the main workshop of reporters, copyreaders and news editors) on the fifth floor of the old *Tribune* building at Dearborn and Madison streets. He had not gone to Clifford Raymond's room and started his percolator.

It was one o'clock in the morning; Percy's Sunday article would have to be written by three. When I asked him how soon I could count on getting his copy, he countered by asking me if I didn't think Bert Taylor's column ("A Line o' Type or Two") wasn't the lousiest in America.

I did not think so; and I knew that in his heart Percy did not think so, either; that, on the contrary, Taylor's column was the best in the country, irritating at times, as all personally conducted columns are bound to be, but maintaining a high average of wit and readability.

So, instead of answering Percy yes or no, I asked him what was the trouble now. I knew he was mad at Taylor about something, although they had been playing golf together only the Sunday before and they had been pretty close friends.

"But, I ask you," he demanded, "is it, or is it not, the lousiest column in the country? I don't know why Joe and Beck stand for it. I give you my word, I can't read it. It is always filled up with tripe from a lot of nance college professors."

These last two statements were patently untrue. I knew Percy had not only been able to read the column but had read very carefully the column in the edition just off the press. The paper lay spread out before him, opened to Taylor's column. Moreover, although Taylor did have among his contributors some college professors, they were by no means nancies; they were men of masculine and vigorous wit, scholarship and poetic talent, men such as Professor Paul Shorey, who was a famous Greek scholar, Keith Preston, who was a clever versifier as well as a teacher of Greek and Latin, Richard Atwater, who was a protégé of Professor Shorey's in Greek at the University of Chicago, and several teachers in English at Oberlin, Northwestern and other schools.

So again I asked Percy what was the trouble.

With his pencil he ringed two words in a contribution to Taylor's column signed "J. U. H."

This was the signature of J. U. Higginbotham, who was not a college professor at all but a Detroit wit, after-dinner speaker and man-about-town. He contributed amusing pieces to Taylor's column, usually in a mock-solemn manner, employing words quaintly for humorous effect. The two words Percy had ringed were "quaint patois."

Percy demanded of me belligerently, "Do you think I write a quaint patois?"

The whole phrase J. U. H. had used was, "the quaint patois of Percy Hammond."

Percy *did* use in his writings a quaint patois; that was the charm of his stuff; but I was not going to imperil my friendly relationship with Percy by saying so.

I let him fume until the heat of anger in him was incandescent, knowing that when the heat was high Percy would go off to his percolator and other paraphernalia and turn out in fairly short order a piece apropos of the current offerings in the theater in which there would be embedded a searing phrase contrived to wound Taylor to the quick.

Frederick Donaghey, who was, at the time I first knew him, a theatrical press agent and later was the *Tribune's* music critic and, for a brief time after Taylor's death, one of the several tried out as Taylor's successor, had been for many years Percy's closest friend.

Donaghey could imitate Percy's style so cleverly that he could write and sign articles and news notes for Percy and few people could detect the imposture. Percy often trusted Donaghey to prepare his entire half-column or column of "oddments and re-mainders" because not only could Donaghey imitate Percy's style: he could also throw himself into Percy's position of responsibility as a dramatic critic. He might work into the notes some publicity matter for his own theater, but it would be legitimate news and there would be no preponderance of material to Donaghey's advantage.

If Percy were unwell or on a party or otherwise indisposed to write his Sunday lead and notes, he would call up Donaghey and ask him to bat for him. Donaghey would write the article and the news items in his own office or at home and bring them in, signed by Percy, so that others at the office would not know of the decep-tion. I knew of it, and I imagine Mr Beck did, but that was because I could recognize the slight distinction between the good imitation and the real thing from that slight difference in individual and personal rhythm from which no writer can escape even in good imitation of another.

But after Donaghey came to work on the paper as music critic he chanced to offend Percy thoughtlessly and without intention. Percy had gone to White Sulphur Springs for a short vacation, and one night when one of the printers in the composing room asked Donaghey where Percy was, Donaghey replied facetiously that he had gone away to take the gold cure.

The printer kiddingly repeated this to Percy when he came back, and thereafter Percy not only never spoke to Donaghey again but carried on an active and continuous one-sided feud with him.

The first page of one of the Sunday feature sections of the *Tribune* was devoted to a two-column leading article by Percy on the left-hand side and a two-column leading article on music by Donaghey on the right-hand side, with a layout of drawings or photographs of musical and theatrical stars in between.

It was my duty as editor in charge of make-up for the Sunday sections to allot space to both Donaghey and Hammond and give them a schedule of the space they would have to fill not only on the first page but in the second- and third-page run-overs. The first-page schedule was determined by the size of the picture lay-out, and the second- and third-page schedules by the space occupied by advertisements.

After their stuff had been set and already in the page form on a movable form table in the composing room, Percy and Donaghey would both come up and stand around it to read proof, make revisions and watch the final lock-up of the forms.

I had to stand between these two men who were not speaking to each other and who glared at each other from a distance of two or three feet. Donaghey was hard of hearing, a circumstance which caused Percy to bandy about the quip, "Joe Patterson has hired a deaf music critic; his next eccentricity will be to hire a blind movie critic."

Taking advantage of Donaghey's slight disability, even taking more advantage of it than the affliction warranted (for Donaghey could pretend not to hear even if he heard distinctly), Percy would say insulting things about Donaghey to me in a growling under-tone loud enough to be heard by anyone much harder of hearing than Donaghey was.

Percy was not, for most people, a reliable guide to the theater; his taste was too shallow from a cultivated point of view, and yet his standards of entertainment were too severe for the average theater patron; his snobbery was specious, inverted and embittered; his prejudices were too picayune and personal to have any genuine universal validity.

One read him, not as a critic and guide, but as an essayist. And, as one reads him now in the volume of collected reviews and essays published under the title *But—Is It Art,* one is astonished that so much sheer talent in the use of words should have been frittered away in comment on second-company performances and theatrical ephemera generally.

In spite of the clever writing the events which called the pieces forth are so dated that even the comment on them seems tarnished.

Since Percy Hammond's death there has been published a volume of encomiums on him by way of an obituary; and in these there are many fine things said about him as a man and as a critic, but the point is missed that he evaded his proper destiny.

Before we got into the war, Percy was violently pro-Ally. This may have been from a genuine emotional sympathy for England and France as against Germany, or it may have been because it was the fashionable attitude adopted by the wealthier classes, particularly those who were socially secure or pretentious in Chicago and New York—and Percy was socially a snob.

At all events it was not, with Percy, a rational feeling or, as events later made clear, a very deep matter emotionally. In his column and elsewhere he denounced President Wilson, damned his cabinet, uttered maledictions against his country as craven and cowardly, yellow and usurious, battening upon the profits made out of civilization's dire plight.

But the moment we did get into war, his own son had to run away from home to enlist because Percy was so frantically opposed to his going to war. Even after John Hammond had joined the Marines, Percy embarrassed his son by pulling every political wire to prevent the boy's seeing action. He was, then, anxious that other fathers' sons should go to war and denounced the government for tardiness in commanding them to do so; but when his own son was involved, it was another matter.

This, of course, was not an attitude idiosyncratic with Percy at the time. I saw examples of it among fathers and mothers on every hand. It showed a touching parental devotion and solicitude but not a high sense of social responsibility.

When we got into the war I had for some time, among my other duties, been covering the theater as second-string dramatic critic, and I was Percy's choice as his substitute when the Chicago *Tribune* decided to send him abroad to report the Peace Conference. When

I was given the post I was not at all diffident about my qualifications for the job. I was young enough (twenty-six) to feel a little superior to it, for it was only an odd job among so many I now was doing.

I was assistant Sunday editor, which meant that I was responsible for many things, including the art layouts of Sunday features, editing, cutting manuscripts, writing proof heads and picture captions and making up, with the assistance of "Andy" Anderson in the composing room, all the feature sections of the paper. I was also rotogravure editor, which meant I looked through all the pictures submitted each day by the news picture agencies, made a selection to submit to J. M. Patterson and, after he had made a final selection, arranged the layouts, wrote the captions and saw the roto section through the press.

The Chicago *Tribune* installed the first rotogravure press in America. I was, then, the first rotogravure editor. I learned later that the rotogravure editor of the New York *World* got $10,000 a year and that was his only job. I got sixty dollars a week after I was made dramatic critic, and the rotogravure editorship was only one of my many jobs.

I was also editor of the "highbrow page"—a page opposite the Sunday editorial page, instituted by J. M. Patterson and later imitated by Herbert Bayard Swope in the New York *World* in his "opposite-editorial" page in which figured F. P. A., Heywood Broun, Deems Taylor, Laurence Stallings, Frank Sullivan, Elsie McCormick, William Bolitho, St. John Ervine, Harry Hansen, *et al.*

I was also editor and chief critic of the Saturday Page of Book Reviews which had already aroused considerable attention and controversy. I was called upon to write the two-column display advertisement of our Sunday features to be run in the daily. (Mr Beck called me the Pooh-Bah or McAdoo of the paper. William Gibbs McAdoo was famous at that time for the number of important jobs he held under the war administration in addition to his position in Wilson's cabinet.)

So I took dramatic criticism in my stride. But there were two other and somewhat older men in the office who were more experienced in writing about the theater than I was, and both of them wanted the job. One of them was James O'Donnell Bennett, a man who had attained some eminence as a drama critic on the *Record-Herald* but who, unfortunately and unfairly, was then under a cloud which would have made his appointment as dramatic critic inadvisable from a publishing point of view, even if such an appointment had not been fought tooth and nail by Percy Hammond, which it would have been, of course.

Percy would have refused the European assignment—his chance to report the Peace Conference at Versailles—rather than have Bennett bat for him in his absence. He would have been afraid that Bennett would win too many admirers. Young and inexperienced as I was, I realized that it was no compliment to me that Percy should nominate me as his substitute. He did not want anyone in there who would jeopardize his popularity.

Vaguely it may also have been in his mind that I then regarded dramatic criticism as one of the lowest forms of ambition, a step lower, if anything, than literary criticism if practised as a form of journalism, requiring words for or against the day-by-day products of the pen and typewriter and not as considerations of such absolute and relative values as you find in Aristotle, Longinus, Liebnitz, Lessing, Hazlitt, Sainte-Beuve and, occasionally, Shaw, Walkley and George Jean Nathan.

Percy was also percipient, and he probably figured that I, with my irreverence for sacred cows and my negligence in the matter of making social connections and pushing ahead in the way of salary demands, should probably last just long enough for him to get back and take over the reins. I didn't last that long.

James O'Donnell Bennett was there in the local room, with a salary, of course, but with nothing specifically to do. He should have had the job Percy turned over to me. His whole ambition had been concentrated on being a great dramatic critic. Patiently and conservatively he had gone far toward achieving that ambition. Then the war had broken out just when James Keeley had scored such a bust in running the *Record-Herald* as a competitor to his old paper, the *Tribune* (on Rosenwald and other department-store money), and Bennett had been drafted by the *Tribune* as their correspondent with the German armies.

Bennett had been a correspondent for the Chicago *Journal* in the

Spanish-American War and, although his heart was in the theater, he readily took up the active journalist's life to report a war instead of pining for the sedentary work of dramatic criticism, especially since that was about the only job available to him at the time.

Bennett, as a war correspondent during the World War, made the explicable but fatal mistake of assuming that we, so long as we had not declared war upon Germany, were neutral and that his dispatches, therefore, should have a flavor of truth so far as he was able to discern the truth.

Attached as he was, as an accredited correspondent, to the German Great Headquarters and there made comfortable and given limited facilities for getting news, he neglected to report that the Germans were degenerate ogres who cut off the breasts of virgins and were so inefficient that they were defeated in every brush with the Allies—he admired dispassionately the impersonal German war machine and accurately reported its victories—victories so great that Paris was within an ace of being taken.

Other reporters were swallowing the leaflets of the British agency for propaganda.

It may have been that Bennett was so well taken care of by the Germans that htere was at times an adulatory tinge in his dispatches.

I never noticed this, but my friend, Keith Preston, wrote a privately circulated verselet against Bennett. All I remember about it was that Bennett had visited Great Headquarters and had been kissing Great Hindquarters ever since.

Knowing Keith, I don't think he had any feeling against Bennett at all, but that "headquarters-hindquarters" offered him a happy opportunity to make a funny quatrain.

But, anyhow, Bennett was in the doghouse at the *Tribune* shortly after we entered the war. He had been recalled, and so high had run the feelings of those who were against the Germans (and they were in the majority, or we should never have entered the war) that the Chicago *Tribune* was afraid to sign his name to anything he wrote.

H. L. Mencken wrote me at the time that Bennett was the only American war correspondent before we got into the war who had any sense of responsibility about his job. Mencken, of course, was pro-German, as he had every right to be at a time when we were officially neutral but when even German-born American patriots were physically and emotionally pro-Ally.

John Reed, Harvard graduate, romanticist, amateur of excitement, was posted then as American war correspondent with the German troops reporting for the *Metropolitan* magazine. Alongside him in the trenches was Robert S. ("Bobby") Dunn of the *Saturday Evening Post*. Reed saw a French helmet, and it occurred to him that this was a good target. He asked for a gun. He aimed and fired. He committed a murder in cold blood, because he was not even a combatant. And he wrote about it to his magazine as though it were a lark. The French officials went up in the air with indignation and made John Reed *persona non grata* on French soil.

When I read Reed's account of this escapade in the *Metropolitan* (reaction had not then set in against it) my stomach turned several flip-flops. It was, indeed, one of the most violent responses I had ever experienced in watching the activities of those who professedly are out to do the most good for us.

I had seen Reed just once. He was then a lad not long out of college, with great personal charm and animation. But, Socialist as I was then—as, I think, all decent persons must be who have in mind the central promise of the Messiah proclaimed two thousand years ago that all men and women shall have equal chance and equal justice in this world, in a realization some time to mature—I could not look upon him as a leader. I was much too serious for that.

We were at a labor meeting on the West Side, Chicago. I was a reporter he wanted to provide copy for. The event he had invited me to had proved to be routine, parliamentary. We went out together to the Men's Room. He stood there buttoning up his fly in a urinal, and then turned to me in excited impatience. "This is a bum show," he said. "Let's go over to another place where there will be some excitement."

He had taken me to a labor meeting, as a reporter for the *Tribune,* on the belief that the labor leaders would work up into a fight among themselves about something and that I should find a story. I had got one and was ready to write it. In fact, I did write it; but Jack Reed didn't think the show was exciting or *funny* enough. He wanted to show me some real rough stuff. He thought that what I had seen and heard wasn't exciting enough for a newspaper. The next day he learned differently, because what I wrote about the meeting had its own quiet, tremendous drama.

Reed wanted noise, fist fights and raids by the police. I did not follow him. I went back, told my city editor there would be another meeting and what might happen and wrote my story. It was given column space on page four, just what it deserved. Jack Reed's exciting meeting did not pan out. No bones were broken, no skulls smashed by the warring proletarians.

John Reed, dead of typhus in Moscow, is now only slightly less important as an ikon than Lenin himself. And this, I think, is sweet, justifiable tribute to a man who loved life, but something of a grim joke on the Russians.

The other tacit candidate for the job as Hammond's substitute was Sheppard Butler, who had been Bennett's assistant on the *Record-Herald* and who, after the sale of the *Record-Herald* to Hearst, had come back to the *Tribune* as a special-assignment reporter and attaché of the Sunday room.

Sheppard's first assignment on his return to the *Tribune* was one he gave himself. It was an exposé story of the South State Street hootchy-kootchy and "come-on" shows.

About six months before this I had written a series of exposé news stories on this poor racket, but it was always good for a feature story, like the circus or Coney Island.

Just south of the Loop on State Street there were some old nickelodeons, hang-overs from the days when you could see a Keystone comedy and hear a contralto sing "The Rosary" for a nickel.

The contralto was usually hired in reverse recognition of her artistic abilities. That is, if she was awful she got the job; if she could sing at all, she didn't. Her function was not to charm the audience but to get them out of the theater.

The profit in the nickelodeons lay entirely in a quick turn-over— a new audience every hour all day long from eleven in the morning to midnight.

Bums had the habit of using the theater as a place to sleep, and other people used it as a place to kill time. The contralto was hired to make it unpleasant for anyone who had come in for anything except to see the show—once—and leave.

By the time Butler came back to the *Tribune* the movies had developed so rapidly as a recognized form of popular entertainment that motion-picture theaters had opened in the Loop, charging ten and fifteen cents for admission. *The Birth of a Nation* had been shown in the Illinois Theater in an atmosphere, on the opening night, like that of the annual première of the Ziegfeld Follies. Patrons attended in tail coats and tuxedos, collapsible opera hats and shiny toppers, low-cut backs (on the women) and trains.

The *Tribune* had taken note of the phenomenon by appointing a motion-picture critic with the trade name of Mae Tinee. That name was supposed to suggest to the average reader the French-English word, "matinee." This was an assumption that if people went to the movies at all they would go there only on afternoons.

Or it may have been a bit of *blague* on the part of Joseph Medill Patterson, whose sense of fun was so juvenile that he thought people would take delight in recognizing the pun on the word "matinee."

Patterson himself never went to the movies until four o'clock in the afternoon, at which time he dragged Clifford Raymond or Tiffany Blake away from their work to accompany him to a showing of a picture of Mack Sennett bathing beauties. He would take his place in the queue, with Clifford (who did not want to see the show anyhow) just behind him, and he would plank down his dime, leaving Clifford to dig down for his dime also.

Later Patterson might take Raymond to Schlogl's Restaurant and, having ordered for himself the rarest vintage wine in the Schlogl cellar (Raymond loathed all wines and took only whisky), would propose to Raymond that they split the check. Raymond would pay his half, even if what he consumed was only about a tenth of the total bill, because Patterson was his boss.

Mae Tinee's stuff, however, became one of the most popular features of the paper. I don't know how many times I purred with satisfaction in reply to persons who learned I was on the *Tribune,* and said, "Yes, I know her very well," when I was asked if I was personally acquainted with May Tinney.

She got her audience agog largely by printing, week after week, a question from one of her readers and answering, "Francis X. Bushman *says* he is not married."

Mr Bushman was married, and he had a wife and some children; but it was thought then that a male movie star would lose box-office value as an attraction for women if it became known that he had a wife and, therefore, was not generally available to the several million women who thrilled at the display, on the screen, of his magnificent physique and beautiful profile.

Mr Bushman's women admirers were jealous of his beautiful co-star, Beverly Bayne, and they demanded to know if it was true that he was married to her. Mae Tinee would reply, "Francis X. Bushman *says* he is not married."

It would seem that, in sheer self-defense, Mr Bushman did get rid of his wife and marry Miss Bayne. And when he did, that was about the last any of us ever heard of him as a star attraction. And he was beautiful (in the Greek tradition as we have had it from old vases, bits of sculpture and Alma-Tadema); and Miss Bayne was beautiful, also, by almost any standard.

The movies, therefore, had just begun to lose out as attractions for the cloaca maxima of South State Street.

The managements not only could not pay the price demanded by the distributors for the better films; they could not even continue to live without offering to the sailors and other floaters something to bring them into the theater. Whereas they had had to employ contraltos who screeched to drive the patrons out, they now had to offer some form of entertainment to bring them in.

They hired hootchy-kootchy dancers. The hootchy-kootchy dancers displaced the film offering as the object of entertainment.

The films as they were run off were spotted, faint and jerky; they justified Percy Hammond's snobbishly sarcastic reference to all movies as "the hopping pictures."

But the hootchy-kootchy dancers gave full value for the money. They were elaborately sensual and, in the technical definition of the word, obscene. In their movements they portrayed all the provocations and consummations of lust.

In their domestic life, however, these women were very proper. I made it a point to know several of them, and one of them, as an example, had three children and a husband who worked in the steel mills, and she got in salary twelve dollars a week.

As a reporter I had known all this before Sheppard Butler came on the scene.

During the year 1913 the Chicago Woman's Club was active in reforms of all sorts. In the autumn of 1913 the club inaugurated a campaign against sex in literature and drew up a "black list" of authors.

As a reporter I covered these proceedings, and in Appendix II will be found a verbatim reprint of the first-page story I wrote for the *Tribune* when the clubwomen drew up the "black list."

It may now seem incredible to read this report and learn the names of the authors put on the "black list" as "sexy" authors— Edith Wharton, Winston Churchill, Joseph Conrad, E. Phillips Oppenheim, Robert Herrick, Robert W. Chambers, Harold Mac-Grath and Hall Caine!

One phrase of Mrs Edwin Theodore Johnson's remarks taken from this news story was seized upon by liberal editorial writers and liberal literary critics in various cities and derided: "A good criterion upon which to judge a book, to my notion, is ask yourself whether you would tolerate the hero or heroine in real life. The situation today is such that we would not relish the acquaintance of the characters of our novelists."

To this foolish pronouncement liberal writers answered with sarcasm and invective, flinging at the imperturbable woman (imperturbable because she was wealthy, of assured social position in the suburban community of Oak Park, and a member of that powerful organization, the Chicago Woman's Club, which could scare the chief of police into the feverish activity of harrying harlots, intimidate aldermen and give orders to members of the school board) such names of heroes and heroines of sacred and classical literature, as Delilah, Jezebel, Bathsheba, Lady Macbeth, Iago, Falstaff, Richard III, Moll Flanders, Emma Bovary, Anna Karenina, Lilith and Mother Eve herself.

Such a "black list," of course, merely gave free advertising to best sellers which stood in no special need of advertisement; but it was the sort of thing to frighten publishers, because women make up the bulk of the book-buying public; the example of the Chicago Woman's Club would stir women's clubs in smaller cities to censorship activities; books would be burned and banned (as they were), and publishers themselves would be branded as conducing to immorality.

Meanwhile, one of the many reform activities of the Chicago Woman's Club undertaken during 1913 was to close up the hootchy-kootchy shows on South State Street. Mrs George Bass, president of the club, told me over the phone of an investigation the club was about to make and asked me if I would accompany one of the members of the club on a tour of investigation. I asked the day city editor, Captain Stott, for the assignment and got it.

A young Gold Coast matron came to the office on the first evening of our tour, and we started out. She had obviously led the sheltered life of a typical daughter of Chicago society—private school, finishing school, trips abroad, perhaps presentation at the Court of St. James's, coming-out party, marriage to a socially eligible young man, children and, being of a serious turn of mind, a dilettante in social welfare.

She had doubtless volunteered for this excursion into the underworld of Chicago. I took her to the first show on the right two blocks south of the elevated on South State.

The show was the usual one. An "aesthetic dancer" came out and did a version of "The Dying Swan" and, on encore, a Vishnu dance with arms and hands while sitting cross-legged on the floor. Two broken-down comedians did a slapstick bit, then the first of the hootchy-kootchy dancers appeared. She was youngish, rather pretty, and her job was to be demurely provocative, for the program of such shows is a work-up to real animal sensuality.

The house was three-quarters full of blear-eyed, unkempt men, sailors on leave, and a spattering of ill-dressed, drab young women, most of them probably picked up on the streets by their escorts. Many among the audience had no doubt come in, not to see the show especially, but to get warm (at the cost of five cents), for some of them were dozing and others were sound asleep throughout the performance.

But my companion was not dozing or asleep. She was visibly struggling with the emotions of shame, curiosity and excitement. She was blushing, but her eyes were glittering; she gasped and kept muttering, "How awful!"—"How terrible!"

But her excitement grew as the show went on to its climax.

Outside (after the show, which lasted only twenty minutes) she asked where the next show was.

I told her it was only three doors down, but that she didn't need to go there, because it was almost exactly like the one she had seen—all of them were—and she could write her report from that one show and merely list the others.

I had a list ready for her.

But no, she wanted to see them all, and see them all she did, not only once but several times, almost every night for nearly three weeks, sometimes seeing only one show, but seeing one she especially liked four times.

I, of course, was pledged not to write anything about the investigation until the report was in and the club had decided upon what action to take.

So I had no work to do except see hootchy-kootchy shows with this silly young woman who was getting the thrill of her life and yet was going to write a report which would result in a raid that would throw a lot of poor unfortunate women, ushers, screen shifters, candy peddlers and ticket sellers out of work.

It took her four weeks to write her report, and for all I know she may have found it necessary to see, in company with someone else, some of the shows more times than she had seen them with me.

Meanwhile I had made acquaintance with the managers, who were usually rat-faced, suspicious individuals, and through them, with the performers, visiting their homes, learning what their salaries were and how they lived.

Most of the hootchy-kootchy dancers were married and had children; moreover, they were mostly very religious and sticklers for the bourgeois conventions, which is true also of harlots as a class, clinging more closely to the conventions of a society of which they feel themselves outcasts than possibly they would if they were as respectable as they would like to be.

I warned the performers of the raids to come and told them to seek other work if they could get it.

Most of them received this news with sunken and dismal countenances, saying there was no work for them to find—they had tried it—for this was the year of a depression which was not in-

terrupted until a few months later by the outbreak of the war in
Europe.

So I warned the managers that they had better tone down their
shows.

But the young matron's report was finally in. I think it was about
one typewritten page long, including the names and addresses of
the theaters; it was almost illiterate and said nothing except that
what she had seen was "appalling, demoralizing, a pandering to the
lusts of men, and a disgrace to the city."

The report was read, recommendations were made and the chief
of police was notified on the authority of the Chicago Woman's
Club that he would have to close the shows or the club would demand the mayor to remove him. The chief of police probably went
to Alderman Michael ("Hinky Dink") Kenna and Alderman
("Bathouse") John Coughlin and told them about it.

The theater managers were doubtless paying tribute to the
First Ward organization controlled by "Hinky Dink" and "Bathouse John," so the stage was set; the raids took place; the women
were rushed in Black Marias to the police station, booked and
jailed, and later released—wageless—until the agitation should die
down.

The newspapers carried news stories of the spectacular police
action; the Chicago Woman's Club received credit for cleaning
up a section of the city; the chief of police was praised for his
efficiency and moral stamina.

In my story in the *Tribune* I was careful to work in what I had
found out about the kind of women employed as hootchy-kootchy
dancers, the wages they received, how respectable their personal
lives were, and how they would now be thrown out of work at a
time when work was hard to get—not with any editorializing, however, because it was then the pride of the *Tribune* and its reporters
that the paper published facts, not opinion, in its news columns.

By the time Sheppard Butler came back to work on the *Tribune*
the hootchy-kootchy shows had been supplanted by the "men-
only" "come-on" shows.

Butler, who had come back as general assignment man for both
the daily and Sunday sections, proposed as his first assignment an
exposé of the "come-on" shows.

At these "men-only" shows the patrons, who were mainly yokels from towns, farms and villages and suckers of all kinds, were victims of a crude duplicity. The "men-only" shows thrived upon the publicity that a moral wave had just swept the city and, therefore, they were prurient and dishonest, whereas the hootchy-kootchy shows preceding them were merely openly sensual and vulgar.

Only males over eighteen were admitted—much point was made of this—and the ballyhoo was a loud-whispered one, inexplicit and suggestive, about "revelations of the female form divine and the portrayals of passion."

The customer paid a nickel for a ticket and, standing up (for there were no seats), saw three youngish women clothed in tights and bloomers, almost fully clothed in fact, go through about a three-minute routine of shaking their hips. The show was purposely disappointing; the ballyhoo man would seize upon the very disappointment he had created by telling about "the real thing, Oriental dances, voluptuous women," which might be seen inside the next curtain for fifteen cents more. He proclaimed that he did not dare advertise this performance outside because of the vigilance of the police.

The suckers who had fifteen cents usually were drawn into the second show, which was also a three-minute performance, somewhat like the hootchy-kootchy shows described above, but brief, to create more disappointment.

Then the spieler would describe in his most enticing rhetoric the daring, the dazzling, the bawdy performance to be seen downstairs for a quarter. This last, also, took only a few minutes and was very like the second performance, only there were more women, all older, fatter and more haggard-looking than the others. A door would open into the alley, and the spieler would hurry the crowd out.

When the duties of a dramatic critic were added to my other duties, I wrote this apologia, with, I am afraid, a touch of tongue-in-cheek humility:

Mr Hammond is now nearing Belgian shores, bound upon his errand of mercy and of joy to the tortured readers of cable dispatches. Soon, if Mr Creel is just and the telegraphers careful, we shall have from him news that is literature. He will look about him in Brussels and in Paris and observe matters of deep human interest which have escaped the others, and he will write about them in a fashion which no one else has done, or, I think, can do.

There is no one in this country who, in the common phrase, can touch him at writing of the drama, because there is no one so writing who has at once his endowment of wit, his sense of prose style, his knowledge of life, his instinct for values, and his general cultivation. And with this in mind, the reasons should not be far to seek why he, of all foreign correspondents, may be relied upon for the most distinctive, the most readable, and the best written articles from abroad.

Were he dependent solely upon the arid soil of the current theater for the fruition of his pen it would never yield that cornucopia of sapient and piquant epigram with which he so delights us. Happily his thought takes root in the subsoil of life, and, seeming to spring from the barren crust, it actually does not. To unscramble the metaphor, he uses criticism of the theater largely as an excuse for talking of more vital things, the while giving the lesser interest the attention it merits and the criticism it deserves. Now comes his opportunity to dispense with the frail pretext and to deal freehanded with a larger theme.

"Genuine humor and true wit," says Walter Savage Landor, "require a sound and capacious mind, which is always a grave one." Beneath the subtle fun of Mr Hammond there is that gravity of which Landor speaks. It is the mark of the satirist, and the satirist is society's greatest friend because he is its frankest critic: his strictures arise not from misanthropy but from sympathy, a fine and hopeful sympathy. A scourge of mediocrity, a nemesis of pretentiousness, a flagellant of the vicious, the evil, and the unjust, the satirist is so out of pity, vision, and of hope. His praise is valuable because it is always a tribute to true worth; his sentiment affecting because it is without trace of the maudlin or the sentimental; his convictions sound because they are rationally considered.

In the great company of gallant gentlemen, the gentle satirists, Mr Hammond is one. That is one reason why, unless you are a potential recipient of his thrusts, you will miss him each week of his absence from this column.

Meanwhile, I ask you to be patient with the substitute he has left behind to make shift at doing his dramatic work. The *Tribune* was reluctant, I assure you, to relieve him even temporarily of these duties, but it had need of his services in the gathering of the momentous news which is to attend the settling of the problems over there. It could not well retain him in both offices, so in the emergency I was asked to occupy with what grace I might the capacious chair he left behind.* He will be back ere long and in this interlude the loss to this department will be the news section's gain.

Already admirers of Mr Hammond are writing of me to the managing editor: "Throw him out! Give us Hammond!" I don't blame them in the least; but they are under a slight misapprehension: this evil is unavoidable. It is an expedient, not the grotesque displacement they very irrationally assume it is. Did some presumptuous pantaloon attempt to don Mr Hammond's robes in permanent office I would be howling for the culprit's hide with the best of them, and not anonymously but with full name and address. But I was requisitioned from the realm of books to do sentry at the drama because, unfortunately, Mr Hammond cannot be in Belgium and in Chicago at the same time.

To those outraged but timid clamorers for the absent critic I extend not merely my heartiest sympathy (for I shall miss his criticism of the drama as much as any of you) but I so heartily agree with their position as profoundly to wish that something might be done about it. Since nothing can be, let us sit like patience on a monument, waiting with a green and yellow melancholy the real critic of the drama's return. And if my stuff gets too infernally bad, let's stop reading it.

Being a dramatic critic was fun (of a kind) while it lasted. Percy Hammond had accustomed his audiences to expect big words: I would give them bigger ones. I called upon my knowledge of Greek and Latin for Anglicizing Greek and Latin compounds not to be found in any dictionary. Such tongue-in-cheek japery as this brought me many letters of admiring and friendly inquiry as to what the words meant. Even my use of the word "lamp-sacene," which is to be found in all unabridged dictionaries, in the following first paragraph excerpt of my review of a Raymond Hitchcock show caused a dispute to break out among B. L. T.'s contributors:

Well, Raymond Hitchcock is back in town with his 1918 model *Hitchy Koo*. And at the Illinois last night he proved an intimate and solicitous chauffeur to a commodious and gaudy bus, which was filled with jokes and jazbo, shapely girls and roughhouse comedians,

*When I wrote "capacious chair," it occurred to me to add, in parenthesis, "His behind is as big as that of a rhinoceros"; but to do so would have destroyed the sweet, solemn effect of my bogus tribute.

soloists in song and in the hootchy-kootchy, experts in the clog and graduates in the pinwheel and handspring, collapsible scenery and Byzantine gowns—all the prismatic contrivances and funny didos that go to make a success of the Hitchcock shows. It was a tuneful, ridiculous and lampsacene evening, running far beyond the time when theater critics should be back to their jobs. . . .

Percy Hammond had accustomed his readers to a show of learning: I would go him one better. For my leading article on Sundays, I drew upon Professor Roy Flickinger's magnificent work of scholarship, *The Greek Theater and Its Drama* and my knowledge of Athenian comedy for mock-solemn disquisitions on the psychology of laughter and on the intellectual superiority of the better musical comedies to the better operas and the better offerings of serious drama, apropos of Raymond Hitchcock and also apropos of a letter some noodle had written to the New York *Sun* saying that musical comedies insulted the intelligence of the audience. After writing a column and a half of rebuttal to the *Sun* correspondent who had unwittingly given me something to write about, I wrote:

And what of Mr Hitchcock? Here is a man who knows that the very enunciation of the name, Vincent Geranium, will bring a laugh; that calling one man Pew-eblo Pete and another Don Oleo, and another Capt. Frijole is funny; that a kick in the rear, the mispronunciation of a word, a reference to Flatbush, Brooklyn, the hives, simple-mindedness, the unexpected, a play on words, or the spectacle of a man in a top hat and frock coat pushing a perambulator tickles the midriff and sets laughter going. Why, I don't know, but it does.

And that is all he wants to do: he has no fancy for making you believe that a particularly abandoned Cyprian of his chorus was suddenly transformed into a self-sacrificing angel, capable of the moral decision of sacrificing her lover to save an army which has been cut off, or of believing that such a thing was possible on the part of a girl telephone operator during the war—vide, *The Crowded Hour.*

No. Mr Hitchcock is merely a man who has figured out the psychology of the laugh to a finer degree than any nine out of ten dramatists have figured out the psychology of human relations, a more acute observer of human reactions to the risible than the average dramatist is of such plain matters as the war orders and newspaper reports. He knows where the risqué ends and the coarse begins and treads not there. He knows that the marriage relation is a greater mine for laughter than for problem plays; that to be chummy with your audience means to win them to your drolleries and put them in the right mood for your fooling; that the success of burlesque is in direct ratio to its harmless violence, and that the sight of himself as a stage father knocking a crying baby out cold with what he calls a nursery blackjack is a scream. It is not an insult to the intelligence to watch him work: it is profoundly interesting—if you can stop laughing long enough to concentrate.

Of course Mr Hitchcock's method, and that of his librettist, is the tried and honored method of Aristophanes, which consisted and consists mainly of the use of the *para prosdokian* (the unexpected) and of the *paronomasia* (the play on words). When Mr Hitchcock speaks of a Tudor house as having an entrance in the front and another in the back, he is employing the same device that knocked them out of the stone seats in the Theater Dionysius in Athens about 450 B.C.; and when he has himself introduced as the Prohi speaker, Mr Raindrop, he is doing the same thing in another way that the author of *The Frogs* did when he had Dionysius, customarily referred to as the Son of Zeus, call himself the Son of the—Winejug. But it just happens that the possible comic situations and tricks are only about two dozen in number, and it also just happens that slight variations of them are perennially funny, and that the kick *a posteriori* will bring a laugh in 2000 A.D., as it did when the sublimated slave directed it against the Wine-god, and as it does when Miss Ray Dooley directs it against Mr Hitchcock during a comic spasm in *Hitchy Koo*.

It is not the suave and more lasting humor of the comedy of manners, of Congreve, Molière, Sheridan, Wilde, and Shaw. It gives not the delight of an epigram, or the pleasure of an ingenious paradox. It is not "a singular and unavoidable manner of doing or saying anything, peculiar and natural to one man only, by which his speech and actions are distinguished from those of other men." It is not "cogency in a modish cynicism." But it has the dignity of age and the virtue of making people laugh. And who would say that Aristophanes' turn for uproarious farce is not a greater attribute than the turn of the later comedists of ideas; and that Mr Hitchcock's provocation to laughter by burlesque is not as important a matter as A. E. Thomas' stimulation to "thought" in *As a Man Thinks?*

Often I would be stuck with a Sunday "lead" to write and no ideas in my head. I had not trained myself like contemporary New

York columnists and contemporary political commentators like Walter Lippmann not to let that deter me, so I had sometimes to scurry around in search of something I could use. On one occasion, for instance, my job as literary editor as well as dramatic critic stood me in good stead. I came upon an anthology of theatrical criticism from Aristotle to modern times, compiled by Barrett H. Clark, just in time to save me worry one December afternoon in 1918. As I read these theories and opinions of the drama by famous critics of ancient and recent times, I was struck by the fact that nearly every one of them was possessed by the illusion that, whereas in his own day the drama had fallen into decay and was a mere pandering to low public taste, the drama of a former day (drama the critic had not witnessed) had been of a very high standard.

I wrote an introduction and a final line and put as a heading to the piece, "The Theater Isn't What It Used to Be, and It Never Was." (I have since seen New York critics and columnists use that quip, but I think I was the first to make it.) Clark's book, a valuable one still, was entitled *European Theories of the Drama*. The excerpts I quoted are so instructive and they make such a *reductio ad absurdum* of critical estimates of contemporary drama at any time that I quote them:

FERDINAND BRUNETIÈRE: "That the contemporary drama is inferior as a whole to the drama of only twenty or twenty-five years ago, it seems to me difficult not to admit. People no longer know how to exert their will. We are broken-winded, as the poet says. We are abandoning ourselves." [1894.]

RICHARD WAGNER: "We are primarily concerned with the purification of a great and many-sided department of art—that of the drama as a whole—the errors of which are today both increased and concealed by the influence of the modern opera." [1871.]

CHARLES LAMB: "The artificial comedy or comedy of manners is quite extinct in our age." [1823.]

GOETHE: "Intellect and some poetry cannot be denied to our modern tragic poets, but most of them are incapable of an easy, living representation; they strive after something beyond their powers, and for that reason I might call them forced talents." [1823.]

DIDEROT: "Thus has the art of the drama become surcharged with rules; and the dramatists, in servilely subjecting themselves to them, have often gone to much pain and done less well than they might have done." [1758.]

OLIVER GOLDSMITH: "Honor at present seems to be departing from the stage, and it will soon happen that our comic players will have nothing left for it but a fine coat and a song." [1772.]

CARLO GOLDONI: "It is now time for Italy to proclaim that in her the seeds of good authorship are not dried up." [1751.]

JOSEPH ADDISON: "The English writers of tragedy are possessed with a notion that when they represent a virtuous or innocent person in distress they ought not to leave him till they have delivered him out of his troubles. This error they have been led into by a ridiculous doctrine in modern criticism." [1711.]

JOHN DRYDEN: "I can never see one of those plays which are now written but it increases my admiration of the ancients." [1679.]

JEAN RACINE: "We should like our works to be as solid and full of useful instruction as were those of antiquity." [1669.]

MIGUEL DE CERVANTES: "I was discouraged, too, whenever I reflected on the present state of the drama and the absurdity and incoherence of most of our modern comedies." [1605.]

SIR PHILIP SIDNEY: "Our tragedies observe rules neither of honest civility nor of skillful poetry." [1595.]

HORACE: "Our poets have left no species of the [dramatic] art unattempted; nor have those of them merited the least honor who dared to forsake the footsteps of the Greeks." [24 B.C.]

ARISTOTLE: "It [the happy ending] has had a vogue only by the imbecility of the judgment of the spectators, and those who practise it are gratifying the tastes of the populace and write according to the desires of their audiences." [384–322 B.C.]

Q. E. D.: The drama has always been bad art.

The fun of reviewing plays and of writing Sunday essays on the theater, however, soon wore off, especially when it was only one of six exacting jobs I was holding on the paper at the same time, each one of which would ordinarily be described as "full-time." After a while it became a chore of the most onerous kind.

Chicago was then, and throughout the first two decades of the century, second in importance to New York as a theatrical center; and at the opening of the season and through the height of it I had to cover as many as five openings a week, and every week I had to write a Sunday essay and get up a column or more of news notes by selecting and rewriting material sent in by the theater press agents.

This meant that, with my other jobs, my day began at eight o'clock in order that I might be at the office by nine for my other duties and that it lasted until three o'clock the next morning, since I rarely left the office until two in the morning (because I always read proof on my copy for the final edition) and it took me an hour to get home and to bed. On Thursday and Friday nights, which were make-up nights for the Sunday sections of which I was in charge, I often never went to bed at all. On these nights I did not finish my work until five o'clock in the morning; so went home merely to take a bath, put on fresh linen and have breakfast. On Sundays I could sleep for twelve or fifteen hours, but on Saturdays never, so my daily average of sleep was less than five hours.

I shall never cease to be astonished at those perennial Peter Pans of dramatic criticism, such as Ashton Stevens, for instance. Stevens has been drama critic for the Hearst papers in Chicago for thirty-four years and yet has never lost any of what must have been his first eager wild-eyed delight in the things concerning the theater. He never seems bored either in the lobby on a first night or in his review the following morning. He appears to approach each new performance with the happy expectation of a young girl at her first party; and if he suffers disappointment, he seems to say to himself and in his review, "Well, better luck next time!" He has probably seen more theatrical performances than any other man living or than any two other drama critics still active in the profession; his judgment and taste are sound; he knows a good performance from a bad one; his criticism can be as severe in actual point as anybody's. Still, his urbanity and tolerance never forsake him; his style remains fresh and sprightly; he admonishes gently, he does not scold or turn waspish; he does not waste energy and adjectives by getting wrought up over a bad play which, experience has taught him, will have a brief enough life anyway without his having to exert himself by whamming at it with might and main.

I couldn't do it. After a term of one season as a critic of the drama in Chicago I could not be dragged into the theater for five years to see anything except the Ziegfeld Follies (in the brave days of Fannie Brice, Bert Williams, W. C. Fields, Will Rogers, Jack Donahue, Eddie Cantor and Marilyn Miller). After going to the theater with me on opening nights four or five times a week for two months, my wife simply refused to go with me any more unless she knew pretty well beforehand that it was something she was going to like; and I did not blame her in the least.

In those days, before Chicago was reduced, as it is now, to practically only one theater for musical comedy or dramatic performances by the turning of nearly all the theaters in the Loop into motion-picture houses, Chicago was almost as much a producing center as New York. And a phenomenon existed: plays which were great hits in New York would flop in Chicago and vice versa, excepting always the Ziegfeld, George M. Cohan, Raymond Hitchcock and Al Jolson shows, equally popular in both cities, the casts and ensembles of which came to Chicago intact. *Abie's Irish Rose,* which enjoyed a record run in New York, was a comparative bust in Chicago. Two plays of distinctive merit (to recall but two), *A Pair of Silk Stockings* and *Hindle Wakes,* after New York would have little of either, came to Chicago and enjoyed long prosperity. *Eyes of Youth* had its première in Chicago; ran for a long time there; folded rather quickly in New York; and ran for more than two years in London—with the same company. Chicago was hospitable to the Irish Players of the Abbey Theater, whereas New York was hostile to them.

Players would be drawing cards in one city and box-office failures in the other. Mrs Minnie Maddern Fiske, for instance, was a pet of New York playgoers, and it was the fashion to admire her there extravagantly; on the last occasion she played in Chicago, as I recall, her art was so lightly esteemed she had to take her vehicle to McVicker's, immemorially a vaudeville theater, for a not very profitable week. Nijinsky, Mordkin and Pavlowa enjoyed more popularity in Chicago than they did in New York: Pavlowa, indeed, was such a hit in Chicago that the Eckstein brothers (restaurant owners, entrepreneurs, publishers of the *Red Book, Blue Book* and *Green Book* magazines, and producers of open-air operas by the Chicago Opera Company and open-air symphony concerts by the Chicago Symphony Company and open-air Shakespearean productions by the Ben Greet Players at Ravinia Park) gave her a year's contract at a startling salary to dance nightly at their newly completed Edelweiss Gardens at the corner of Cottage Grove Avenue and the Midway Plaisance on the South Side.

These Gardens were probably the most disastrous venture of the Eckstein brothers, financially. They engaged Frank Lloyd Wright, the architect, to draw up the plans for an elaborate open-air restaurant, with terraces and porticoes, an outdoor stage and dance floor and an inclosed dining room with stage and orchestra pit to be used in inclement weather. Wright produced one of his masterworks. The Gardens were, in every way, of restful and relaxing beauty. But after a brief spell of curiosity patronage, the Gardens were practically deserted night after night. I had day work then in the Sunday department, and we lived two blocks away from the Gardens; prices at the Gardens were reduced to figures within our means in a vain effort to draw patronage; so we went two or three evenings a week to watch the incomparable Pavlowa dance. There might be no more than a dozen other couples in the place, yet her performance was ever flawless. The fault was not Pavlowa's: it was simply that patrons of the better-class restaurants with floor shows and dance orchestras lived on the North Side; residents of the higher class on the South Side dined at home; those who went dancing on the South Side were office workers, salesmen and clerks, who preferred the beer-and-dance halls and the jazz orchestra cabarets. The Gardens were closed; Pavlowa was paid the full amount of her contract; and after a while the white elephant was demolished.

New York theatrical producers never seemed to make this elementary and obvious observation of the difference between the tastes of New Yorkers and Chicagoans for the drama. As a result they would compound error with error. No sooner would some trashy piece of playwrighting prove to be a success in New York than they would hastily organize a road company of second-rate actors and shoot it out to Chicago. There it would meet with the venom of Percy Hammond of the *Tribune,* "Doc" Hall of the *Journal,* Charley Collins of the *Post,* James O'Donnell Bennett of the *Herald* and with the polite dismissal of Ashton Stevens; the public would avoid it; and in a day or two the show could curl up and die.

In those days of the Nineteen-twenties the record would seem to indicate that the standard of taste in the drama was much higher among Chicagoans than it was in New York. But this was not, I think, the explanation. The explanation lies more probably in the fact that whereas the daily influx of sightseers and buyers from out of town is vast in New York, it is small in Chicago. Sightseers and buyers have to do something with their evenings, so they go to the theater and night-club shows, good or bad indiscriminately; if they can't get tickets for one show, they will go to another one.

Chicago patrons of the theater, except for an inveterate group of first-nighters, stayed home unless there was something in the theater they were fairly certain they would enjoy. The failure of New York producers to take cognizance of this and think twice (or, if that was too much of an effort, once) before sending to Chicago a road company in a Broadway show that was primarily put on in hope of a sale to Hollywood, is doubtless the reason why the theaters of Chicago's Rialto, once prosperous with the best then current in American drama, are now motion-picture houses and there is usually only one legitimate theater available to producers.

This situation would have suited me fine when I was drama critic in Chicago. To go to the theater night after night and find three out of five shows a bore; to rush back to the office and write a sizable review in forty-five minutes—that got on my nerves, especially since I was conscientious and strove to make my review not only informative but readable and entertaining in itself. I always made the deadline of the first city edition, and when it came off the press I would go over it carefully for correction and improvement for the final.

As a result of this I got to having hair-raising dreams about the stuff: dreams that I had got the roles and the players mixed up; that my review had appeared spattered with misused co-ordinates and dangling participles, or that type lines had got so transposed that they made me sound like an imbecile or that the linotype operator had accidentally dropped a letter, thus making an obscene word that would stand out as though it were aluminum-painted in the exact center of the column.

I could not bear to look at the review in the morning. Moreover, I got so I could not bear to have my wife read it at the breakfast table. She had a habit of turning to my review first thing and reading it while I went white and my appetite just went. If she laughed or chuckled as she read, terror would seize me, and I would ask agitatedly, "What's wrong?" I could not remember anything funny about it, so I always thought I had made some grotesque mistake that was accidentally comic. I got to the point where I could not stand this morning ordeal any longer. We lived in an apartment on the second floor. The paper was delivered rolled up at the kitchen door from steps leading into the basement. I would arise before my wife was awake, sneak out to the door landing and kick the paper out of sight down the steps.

This worked for a while, with morning vocal wonderings on the part of my wife: "Is some neighbor stealing it?—Do you suppose there is a new carrier on the route?" etc., etc. After breakfast she would go to the newsstand of the Sherwin Avenue station of the elevated near by and I would go to the office.

Just when she was going to do something about the nondelivery, Patterson summarily removed the post of dramatic criticism from my hands and arms, leaving me to struggle with the other five. His action was not humanitarian: it was a rebuke. Had he been humane, he would have taken at least two more posts from my burden and raised my salary.

Instead he was shortly to take all the posts away and remove the salary also, in a manner to be described in the following chapter.

During the years of our participation in the war and the return of soldiers to civilian life, there had been an acute shortage of trained newspapermen; I had been well trained in every department on the editorial side, including that of sports and that of making layouts for the art department; and, because I *was* reliable and efficient (in fact, in some instances, the only available member of the staff who could be called upon to fill a breach reliably without giving up whatever else he was doing or without extra compensation), and because I was young (the youngest member of the entire staff of editors and reporters, except a few cubs like Donald Culross Peattie who were inexperienced), eager, inacquisitive, they piled job after job on my already burdened shoulders as a series of temporary extra chores, such as getting up the "Bull Pup" Sunday news edition in the illness of the regular editor, getting up the "Voice of the People" in Peattie's absence on vacation, and writing advertisements of the features that would be found in the newspaper on the following Sunday.

I even imposed extra work upon myself, out of desire to enhance the glory of the paper: when cable dispatches announced that Ludwig Fulda had written a sensational *Haszgesang gegen England,* I knew readers who knew no German would want to know what was in it, so I translated it into English verse; I found articles of topical interest in the *Mercure de France* and translated and abridged them.

It was all good experience, you will say, and it was, indeed. It would also be good experience, I imagine, to buttle for a while for mere board and room, or to dig ditches with a labor crew just for the exercise; but I don't see men trained in the two techniques going around doing it. Most employers know of this eagerness for experience and responsibility among men as adept and as young as I was then; and they play upon it, even some of the justest and humanest of them, especially when they know the employee's wages are so low and his obligations so great that he cannot afford to take a chance on seeking a job elsewhere.

I had a wife and two children to support and was twice in debt to loan sharks, paying as high as 25 per cent a month—once, to pay my federal income tax (an embittering experience, I can tell you, which did not cause to rise in me any sweet feelings about the justice of my country; for I knew of the enormous fortunes arising from the execution of government war contracts, of some patriotic dollar-a-year men who did not neglect to use such advance information as came to them in a private way to reap heavy winnings in stock speculation)—and I was getting $50 a week for several jobs, the minimum wages for any one of which should have been at least $75, considering the current high prices for food, clothing and especially shoes.

I was never one to ask for an increase in salary. It is something I have never done. But after that early experience of having the then much-preached "loyalty to your employer" so cruelly rewarded, I have since tried to make it a point to be well heeled enough to be just as loyal to an employer as he is to me and prepared to walk out on him in the event that he imagines the obligation of loyalty to be entirely on my side, or in the event that he does not recognize what I consider to be the value of the services I have rendered him.

I did not ask for a raise in salary; but during 1918, while Miss Mary King was in hospital and I was obliged to take over her work as Sunday editor in addition to my other duties, and while Patterson was still in France, Beck, the managing editor, humane man, voluntarily jumped my salary from $50 to $60 a week, probably with the enthusiastic consent of the late William H. Fields, the business manager, who had, like Beck, often been complimentary to me about my writings.

My removal from the post of critic of the drama was, as I have said, not an act of humanity in relieving an overworked and under-paid young man of one of his duties, but a rebuke and, moreover, a rebuke in response to an outside demand, which lessened my admiration for Patterson. It came about in this way: When Frank Craven opened his Chicago engagement in what had been a smash hit in New York, *Going Up,* receipts for the first night were donated to a pet charity of the Gold Coast (although I did not know this), and Chicago society had attended en masse in high hats and ermine. Moreover, they had liked the show immensely. I had not—except for the singing and dancing of Miss Edith Day and the dancing of Miss Marion Sunshine. I thought the book was so witless that not even Frank Craven's comic countenance and strenuous antics or the good musical score could redeem it. I made the mistake of saying so.

Petty-minded Gold Coasters of Chicago, like petty-minded Gold Coasters everywhere, whenever they think their egos are affronted or their perceptions challenged, always try to get somebody fired. Hotel managements have to contend almost constantly with such people, whose way of showing their importance is to demand the discharge of a waiter or headwaiter for "insolence." Every large department store employs at least one man whose sole job is that of getting himself audibly "fired" whenever a customer who boasts of his or her expenditures in the store demands, as a means of showing power and importance, that the person in charge of a department be discharged at once for some fancied affront to the patron or for some slight, easily rectified error on the part of the store. Sometimes he gets "fired" three or four times a day. He is summoned by a floorwalker before the complaining customer and is given severe treatment; he acknowledges he is responsible for the disgrace to the store, whereupon he is ordered to call at the cashier's desk for his pay, get his coat and get out. Sometimes the floorwalker tells him angrily that he will see to it that the miscreant is blacklisted by every department store in town. This often pleases the customer very much; he or she may purr with pride and boast how he got a man fired.

People such as these among the Gold Coasters of Chicago demanded my removal as critic of the drama. Patterson complied with their demand. He appointed, to succeed me, Sheppard Butler, who should have had the job in the first place. With relief, I was now able to get a few more hours' sleep at night. It was almost too late, for I was on the verge of a nervous breakdown. Being literary editor, writing of books, staging fights among the literati, hailing meritorious new authors, stirring up the intellectuals, attacking the censorship, fighting what I believed to be the good fight for life and literature—that was what pleased me most then; that was what I considered true fun.

CHAPTER XIX

Literary Editor

How I Became Literary Editor of the Chicago *Tribune*. The American Scene in 1912. The Chicago Literary Renaissance. The Dramatis Personae. Brawls of the Brainy. War Reactions. End of Chicago Period.

CHICAGO IS PERIODICALLY in a state of having a cultural renaissance which outsiders are quick to see and comment upon, but which Chicagoans are never conscious of until it is brought to their attention. Then they become self-conscious, diffident and embarrassed. They try to remedy the defect. It is to them as if someone said, "What a loud suit you are wearing!" Colorful and attractive though the suit may have seemed up to that moment, even the hardiest temperament is now likely to take stock of itself with grave, subjective suspicions that something is wrong, and set about achieving a more effacing and conservative aspect.

There is something about the air, the atmosphere, of that metropolis which makes it, to me, at once the most attractive and the most repellant of cities. It is dynamic and energizing. I feel it the moment I step off the train at the La Salle Street or the Union station. It is almost like going into a huge hydroelectric plant and absorbing, at the same time, some of the generated energy.

This is probably because of the city's location on the shores of a vast and frequently tumultuous fresh-water lake, a lake which absorbs the iodine of the air and thereby creates a hyperthyroid condition among many of the city's inhabitants. One sees more goiterous necks among the young women on the streets of Chicago than in any other American city, unless it is Cleveland; and a goiterous condition exists, I am told by the medicine men, when the thyroid gland is functioning excessively and the energy it creates is not used up in love or work.

Chicago is beautiful and ugly, formidable and forbidding. If its people are kindlier, friendlier, more natural in their personal relationships than people in New York, say, and more savage toward the world in general, more given to a direct expression of warmth of feeling in social intercourse and more brittle and challenging to outsiders than are people in New York, the reason, I believe, is that the geography of Chicago makes its inhabitants lonelier than are the inhabitants of the tight, constricted, rapidly traversed little island of Manhattan; and that Chicagoans make their friendships a family affair against the terrifying aspects of a city that booms and brattles, roars continually with the cacophonous rhythm of the elevated trains of the Loop.

If you are a resident of Chicago and have no car, it is very likely that the congenial acquaintances you make, whom you would like to see often, frequently live so far away from you that, if you have a job, you can't even invite them to your house for dinner; and, if you accept an invitation from them, it is a momentous event to be prepared for. It may take you two or even three hours to get there by streetcar or elevated train or by taking the Illinois Central suburban train from the South Side, going crosstown and taking the Chicago & Northwestern to the North Side.

If your friend lives on the far West Side, in Austin, Oak Park or Western Springs and you live, say, in the neighborhood of the Midway Plaisance on the South Side near the University of Chicago, or in Rogers Park or Evanston on the North Side, you are many miles apart; and, if you have a job, you can go to see him and dine with his family only on your day off, and your day off may not correspond, and usually does not correspond, with your friend's day off.

Thus, in Chicago, I knew, liked and admired Harry Hansen; we had gone to the same university; we had covered many stories together as reporters; and we had met at lunch at Schlogl's or in the Marshall Field's Grill, with others, once a week. Yet Harry was never in my house as long as I lived in Chicago, nor was I ever in his. He lived in Winnetka and I lived in Sixty-second Street. Our homes, since neither of us had cars, were nearly three hours apart.

I knew and had a great affection for Carl Sandburg. I saw him and had luncheon with him often, but his wife and my wife never met because he lived in Hinsdale on the far West Side and we were therefore so far away from each other that we could not visit.

Edgar Lee Masters I saw only once during the nine years I was in Chicago, although I have come to know him in New York; and yet, in Chicago, I had occasion to know, better than I knew Masters, Georg Brandes, the great Danish critic; Maurice Maeterlinck, the Belgian Nobel Prize winner; John Galsworthy, the British novelist; William Butler Yeats, the Irish Nobel Prize winner; Rabindranath Tagore, the Hindu Nobel Prize winner, and a host of foreigners, including St John Ervine, Robert Nichols, Hugh Walpole, Jacques Copeau, G. K. Chesterton, Arnold Bennett —in the line of duty as newspaper reporter and, later, as sentinel in literature.

I never saw, except occasionally at luncheon or at a public function or at a rare literary banquet, many of the men and women engaged in the fine arts in Chicago during the time I lived there— and that was because distances were so great between their homes and mine. One gave parties in those days in Chicago or attended parties, but they were rare and memorable events.

Men and women who were lonely and isolated create. Those who are gregarious rarely do. It is much easier, it is much more fun, if you have talent, not to exercise this talent, but to skim along on the surface of life, negligent, carefree and convivial. Any poet would rather bed with a girl than write a poem about her; any novelist would rather participate in heroic events than imagine them and bring the image to life on paper; any musician would like to experience a life as harmonious and melodious, as exalting as he can express in counterpoint. All art is the result of frustration in which the creator seeks to give pattern, meaning and significant or beautiful design to imagined life through the symbols used by

[314]

the poet, the prose writer, the painter, the composer of music, the master of pantomime.

Art is energy deflected from its normal course in action. It is escape and protest, daydreaming, the oblique comment of a *sensitif* acting as a medium for a force higher than himself and yet attempting to order and regiment that force. A good novelist or playwright can make his characters obey his will—which he cannot do with characters in life. He can direct the destinies of men and women in play or story. In life he cannot do this.

In the late Eighteen-eighties and the late Eighteen-nineties, Chicago was, in the main, crude, vulgar, vital and grasping—"hog butcher to the world." The Armours, the Swifts, the Libbeys had established the Stockyards with its slaughterhouses, its canneries and its elaborate machinery for drawing beef, lamb, mutton and pork from the farms and ranches and distributing the meats and by-products of these to all parts of the country and the world.

Montgomery Ward and Sears, Roebuck & Co. had developed their great plants for expediting by mail and express and freight at low cost all the products of the factories of cities to remote and isolated farmers. The International Harvester Company, arising out of the invention of the McCormick reaper, was making and sending to the four quarters of the globe new and efficient implements for the development of agriculture.

The whaleback steamer had been invented to weather the waves of the cross-wind storms of the Great Lakes, storms which few salt-water ships could survive, and these brought to the tall grain elevators along the Chicago River wheat, oats and corn from the Northwestern prairies, from Canada, from Wisconsin and Michigan to be converted into flour, starches, cattle feed, breakfast cereals, paste and hundreds of new products brought to light under the development of chemistry. Meat products, Pullman cars, soaps, starches, shoes, farm implements, men's clothing, chewing gum, chemicals, canned goods, iron, steel and coke became the great factors of industry in Chicago because of its central location, its railroad terminals, its cheap waterways transportation. Chicago was a place where wealth accumulated but men did not decay. On the contrary, they asserted themselves with energy and magnificence, creating, out of their profits, within a brief time, the

Art Institute of Chicago, the Chicago Public Library, the Field Museum, the Auditorium for opera, Orchestra Hall for concert music, the Theodore Thomas Symphony orchestra, the Rush Medical School, the University of Chicago (out of a one-building Baptist theological seminary), a great system of parks for all of the people, a zoo and a botanical garden, a series of aesthetic memorials, including the beautiful St Gaudens statue of Lincoln. They brought to pass the World's Columbian Exposition, put up the Monadnock Building as North America's first considerable contribution to architectural art.

In the efforts of some of those who grew rapidly rich there was a display of bad taste, but not as bad taste as effete critics, infected with cultural *clichés* from Europe, contend. There is the brownstone Potter Palmer mansion on Lake Shore Drive, which is to me an affliction to the eyesight, but no more so to me than Buckingham Palace, L'église des Invalides or the Pantheon in Paris, the Kremlin in Moscow, and many another edifice that has been accepted without rancor.

Much has been made, too, of the use of silver dollars in the masonry of the floor of the barroom of the old Palmer House hotel. The legend persists that this floor was paved with silver dollars. That is untrue: silver dollars were inserted at the joining of every foot-square slab of marble.

The symbol of this architectural gesture seems to have escaped those who have commented upon it. They take it as a gaudy display of wealth. It was not. It was a contempt of wealth. What could be more contemptuous of wealth than that of using a silver dollar—a symbol and a medium of exchange of wealth—as something for people to trample upon?

This use of silver dollars was probably not Potter Palmer's idea—Potter Palmer was an acquisitive man to whom the dollar was undoubtedly sacred—but the idea of the architect who may have been acutely deficient in acquisitive instincts and who may have wished to express a contempt for the dollars he did not have a faculty for getting; but the aesthetic result was the same, for Potter Palmer had to okay the notion, and he probably did it with a chuckle of approval.

In this vibrant and commercial city of Chicago there were, and always have been, those for whom the things of the mind and spirit are more important than matters of commerce and "reality." In the Nineties and early Nineteen Hundreds there were Theodore Thomas, the orchestra leader, Harper, the Greek and Semitic languages scholar and creator of the University of Chicago, Moody, the theologian, Jane Addams, creator of Hull House, the Rev. Jenkin Lloyd Jones, founder of Abraham Lincoln Center; painters, musicians, scientists, architects and the writers: Eugene Field, George Ade, John T. McCutcheon, Henry B. Fuller, Opie Read, H. C. Chatfield-Taylor, Finley Peter Dunne and Herbert Stone. Herbert Stone was the publisher of the *Chapbook*. This little magazine is an almost inconceivable phenomenon, more incredible than the *Wave* in San Francisco.

The *Chapbook* was antecedent to, and anticipated, the *Yellow Book* and the *Savoy* in London, those brief-lived organs of the aesthetes and decadents who were in protest against the smugness of Victorianism. In the *Chapbook* were translations of Baudelaire, Rimbaud, Verlaine, Mallarmé, and essays in the mode of prevailing spirit of the literature of France which England was only later to become aware of. This in the Chicago of the noisome stockyards and the noisy Loop!

The Whitechapel Club, made up of poets, novelists, painters, musicians, who derived their living from precarious routine jobs on newspapers, was a fantastic, bohemian organization, which erected a huge pyre of creosote-soaked crossties on the sand dunes of South Chicago to cremate the body of one of its just-deceased members, whose last request was that they do this and to celebrate his extinction by getting drunk on champagne when his body had been thus reduced to ashes.

A beautiful, dainty girl of eighteen, clad in starched white linen, read, on October 21, 1892, her "Columbian Ode" at the dedicatory ceremonies of the World's Columbian Exposition. She had been requested by the committee on ceremonies for the exposition to write a poem for the dedication. Chicago had expected to have its world's fair ready for display on the anniversary of the discovery of America; but apparently nobody, except "Little Egypt," the hootchy-kootchy dancer, who was to make the fair as famous as Sally Rand, the fan dancer, was to make the later one, was ready. Opening of the fair was postponed until the following spring. But the "Columbian Ode" was read and later sung (for it had been set to music) before a great and gratefully enthusiastic crowd as the principal event in the ceremonies held among the litter of a toy city of cardboard and plaster that was in the process of being erected.

The girl who wrote and who read the "Columbian Ode" was Harriet Monroe, a graduate of Visitation Academy, Georgetown, D.C., although a native of Chicago. She not only gained immediate fame: she came, by a suit in law, into a considerable amount of money. The New York *World* published her "Columbian Ode" prematurely, against express instructions that it was not to be published until *after* it had been read at the ceremonies. In her suit against the *World* she was awarded $5,000.

Within almost a year after I went to Chicago, Miss Monroe had got more than one hundred rich Chicagoans to endow a magazine she was to edit under the title, *Poetry: A Magazine of Verse*. She had, as sub-editors, a succession of talents—Ivor Winters, Alice Corbin Henderson, Eunice Tietjens, Marion Strobel —and she began to publish the work of such new spheroids in the poetic heavens as William Butler Yeats, Vachel Lindsay, Sara Teasdale, Carl Sandburg, Alfred Kreymborg, Edgar Lee Masters, Amy Lowell, Ezra Pound, James Stephens, "AE," Padraic Colum, Conrad Aiken, Maxwell Bodenheim, Louis Untermeyer, Edna St Vincent Millay, Arthur Davidson Ficke, Eunice Tietjens, and dozens of other poets whose names have faded, perhaps only temporarily, from the public's memory.

The literary page of the Chicago *Evening Post* was already an intellectual institution when I arrived in Chicago. It had been created by Francis Hackett, an immigrant from Ireland, whose prose had such freshness and power and his information had been so wide and his untutored learning so great that he was called to New York as literary critic for the *New Republic,* when that magazine was established in 1912 under a guarantee against deficits by a rich Liberal, Willard Straight.

Hackett's successor on the Chicago *Evening Post* was Floyd Dell, a flaming youth from Iowa, whom I did not meet for many years and only after he had calmed down a bit, who left Chicago to become a bohemian in Greenwich Village and an editor of *The Masses,* the oriflamme and organ of the radicals.

Dell was succeeded by Lucian and Augusta Cary, a strange (to me) pair, who disturbed my Kentucky- and Oklahoma-conditioned prejudices by their very vocal disavowal of any standards of marriage and human conduct that seemed reasonable and natural to me. They talked of Bertrand Russell and Sigmund Freud and of the necessity of an open covenant between man and wife for each to go to bed with any other person who happened to strike his or her fancy.

Adultery had been current and common, as I understood history, from the days of our first knowledge of human relationships, but it had been condemned by general consensus on the reasonable grounds that people have a habit of being jealous of those they love and even of the things they love; they have egotism, pride and vanity; therefore if either a male or female who is in a conjugal state is going to find some satisfactions elsewhere, he or she will find it troublesome if he or she does not keep quiet about it.

Lucian and Augusta Cary preached, at the time, the doctrine that a wife should have a lover and a husband should have a mistress whether either wanted an extra sweetheart or not—merely as a social and biological necessity. Moreover, that they should crow about it.

I think they were both just talking; for I knew Lucian but I did not know Augusta except casually. When I was a reporter on the *Tribune,* Lucian was a reporter also. He did not like being a reporter, whereas (for quite some time) I thought being a reporter was thrilling. Lucian was an intellectual, and he was at pains to let all of us other reporters know about this.

When any of the rest of us got an assignment from Captain Stott or Walter Howey, even if it was an assignment that didn't make sense or was a mere picture-chasing chore, we hotfooted it and did what we were asked to do. Lucian did not. When he got an assignment, he let his cigarette droop from the left side of his mouth in such a way that the smoke swirled into his eyes, and he would squint for a while and then have it all figured out. He had been waiting ever since coming on duty for a chance to go over to the public library to read something by Dostoievsky or by

Havelock Ellis, and this assignment gave him the chance. If it was a picture-chasing assignment, he would figure out that the chances were that the picture would not be used even if he went out to Oak Park and got it, so he could read for three hours and come back and report that the door had been slammed in his face, that he could not burgle the house because he found all the windows fastened, and that his canvass of the photographers showed that the person in question apparently had a violent phobia against having a likeness taken.

Or, since Lucian knew the City Press Bureau's reporter was likely to get all the facts—which the City Press Bureau's reporter usually did, because he would be hoping to get a job on a newspaper sometime and therefore was extremely conscientious—Lucian would go over to the library and get in a few hours of reading, knowing that when he came back he could ask Jimmie Durkin for the City Press mimeos on the story he was supposed to have been on, and out of this stuff he could write a better story than if he had gone to the spot and confused his mind with all the irrelevant information that comes to a reporter from cops, eye-witnesses and plain morons who were impressed by talking to a reporter.

The Chicago literary renaissance was occurring; but none of the participators in it knew about it. Edgar Lee Masters was still in the practice of law in partnership with Clarence Darrow, even though his fame was widespread through the publication of *The Spoon River Anthology*, the poems of which had originally appeared anonymously in *Reedy's Mirror*, a literary magazine published in St Louis. Carl Sandburg was reading his poems, or crooning them, before small audiences and working as a reporter on the Chicago *Daily News*, along with Ben Hecht, Wallace Smith, Vincent Starrett, Harry Hansen and Henry Justin Smith. Ring Lardner was a sports writer on Hearst's Chicago *American* who had recently come to the Chicago *Tribune* to conduct the column, "In the Wake of the News," which had been inaugurated by H. E. Keough, who had just died. In Ring Lardner's ancient and battered roll-top desk at the office were accumulating the letters from illiterate baseball players which were to furnish him with the basic material upon which his imagination was to play in the creation of his Busher stories and his special, engaging American use of language. Charley MacArthur was a peripatetic reporter, getting bounced like a ping-pong ball from one city editor to another: he was completely engaging and completely irresponsible, a clever adept in the writing of the Hearstian style of shock, horror and sentimentality and despising the formula so much that from time to time he would take an important assignment as an excuse for playing a practical joke on the city editor; for which, of course, he would be fired, only to be hired back when he was fired from his next job. Sherwood Anderson, in an advertising agency, was writing copy on canned soup and on the merits of real burley tobacco for pipe smoking.

The venerable *Dial,* founded in Boston as an organ of opinion expressed by the sages of the "Concord Group," had been brought to Chicago, and it was there carrying on the sentiments, the traditions, the ideas and the style of Holmes, Emerson, Parker and Longfellow, almost unchanged—an anomaly in that gusty city, patronized by a few oldsters. On the campus at Northwestern University the serious-minded co-eds and in the streets of Evanston the women who wanted to warn people they were cultured carried copies of the *Atlantic Monthly* around with them, with the front cover of the magazine conspicuously visible.

In the East, literature was being led by the hand by William Lyon Phelps, and he was followed, even shadowed, by Richard Watson Gilder, Henry Mills Alden, Hamilton Wright Mabie, Brander Matthews and Walter Hines Page to see that he did not get too familiar with it. They had avoided the impropriety themselves.

Frowned upon and sneered at by these "intellectual leaders" was Elbert Hubbard of East Aurora, who, whatever may have been his limitations (he was a superb showman, and all showmen have a degree of charlatanry in their make-up) *did* have a deep sense of the essential values of a living literature and was committing (in their eyes) the vulgarism of interesting the masses in the arts of literature, music, sculpture, painting, architecture and in the handicrafts of printing, typographical design, furniture making and tannery.

Hubbard in his enormously successful magazines, the *Fra* and the *Philistine,* and in his lectures (he achieved the superb publicity stroke of getting himself billed as a speaker on the arts, along with the comedians, hoofers, acrobats and trained seals of a variety program at the largest vaudeville theater in Chicago—and he packed the house night after night) had called attention to the life and work of Leonardo, Michelangelo, Erasmus, Voltaire, Luther, Montaigne, Pascal, Ruskin, Morris, Tolstoi, Bach, Beethoven, Brahms and many other painters, poets, novelists, composers and seers. The arbiters of taste and elegance in Boston and New York did not like to acknowledge the existence of these geniuses, because they had heard that their private morals were not as circumspect as the standards set by Queen Victoria and her consort during their blissful and expansive reign in which, for instance, the Transvaal Boers were killed off in vast numbers, African natives were enslaved and their lands expropriated in the interest of Cecil Rhodes, a British bandit statesman who in 1888 gained from his queen and government a monopoly of the diamond industry in South Africa with an unlimited charter, and from this humble beginning proceeded by plain banditry and murder, with the help of Her Majesty's troops, to accomplish much in his dream of seizing the agricultural and mineral wealth of Africa and then of the whole world for himself and his queen.

The late queen's taste in literature was also still venerated by the arbiters of American taste in the magazine- and book-publishing world of New York, Boston and Philadelphia. Queen Victoria's favorite authors were Marie Corelli and Hall Caine. And the moral preachment inherent in the novels of Marie Corelli and Hall Caine was precisely the first and almost the only standard of literature set by Richard Watson Gilder, Hamilton Wright Mabie, Walter Hines Page, Irving Babbitt, Paul Elmer More, Henry Mills Alden, Barrett Wendell, William Dean Howells and William Lyon Phelps.

Alden in his younger days as editor of *Harper's Magazine,* had been whammed over the head and slammed about so thoroughly by the moralists for publishing even a censored version of Thomas Hardy's *Jude the Obscure* that he was immediately tamed and whipped into line. Howells and "Billy" Phelps were permitted to write with enthusiasm about the Russian novelists, Turgeniev, Tolstoi, Chekhov, Gogol, Dostoievsky, Sologub and Andreyev; but it was useless for an American writer to offer a manuscript to an American magazine or to an American publisher dealing with life as frankly as the least realistic of these Russians; and it was fatal for both author and publisher to make the mistake of challenging the taboo.

In the Nineties, the cultured and timid Henry Blake Fuller had been so frightened by the denunciations of him as a moral leper for writing so innocuous and semirealistic a novel as *The Cliff-Dwellers* that he gave up writing altogether for nearly twenty-five years, lived as a recluse with but a few intimates and occupied himself in collecting the rents on some property he owned.

When Theodore Dreiser's *Sister Carrie* was published by Doubleday, Page & Co. in 1900 on the insistence of one of its manuscript readers, Frank Norris, about four hundred copies of the book had been sold before the wife of one of the officials read it and was so scandalized that the book was immediately withdrawn. The lady's apprehensions, considering the times, were justified; but the evil had already been done. Norris had naïvely sent out one hundred review copies to a select list of critics and reviewers, and the four-hundred-odd sold copies were already on the counters of bookshops. The storm broke: cries from press and pulpit went up that Dreiser should be hanged, drawn and quartered, or tarred and feathered and run out of the country on a rail as a blasphemer, corrupter of youth, false witness to the character of the American people.

Dreiser was cut dead on the street by friends and acquaintances; magazine editors who bought his stories regularly closed their doors to him; he was to be so discouraged by this and so frightened economically that he was not to publish another novel for eleven years, *Jennie Gerhardt,* and when Harper & Brothers took courage to publish that novel and to reissue *Sister Carrie* in 1911, the storm of vituperation and abuse against Dreiser broke out again.

One of the shrillest, most vituperative and vindictive of these anti-Dreiserians in 1911 and for several years afterwards was Mrs Elia W. Peattie, literary critic for the Chicago *Tribune*. Mrs Peattie was a formidable bluestocking, who had written some successful novels for young girls, and who dominated the Fortnightly Club, a culture group of women in Chicago society, and rather ran the literary roost in Chicago. It was Mrs Peattie who was later to furnish a youngish, clever and ambitious professor of English at the University of Illinois, Stuart Pratt Sherman, with most of his ammunition for his essay, "The Barbaric Naturalism of Theodore Dreiser," in the *Nation,* which was to be one of a series of denunciations of modern writers included in a volume called *On Contemporary Literature.* Mrs Peattie among other things called Dreiser "the tomcat of literature," and by a comparison of Mrs Peattie's reviews of Dreiser's novels and what Sherman had to say about them it seemed (and seems) to me that Sherman had not troubled to read Dreiser but merely Mrs Peattie's reviews.

During the eight years I was on the Chicago *Tribune,* Mrs Peattie's husband, Robert Burns Peattie, was one of the best friends I had there and one of the most enjoyable companions I have ever had anywhere. When I joined the staff of the newspaper he was literary editor of the page of which his wife was the chief critic. He also wrote reviews for the page which he signed "By Herbert Caxton" and "By Ben Trovato": he never used his own name. He was also exchange editor, editor of "The Voice of the People," writer of occasional editorials and writer of premature obituaries.

Some of these duties performed by Bob Peattie, as everyone affectionately called him, perhaps had better be explained. To the office of an exchange editor come newspapers and magazines from all over the country and all over the English-speaking world, small-town dailies, metropolitan newspapers, country weeklies sent in exchange for being on the free list of the newspaper. The exchange editor goes through all these newspapers and magazines rapidly, but with an unerring eye for items which will be of interest to various editors and writers on the paper—topical or contentious editorials to the chief editorial writer; local murder or other crime stories in remote cities which do not get into Associated Press dispatches to the "bull-pup" editor, who must send to press on Thursday night a complete news section with what looks like Sunday-morning news for the "bull-pup" edition—a complete Chicago *Sunday Tribune* on the stands in Miami, Portland, San

Diego and other cities remote from Chicago on Sunday: news and criticism of the drama, music, and the other arts to the heads of the respective departments; features which may give hints to the feature editor; cartoons to be used to express political sentiment in various parts of the country. The editor of "The Voice of the People" goes through the hundreds of letters to the editor from cranks and indignant persons, persons of good will, persons who are aroused over some public question and have no other forum except the newspaper in which to express their views; selects the most interesting of these, edits and writes captions for them. In every large and efficiently run newspaper office biographies of every person of any prominence are kept on file and up to date for use as an obituary in the event that the person dies suddenly. Some of these are brief, and some of them, like that of the late Theodore Roosevelt, run to two and three pages of type. Peattie wrote most of the premature obituaries on file at the Chicago *Tribune* and kept them up to date by occasional revisions. (Joseph Medill Patterson, incidentally, when he went away to the wars, wrote his own obituary and had it set in type with orders that it was not to be tinkered with nor embellished: it was a marvel of succinctness and good writing, neither overly modest nor otherwise, a competent, comprehensive, informative job of objective recording.)

Robert Burns Peattie was a Parisian boulevardier *manqué*. All of his sentiments, his point of view, even his manner were French and were comprised of *élégance, sang-froid,* urbanity, a taste and respect for wit, and an eye for feminine charm and beauty. In these respects he was the exact opposite of his formidable wife, for whom he had, however, a deep admiration and affection. He wore a beard in the French manner of the Nineties; his clothes were cut with care and, for Chicago, were a little exotic. He was immaculate always, and conversation to him, as with the French, was the breath of life, especially anecdotal conversation in which there were opportunities to make a happy phrase.

He presented me with the first tail coat I ever owned. I have it yet. He never developed a paunch in all his seventy-odd years; yet at the time he gave me the coat his shoulders had drooped somewhat from bending over a desk for so long and, because he required that his clothes fit him perfectly, he had to order a new tail coat, though he retained the trousers. I had to order trousers. The tail coat was tight-fitting and cut that way, tapering neatly from shoulders to waist, and to emphasize the slimness of the waist, the front buttons were caught across the waistcoat by a braided silk cord with loops at both ends. . . . It was Bob Peattie's tragedy that circumstances and the exigencies of newspaper work never permitted him to visit France, much less go there to live the life of a boulevardier, although it may have been a blessing, not a tragedy, because he might have been bored and disillusioned by the life, especially since he was constitutionally incapable of mastering the pronunciation of simple French sentences, valiantly as he tried to learn. He could read French with a degree of ease; and he read French books almost to the exclusion of all others, even though he *was* literary editor of an American newspaper. But his tongue could not manage simple words like *soir, nuit, Dieu, menu, garçon, addition* and *absolument* which he would have found rather necessary in the life of a boulevardier.

I was introduced to Peattie by Bert Leston Taylor, the humorist, essayist and column conductor, who, under the initials he made famous, "B. L. T.," conducted the column "A Line o' Type or Two," not long after I joined the staff of the paper and while I was in my first year at college. I had met Taylor through an urgency. One day he had received from one of his contributors a poem in Latin. He couldn't read Latin, although whenever he could get someone to translate it for him and he found it was all right, not smutty, he would publish a Latin contribution in either verse or prose to the annoyance of his readers who knew no more Latin than he did. This poem was from one of his most trusted contributors, perhaps Professor Paul Shorey (a model of decorum) or Keith Preston (impish but with a regard for his own reputation) or Richard Atwater (a protégé of Shorey's at the University of Chicago who had specialized in Aristophanic comedy but was not Aristophanic in his verse or prose); but Taylor was not taking chances.

Once he had received three very lovely quatrains. He had run them at the head of his column in ten-point Caslon Old Style. The first letter of each line formed an acrostic which resolved into an obscene command. Thousands of letters poured in; telephone calls drove the editors frantic; Taylor disappeared from the office and went on a terrific binge, although he had been a tee-totaler for years.

Thereafter Taylor never read a poem in the ordinary way: he read the initial letters down, and then looked out for capital letters across, and examined it in other ways for cryptograms. Then he would read the poem, and if he liked it he would publish it.

It was late at night; Taylor had been golfing all afternoon and had dined before coming to the office to get up his column. He found himself short of good, available material. This Latin poem would serve just the proper space and balance of his column material, if it wasn't smutty. Time was short. In those days, before the city room on the second floor of the old *Tribune* building at Dearborn and Madison streets was moved to other quarters on the same floor, the cable editor, night editor, telegraph editor, telegraph copy desk, Bert Leston Taylor, the managing editor and managing editor's assistant were all huddled together in a partitioned-off corner of the composing room. Guy Lee, an office versifier, was on the telegraph copy desk; so when Taylor yelled out to ask if there was anybody around who could read Latin, Lee said there was a reporter named Rascoe down in the city room who could.

I was sent for. I was introduced to Taylor. I translated the poem. It was an easy one, I was relieved to discover; and its sentiments were pure. Taylor was vastly relieved, too. He marked it to be set and sent it to the compositor. Thereafter whenever he had a contribution in Latin he called upon me to translate it. Thus we became intimates, more or less, through our community of interest in intellectual matters, especially concerning Latin, of which he knew nothing.

He was a grouchy man, grouchier even than Hugh E. Keogh, who conducted the humor column on the sports page; and he was a snob about the office, disdainful of or ignoring everybody except E. S. Beck, Percy Hammond, Guy Lee, John T. Mc-Cutcheon, the cultivated and erudite head of the proofroom whose name I unhappily forget and whose education and knowl-edge of words were much greater than Taylor's and upon whom Taylor relied, Robert Burns Peattie and myself.

It was perhaps largely because I was useful to him in his quandaries and an occasional contributor to his column that Taylor ever condescended to become intimate enough with me to invite me to lunch with him at the Cliff-Dwellers' Club, grouse to me about Patterson and about Patterson's deplorable sense of humor, show me some of his more unprintable contributions, introduce me to Robert Burns Peattie and sit in with Peattie and me when we were killing time with conversation.

No one, I believe, has ever had as large and as literate a following as a columnist as Taylor had during the ten years before his death; although when Richard Henry Little succeeded him with a vastly inferior column in which he printed inanities of all kinds, feeble witticisms, and atrocities in verse form, he attracted much more mail than Taylor received because the *Whizz-Bang* and *On a Slow Train Through Arkansaw* type of humor was understandable to more people than was Taylor's column and hence inspired more people to efforts in verse and prose as contributors.

There was intellectual snobbery in Taylor's column, arrogance and a conscious pose of superiority that were irritating and antagonizing, especially when Taylor issued *obiter dicta* on subjects about which he was badly informed. But his own sense of humor was subtle and comic; his verses were correct, distinctive and various; he had a sly technique of making bawdy inferences without being baldly bawdy; and he wrote the most inspired and amusing captions to his contributions I have ever seen anywhere. He was so well known to postal employees all over the world that letters with no other wording on the envelopes than "B. L. T." or "The Line o' Type" came to him from the four quarters of the globe. He would make enemies one day and reconcile them the next; many readers hated him but did not fail to turn to his column the first thing in the morning even before they looked at the front-page headlines.

Part of his success was due, no doubt, to the fact that he never took his job with the least seriousness, except on the few occasions when he attempted to write serious, stylistically mannered essays —and then he was monumentally dull. When Taylor was an editorial writer on an Eastern newspaper, according to his protégé, Franklin P. Adams of the New York *Herald Tribune's* "Conning

Tower," whenever he could think of nothing to write about he would go through the latest Springfield *Republican* or Boston *Transcript* or rival newspaper and clip out the longest editorial, paste it up without reading it, write above the editorial, "What does our esteemed contemporary, the Springfield *Republican,* mean by this?" and below it, "We pause for reply" and call it a day. However, he did this once too often and got the bounce.

During my last year on the *Tribune* I shared a suite of two rooms on the fourteenth floor of the old *Tribune* building with Taylor and Leo MacGivena, an advertising copywriter, far above the madding crowd of the city and Sunday rooms. MacGivena and I had the large room, and Taylor had the smaller room opening into ours. On the floor of the large room was a magnificent large green rug with a deep nap. This rug and this room proved to be one of the happiest delights of Taylor's last years—a delight which made work in the room impossible to either MacGivena or me whenever Taylor came to work.

Taylor was a golf bug. It occurred to him that this rug would provide most of the recreation of a golf course and none of the inconveniences of traveling to and from the course; and that also, because it was in his office, he could pretend he was at work. He brought golf balls, a mashie and a putter to the office, and for hours at a time he would practice putting and mashie shots on that rug. He placed a wastebasket in the corner opposite Mac-Givena and from my corner of the room would try to drop the ball into the basket with the mashie, which he did, often. Sometimes he would miss, the ball would bang against the wall, ricochet and hit MacGivena on the head, knock his drawing pencil out of his hand or roll under his feet, to be retrieved by the earnest and preoccupied golfer. About five o'clock in the afternoon or thereabouts Taylor would take some paragraphs out of his coat pocket which he had scribbled at home, paste up some contributions, write heads and mark type faces, take the batch to the printer and go home, to return sometime in the evening to read proof and direct a printer in the arrangement of the items in the column.

Taylor introduced me casually and without intention to Peattie one day; and on the first day of that introduction Peattie and I became friends. When I started to leave the office he asked me if I wouldn't like to write some book reviews for him. This was something I had been very eager to do but did not know how to go about getting an opportunity. Nor was I in the least confident that I should be able to write book reviews which would be acceptable to the Saturday book pages, since my ideas about the merits of books were so remote from, and so hostile to, those expressed by Mrs Peattie.

I would write about such books as were given me to review just as I felt about them, honestly and conscientiously, I said to myself, and if the reviews were unacceptable, I should have had my trial anyhow and no bones broken, because my living did not depend upon book reviewing and the only pay I should receive was a free copy of the book. The first book Peattie gave me to try my hand on was *The Children of the Dead End,* by Patrick MacGill, a writer I had never heard of, which is not strange, because MacGill was just twenty-four years old and this was his first book. It was a novel of the peasantry of Donegal and of the navvies of Kinlochlevan, autobiographical in the main, with some of the usual faults of a first and autobiographical novel, but shot through with the power and intensity of youth's deeply felt emotions. And in my review I said just that. What I wrote about that novel I feel about it now; and it is about the same verdict later reached by the authors of books about the modern English and Irish novel.

Peattie expressed delight with the review when I turned it in to him the next afternoon. I had got off from work in the local room at between midnight and one; and I had stayed up the rest of the night to read the book and write the review. He said, "And now suppose you take a whirl at that," handing me *The Ragged-Trousered Philanthropists,* by Robert Tressall, another writer of whom I had never heard, which also is not strange, inasmuch as that was the first and the only book he was ever to write, for he had died before the book was published. To my amazement and pleasure I opened the newspaper on Saturday morning to find that Peattie had given my signed review of the MacGill book preferred position on the book page; as he was on the following Saturday with my review of *The Ragged-Trousered Philanthropists;*

and by his subsequent actions it became clear to me that he was going to call upon me to do one full-length, importantly placed, signed review each week. Moreover, he invited me to his home on the South Side for dinner, where I met Mrs Peattie, who was friendly, almost maternal, toward me, complimentary and encouraging; and there I met also a skinny, awkward and indolent-looking high-school lad called Donald, a son of the Peatties.

(This same Donald I was to see a few times in the local room four or five years later during the brief period wherein he proved most successfully to himself, to his parents, and to the city editor that he didn't want to be a newspaperman and wasn't cut out to be a newspaperman. He was still lanky and indolent-looking; and on his face there was perpetually an expression of sullen resentfulness. His parents were not wealthy; they had spent much in the education and advancement of the older and more promising brother, Roderick, who was unusually personable and had made a brilliant academic and social career at the University of Chicago, been marshal of his graduating class, co-author of Blackfriars music comedies, editor of student publications and had then gone East to write plays; and his parents had got Donald a job as a reporter in order that he might begin to make a stab at earning his own living. I spoke to him one day, and he looked up from the copy of *Wuthering Heights* he was reading and politely but rather impatiently acknowledged the interruption. The next time I was to speak to him was at an elaborate breakfast in his honor in the Sert Room of the Waldorf-Astoria in 1935. I was on a committee with Carl Van Doren, Joseph Wood Krutch and Harry Hansen which had awarded him the Limited Editions Club's gold medal for having written the American book published during the preceding year which, in our opinion, was the one most likely to become a classic, *An Almanac for Moderns*.)

Following the depression which began in 1930, there arose a concerted demand for a literature of, and by, and presumably for, the proletariat, on the part of young Left Wing critics and reviewers in New York. It started among the radical and Communistic publications and penetrated into the reviews and comments of those who were drawing substantial, even munificent, salaries, on the capital-owned newspapers and magazines. The demand was stated in terms which not merely implied but expressed the naïve view that in British and American literature no novels had ever been written of and by the proletariat, and that it was high time this situation was rectified. This demand was taken cognizance of by various publishers who soon began to issue any novel, however mediocre or downright tripey, that came to them in manuscript form that was about manual laborers and the proletariat. Perhaps out of all these there were two or three which might compare in merit with *The Children of the Dead End,* written by an Irish navvy, and *The Ragged-Trousered Philanthropists,* by an English house painter.

In both of these novels, the class message demanded by the young, ill-read, appallingly ignorant but dogmatic and obstreperous Left Wing critics was there in abundance, so much in abundance that they interfered with the effectiveness of the novels as depictions of sordid poverty, misery, exploitation and the crying need of economic reform implicit in the narratives, although considerably less so in Tressall's novel than in MacGill's. And this I said in those first two book reviews I wrote for the Chicago *Tribune.* Of MacGill's novel I wrote: "While in the earlier chapters the story is so simply and so effectively told that the reader feels inclined to preach about what he has learned, the author in the later chapters undertakes to do the job himself." In these later chapters MacGill forsook his narrative to inveigh against capitalism and hypocrisy and to announce his personal revolutionary philosophy, alternating his preachments with a glorification of fistic encounters —of which, I wrote, "there are far too many in the book."

The Ragged-Trousered Philanthropists remains a unique, moving and too little known masterpiece of London's *les misérables.* In closing my review of this novel I wrote: "For those perennially youthful revolutionaries, Tressall's novel is perhaps the most effective weapon that has come into their possession for their logomachy with the conservatives and reactionaries who are the enemy." I deem it probable that not one of those in England and America who began in 1930 to demand a proletarian literature (as if it were something that had never yet come into print) has ever read or even heard of *The Ragged-Trousered Philanthropists.*

LITERARY EDITOR

I wonder, too, how many of these young critics of the Nineteen Thirties, with their amusing jargon of "bourgeois ideology" and "dialectic materialism," ever read or heard of some of those other books I was presently to review with enthusiasm for Robert Burns Peattie nearly a quarter of a century ago: Abraham Cahan's realistic and bitter masterpiece of Ghetto life in New York and of the emergence from it of a crushed idealist as a shrewd, resourceful, predatory and hollow man, *The Rise of David Levinsky;* Nathan Kussy's *The Abyss,* a narrative, so I wrote, "which begins with the author's childhood in the Ghetto, recounts his negligible schooling, his premature struggle for a living, his association with thieves and underworld characters, his participation in sordid acts, his conviction on charges of embezzlement and theft, his various attempts to live by honest labor, and the failure of these attempts through the hounding of him by detectives," a vivid and poignant document, marred, I wrote, "by an obsequious servility toward material success that seems to me unnatural, distasteful and inept in a work which purports to be a human document and which reflects, for the purpose of bettering them, the miserable condition of the slums"; or of the English translation by Lloyd Morris of Georges Eekhoud's appallingly realistic masterpiece of life on the Antwerp waterfront, *The New Carthage.*

On looking over the scrapbook containing some of those earlier reviews I wrote for Robert Burns Peattie I find that my impatience with most of the best sellers and much of what I considered literary shoddy was enormous, messianic and somewhat misplaced. It outraged me that novels such as Harold Bell Wright's *When a Man's a Man,* Eleanor H. Porter's *Just David* and her Pollyanna stories, Gene Stratton-Porter's *The Girl of the Limberlost,* etc., Winston Churchill's *Inside the Cup,* and Samuel Merwin's *The Trufflers* sold into the hundreds of thousands, whereas Theodore Dreiser's novels were condemned and neglected and his *The "Genius"* suppressed; and that W. Somerset Maugham's magnificent *Of Human Bondage,* D. H. Lawrence's *Sons and Lovers,* Willa Sibert Cather's *O Pioneers!,* and the translations of a vital new literature from Russia, Poland and Germany being brought out by Ben Huebsch and by Alfred Knopf should be greeted with condemnation by the bigwigs of the Eastern press and remain generally unread. Instead of taking those best sellers for what they were as ephemeral popular entertainment, opiates and anodynes and dream-fulfillment for hard-working and harassed people, I considered these books dangerous, immoral, perverting and corrupting, and I sailed into them with all the searing fire of invective and satire I could muster.

Curiously enough Peattie and Beck and others in executive positions about the place encouraged me in this. When I wrote a column-length, scathing review of a Harold Bell Wright novel which had sold 600,000 copies in advance, calling it in the heading, "A Nickel Novel in a Dress Suit" and denouncing it as immensely inferior in style, story, logic, observation and common sense to the jitney fiction such as *Pluck and Luck, Diamond Dick, Light Horse Harry: The Hero of Dead Man's Gulch* formerly read by boys in haylofts who got their backsides whanged by their dads if they were caught at it, Beck read it in proof (because I asked him to: I was afraid there just might be some kick-back from it); he chuckled as he read it, laughed out loud, and said, "That's swell!"; and two days after the review appeared William H. Field, the business manager (of whom I was somewhat in awe), sought me out at my desk, instead of asking me to come to him, and said: "Harold Bell Wright's publisher has just canceled a $5,000 advertising contract with us." . . . (I began to tremble: I thought it meant the boot.) . . . "I want to congratulate you upon being the only means we have found of keeping advertisements of Harold Bell Wright's novels out of the paper. I enjoyed your review very much."

Early in 1916, about a year after Robert Herrick had been writing his furious denunciations of America for not entering the war on the side of the Allies and we had been publishing them on the "highbrow" page which I edited, he brought under book covers a selection of his weekly tirades under the title, *The World Decision.* I wrote an ironical review of it, heading it, "Sound and Fury Signifying—Mr Herrick" (see Appendix III). I was somewhat doubtful about the propriety of my denouncing a book by a regular contributor to the paper, especially a book largely made up of articles which had appeared in the paper; so I sent a proof to Patterson with a penciled query: "O. K. to run this?—B. R." The proof came back marked, "O. K.—J. M. P."

Such complete freedom for the expression of opinion as then prevailed on the Chicago *Tribune* made that newspaper a genuine forum for ideas.

Not long after I arrived in Chicago I made the discovery of a bookshop which was to be a haunt of mine as long as I remained in Chicago. There, too, I made friends with men who have remained friends of mine to this day and to whom I feel attached with ties of genuine affection because of the intellectual stimulation they gave me and the opportunities they afforded me to keep alive my interest in, and curiosity about, all the literature that was then in being, whether American or European. This was the small bookshop operated on the south side of Monroe Street between Wabash and Michigan avenues by A. Kroch, who has since become, I believe, the most important individual retail bookseller in the country, with the ownership of McClurg's, once known as the largest bookshop in the world—not the A. C. McClurg wholesale house—and the ownership of a large and magnificent parent bookshop on North Michigan Avenue, Chicago, where he has his main offices.

In those days, in 1912 and until sometime after the war, Kroch's bookshop was an intimate little store specializing in the importation of foreign art prints and books in foreign languages. The proprietor was an amiable, slim little man, with beaming and alert brown eyes, who was well educated, cultivated, intelligent—and a linguist—who had emigrated from Lemberg when it was in Austrian Poland. In Europe he had known Przybyszewski, the author of a sensational and bitter novel, *Homo Sapiens,* which was suppressed in this country when it was published in translation, Richard Dehmel, Frank Wedekind, Arthur Schnitzler and other poets, playwrights and storytellers who participated in the Über-brettl movement in Austria and Germany—a movement to take art away from the patronage of the well-to-do, who made the same use of it as they would of a top hat or a tiara, and give it to the masses, the petty bourgeoisie and the workers whose hours of recreation were spent in the beer halls and variety theaters.

"Papa" Kroch, as all his intimates were later to call him, had and has excellent taste in literature. In those days he simply would not stock what he considered trashy and ephemeral novels such as

[335]

ordinarily enough were best sellers—novels by Harold Bell Wright, Robert W. Chambers, Eleanor H. Porter, etc., etc. Nor did he encourage the patronage of those whose tastes in books were shallow. He was polite about it but also unyielding. He was the despair of book salesmen from the Eastern publishing houses who could not understand why a man in the retail book business would not handle novels which were in large and persistent demand, and, moreover, who chose to order books out of their samples which they had had little luck with elsewhere. The answer is that "Papa" Kroch has grown rich and influential and has had a marked influence upon the taste of his time, whereas many of the publishing houses which then battened briefly upon best sellers have long since gone out of business and the books of some of their best sellers have been entirely forgotten.

In Kroch's bookshop were three salesmen, Lewis Galantière, Benjamin Silbermann and A. van Ameyden Van Duym, all linguists, all keenly interested in the best literature of the day. On the counters were the latest magazines from France, Italy, Germany, Norway, Sweden, Spain and Italy; on the shelves were contemporary books in nearly every European language. Kroch and his salesmen were not mere salesmen: they read the books they sold and could talk intelligently about them; each regarded himself as an implement in the inculcating of cultivated taste among the book buyers of America, and the taste among the book buyers at the time, as attested by the lists of best sellers, was limited and provincial. Kroch and his salesmen were instrumental, in Chicago, at least, in arousing curiosity over general ideas, the development of literature and art in England, Ireland and on the European continent, and in the translations from the literature of contemporary Europe which the publishers, Huebsch, Knopf and the young firm of Boni & Liveright, were trying to introduce to the American public. (Macmillan published translations of Dostoievsky and Chekhov, and they were bringing out a translation of the complete works of Friedrich Nietzsche under the direction of Dr Oscar Levy when the outbreak of the war suspended this enterprise; Harper & Brothers published the translated works of Turgeniev; Doubleday, Page & Co., Selma Lagerlöf; Dodd, Mead & Co., Maeterlinck; John Lane & Co., Anatole France; and Henry Holt,

Romain Rolland's *Jean Christophe*. But it remained for the newer and smaller houses to bring out the work of lesser known contemporary Europeans—Gerhardt Hauptmann, Herman Sudermann, Leonid Andreyev, Alexander Kuprin, Michael Arzybashieff, Pedro Alarçon, and Gabriele d'Annunzio).

My closest friend in the shop was Lewis Galantière. He and I lunched together two or three times a week at the near-by Tip-Top Inn on the top floor of the Pullman Building. Our luncheons together were singular in that often neither one of us said anything throughout the meal: we each sat with some European book or magazine, perhaps the *Mercure de France,* the *Revue de Deux Mondes,* or the *Nouvelle Revue Française* (with which a group of new and talented Frenchmen were doing such exciting things). We were in agreement over so many things that we rarely had any arguments: our conversation was, when it took place, rather to give each other items of intellectual information or to call one another's attention to stimulating things to read—the sparkling work of a new critic, Dixon Scott, on the *Manchester Guardian,* the beautiful and ironic essays of the brilliant young Irish Catholic writer, Thomas Kettle, the essays of Jacques Rivière in the *N. R. F.* (Scott, Kettle and Rivière were killed early in the war), a new book of poems by James Stephens, whose *The Crock of Gold* and *Demigods* we delighted to quote to each other and chuckle over, the work of the new young Englishman, D. H. Lawrence, Compton Mackenzie, Gilbert Cannan, Oliver Onions, H. M. Tomlinson, J. D. Beresford and Hugh Walpole, the good things we had found in the latest *Smart Set* or in Mitchell Kennerley's *Forum* or in Frank Harris' old magazine, the *English Review,* later edited by Austin Harrison, or in *Simplicissimus.* The *Mercure de France* was a thrill in the days when it was edited by Rémy de Gourmont, but it became so stodgy after Gourmont's death that the younger generation decided to bring out a magazine of their own, the *Nouvelle Revue Française,* (shortened, in references to it, to *N. R. F.*). It was also to Galantière and me an experience very much like Keats's when he first came upon a copy of Chapman's *Homer,* when we discovered Van Beaver and Leautaud's two-volume anthology of modern French poetry and read the works of Jules Laforgue and Tristan Corbière which were later so greatly to influence Ezra Pound and still later T. S. Eliot, and the work of Verhaeren, the Belgian who had been so influenced by Walt Whitman that he was responsible for the inauguration of a school of French poets who called themselves Whitmanistes; the declamations of Paul Fort, "the Prince of Poets," the tender work of Albert Samain, and Gourmont's haunting *Pélérin du Silence*. Anatole France was our favorite in prose; but we were alive to the merits of the poets and playwrights of the Irish literary renaissance, particularly Yeats, Stephens and Colum; yet with what vast delight did we greet the successive volumes of George Moore's *Hail and Farewell* wherein Moore created so charmingly the whole atmosphere of Dublin during the literary renaissance and all the participants in it, and killed all of them, excepting "AE"!

When the European war broke out, things of the mind and spirit went by the boards in Europe. The brave new literary magazines died; and soon most of their editors and contributors were dead also in the slaughter. The ancient friendship between the great Danish critic, Georg Brandes, who had done so much to further the fame of his European contemporaries in England, France, Germany and the Scandinavian countries and to make literature a universal enjoyment, and Georges Clemenceau, who was a scholar as well as a statesman, went upon the rocks in acrimonious recriminations when Clemenceau became the Tiger of France, bent upon revenge for the "rape" of Alsace-Lorraine.

D. H. Lawrence was harassed on suspicion of being a spy because he had married a German baroness, sister of Von Richthofen, the German war ace; Gilbert Cannan and other promising young British writers were interned as conscientious objectors, to be so broken by the humiliations of the experience as thereafter to create little. Romain Rolland, both French and German in his sympathies, sent out his sad, philosophic challenge to the good will in men, *Above the Battle,* from Switzerland, begging the combatants in the name of civilization and humanity to stop killing one another—only to have his name stricken off the honor rolls of learned and literary societies in both France and Germany, and his work execrated on both sides.

Just before the war Frederick Stock, the conductor of the Chicago Symphony Orchestra, had arranged with Gustave Mahler, the

Austrian composer, to stage in Chicago the world première of
Mahler's so-called "Symphony of a Thousand" with its score calling for masses of vocalists on stage, in the boxes and in the balcony
singing antistrophically to the accompaniment of an augmented
orchestra. Mahler mailed the score to Stock just before August 4,
1914; the score was seized in England and held there for the dura-
tion of the war in the belief that it was an elaborate cypher message
to German spies.

All the papers of Dr Oscar Levy, translator of Nietzsche and
editor of the complete translation of Nietzsche in English, were
impounded in England while he was stranded in Switzerland for
no other reason than that Nietzsche, dead fourteen years, was
being accused by G. K. Chesterton, William Archer and lesser
raging journalists of having started the war—Nietzsche, who had
uttered more resounding maledictions against the Germans than
any enemy of the country before the war, as I was at pains to
point out late in 1914, with voluminous extracts from Nietzsche's
work published on the "highbrow" page, with an explanation by
me.* G. Bernard Shaw was taking happy advantage of the fact
that he had been regarded as a clown in England; as a privileged
jester he dared to speak cutting truths which drew upon him the
wrath of his old friend William Archer and of petty journalists
everywhere.

Hysteria ruled the world. I had profited from the creative minds

*Among those to whom Friedrich Nietzsche is merely a name, he has, since the
war, taken on the character of an avatar of terror, rapine and vicious doctrine. By
hack journalists in England the entire responsibility for the war was early laid at his
feet. The singular attribution, made by sensation writers who, it is evident, were
acquainted only with a few of the isolated phrases used by Nietzsche in a context
that utterly changes their complexion, such as "A good war sanctifies every cause,"
and "Goest thou to woman? Don't forget thy whip," has gained currency not only
among people generally but among college professors and writers of standing, who
accept without verifying and who, by parroting catch phrases, show themselves less
responsible intellectually than the yellow journalist who is quite frank about his
yellowness. Mr William Archer, for instance, in his *Gems of German Thought*,
quotes some Nietzsche and pages of a "Pastor Lehmann." Now, Pastor Lehmann in
Germany has the same significance as "the Rev. Mr Smith" in our country, that is to
say, it is the most common of names, and someone thus referred to, with initials
omitted, would mean a nonentity quite as vague as "Mr Whatsisname." Mr Archer
and others link Nietzsche with Treitschke, a man for whom Nietzsche had the
utmost personal contempt and whose jingoistic writings Nietzsche lampooned on
every occasion that offered. For such imperialistic authors as Bernhardi, Nietzsche
had and would have nothing except utter disgust. Against the materialistic aims of
Germany, against rabid nationalism in all its aspects, against insensitiveness to the

of Germany just as I had from the creative minds of France; I had made myself proficient in German not merely to read Goethe and Heine, whose work had meant so much to me, but to read things like the contemporary Hauptmann's *The Sunken Bell,* work of the current poets and novelists, the wit of such great satirical papers as *Simplicissimus,* the stimulating and often thunderous essays by Maximilian Harden in his weekly, *Die Zukunft;* and hardly had the war begun than it was no longer possible to receive in America this stimulation of European minds and, when the hysteria spread and swept us into the war, it became dangerous to speak German or to be seen reading a German classic. Thus from lack of exercise my German left me, and now I can read it only with difficulty.

Something in the French spirit seemed to die in the war, but not to become so dead as all of that spirit of the Germans which was once so humane, so homey, so full of *Gemütlichkeit,* so friendly and so at peace with the world. The *Junker* spirit alone survives generally in Germany—that and its concomitant, robot obedience to command. A comic-opera kaiser, with upturned mustaches, who merely believed that he ruled through Divine will, is now displaced by a low-comedy kaiser with a Charlie Chaplin mustache who wishes to revive the ancient German theology of Wotan and to be worshiped alongside of Wotan as a god.

After the war it was distressing to watch the strange crack-up of the sensitive, the talented and the intelligent, the artists, the poets, in Europe in an antisanity movement in the arts, expressed by Dadaism and later by Surrealism in Germany, Austria and France. This withdrawal of artists from the symmetry, order, form, har-

benefits of the arts, and against the prevailing indifference to human development, Nietzsche was forever hurling his catapultic apothegms, his withering sarcasm and his vitriolic wit. That many Germans misapprehended the philosophic message of Nietzsche's Gospel of the Superman, and falsified this doctrine to subserve imperialistic ambitions; that, indeed, this message in its superficial aspects fitted in with the German dream for "a place in the sun," is likely. But it is rather more than Nietzsche, in his unhappy and lonely life, could have wished for, to be honored with the authorship of a world cataclysm. It is this same Friedrich Nietzsche whom some conceive to be the power behind the German general staff, who has offered the most adverse criticism of Germany and the Germans, who has, in fact, said nearly all that is to be said against Prussian junkerdom. As examples may be quoted these few passages selected from among the great body of similar expressions in *The Collected Works of Friedrich Nietzsche,* translated by various hands, edited by Oscar Levy and published in this country by the Macmillan Company.

mony and significance which had been the marks of a work of art before the war was not, I think, as so many people believed it was, merely the prank of exuberant young men thumbing their noses at the world, but more or less an unconscious expression of the civilization of the time. Nothing they did was as lunatic as the normal actions of responsible statesmen at the Peace Conference at Versailles, nothing as crazy as the deliberated and wisely considered policies of the men in whose hands lay the fate of Europe.

Yes, presently the war was upon us in America also, like a swift blight, galvanizing the eager young men into action all over the land, their eyes alight with the thought of adventure, their hearts stirred by the music of military marches, their spirits aroused and canalized in the belief that in giving up humdrum jobs and routine amusements and going across the seas to shoot and stab and gas and bomb other lads and men they were defending their country, saving the world for democracy.

Those who took the war as a lark, as a comradely adventure utilizing their youthful energies, when they returned—*if* they returned—still regarded their participation in the war as an adventure, an adventure full of danger and discomforts, as are all adventures involving the possibilities of death. Yet even to these the war did something greatly disillusioning and disrupting; for they were a long time readjusting themselves to civilian life; to some this readjustment was more difficult, more arduous, more excruciating than anything they had experienced in the war, and they went down in their efforts, baffled and defeated, as they had not been during the war.

Some had been keyed to such a high pitch of constant excitement and had come to have so little regard for human life that only the banditry and the chances of killing and being killed which were opened up by the era of lawlessness following prohibition could bring them alive. The sensitive, the idealistic who had gone to war with brave hearts, sincerely believing they were warring for a better world, returned shattered, embittered, apprehensive, considering themselves to have been dupes and so humiliated at the thought of it that they had vague hatreds and resolutions thereafter to live in contempt of all the prettier sentiments which men had hitherto held up as the ideals of a human society.

To many civilians the war did something worse even than it did to those who went overseas and returned. It made some women gloat with pride that their sons or sweethearts were engaged in mass murder; it caused them to develop active hates for those who bore German names, even though their great-grandfathers were born in this country; upon others it inflicted false sentiments, irrationally expressed, which were neither true to fact nor true to what they felt; for they truly felt only grief and fear, these poor women, and they wanted their sons, their brothers, their sweethearts back, safe and sound, at the speediest moment possible, whatever they said. In men it brought out either innate cruelty or hypocrisy or despair. It troubled and saddened me. As long as the war was over there, and we were not in it, it was almost like the repeated great famines in China or a disastrous earthquake in a remote part of the world: one does not feel such things emotionally; one takes them negligently, gives a contribution to the Red Cross and that is the end, so far as they touch one.

For nearly a year after we entered the war I could not arouse myself from an inner despondency, my feeling that rationality had gone from the world and that all my bright dreams of a happy and useful life were shattered in a collapsing civilization. Typical of the mood I experienced at the time is this entry in my diary on May 20, 1917. It reveals that at twenty-five years of age I was thinking of all joy and happiness as being in the past and that, in resentment and harassment, I was trying desperately to find some spar of reason and hope to which to cling:

I am getting old, old. I look back over these pages in this journal tonight and fondle them affectionately. Regret, sadness, delight pass alternately through my thoughts. Here is set down the record of a boy's soul—a soul that I do not now possess: it may be a larger and it may be a smaller soul that I now possess—at least it is not the same. The girls, the women I have loved, the depressions and the joys of adolescence, the constant striving toward some vague goal—these are here revealed to me. They would, of course, not be obvious to another one on earth, so false and inept are feeling and emotion and even thought when they are expressed in words.

Tonight I should give worlds to live through the experiences any one of a half-dozen of these pages record. To touch the hand of this or that one in silence even now, if I were sure he or she could feel as I at that moment the beauty of the past, that, indeed, would be a solace and a benefaction. I have been here simple and naïve, but I have expressed throughout, I feel, the deepest reaction to all with which I came into contact.

The tremendous rush of time! It was only yesterday that I lay in bed and while the rain beat upon the windowpane scribbled down the verses on that page underneath this one. And yet in this short lapse of time has so much happened.

I have been to college, loved, worked and suffered there, tasted there the first bitter fruits of life—and life's joys. I have gone into a profession nearest akin to my ambition's bent, have married and have now a boy—three years old in July. We are at war with Germany. My brother, George, is in barracks at Fort Sill, a mounted orderly. Stevers (Martin D.) is training for the officers' reserve corps at Fort Sheridan. War was declared on Good Friday, April 6th, and on that day my whole psychology took a tumble. To me weeks of adjustment were necessary before I was even two days of the same mental attitude. It was, and has been, to me absurd that we should say what is now being said: "We enter the war for liberty; Prussianism must go."

The direct cause, the sinking of American ships by submarines by a blockaded country whose only effective weapon for combating the blockade is the submarine, seems to me illogical and inane. It is as if we said, which in truth has been said, the submarine is an immoral weapon and we propose that Germany shall not use it. Of course, it all goes deeper than that. These facile phrases for justifying entrance into war are delusions.

What we really are in war for is that our own political and economic integrity is threatened by a German victory. And in the eternal flux of things, I suppose, it is in the order of nature that even so excellent a human mechanism as the German people have built up shall perish by its own incapacity to do more than that for which it was built. . . .

To get back, war has entered my sphere and that of my neighbor since the pages in this journal were written. And with it grayness— of the twilight or of the dawn? Revolution has, in Russia, dethroned the czar—a momentous achievement in the history of the world— momentous and portentous. It may mean the rise of a powerful democracy whose hunger and human greed my son, in his nation's hunger and greed, may find it necessary to contend with in war.

Peace? Idle, idle mumblings of idealists. There is no permanent peace, can be none. It is not in the nature of men or nations to stay at peace until they are one with Nineveh and Tyre. . . .

War prices already obtain, though food has so long been so costly that I cannot see how men with families exist on small salaries. I get $50 a week, and we live almost from hand to mouth, putting away only a small sum in the bank every week. Potatoes are 9 cents a pound, flour is $16 a barrel, and even round steak is 30 cents a pound. Bread sells at 15 cents a two-pound loaf in most markets, milk, fuel, clothing, furniture, all the necessities of life have gone up to almost prohibitive prices.

We are living now at 3741 Broadway, having moved from 1536 East 68th Street on the South Side of the city about a month ago. We are just getting settled. I have sandpapered the bird's-eye maple bedroom suite and reshellacked and revarnished it. I have stained and rubbed for a dull black effect the furniture in the living and dining rooms, and I have made very pretty chairs out of commonplace kitchen ones by giving them coats of white paint and then two coats of green enamel.

Hazel has made curtains and sofa pillows for the flat, shirred and covered a box in the hall with burlap and otherwise made things homey and comfortable. I have new bookshelves running along one wall of the room: these I have painted a dull black, as also I have painted the frame of the etching by Henry Ferrer. . . .

Last night Sherwood Anderson and Mrs Anderson, Lewis Galantière and Elaine Edel and Imogen Frizell were here for dinner. We ate by candlelight. Sherwood was in dinner dress—repaying, I suppose, the compliment of my first dinner at the home of Mrs Anderson in Division Street. Sherwood and Mrs Anderson live in separate apartments, he several blocks away in Cass Street. He comes to see her in the evenings, has dinner at her house and altogether they maintain a unique relationship. . . . He is a man with a marvelous softness in his voice, kindly, contemplative eyes, an intense emotional capacity and a calm manner.

After dinner Sherwood, Galantière and I soon were involved in a three-sided argument with the women only an audience to our fruit-less debate: Mrs Anderson reclined in the big chair, smoking one cigarette after another, throwing in a jibe at Sherwood now and then but taking up not at all any thread of the argument and weaving it. Elaine contented herself with watching with interest, she said, the expressions on our faces. Hazel, with her bright, deep brown eyes, was mentally keeping score, I suppose, upon the game, so eagerly did she follow every word.

Sherwood told me the first impression he had of me was that I was of an isolated, poetic temperament, austere and self-satisfied, that he looked every moment for me to pronounce a final word about life or literature and walk out, leaving him and Galantière amazed. How he got so absurd an impression he does not know: Hazel suggested that it was because I was tired and that I could not react on that day with my customary energy. I, on the other hand, know that two things were responsible for that impression: Sherwood's vanity and my own inability to praise anyone to his face, even when I think one is most deserving of praise. I am on my guard lest someone will mistake a word as flattery. Sincerity is overdone to the point of silence; but I cannot help it. Sherwood was expecting me to be as eager as was Lewis in meeting him and of talking about his work: I was indifferent from this constitutional defect, and he misunderstood it.

During the argument Sherwood said I intellectualized life too much, that I sought causes and traced effects, that I did not "lie fallow" enough. "My whole philosophy of life is made up," he said, "of the contention that two and two do not make four, that the mathematician's idea of life is wrong. You believe two and two make four and act on that principle."

We talked of the war, of Nietzsche, and of social life, never getting anywhere, of course, but Sherwood left an impression on me and I hope that I did on him, because that is the only value of such arguments. He has a beautiful idealism, a great depth of poetic feeling; he is more religious than I have been, even though he has never been to church. He said, in fact, that he believed he was an old-time Christian, that "Christ was righter than any man I know of." "What we need in this country is more sorrow, more prayer, more reliance upon something outside ourselves," he contended.

Well, we shall get it in war.

Things were to grow worse, not better, during the next two years, at least for me. Prices were to go higher and higher still; another child, a daughter, was to arrive on January 30, 1918, and her coming had filled her mother and me with anxiety and, at the first intimation of her arrival, with the terrified and pitiable expedients of the desperate. That winter was one of blizzards and of snow six feet deep in the streets; streetcar transportation was entirely suspended in those last weeks of January—only elevated trains were running. Our family doctor was ignorant and cruel, senselessly torturing my wife and me in his ignorance; his first diagnosis was that in my wife's womb were twins, which was terrifying to a young couple who were already in debt to a loan shark and with hospital and physician's bills to be met somehow; and his second diagnosis was that the child was abnormal, hydrocephalic, that maybe a Caesarian operation would be required and at all events he would have to use forceps, that from the indications of the heartbeat, the child was a boy, that he probably would not live and that if he did he would probably be an imbecile. During the raging blizzard he sent my wife to the hospital prematurely and returned her after a week; then labor pains came on her suddenly one morning and I had to take her to the hospital in a taxicab through slippery streets, deep with ice-glazed snow. I stood in the writing room numb and dazed with anxiety, suffering agony with every groan of pain my wife gave. The child came naturally, without undue effort on the mother's part. It was a normal girl baby, sound and healthy in every way; she weighed eight and a half pounds—the largest girl baby that had been born in that hospital in eight years. The doctor admitted he had been wrong in his diagnosis; and such was my own relief, so easily is pain followed by joy in the young, that I forgot the torture he had inflicted upon my wife and me; I forgot the desperate plight of my finances; I forgot the fear that in the midst of all this I might lose my job; I forgot the war and the miseries of the world in my exultant pride in this beautiful and precious bit of new life which was of me and in my gratitude that my wife was again free from anxiety and pain, radiant with pride and happy in the praises the nurses who gathered around her bed had for her new baby.

Three months later harrowing anxiety and trouble were to descend upon me. We had arranged to move to Rogers Park on May 1. The movers had been contracted for. A maid of general work had been in service with us since the birth of our daughter. My wife grew desperately ill in the early morning of the day before we were scheduled to move: most of our movables had been packed; my wife had walked across the bare floor on a chilly night. The doctor came and ordered her taken to the hospital at once: it was double pneumonia and pleurisy. The maid was so frantic that she was useless. The rest of the packing I would have to do myself and yet attend to my jobs at the office, for there was no one I could call upon to substitute for me: I directed the maid to confine herself to the care and feeding of the children.

At the office I could get no reassuring word from the hospital, except the perfunctory one, "The patient is doing as well as can be expected." I slept none that night and, next morning, to add to the difficulties of my plight, the movers of our successors in the apartment started moving their furniture into the place before our movers arrived. However, we did, in time, vacate. I bundled the maid, the children, my typewriter (which I had paid for long ago, $5 down and $2.50 a month—$40 in all for a rebuilt second-hand Underwood) and myself into a taxicab, and we all went to the new apartment where, as soon as the furniture arrived, I worked in a fever of activity, setting up the beds and unpacking food and kitchen utensils, so that at least the children and the maid might sleep. Thence I went for the first time to see my stricken wife, in whom the crisis was rapidly developing. Fatigue poisons were filling my blood, heightening my sensitivity and my consciousness feverishly. My wife was delirious. For four or five days her temperature of 105 degrees remained unabated; the doctor was without hope for her and intimated as much to me; then suddenly the fever subsided rapidly, and after a week's convalescence my wife was allowed to be removed to our new home, which the maid and I had endeavored to set tidily in order.

It is astonishing what the human spirit can endure privately and still function normally in work and give no outward indication of the terrors and desperation within. I say this because my records show that, at the very height of these various difficulties, I continued to write and to edit with gusto.

If I was melancholy at the office or afflicted with a mood of worry, or self-pity, I would stroll into Bob Peattie's office, seat myself on the desk near him and say nothing beyond a mere greeting. He would sense my depression and know what I had come in for—to be cheered up. He might lay aside his shears, turn around in his swivel chair and begin by saying, "Did I ever tell you about the time Mark Twain was entertained at a dinner given him by the Press Club? . . . No? Well, they were all so awed by being in the presence of their great hero that they were silent and stiff as boards. Mark endured this for a little while and then said, 'I don't know how you fellows feel about it, but I am in just the right mood to tell a dirty story.' And he proceeded to tell one. That broke the ice; the fellows relaxed and became natural, and what with drinks and all it turned out to be a merry evening." Or he would tell me about the pranks played upon him by his friend, Eugene Field. The Peatties had a large library, as persons who review books usually do. Field went to the Peattie home rather frequently for dinner, and while he was there, whenever he was alone in the library, he would busy himself writing on the fly-leaves of the books inscriptions to Robert Burns Peattie with his own signature as the donor, inserting comic variations on the sentiment and on the theme of the occasion of the gifts. More than half of the Peattie library had been thus inscribed before they discovered the joke. This joke proved to be valuable to the Peatties when they decided to part with the bulk of their library, for Eugene Field's signature had cash value among collectors, and presentation copies of books with Field's signature were especially rare, for there was Scotch blood in him and he was not known, Peattie said, ever to have given anybody, except his family, anything. Or Peattie would tell me the expedient Field used to pry a raise out of the notoriously tight-fisted Victor Lawson, owner and editor of the Chicago *Daily News* on which Field conducted his famous humor column "Sharps and Flats." After repeated unavailing efforts to extract a raise of salary out of Lawson, Field gathered up from the streets twelve of the dirtiest, raggedest urchins he could find and promised them each a nickel if they would sit quietly on a bench in the editorial rooms of the *Daily News* until he told them they might go. The boys tagged after him as he entered the *Daily News* building and up the stairs behind him. He sat them down on a bench just outside Lawson's door. His own desk was near by. Lawson soon emerged from his office, looked at the children with surprise but said nothing. He went about giving orders, but just as he was about to enter his office again, he paused and asked Field what those children were doing there. Field said they were waiting for him; they were his children. Lawson asked him why he didn't keep them clean and give them some decent clothes. Field declared with a tragic air that his children were motherless, that so much of his time was taken up with work at the office that he could not personally look after them and that, besides, his salary was such that he had barely enough money to feed and house them, let alone clothe them properly. Whether touched by the story or afraid Field would perpetrate a more embarrassing joke, Lawson gave Field a raise.

One evening in the fall of 1917 I was in Peattie's office and was idly looking over the books that would go unreviewed. Space for book reviews was limited in the *Tribune* to three or four columns during those days of war news. Since only a few books could be treated in such inadequate space, it was Peattie's habit to award this space to publishers who advertised in the *Tribune*. Review copies of other books he locked up in a tall bookcase with glass doors until the case was full, whereupon he shipped them out to the Cook County jail and the Cook County hospital. Robert M. McBride & Co. were at that time not advertising in the *Tribune,* nor, to be sure, were they advertising conspicuously anywhere else. Looking over these books by hopeful authors whose hopes would be dashed as far as any notice by the Chicago *Tribune* was concerned, I was so struck by the title, *The Cream of the Jest,* by an author named James Branch Cabell, that I asked Peattie if I might take a look at it. That night I read it in that state of exalted excitement which comes from discovering something new, rich and exciting. I considered it one of the drollest books I had ever read and that not the least droll among the author's ideas was that of setting himself down in the front of the book as the author of twelve nonexistent books, with such fantastic titles as *The Rivet in Grandfather's Neck, The Cords of Vanity* and, among genealogies, *Branch of Abington* and *The Majors and Their Marriages.* The next morning I communicated my enthusiasm to Mr Peattie, who told me I could have space to review the book if I kept the review "within half a column." I looked up Cabell in *Who's Who in America.* I could not find his biography in the copy available, although it had been included in previous issues. (Not until later did I discover that Cabell had written all the books he ascribed to himself.) Then I called up Lewis Galantière at Kroch's bookstore and asked him if he had ever heard of Cabell. He said he had and not only that but had mentioned to me the fact that Guy Holt, of Robert M. McBride & Co., was particularly enthusiastic about the book and had asked me as well as Galantière to do him the favor of reading it. I had forgotten this: so many books were being called to my special attention by publishers.

The heading on my review was: "Here Is Your Chance to Own a First Edition" and, within the limits of the space given me, I made an impassioned exhortation to the reading public to treat themselves to this book which had given me so much pleasure.

Shortly thereafter Mr Peattie was retired on a pension, and I became literary editor in addition to my other duties as assistant Sunday editor and editor of a page opposite the Sunday editorial page which was set aside for essays and called (in the office) the "highbrow page." In this I serialized parts of Cabell's next book, *Beyond Life,* and thereby provoked one of the most entertaining literary dogfights ever staged in this country. Rupert Hughes attacked what he misunderstood to be Cabell's aesthetic tenets to the extent of three columns; Cabell replied with merciless and malicious humor; Hughes countered with an extraordinary document largely devoted to his career wherein he said he had learned Greek art at his mother's knee and had been an encyclopedist as well as an acknowledged scholar in many fields; and Cabell replied in a brief but malicious quip (see Appendix IV). Bert Leston Taylor, Keith Preston, Richard Atwater and Ben Hecht joined in the squabble.

Robert Nichols, the English poet, came to town as a litterateur-propagandist for the Allies, and after his first lecture he asked me to dinner. I went only to berate him as an illiterate, condescending Englishman over here to boost fifth-rate English writers without ever having read American writers like Sandburg, Masters, Aiken, Dreiser and Cabell. I bawled him out for not having read *The Cream of the Jest*. He got a copy of the book and read it (he wrote me) all night long in a Pullman berth: it was, he said, a work of genius—a fine flowering of a rich subconscious. I printed the letter. Then Aiken and Galantière each wrote me letters praising Cabell but criticizing the "unrestraint" of my enthusiasm. I replied with two long blasts. In his column, "A Line o' Type or Two," B. L. T. wrote:

THE SEETHING QUESTION

In all literary gabble
Concerning Mr. J. B. Cabell
No one has yet got up to tell
If it be Cabell or Cabell.

I replied:

You may slip it to the rabble
That his name is James B. Cabell.

I attacked Wilson Follett for bringing out a book on the contemporary novel without mentioning Cabell. Follett made haste to make amends with a glowing article on the entire work of Cabell in the *Dial*. Floyd Dell reviewed *Beyond Life* extensively and sympathetically in the *Liberator* under the title "The Importance of Being an Artist."

H. L. Mencken observed the Chicago battle from afar and devoted his monthly article in the *Smart Set* entirely to it, saying (in part): "Out in Chicago, the only genuinely civilized city in the New World, they take the fine arts seriously and get into such frets and excitements about them as are raised nowhere else save by baseball, murder, political treachery, foreign wars and romantic loves . . ." (here follows a tirade against New York, Boston, Philadelphia and other capitals as "intellectual slums," then): "But what I started out to do was to call attention to the uproarious critical battle that has been going on in Chicago over James Branch Cabell —a battle full of tremendous whoops, cracks, wallops and deviltries, with critics pulling the nose of critics, and volunteers going over the top in swarms, and the air heavy with ink, ears, typewriters, adjectives, chair legs and strophes from the Greek Anthology. And the question, what is it? One of morals—Cabell vs. the Comstocks? Nay. One of sales—Cabell as a best-seller? Nay. One of patriotism, politics? Cabell as a Socialist, a forward looker, an agent of the Wilhelmstrasse? Nay again; the question is simply one of style. . . . A question of style—and within one verst of the stockyards! Almost one fancies the world bumped by a flying asteroid, and the

Chicago River suddenly turned into the Seine. . . ." The rest of the article is devoted to praise of Cabell as "a man of novel and ingenious ideas, a penetrating ironist, a shrewd and infectious laugher, a delicate virtuoso of situation, an anatomist of character, one who sees into the eternal tragicomedy of hope and striving, above all, a highly accomplished doctor of words."

The upshot of all this furor was that the sale of *Beyond Life* was only a little over 3,000 copies, mainly in Chicago and environs. But still, not a bad sale for a book of essays.

Jurgen came next. Before it was published I had to plead with Guy Holt not to cut out the Anaïtis episode and otherwise emasculate the novel—not that Holt wanted to, but pressure was being put upon him by his employer-publisher to kill the book altogether. Cabell wanted to call the book *The Pawnbroker's Shirt,* which title I liked, but Holt was adamant in contending that this title was unsalable. When the book was published I was handicapped, if gratified, that Cabell had dedicated it to me. But I did not let modesty stand in my way. I wrote of the novel glowingly in the Chicago *Tribune.* Echoes of the Chicago battle drew attention of reviewers all over the country to Cabell's latest work; Sinclair Lewis, Joseph Hergesheimer, H. L. Mencken, Carl Van Vechten, Waldo Frank, John Macy and Emily Clarke visited Cabell in Richmond; Frances Newman wrote adulatorily about him in the Atlanta *Constitution.* Hugh Walpole came to Chicago to lecture and to autograph books at Marshall Field & Company's store. I went over to see him and told him I had read his "imbecile remarks" (and they were that exactly, because he had not troubled to inform himself of any American novelists later than Jack London except Edith Wharton and Upton Sinclair) about American literature to reporters for the New York papers, and that I would have no respect for him until he had taken the trouble to learn the contents of some American books issued since Mark Twain. Walpole was both patient with and impressed by my assault upon him—even if he did grow red in the face. He asked me the names of some books he should read. I jotted down a few, with special emphasis on Cabell. A few days later I received a letter from Walpole thanking me for calling attention to Cabell, describing *Jurgen* as a masterpiece of a "talent as original and satisfying as anything our time has seen" and saying he had ordered all of Cabell's books and was going to visit Cabell preparatory to writing an article on him for the *Yale Review,* which article duly appeared under the title, "The Art of James Branch Cabell," and was later used as a pamphlet and as an Introduction to the book.

Others jumped on the band wagon—John Macy, Edward Hale Bierstadt, H. L. Mencken, and the news percolated to the intellectually comatose and provincially self-satisfied New York. There Heywood Broun, then literary editor of the *Tribune,* ignored *Jurgen* but printed a letter from a vaudeville press agent, Walter Kingsley, in which letter was the sniggering statement that "James Branch Cabell is making a clean getaway with *Jurgen,* quite the naughtiest book since George Moore began ogling maidservants in Mayo," and which went on to describe the book as "thinly veiled episodes of all the perversities, abnormalities and damn-foolishness of sex." Someone sent a clipping of Kingsley's letter to John S. Sumner, secretary of the New York Society for the Suppression of Vice; Sumner procured a warrant and descended upon the publishers, seized the plates of *Jurgen* and summoned the publishers to defend themselves on a charge of publishing and selling "a certain offensive, lewd, lascivious and indecent book." The book was suppressed and impounded for two and a half years, when, at the conclusion of a three-day trial, Judge Charles C. Nott of the Court of General Sessions directed a jury to bring a verdict of acquittal.

Jurgen was released. It sold like wildfire. And thereafter, for several years, Cabell's succeeding books stayed in the best-selling class until Cabell himself ceased to write of the descendants of Don Manuel, and up to the publication of *The Nightmare Has Triplets,* wrote under the name of Branch Cabell.

After *Jurgen,* Cabell was so indelibly marked as the author of *Jurgen* that reviewers failed to observe that in *Figures of Earth* and in *The High Place* Cabell essayed more difficult and profounder tasks than he had in *Jurgen* and acquitted himself in these tasks majestically; some reviewers complained, in effect, that Cabell's later books were not as full of lechery as *Jurgen.*

That is the real cream of the jest. *Jurgen* is, essentially, a novel of the poetic attitude wherein all the adventures are of the mind and spirit. Its ultimate moral is a plea for monogamy, a poetic counsel

[353]

to the young poet never to put his dreams to the unfair and disastrous test of relating them to reality; let the poet apostrophize in haunting verse diverse perfect mistresses of the imagination, but let him not seek in the flesh to find one lest he, in Flaubert's phrase, find in adultery all the platitudes of marriage.

Cabell wrote of a hero who was all action, Manuel, an extravert par excellence, a man in whom dreams did not dwell but who translated into action every impulse as it arose. Reviewers, most of them, ignored this. Cabell remains, in their minds, only as the creator of Jurgen, and this harmless, ineffectual, timid, henpecked poet, Jurgen, reigns in their minds incomprehensibly as the paragon of potency and profligacy.

This dismayed me as well as Cabell while it was going on. But Cabell learned early to smile at it all, and he smiled in *Preface to the Past* to recall those brave, exciting days, and to recall that he accurately prophesied the waning, when the 'thirties were ended, of reputations as well as the creative powers of those who figured so prominently then in the limelight.

My opening blast as literary editor* in the Saturday pages of book news and reviews, which I decked out with new hand-lettered engraved streamers across the pages, new type heads, line

---

*I wrote H. L. Mencken, with whom I had begun to carry on a voluminous correspondence after the appearance of my article "Fanfare" in review of his *A Book of Prefaces,* telling him I had just been made literary editor. He answered with a lengthy letter of which I quote (Mencken dated none of his letters, but it was written in the latter part of February 1918):

"I congratulate the *Tribune* and God upon your ordination, but not you yourself. You will sweat for authors, and they will drop purgatives in your coffee. You will do filthy favors for publishers, and they will curse you in the miserable taverns where they meet. But remember this: there is a lot of fun in the job."

Mencken's prophecy was accurate. With a few noble exceptions (and as it happens these few were all first rate), I was to find that the more you sweated for authors, the more eagerly you sought to widen their audience and defend them against their critics, the more likely were they to turn on you and go out of their way to do you harm—which, however, never affected my attitude toward their work when I thought their work was good. I was also to find that you might write five leading articles in succession in praise of five books on a publisher's list, grant him permission to use the reviews in broadside reprints, work in various ways to drum up sales for these books voluntarily and for the love of doing it; and then you might write a roast of a book on the list of the same publisher and he would write to your boss trying to get you fired. (The boss always sent the letters to me, after formally acknowledging receipt of them, often with a penciled comment such as, "Note contents and drop in wastebasket.")

drawings and caricatures, was called "On a Certain Condescension in Our Natives," in allusion to James Russell Lowell's famous essay, "On a Certain Condescension Among Foreigners" (see Appendix V). I was genuinely worked up with irritation over the opacity and dunderheadedness of the reviewers of the New York press and the bigwig critics for the more serious literary magazines in the East. They all seemed to me to be eager enough to pay glowing tributes to the dullest mediocrity among English novelists and yet to begrudge the space they gave even to a curt dismissal of the talents of American men and women who were producing really notable work. The bigwig critics seemed actively to hate literature.

The whole literary scene in New York seemed to me to be dominated by men and women who were shallow, pompous, uninformed, either frivolous or full of the wrong kind of solemnity, playing into the hands of the private organizations bent on censorship, like the New York Society for the Suppression of Vice and the Boston Watch and Ward Society, and also into the hands of the militant upholders of the genteel tradition in letters. In New York only the *New Republic,* the suppressed *Liberator,* the *Dial* and the *Smart Set* had seemed to be aware of a living and vital literature emerging in a distinctly American language. Dreiser was denounced and persecuted; Willa Cather, Joseph Hergesheimer, Frank Moore Colby were not recognized for the merit they possessed; Sherwood Anderson's *Winesburg, Ohio* came out, and although it was treated in the Chicago Press for the notable event it was, it was a long time before Anderson was recognized and taken up by a small clique in the East, who then almost ruined the simple and unlettered man by writing turgid, involved and polysyllabic tributes to him in the *New Republic* and the *Dial.* Anderson understood scarcely a word of these tributes, but he purred with satisfaction at knowing that the highbrows and intellectuals of the East had taken him up. One word describing himself and his work he understood, and that was "naïve." He began to use the word repeatedly in conversation and grew to be so self-consciously naïve that he seemed to me to drool; he was several years getting over this attention from the intellectuals and becoming himself again.

H. L. Mencken, who was stimulating and invigorating, a portent and a figure in American letters to us in Chicago and, indeed, to young men with a taste for life and letters everywhere but in New York, was dismissed as a cheap-jack by both the intellectuals of the liberal magazines and the literary editors of the New York newspapers until I wrote the first lengthy appreciation of his work, treating him seriously and with respect in an article under the title "Fanfare," published in the Chicago *Tribune* in November 1917, apropos of the publication of his first book of critical essays.

Mencken's most formidable rival as a writer of polemics was Stuart Pratt Sherman, a professor of English at the University of Illinois, who was performing in the *Nation* under the editorship of Paul Elmer More. Sherman saw the rise of Mencken's popularity and influence in the Middle West, where it was more obvious than it was in the East, broke the rule of the academicians to ignore Mencken and cracked down upon him in an article in the *Nation* which filled me with dismay and horror. It purported to be a review of Mencken's *A Book of Prefaces* and was called "Beautifying American Letters." There was no indication of the contents of Mencken's book in this review; it gave not the slightest glimmering as to what the book was about. It was a denunciation of Mencken as a German (although Mencken was a third-generation American)—at the very height of the war hysteria, the wholesale internment of innocent Germans as spies or enemies of the country; it was, it seemed to me, cunningly designed to silence Mencken by internment or arouse the rabble against him and not only against Mencken but all American writers who bore German or German-Jewish names. The review was also anti-Semitic to a high degree, linking the Jews with Germans as inimical to the American tradition. There was nothing in Mencken's book about the war; nothing political or pro-German in it: the principal essay in the book was *Puritanism as an American Literary Force,* which was directed against the activities of the Comstocks, but the essays were in appreciation of Mencken's contemporaries, notably Joseph Conrad and Sherman's dog-to-be-beaten-with-any-stick, Theodore Dreiser.

Not long afterwards Sherman published a selection of his fulminations against the writers of the time, including his attack on Dreiser but omitting his act of dangerous malice against Mencken, as though he had thought better of it. (He never republished this essay in book form, I believe, although he made books out of nearly all of his journalistic writings.)

I was still angry with the advantage Sherman had taken against Mencken, and I thought that such tactics on the part of a man in high academic repute and in a position of power should be opposed with the utmost vigor. Therefore when Sherman's *On Contemporary Literature* appeared I wrote a review of it which was but little more of a review of his book than his review had been of Mencken's. I gave it the heading, "Prof. Sherman Gives Asylum to His Brood" (see Appendix VI).

This review wounded Sherman to the quick; it caused him to write Paul Elmer More some curious untruths and to complain that he was set upon by a mob of Chicago gangsters. It started a feud between Sherman and myself which lasted, on his side, until after he came to New York. His biographers, Woodbridge and Zeitlin, without troubling to check on the statements made by Sherman in his letters, took them at face value, and Zeitlin, who wrote the part of the biography relating to this episode, wrote malignantly about me and so stupidly misread an important "humorous" letter of Sherman's that one wonders to what extent he has further traduced his subject in his zeal to do him honor.

Chicago was enjoying the literary excitement without knowing or caring much what it was about, and Eastern writers were following it closely. I engineered dogfights and got up controversies. Robert Nichols, the poet, returned to town after a lecture tour and uttered some inanities in that condescending manner which many Englishmen do not know they possess because a feeling of superiority to all other peoples is so natural to them that condescension is not conscious. Conrad Aiken, much superior to Nichols as a poet, had come to town and was staying at my house because a small lecture engagement had been arranged for him; and because Aiken was an American, he was shown none of the attention accorded Nichols. I brought Nichols and Aiken together at lunch. Later I showed Aiken a clipping of a newspaper interview Nichols had accorded. Aiken grew red with resentment. He seethed over the matter for a while and wrote a lampoon in verse, dedicated to Nichols, entitled "Verbum Saphead." I printed it. This caused Nichols to call upon me, with a wounded and humble letter in reply to Aiken, saying he had stayed up all night on a train to read Aiken's "Senlin," which he said was a poem to place Aiken's name beside that of Poe. Aiken was contrite, and so I published his letter of contrition.

I was championing Aiken, Alfred Kreymborg, Maxwell Bodenheim and several of the lesser poets in my column as well as Sandburg, Masters and Lindsay. Aiken and Louis Untermeyer were rivals for the post of critic of poetry in the *New Republic,* and a feud started between them in the columns of that magazine. I thought Untermeyer had been unfair to Aiken's work in a book of essays on modern poetry, so I attacked Untermeyer on this score. But soon Aiken also brought out a book of critical essays entitled *Scepticisms,* in which I thought he was unduly severe upon his brother poets, particularly Kreymborg. I wrote a severely ironical piece about Aiken's book, which precipitated an acrimonious correspondence between Aiken and myself, which ended with our being friends again until, he whom I had known as full of adulation for James Branch Cabell, wrote an article review for the *Dial* which I thought was smug and misinforming about Cabell's work, and our feud broke out again, to last for several months.

Ben Hecht, annoyed that anybody should praise anyone but himself, wrote a brief diatribe against Cabell for Henry Blackman Sell's book page in the Chicago *Daily News* which enticed me into some sarcasms about Hecht. I had never met Hecht. Tennessee Mitchell, then the wife of Sherwood Anderson, invited Carl Sandburg, Llewellyn Jones, Anderson, Hecht and myself to dinner to meet Waldo Frank, an earnest-minded New York intellectual. Tennessee had purposely brought Hecht and me together without telling either that the other was to be there. Hecht and I were polite enough during the dinner; but we had no sooner gone into the drawing room than a heated argument arose between Hecht and myself over some matter of preferences in literature. We hurled epithets, quotations, names of European writers and titles of their books at one another's heads, our voices rising crescendo, for more than an hour, giving no one else a chance to say a word.

Frank sat in wild-eyed astonishment. Later he told us that he was enchanted, impressed, that nowhere in the world, except in Chicago, could literature be such an alive and burning issue; that New Yorkers in comparison were apathetic and uninformed on the subject of literature. Hecht and I became friends after that night, and thereafter it was only with difficulty that we could appear to be enemies in print. Keith Preston, a professor of Greek and Latin at Northwestern University, who was conducting a column of humorous verse and comment on literary subjects under the heading "The Periscope" in the *Daily News,* joined in the fun, and he and I gleefully engaged in some prodigious scraps in print, hurling classical allusions and items of Greek scholarship at each other once a week and visiting alternately at each other's home for hours of whisky and soda and loud laughter over the antics of the literati. We were serious enough, all of us, in the importance we attached to literature and jealous in guarding it against its enemies; but we did not take ourselves too seriously.

As literary editor I was sent to New York, Boston and Philadelphia two or three times a year to call upon the publishers and get advance news of their publications. On the first of these trips I dropped down to Baltimore to meet Mencken and was taken by him to one of the beer-and-music evenings of his cronies. I later wrote an informal character sketch of Mencken as he was then. (See skit on Mencken among the Unconventional Portraits in Appendix IX.)

One of these trips to New York happened to coincide with one of James Branch Cabell's rare visits to New York. Joseph Hergesheimer was also in town. Howard Cook, then an editor for the firm of Moffat, Yard & Co., brought the three of us together. Cabell and Hergesheimer had never met, and I had not met Hergesheimer, although I had written much about him. Hergesheimer, throughout the luncheon, was so earnest and so well protected by his egoism that, as he talked about how much alike in their art and ideas he and Cabell were, he did not realize that Cabell in his replies was slyly but patently kidding him. I was so amused by this session that I went back to my hotel and wrote of it in the form of a theatrical skit, heading it " 'Jim and Joe, Authors,' a One-Act Play Without Punch or Point" and dropped it in the mails that night to be run on my page the following Saturday (see Appendix VII).

On my first trip to New York I was invited by George Jean Nathan to come to his apartment at the Royalton for cocktails, and while I was there he asked me to read a short story he had just bought for the *Smart Set* to see what I thought of it. He folded over the page containing the title and the author's name so I could begin at once. I read with mounting excitement and finally handed the story back to him. I told him it was marvelous, a modern version of *Thaïs,* but a magnificent piece of work. Nathan said he thought it was the best short story that had ever come into the *Smart Set* and asked me to guess who the author was. I had no idea. "Somerset Maugham," he told me.

It was Maugham's story, "Miss Thompson," out of which the famous play, *Rain,* was made. It had been the rounds of the magazines, including *Cosmopolitan,* in which Maugham had always had a ready market at a high price for his stuff. But all of the magazine editors in New York were afraid of it—afraid of the Comstocks and of the squeamish. That is how the *Smart Set* got it at the magazine's notoriously low rate of payment for material. . . . As a sequel to this, John D. Williams, the theatrical producer, cabled Maugham, asking him to make a play out of the story, saying he would like to produce it. Maugham, an expert playwright with many stage successes to his credit, cabled back that it was a short story and did not lend itself to adaptation for the stage. Williams then cabled asking Maugham's price for the dramatic rights to the story. Maugham cabled that he could have them gratis. John Colton adapted the play; Williams produced it with Jeanne Eagels in the leading role. Maugham had come over from London to supervise the production of a play of his of the success of which he was highly confident. He thought so little of the possibilities of *Rain* that he did not attend the opening performance. The play he had his heart on was an expensive failure. On the opening night of *Rain* the last curtain rang down to what was probably the greatest spontaneous ovation of an audience in Broadway history.

Once, on those trips East, I spent an evening with the aging John Butler Yeats at his corner in the dining room of the

Petitpas Restaurant (see Appendix VIII) in New York. And once I went down to Richmond to visit Cabell in his large colonial-Virginia house with mullioned windows, in Dumbarton Grange, where he wrote most of the biography of Dom Manuel. Mrs Cabell was away visiting one of her daughters at Randolph-Macon College. Cabell cannot drive an automobile; Mrs Cabell was family chauffeur. He met me at the station, and we boarded a streetcar. I did not notice the Jim Crow signs and started to sit down in the section reserved for colored people. Cabell said, "You'll get arrested if you do that," and smiled. We found a seat and rode to the end of the car line. Then we had to walk about half a mile to the house.

It was wartime, and servants had left their service and were drawing high wages in the munitions plants. The Cabells were without hired help in that big house. Mrs Cabell's daughter Virginia cooked a marvelous dinner of fried chicken, cream gravy and hot biscuits. We went into the living room for coffee. Cabell had warned me that he had had little experience in conversation. That night it would seem that neither he nor I had had any. There had seemed so many things I wanted to talk about when I should meet him, but there we were sitting together and I could think of nothing.

Occasionally he would break the silence with a grieved neighborly statement about the sorrow already inflicted thereabouts by the deaths of Richmond boys at the front and of influenza in the training camps; or he would say something about the difficulties of writing when the young folk were having parties at the house; or he would drum into me vocally the demand he had already made and was to continue to make for ten years or more: to get out a book or books made up of my journalistic writings, as Mencken, Nathan, Van Vechten and others had done. (Guy Holt, of Robert M. McBride & Co., had also urged me to do this, saying he would publish the first and later books; but I lived so actively in the present then that to reread old clippings, paste them up, arrange and revise them was something I had neither the stomach nor the leisure for.)

Then, with an air of real curiosity, he looked at me suddenly and asked, "How do you manage to avoid being assassinated?"

He subscribed to the Saturday issue of the Chicago *Tribune;* and he had been reading of the squabbles and controversies I had been engaged in. His manner is quiet and rather humble; his accent is that of Tidewater Virginia; he seemed then to me to be a man who outwardly fitted himself perfectly and unobtrusively into the whole social scheme of things domestically and communally in Richmond and yet lived an inner life that was realized in the dreams of his novels.

In the room in which I slept that night there was a photograph of Cabell when he was at the College of William and Mary: he was then a fat boy with eager and challenging eyes; now he was thinnish and wore glasses and was losing some of his hair at the sides of the top of his forehead; and his face had taken on angles and lines of quiet dignity and inner serenity. I arose so late that I scarcely had time to snatch a bite of breakfast and drink a cup of coffee and make the train I had planned to catch back to New York. When Cabell waved to me from the platform while I stood on the steps of the train there was an expression on his face which told me that I had found a personal friend in Cabell as well as an author whose work I admired greatly and meant much to me.

There had been but six men in the East whom I had wanted to meet particularly—Frank Moore Colby, H. L. Mencken, James Branch Cabell, George Jean Nathan, James Huneker and John Macy. Huneker I never succeeded in meeting: at the time he was living in Flatbush, Brooklyn, and commuting all the way to Philadelphia and back every day as music critic and "steeple jack of the five arts," as he called himself, for a Philadelphia newspaper. Stimulating and prodigiously informed in all branches of art as he was, he was a humble man who deprecated his abilities and thereby convinced New York editors that he was not as sound as stodgier and more solemn critics; and thus he was always being hired as a fill-in at some post when the staff critic of a New York newspaper was abroad, or he would be hired to write a daily column for a year and then dropped. No New York newspaper editor was perspicacious enough to give him a permanent berth and a spot in the paper Huneker's followers could always turn to. He and I corresponded occasionally at great length, he writing in his fine, small, careful penmanship; and he once wrote in his *World* column that I was one of the three or four critics in America to whose opinions he attached any value and once quoted with credit a quip of mine, "The wages of sin is art" with more pleasure than I had had in writing it (for I didn't think it was a good quip); but I never met him.

To Frank Moore Colby I have devoted a sketch in Appendix IX.

The man I wanted to meet most in Boston was John Macy, whose fine book of criticism, *The Spirit of American Literature,* had been a treasure, often reread by me. So eager was I to meet him on my first morning in Boston that, not being able to find his name in the telephone book, I did not wait to write asking for an appointment. I had his address, and at about ten o'clock I was sitting in the Victorian parlor of an old Boston home near the Common, then used for paying guests. I was surrounded by a whatnot and other weird items of furniture of a vanished era, while the white-haired hostess went upstairs to announce me. I was shown to Macy's room. He had been lying on a pallet in the center of a room otherwise almost bare except for stacks of books on the floor, and he had been reading Blasco Ibáñez in Spanish. He was still in pajamas and lounging robe, with a great shock of beautiful white hair, a hawk face, amused, quizzical eyes peering from behind horn-rimmed spectacles, thin and white and stooped.

As a Socialist and pacifist Macy had been the victim of abuse in Boston, and almost at once he began telling me there was only one civilized man in the whole of Boston, his friend John Koren; there had been civilized men in the town once, he said, but they were all dead now. He dressed and took me to the St Botolph Club, where I met Koren. Neither of them was speaking to their fellow club members, but they had refused to resign, and it appears that the others did not dare throw them out. They both talked volubly of the cruelties and stupidities being enacted in Boston under the guise of patriotism and of the opportunities now offered for writers of cheap and shallow fiction to get themselves exalted publicity by hunting down and denouncing people who did not believe in war or in the necessity of our entering it—opportunities these writers did not neglect.

Macy and I remained friends until the day of his death: he

wrote to me often, especially on hearing I was ill or in any kind of trouble, reminding me that I was his "spiritual godson." . . . On that same visit to Boston I was taken to a tea, where I was introduced to a gracious and lovely little woman past middle age, who was so sweet and pleasant to me that I was heartily ashamed of the misdirected energy I had used in invectives against her books. She was Eleanor H. Porter. If she had ever read any of my reviews or remembered them, she did not remind me of this.

The battles I waged in Chicago in behalf of a rising and distinctive American literature were accompanied by wars against the censorship. Anthony Comstock's vicar or similar in Chicago was a Major Funkhauser, a civic officer appointed by the mayor, who looked for all the world as though he might have later sat as model for Peter Arno, except that his white mustache was not walrus, it was military. He was a dandy in the style of the retired English army officer keeping a pose of enormous dignity. It was he who was duped by the press agent of an art-reproduction firm into arresting an art dealer for displaying a copy of "September Morn" in his window, an action which gave so much publicity to that mediocre work of art that the art-reproduction firm sold millions of the prints. Otherwise Major Funkhauser was an adornment to the town rather than a menace to art.

Censorship there was largely of spontaneous generation among clubwomen—as, for instance, when demand was made by them that the partially nude statue of Goethe be removed from Lincoln Park. The only instance I recall of highhanded vandalism on the part of censors in Chicago was when the federal officers seized a series of panels, only one of two examples in the world of a particular period in the history of Chinese art, very ancient and very precious, and burned all of them despite editorial protests on the part of the Chicago *Tribune* and pleas from the officials of the Field Museum. The panels had been imported by Jerome Bloom, an artist. The series were colored cartoons painted on silk and represented twelve stages in the love life of a Chinese maiden. Only the final one could by any remote imagination be accounted obscene. Bloom begged that the panels be turned over to the museum and shown only to students; when this was refused, the museum officials asked the federal officers to destroy the final panel and let them have the others. But petty officials who like to show their power find in such attentions a magnification of themselves; the more deference or supplication accorded them, the more adamant they become. The panels, all of them, were burned in the post-office furnace.

Censorship was rife in New York, however, during 1917 and 1918. Fearing it would spread and would cripple all freedom of expression, I wrote against specific acts of censorship and against censorship in general. I selected some pertinent excerpts from Milton's noble tract against the censorship of his time and in be-half of freedom of expression, the *Areopagitica,* and published them as an article, signed it "John Milton," without explanation, as though he were a contemporary. It amused me to find John Milton denounced in letters to the editor as a misguided and verbose man who advocated license and not liberty and thus should be brought to account.

Mrs N. P. Dawson of the New York *Globe* was the most mis-chievous of the New York reviewers in abetting the censorship activities because she was diabolically clever. Although James Huneker's *Painted Veils,* after being rejected by Scribner, was brought out by Horace Liveright in a limited edition for subscrib-ers only and copies sent to reviewers only as a present, with the request that they should not review it, Mrs Dawson seized upon it as an opportunity to set off her fireworks; she denounced it categorically and in detail as an obscene, corrupting and horrifying book and Huneker as a monster of depravity. *Painted Veils* was merely a dull, unorganized novel, with a few interesting spots in it, for instance the one in which he described the notorious Girl-in-the-Pie dinner, given in the late Nineties by the flamboyant financier, James Hazen Hyde, which had so scandalized New York at the time. Mrs Dawson's pet aversion for a long time was Ben Hecht; but Joyce, Cabell, Dreiser, Lawrence, Hergesheimer, Bennett and many another came in for severe moral drubbings at her hands.

Shortly after the armistice was declared, the group of us who lunched once a week either at Schlogl's or at a big table in the grill room at Marshall Field & Co.—Carl Sandburg, Sherwood

Anderson, Ben Hecht, J. P. McEvoy, John V. A. Weaver, Harry
Hansen, Keith Preston, Richard Atwater, Henry Blackman Sell
and I—began to scatter. Hansen, who had a correspondent for the
Daily News with the German armies on both the Eastern and
Western fronts and in Stockholm before we got into the war, and
who had specialized in the political history of Europe, was sent
to Versailles to cover the peace conference; Hecht was sent to
Austria and Germany to write feature and news stories on postwar conditions among our late enemies: he witnessed the several
revolutions and counter-revolutions in Munich and Berlin; Carl
Sandburg went on a tour of recitals of his poems to his own accompaniment on the guitar; Atwater was called to the University
of Minnesota to teach English; Preston was immersed in his duties
at the University; I, as dramatic critic and dramatic editor as well
as literary editor and critic and assistant Sunday editor in charge
of make-up and rotogravure editor, had little time for sleep, much
less to talk literature and life for two hours over a lunch table.

And presently I saw appearing, in Henry Blackman Sell's column of news and comment on books and authors in the *Daily
News,* repeated eulogies of Ray Long, who had made a great commercial success of the *Red Book* by the discovery and publication
of the "Tarzan" stories by Edgar Rice Burroughs and of the outdoor stories of James Oliver Curwood and by the judicious use
of romantic-realistic series by well-known authors like Rupert
Hughes. There was less obvious reason for these eulogies than
if Sell had chosen to extoll the editorial merits of Maxwell Perkins
of Scribner's, T. R. Smith of Liveright's, Robert N. Linscott of
Houghton, Mifflin Co., or Eugene Saxton of Doubleday, Page &
Co., so I wondered what was up—until the reason became apparent with the announcement in the press that Ray Long was
leaving the *Red Book* and going to New York to assume complete
editorial supervision of all of the Hearst magazines and edit the
Cosmopolitan, and this news was followed shortly by the announcement that Ray Long was taking Henry Blackman Sell with
him to New York to take over the editorship of *Harper's Bazaar.*

The *Little Review,* edited by the redoubtable Jane Heap and the
exotically beautiful Margaret Anderson in the interest of the
very latest in art and literature, moved to New York. The *Dial,*

purchased by Martyn Johnson, had been changed from a magazine in which ancient literary traditions were carefully embalmed into a magazine espousing liberal politics, with Wilson Follett as contributor of the principal critiques of the novel. The *Dial* had also brought on, from among the disciples of Randolph Bourne, in New York, an alumnus of the *New Republic,* a somnolent young man with a high forehead and appealing brown eyes, named Harold E. Stearns, who, because of the appealing brown eyes and the accounts of his brilliance and deep political wisdom which had preceded him, was immediately taken up by the bluestockings of the Gold Coast, Janet Ayre Fairbank and Mrs John Alden Carpenter, and introduced into Chicago society. Stearns came to my office and introduced himself, and we went out for a drink; thereafter it was his custom to drop in often and invite me out for a drink. He was so serious-minded and preoccupied with weighty problems that he was never aware that the drinks were to be paid for until after I had paid the reckoning. But I ignored this lack of interest in mere financial matters; for he had an interesting mind, and I was curious to discover by what process of mental telepathy he was able to know what was going on in the minds of European statesmen at any given moment. He had seen none of these men of diplomacy and intrigue, yet he seemed to know their minds better than they could know them themselves and tell what each was going to do next week or next month, which is something I am sure they did not know themselves. He would talk of these matters, of which I understood nothing, with an air of lugubrious profundity, with no reservations of dubiety whatever. I was pleased on reading his articles in the *Dial* to find that this air of omniscience and infallibility did not desert him when he shared his information and his wisdom with the generality in the form of prose. One false slip of self-doubt and some of us would have lost faith in him as an oracle.

One day sometime in 1915, a lanky, freckle-faced, sandy-haired, most amiable, most immediately friendly young man, vibrant with nervous energy, had come to the office to see Fanny Butcher, who wrote a column of book news and comment for one of the Sunday sections. Miss Butcher introduced me to him. He was Sinclair Lewis. He acknowledged the greeting with "Hello, Burt!" Soon

[367]

afterwards I was calling him "Red," whereas Miss Butcher stuck to "Hal." He was in town to get a job in a real-estate office, out of the experience of which he wrote *The Job*. I had liked all of his published books, and I had never met anyone more agreeable or more entertaining as a person. We got together every time he came to Chicago until I left there; but it was not until 1920 that he had become a personage, famous for the authorship of *Main Street*. My wife and I gave a party one night, inviting Lewis and Sherwood Anderson, Harry and Ruth Hansen, Keith and Etta Preston, Jerome and Florence Frank and Gene Markey. That evening we called upon Sherwood to tell his famous Mama Geighen story—his best unpublished story and his most hilarious story, published or unpublished. He was in top form about this fantastic binge he went on with George Wharton and about their encounter with the massive and marvelous woman who ran a saloon on the side of the road in Wisconsin, far from town or village. He sent us into gales of laughter, and he smiled modestly in satisfaction that his performance had been good. Lewis left the room. He came back after a minute or so. He had turned his collar and his vest hindpart before, parted his hair severely, powdered his face white. He held his hands before him, tips of fingers to tips of fingers. There was a look of severe piety on his face. He delivered an extempore sermon on the evils of drink and on the evil that women like Mama Geighen do in this world, so realistically that had he delivered it in precisely the same way in a Protestant church where he was not known I am sure it would have been accepted as a very elevating and ennobling sermon indeed. We all paid this manifest genius as an actor, improviser, orator as well as great novelist the tribute of complete silence until he had concluded. Then there was an uproar of laughter and acclaim. Lewis went into a bedroom to remove the powder and change his collar and vest. Sherwood was sitting beside me on a piano bench. Sherwood was jealous and mad as a wet hen because his performance had been capped. He turned to me and said, "It's a pity. He wants it so bad, and he will never have it." I did not ask Sherwood what he meant by "it." I knew. He meant "genius." There is in Lewis the least jealousy of his fellow writers of any writer I ever knew; no one goes out of his way to praise the contemporaries whose work he likes as much as Lewis does. His tribute to Thomas Wolfe in his speech of acceptance when he was awarded the Nobel Prize is but one of dozens of voluntary efforts to enhance the fame of his contemporaries and help them to gain wider audiences. . . . Later on that evening there was dancing, and wines and spirits for those who cared for them; Lewis got exhilarated and demonstrated his ability as a "human fly" by climbing out the window and making his way around the three sides of the sunroom on a ledge not more than an inch wide, and then climbing cautiously down the wall to the ground, two stories below, oblivious of the frightened screams and supplications of the women that he desist.

One day in the spring of 1920 there came to my desk a novel with an interesting title, *This Side of Paradise,* by a new author of whom I had heard nothing. I dipped into it and did not go out to lunch. Here was something fresh, vital, sparkling, new—a novel with faults, surely, but by an eager and observant author who knew the slang of the college campuses, knew that young men and women since the war had kicked over the traces and were exercising a full expression of their youth before growing old; and this young new author had overtones of sadness in his work and a Celtic gift for fantasy and for poetic moods. Here was a "discovery," so I thought. I wrote at once an enthusiastic review urging my readers to read the novel. Going to the elevated station that evening, I ran into John V. A. Weaver, an employee in the advertising department of the *Daily News,* whose verses, later published under the title, *In American,* had been highly praised by Mencken and others when they appeared in the *Smart Set,* and who occasionally wrote reviews for Sell. "Wow! Boy!" he exclaimed, clapping both hands on my shoulders. "Have I read a book! Have I READ A BOOK!" I asked him what book. It was *This Side of Paradise.* I told him I agreed with him. He asked if I had written my review. I said I had. He said, "I'll write mine tonight. Our page comes out Wednesday—yours doesn't come out until Saturday. I'll discover Fitzgerald first. Tee, hee!" Practically every reviewer in the country discovered F. Scott Fitzgerald at about the same time we did.

BEFORE I FORGET

With *Main Street* and *This Side of Paradise* the literature of
the Twenties was inaugurated, and these two books, so unlike,
were to represent the two main characteristics of the Twenties—
the protest against the smugness of the American mores and the
provincialism of American culture, on the one hand, and on the
other the so-called postwar disillusionment on the part of the
young, which was less a disillusionment than an attempt to catch
a new illusion in drinking, dancing, promiscuous flirtation and
love-making and excitement.

A period was closing for me also, and a new one was beginning,
though not of my own choice. There was one rule on the Chicago
Tribune I had scrupulously observed, and that was that Christian
Science and Christian Scientists were never to be mentioned, except
by the religious editor, in any manner which might possibly be con-
strued as a slight or a criticism. We were also cautioned that it
would be better to omit any reference to the church or its members altogether. The reason for this was that the Christian Science
church in Chicago was an organization filled with rich and powerful members; certified Christian Science practitioners were numerous in the city, with loyal and profitable clienteles. Moreover, the
Christian Scientists had, at the head of its bureau of propaganda
and public relations, a man who with his staff was extremely
vigilant in ferreting out any slighting reference to Mrs Eddy or
her following. Whenever he found any such reference he would
write a letter to the editor pointing out numbers and membership
strength of the Christian Science churches in America, the rapid
spread of the religion, the comfort, solace, help and healing it had
brought to countless despairing souls. He would also point out
that one of the foundations of our republic's principles is the freedom of any man to worship as he pleases, without hindrance.
There also might be other letters, hints of reprisals, and a delegation might visit the office. Such occurrences were the bugaboo of
the managing editor's life. His eyes could detect the words
"Christian Science" in the middle of a galley proof three feet
away; and he would seize upon the proof with agitation and cut
the word out if it were possible to do so.

I knew about all this well enough. The only reason it slipped
my mind, I guess, was that I was doing something that was un-

usual for me: I was writing to expose a slip of Mencken's and kidding him about it. Hitherto it was I who had written in praise, even uncritical praise, of Mencken while others were denouncing him. He was editing for Knopf the Free Lance series of books of philosophy, the first of which had been Ed Howe's excellent *Common Sense*. I read the third volume of the series, and at the bottom of the second column of my comment which I ran under the heading, "Presuming You Are Interested," I wrote the following notice:

"We Moderns" (Knopf), by Edwin Muir. This is the third in the Free Lance series under the editorship of H. L. Mencken. There is no connection whatever between the ideas Mr Mencken attributes to Mr Muir in the preface and the ideas Mr Muir sets forth in the text. I have read the book through three times (it is very short) to see if Mr Muir could possibly be the great moral revolutionary heretic and anarch Mr Mencken says he is. Instead, I have found this Muir a crabbed, blue-nosed Scotchman, a stark, humorless Geneva Calvinist, who, if he ever reads that preface, will have the law on Mr Mencken.

In the preface we learn that Mr Muir is a radical philosopher who has gone a step farther than Nietzsche, that he sets out to free man from superstitions, fears, conscience; that he formulates a new aesthetic, and that he is a prophet, critic, and iconoclast. Instead, we find a man who writes in an ape-like imitation of Nietzsche's manner—abruptness, ellipsis, typographical effects, punctuation, and all—but whose ideas are no more like Nietzsche's than I am like Jack Dempsey. A "philosopher," indeed, who would have a man jailed for ever laughing or reading *Mlle de Maupin* or going to a musical comedy; a "philosopher" who says that every drama should end in tragedy, that George Moore will not live because he hasn't Love (the capital is his); that Hardy "fails" because he hasn't Love; that the only men now writing in English who will live are W. H. Hudson and Joseph Conrad "because they have Love." Seldom have I encountered such abject nonsense, so many wild and untenable dicta. The latter part of the book sounds like the most rhapsodical sections of *Science and Health*—Mrs Eddy is a rather better and more original literary artist.

How did Mr Mencken ever fall for this pishposh?

The last sentence in the second paragraph of that notice brought an avalanche down upon the paper. By nine o'clock the next morning a delegation was waiting at the office to upbraid the editor and to demand my removal from the staff.

I had worked until six o'clock that morning and had slept late. The phone rang about eleven, waking me up. It was Mr Beck. He asked me what time I was coming to the office. He and I had left at the same time in the morning. It had long been the custom of Beck, Percy Hammond and myself to gather in Beck's office for a drink and a chat after the paper had gone to press, and now that Percy was in Europe Mr Beck and I continued the custom. We had had a long talk that morning, for he had been reminiscing to me about old days on the paper and amusing personalities that had been on the staff. I knew by the tone of his voice over the telephone that our personal relationship was suffering from a sudden strain. I told him I would be in after the noon hour. I did not ask him what was the trouble. He told me to come to his office at five o'clock.

At five o'clock precisely I went to his office. The fine gentleman was pacing the floor rapidly. Tears were in his eyes. He was trembling. He tried to talk and couldn't. He blurted out how he had always admired me and my work; how he had regarded me almost as a son; how I was one of the boys he had been most proud of; how loyal I had been to the paper. He was performing a duty highly disagreeable to him, under orders. I had compassion for him. It was visibly hurting him to come to the point. I saved him from coming to the point. I told him I understood; that I was young, full of ambition, not in the least afraid of myself and so self-confident that I should probably not continue for long with the paper anyhow; it would be good for me to avoid getting into a rut at my age.

Beck was grateful that I had saved him from the necessity of saying I was fired or why I was fired. His relief calmed him. I knew that the orders had come from Patterson, because in his first stumbling and incoherent mumblings as he paced the floor, looking down, there were the words: "Joe . . . Highhanded . . . Impulsive . . . Damn!"

His face brightened a little, and he told me he knew I would find a better job and go on writing better and better; that he knew he would be proud to have worked with me. We shook hands long and warmly. Then he told me Patterson had authorized him to pay me three months' salary in advance. He handed me a check for the amount. I thanked him and told him to tell Patterson I thought it was considerate of him.

However calm, unconcerned and brave I had been in the presence of Beck's distress, this all left me as I went back to my office on the fourteenth floor. I hoped I would not see anybody. I was afraid I would crack. I cleaned out my desk, throwing nearly everything away. I walked out of the office, never to return. Under my desk I had kept a gunny sack into which I put the clippings of my writings. An accumulation of more than two years was in it. I did not think of it until I was down in Oklahoma a week later. I wrote a friend at the office to see if it was still there, and if so to send it to me. The friend reported that apparently the sack had been thrown out in cleaning up the room for the new occupant. Therefore I have no clippings representing two years' work, and but very few clippings of any kind representing eight years' work on the Chicago *Tribune*.

My wife and children were already on my parents' farm in Oklahoma. They had gone there because my wife felt the need of country life to recover from the aftereffects of pneumonia. I was worried about my books. There were a great many of them, most of them precious and some that could not be replaced. My friend Anthony M. Rud solved the dilemma by suggesting that I store them at his house. In his large open automobile we moved the books by making several trips with the car filled to the gunwales with books. I immediately rented our apartment furnished. The Ruds gave a party for me, inviting a great crowd of my friends. The party lasted all night and part of the next day; and many of the guests returned on invitation the next night and again remained until after breakfast.

A few days later I was in boots, knee breeches and khaki shirt riding about the hills of the Seminole countryside, breathing the sweet air of the country, beginning already to find my strength returning after the strain of work of those last two years. My children were sturdy and healthy; having been on the farm once before, they had never liked city life—nor indeed did they ever come quite to like it. And I was again with my mother, my father and my two brothers. A bad depression was setting in, but I had the check for advance salary intact deposited in the local bank. The money would last a long time, what with fresh milk and vegetables grown there on the farm, hams and bacon and salt pork in the meat storehouse.

I decided to try my hand at building a tent house that would be better than a mere frontier shelter. I bought two large road-camp tents from the county. With the help of my brothers I laid a wooden floor for the living room, cut a square out of the rear of the tent which was to be the front of the house, and inserted a window, making it wind- and leak-proof. I joined that tent with the other tent, which was to have a dirt floor and was to be the kitchen and dining room, made a waterproof passageway between them by joining the front flaps of each. The passageway was also the only entrance to the house and was protected against winds by an elbow passageway, the outside wall of which was a screen of canvas.

I gathered with team and wagon my own wood and began sawing it and cording it against the winter. After summer had gone I was as hardy as a longshoreman. We rented a small upright piano for the tent for the use of my wife. I had brought from among my books nothing except a large collection of the Loeb Classical Library volumes and another large collection of books in French, including Anatole France complete and Rémy de Gourmont complete. I read nothing but Greek, Latin and French literature for nine months.

I attempted no writing until late in the fall. I wrote two short stories, each at a single sitting, at separate times and sold them to the first magazines to which I sent them. I wrote a study called "The Agricultural Proletariat," made up of my observation of the ways of the tenant farmers and sharecroppers I had come to know so well, which I sold to the *Freeman*. I played the role of Santa Claus, with white cotton whiskers, for the farm children at a country schoolhouse, and the whiskers caught fire from the lighted candles as I stooped to get the last present from under the tree. When I ran out into the night so that the children would not see it was I and not Santa Claus, the high wind whipped the fire into swift flame which burned all the surface skin off my

face, but fortunately got no deeper. I was miserable and despond-
ent for a few days until my face healed.

Then, just as I was beginning to get restless and wanting to get
back into harness, a letter was dropped into my lap one morning.
It was from a man I had never heard of. It contained a check for
$300. It asked me to come to see him and talk over a job he had
me in mind for. He said that if we did not come to an agreement,
he would pay all expenses of myself and family to wherever I
wished to go, to Chicago, back to Oklahoma, or to New York.

I had known definitely for many years that I should be someday working in New York, and I had known what sort of work
I would be doing. This was not it; but it was a start, perhaps, I
thought and made preparations for my family and me to leave the
farm almost immediately.

APPENDICES

APPENDICES

CONSUMPTION AND GENIUS

By Burton Rascoe

PHYSICIANS, LIKE LAWYERS, preachers, newspaper writers, bill collectors and others, have their flights of fancy and are apt to be led astray with the influx of almost any novelty into their mental cosmos. The prominent Eastern physician who said that consumption breeds genius and mentions Goethe, Emerson, Schiller, Balzac, Hawthorne, Shelley, Stevenson and Keats as heroic examples not only slipped from the service of his subsidiary intellectual secretary, the encyclopedia, but also flitted in his flight of fancy into a realm of rusty reason. Of course everyone knows that Keats died of consumption, that Shelley left England partly because of lung trouble, that Schiller showed strong symptoms of tuberculosis at thirty and that Stevenson succumbed to a life attack of pulmonary trouble, but we also know that Balzac, Hawthorne, Emerson and Goethe did not gravitate to the Great White Plague. Any pedagogue or pedant will tell you that Balzac died of overwork and mental exhaustion. Nathaniel Hawthorne lived within two years of the time allotted to man, and his death was not the result of an attack of the dreaded plague. If ever the old maxim, "Mens sana in corpore sano" (a sound mind in a sound body) was entirely exemplified it was in the case of that monument of literary genius Johann Wolfgang von Goethe. He was the most perfect man physically that the literary world has ever known. His life was wholly exempt from maladies. He lived to the ripe old age of eighty-three, and but for his dissipations, and that alone, might have been a centenarian. We come to the Concord sage, the American Plato, Emerson. Emerson was not an athlete, but his body was vigorous. Dr Oliver Wendell Holmes, who wrote the best life of Emerson and who was a lifelong friend, mentions nothing of consumption in the biography. And that suffices. Had there been any he would have mentioned it and would have dwelt on it, for the Doctor's long suit is the problem of heredity.

As for pathology of the affections and its relation to consumption and genius, we are not versed enough in the enigmas of pathology to

APPENDICES

"give him the lie direct"; we do know that the blood feeds the
brain, that the brain is the seat of genius, that the blood of a consumptive is disordered and contains poisons, and that if anything is
fed on poison it does not enjoy health; therefore, we think that we
are justified in saying that genius is not a product of tuberculosis. If
a literary landmark has consumption it is neither a pass check to a
lengthy life nor the base of the landmark. If this "prominent physician"
is right in his conjectures let us all court consumption that we might
live ninety years and produce a *Faust* or a *Wilhelm Meister*. (Shawnee
Herald, January 18, 1908.)

SEANCES WITH THE MENTAL MEDIUM

Reports of Visits Made by Burton Rascoe

"GENIUS," SAID THE PROFESSOR as he laid the June *Bookman* on his library table, "carries along with it a certain amount of egotism. Some
men of poetical and narrative genius are not deep thinkers and are not
laden with prodigious intellect. Tennyson and Longfellow might
easily describe their emotions in strains of transcendental beauty, but
to think beyond the depths of a torpid love revery would be next to
impossible for either of them.

"In this month's *Bookman* there is a paragraph relative to the egotism of Victor Hugo which states that upon Laferrière's complaining
of only ten lines to his part in *Marion Delorme,* Hugo shut him up with
'Ten lines of Hugo are something not to be refused—for they endure.'

"This is only a simple instance of Hugo's egotism; he was teeming
with it. He once remarked to his biographer, Stapfer, 'There is only
one French classic—myself. Let M. Victor Hugo be careful. If he
keeps on his work will sink to the level of the *Iliad* and the *Odyssey.*'
He claimed brotherhood to Dante and Aeschylus and, lamenting the
lack of a great French epic, he wrote *The Legend of the Centuries.*
His conceit reaches its height when he wills his drawings to the
National Library. It is strange that he praised Rembrandt and admired
Van Dyck, yet left to one of the greatest libraries in the world drawings in which the moons were made by accidental blots upon his
foolscap. In all his writings his pedantry stands out in a marked degree,
but like Macaulay he never mentions anything of which he is not
entirely acquainted. M. Stapfer assures us that he knew nothing of
the Greek classics beyond Homer and Aeschylus, whom he read in

Latin translations, and as we read his works we notice allusions to passages in Homer and Aeschylus, yet never to Sophocles, Euripides or Aristophanes.

"But with all his egotism Hugo had a right to it. His memory was stupendous, his intellect wonderful and his genius remarkable. He was right when he said that he was the only French classic of his time. He wrote about and for the people, the mass, the makers of heroes as well as about and for the heroes, the educated and the few. Balzac knew only the sordid and described it as the prevailing type of humanity. Hugo said that next to him were Sainte-Beuve and Mérimée. The former was a great critic, but no writer. The latter Hugo described as 'a writer of short breath, a consumptive, one of those for whom the word "consumptive" was invented.' "

When he had finished the professor leaned back in his chair and stared at the long rows of books before him. He finally drawled forth: "Did you read the two editorals on Tolstoy, one by Roosevelt and the other by Lyman Abbott, in last week's *Outlook?* Remarkably conflicting, weren't they? Roosevelt said that the Russian was a good novelist, but a poor philosopher. Abbott said that Tolstoy was a great philosopher and moralist, but not a novelist. Both gave proof for their assertions. Which criticism are we to choose if we rely upon the *Outlook* for our opinion in regard to the works of Count Lyof N. Tolstoy? The editorial by Mr Abbott is by far the most scholarly and convincing. Abbott says that the Russian novelist does not know women and portrays them in a shameful manner. He is right. Tolstoy writes on the order of Balzac. He wrote his novels when he was steeped in the dissipation that he admits in *My Confession,* or soon after. Some time ago the aged author sent broadcast an entreaty to the people, begging them not to read his novels, as they were not morally fit for perusal. He said that if it was in his power he would burn all the novels that he had ever written. So we see that Abbott's criticism will not wound his pride. But Count Tolstoy loves the appellation, 'philosopher'; since he was fifty-five he has been a religious worker, full of the love of those about him, and he will, if he hears of it, feel the sting of an attack by Roosevelt upon his philosophy." (Shawnee *Herald,* 1908.)

MAKES BLACKLIST OF "SEX" AUTHORS

Chicago Woman's Club Criticises Overemphasis of "Problem" in Fiction

SEEN AS PERIL TO MORALS

MEMBERS of the Chicago Woman's Club went on record yesterday as condemning the present-day overemphasis of sex in fiction. A "black list" of authors, described as "prostituting their gifts for gain and pandering to the cheap sensationalism of the day," was drawn up during the club meeting in the Fine Arts building.

Mrs Edwin Theodore Johnson of Oak Park, who talked critically on recent literature, prompted the discussions, which were conducted by Mrs George Bass, president of the club. More than twenty women made extemporaneous speeches against the American fiction writers who are incorporating sex problems in their novels.

"Ragged Hole in Life"

Mrs Johnson characterized the new literature as "ragtime turkey trot," and said "literature in America seems to have struck sex o'clock." The novels have not art, she said, and they are not slices of life as they propose to be, but "rather a ragged hole in life into which the authors have poked an instrument." Of popular authors she said:

"Robert Herrick, University of Chicago professor and author, never is fair to women. He takes a malicious pleasure in showing us up.

"Winston Churchill, in his new novel, has fallen into the sex snare, and gives a recital of free love philosophy.

"Hall Caine seems to be obeying orders to put the most disgraceful of corrupting stuff in his books to satisfy the popular palate. I have not read *The Woman Thou Gavest Me*. I don't intend to read it. I have read reviews of it and must agree with the critic who called it a brief defence of adultery. And yet I know a woman who went to the public library, and finding it was barred, said she didn't see why, 'since it was a fine book to keep young girls pure and wholesome.'

"Mrs Edith Wharton at one time had a fine style and a pleasing distinction in her fiction; but she has prostituted her great faculties to the fad of sex. Mrs Wharton's new heroine has not one redeeming merit.

She is disgusting, disgraceful, and I cannot believe any woman could exist who has the characteristics of the woman Mrs Wharton has drawn. I don't believe any woman could have as many husbands as she had and act in the manner she did in the book.

Touches on Anthony Comstock

"Mr Anthony Comstock, who today is in our city, was responsible for condemning *Hagar Revelly*. I shall let it go at that. A good criterion upon which to judge a book, to my notion, is ask yourself whether you would tolerate the hero or heroine in real life. The situation in American literature today is such that we would not relish the acquaintance of the characters of our novelists.

"Present-day poetry is a bit more optimistic. It is an illuminating fact to know that Palgrave's collection of poems of worth in his time contains only three poems by women, while the *Lyric Year,* an anthology of recent American verse, is made up of 40 per cent of poetry by women. There seems to be some danger that poetry will take over the province of the novel of the last generation."

Sees Immorality as Result

"I believe it is time that our organization should take a stand against the present-day American fiction," said a woman at the conclusion of Mrs Johnson's talk. "The fiction of our day not only is corrupting the imagination of the youth of the present day, but will form a harmful influence upon the next generation. The freedom with which sex is now discussed is responsible for the awful immorality among small children of our time."

"The fault lies largely with changing conditions," said another woman. "The young people become drunk with the freedom which was prohibited us in our day and in our parents' day. The sudden matter-of-fact discussion of hitherto tabooed problems has not allowed our youth to get their bearings. It is hard for them to maintain their wisdom. The sex novels augment the harmful effects of the situation."

Other Authors Draw Criticism

Others expressed similar opinions and named the authors whom they believed "most culpable in the offense against decency." One woman declared some of the books were recitals of "vain efforts to stay married." Conrad, Chambers, Oppenheim, MacGrath, and others were among those condemned by the speakers.

[383]

SOUND AND FURY SIGNIFYING—MR HERRICK

By Burton Rascoe

ROBERT HERRICK, whose verbal mosaics adorn the highbrow frieze of the *Sunday Tribune,* has razed this paper's files and collected some of his gems, polished them and glistened them, and set them up as a permanent entablature for posterity under the title, *The World Decision* (Houghton Mifflin Company). So avid was he to inaugurate the memorial, he neglected to mention that his novice hand had fashioned many of his conceptions originally for the ephemeral frieze aforementioned. That courtesy, of course, is merely a custom, and indifference to it may be condoned in so earnest a foe of bourgeois practices.

Mr Herrick undoubtedly is the world's most thoroughly infected Teutophobe. No poilus in the trenches cherishing revenge for atrocities recited by *Le Petit Journal,* no Belgian separated from his fellows in the prison camp at Halle, no Bersagliere inflamed by the molten words of Gabriele d'Annunzio, no London slacker forced into service under Lord Derby's recruiting campaign, is fevered with so poignant a virus against the Germans as this associate professor of rhetoric in the University of Chicago.

Prussians are, to this ruthless expositor of the innate wickedness of the insinuating sex, worse even than women—like women, they stifle liberty, defeat the noblest ambitions of the male individual, crush the soaring spirit to earth with lies, intrigue and rigid codes; but even women do not chop off the arms of members of their sex, outrage young girls, pillage and burn, and commit wholesale murder. These things, Mr Herrick believes, the Prussians literally do.

And we of America, soulless dealers in stocks and bonds (how many have you?), traffickers in munitions, drink champagne and throw confetti on New Year's Eve while the chivalrous French in the muddy trenches are (I believe I quote Mr Herrick's exact words) fighting our battles for us—fighting to keep the pernicious German landlords with their model tenements out of romantically dirty Naples, to prevent that plague called German efficiency from infesting London's picturesque east side, to stop the flow of serums and anesthetics and coal-tar products from German laboratories to relieve a suffering humanity that is better off, spiritually, without these things.

In France, in Italy, there is poetry, the poetry of the Latin, that, according to Mr Herrick, will have nothing of the blond beast to the north—the poetry in the soul of the people that fires in patriotic passion at the words of an androgynous poet who returns at the right moment from years of exile. Political sagacity of corrupt politicians like Galotti, even the catchphrase "Italia Irredenta," means naught to these liberty-loving children of the sunshine; they would be at the throats of the hated Huns, not for gain, not for the sake of state, not for anything that is base and ignoble, but for the holy cause of exterminating the monsters across the Alps.

In Mr Herrick's tower of ivory the brutality of actual fact has no welcome, no scapegoat of life's actuality is suffered to intrude, like those literary parasites the newspaper interviewers, upon his august presence. He believes, in his naïve way, that the *Lusitania* disaster caused Italy to declare war upon Austria; that the Belgians are glad the war began. One impostor, the reality that this war is largely between two distinct and opposed views of life, has crept into his sanctum and Mr Herrick has embraced it, but he has not admitted the relatives of the reality which knock at his door. Instead, Mr Herrick has gone to his desk and written—beautiful English.

THE HUGHES–CABELL SCRAP

I omit the first very long dissertation in the form of a letter to me from Rupert Hughes, which he had been inspired to write by the serialization of Beyond Life *in the Chicago Tribune. He misapprehended Cabell's contention and made much of the same point in his argument that Cabell had made. I captioned the letter "Literature and Life" and used it as a signed article. I sent it to Cabell, saying I would reserve space for his rebuttal. Came then:*

"Ultra Crepidam"

By James Branch Cabell

THOUGH, INDEED, MY TITLE need deter nobody. It merely indicates that as one result of reading Capt. Rupert Hughes' article on "Literature and Life"—which is a curiously learned performance, even for a Western Reserve graduate—I discovered its most civil summing up in the back of the dictionary, to which I, too, had turned to cull a trifle of erudition. For, of course, I have read this article with all that interest which none but feels at seeing himself rebuked in print, as well as with, I trust, appropriate regret that the captain did not in any way approve of my paper on "Literature and Life."

I very honestly deplore this circumstance in accordance with its actual importance. Still, various causes combine to prevent my entering into any serious discussion of Capt. Hughes' literary ideals, either as explained in his article or as exemplified in his books. The latter, as the phrase is, speak for themselves; and render it superfluous to question that the auctorial virtues which Capt. Hughes especially prizes—such as "grandeur, horror, sublimity, and ferocity"—are very adequately displayed in *The Music Lover's Cyclopedia* and in *The Lady Who Smoked Cigars.*

But about these matters I do not propose to write, however alluringly they tempt consideration. For it seems more to the point quite humbly to explain that these little essays of mine now being printed in the *Sunday Tribune* are extracts from a volume, to be called *Beyond*

Life, which I believe, when published in its entirety, will reveal between Capt. Hughes and myself no difference so wide as to be undesirable. It is merely that Capt. Hughes, in the impetuous way of these bluff military fellows, has seized upon a brick, in part to prove that a building's architecture is all wrong; and incidentally, of course, to heave at the architect's head. I can but dodge him with that deference which is today the captain's due from all well wishers of literature, even though he has but temporarily abandoned novel writing.

Meanwhile, his main contention—that literary affairs in America are not very strikingly dissimilar to what they have always been in every land—is one of the contretemps which *Beyond Life* especially laments; and inasmuch as here as elsewhere Capt. Hughes pursues me along lines of argument which I have very lately traveled, with results that are presently to appear in the *Tribune,* this scarcely seems the happiest place wherein to controvert these arguments. For two of his most telling "points" indeed—as to such dissimilar matters as the employment of grease paints by actors, and of improbable dialogue by novelists—the curious may find that I had actually anticipated, in the second extract from *Beyond Life,* as published a week before the captain was moved to attack me, with an ingenuity hitherto devoted to the contrivance of mysterious murders and an indignation until this reserved for the iniquity of millionaires.

And yet, no less, with the main assertion of Capt. Hughes nobody could possibly take issue. It is undeniable that there have always been writers who were unable to venture in imagination beyond the orbit of their daily lives and substitutes for thought; and so have devoted their talents to the making of ephemeral chronicles of ephemeral conditions, to the delight of a vast number of equally unimaginative readers. And, for my part, I esteem it eminently praiseworthy modesty in the author of *What Will People Say?* and of *Empty Pockets* thus to be the very first to insist that his performances are in no way unique.

Nor would I willingly omit to express appreciation of the fact that to his presentment of truisms Capt. Hughes has loaned the inestimable ornament of humor. For there can be little doubt that the captain's remarkable display of erudition is a joke that was intentional. In our first bewildered glow of astonishment to discover that Capt. Rupert Hughes is interested in and even has theories about literature, any one of us might pass over his comments upon Greek writers, say, as Gradgrindian stuff quite seriously intended.

Yet none upon a second reading could fail to perceive that the humor of it all is very fairly describable as Aristophanic, if but in that a footnote is usually required to explain it. Though, indeed, I doubt it for the captain's jokes a footnote is always necessary. His contention, for example, that Greek tragedy ought not to be appraised "as if Sophocles and Euripides and their contemporaries summed up Greek dramatic art," but only after comparing all the other Attic dramatists, has certainly a ring so plausible that for the moment one is gulled: yet instantly reflection suggests that the work of these other dramatists has perished a many centuries ago; and you wonder how Capt. Hughes proposes to set about making a study of them, and so perceive that he is voicing his sturdy military humor.

Thereafter all is pleasant sailing, once you have recognized that the captain has not taken leave of his senses but merely of seriousness, and is jocosely introducing into an overglum discussion of unread books the literary standards to which he has most advantageously adhered in the *Redbook*. For then it appears not quite inexplicable to find even Homer cited as a thoroughgoing "realist" on the plea that he depicts his characters as eating three meals a day. Nor will the initiated then quarrel with the statement that the lyrics of Aristophanes "were like the musical comedy lyrics of today," and offer to point out some trivial difference between the choruses of "The Clouds" and of "I May Be Gone for a Long, Long Time." And everyone will merrily agree with Capt. Hughes that the "Persians" of Æschylus, with its scene laid at Susa and the main role enacted by a ghost, ought to be regarded as a "realistic" study of Athenian society. For this is just a way, as you perceive at last, that these bluff military fellows have of joking.

Then, too, this granted, it becomes doubly pleasant to note how Capt. Hughes facetiously clinches his Grecian dicta with the statement, "And then there were the unspeakable knockabout farces that ended the show." After that sweeping stroke it seems, of course, the idlest sort of hair-splitting to point out that just one of these satyric dramas remains to us, in the *Cyclops* of Euripedes; that this is based upon a highly romantic episode from the *Odyssey* and is neither "knockabout" nor particularly "unspeakable"; and that concerning no other satyric drama ever produced in Athens can Capt. Hughes or anyone else pretend to speak with any authority save that of casual mentions which indicate these dramas to have resembled *Tommy Rot* and *Excuse Me* far less closely than anybody would image from the captain's description.

Nor equally, of course, will an intelligent person here descend to any such prosaic hair-splitting. Instead, one must continue to fall in with the jest.

APPENDICES

However, Capt. Hughes can very well afford to take these jovial little liberties with logic because the thread of his main argument, I must concede, is sound. The admission goes sadly against the grain, since, being human, I would like intensely to dispute his argument: and it is a comfort to reflect that I have probably damaged it considerably by writing a book to support it.

Thus there seems to be no real conflict between the general contention of Capt. Hughes and the actual trend of that small luckless essay which he has elected very dexterously to assail with his habitual vigor and with his unwontedly clever burlesque of erudition. Meanwhile I have pointed out that there always have been writers who practiced their art quite seriously. And Capt. Hughes has retorted that along with these have always coexisted a far greater number of artisans who wrote amusing and ephemeral plays and books against the needs of honest persons now and then to "kill off" an hour or two innocuously. I question not at all the truth of the captain's statement, but merely what conceivable connection it has with literature. And I take it that the evinced desire to quote a precedent for one's vocation shows honorably enough in both of us.

Anti–Cabellum

By Capt. Rupert Hughes

Mr James Branch Cabell is much more ferocious than I had judged from his work, and I am sorry I attracted his lacerating attention. I have just enough strength—and spite—to revert to the consideration of facts, since there is nothing else that so annoys him. Admitting that I deserved what I got for being foolish enough to interrupt the dreamy babble of his essays, I must ask for a little further space.

I wrote complimenting the *Tribune* on praising so enthusiastically so fine a novelist as Mr Cabell, but I felt called upon to point out that as a historian of Greek, medieval, and Elizabethan art and letters he gave an utterly false and disproportioned account of them. I quoted his statements verbatim and answered them with history.

In his answer to me he ignores all but one or two of my citations, and turns and rends me with his super-Molierian satire. And here also he proves his avoidance of what he so Cabellishly denounces as "a too sparing employment of untruthfulness."

[389]

He rushes to *Who's Who in America* for ammunition to destroy me with and selects a few facts and a few titles for my complete maceration, omitting everything that would mar his caricature.

But as I complained before, he selects too carelessly. I would not spoil his excellent satire by failing to enjoy its fine careless rapture, but I must again call him to account as hopelessly unfitted to deal with what he so frankly hates, and that is the truth.

He says that my article is "a curiously learned performance even for a Western Reserve graduate." This is meant to annihilate both the university and this particular product of it. But Adelbert College has always maintained a high standard in its classical curriculum, which I took both in the required and the elective courses and supplemented with voracious reading, taking second honors on graduation and delivering a salutary in Latin.

I had studied Greek art at my mother's knee. At Western Reserve I studied the Greek philosophers and poets and playwrights. I took a course in Greek archaeology and wrote a monograph on Praxiteles, reading for that purpose every word that exists about him in ancient Greek.

Years after I was concerned in the discussion of an alleged statue of Praxiteles now owned by Mr Rockefeller. I recognized at once that it was not what it pretended to be, yet a very beautiful work, and I visited the principal art galleries of Europe searching for information on which to base its proper ascription. I had quite a wrangle with the papal curator of the Vatican over some Greek fragments.

I contributed many articles on art to *Scribner's* and other magazines and an article on American sculpture to the tenth edition of the Encyclopedia Britannica. This I state to show that I have some right to discuss sculpture.

In common honesty Mr Cabell might have quoted from *Who's Who* the statement that after graduating from Western Reserve I took a master's degree at Yale. I specialized in the history of satire, particularly Elizabethan satire. I spent most of my time in the library, taking home armloads of books to read of nights. I read everything that I could find in Greek, Latin, Italian, early French, Spanish, German and French satire.

I read before the Modern Language Club a thesis on Bishop Joseph Hall's *Virgidemiarum,* which Hall erroneously claimed to be the first English satires. I remember blandly stating that Hall was greater than Pope, because Pope attacked the individuals of his own time, while Hall satirized the vices in general. Prof. Lounsbury, a great scholar,

whose knowledge made him the more human and reasonable instead of
affected and superior, rebuked me gently, and stated that anybody could
berate evils in general, but it took art and courage to deal with one's
own contemporaries minutely. And that such contributions to literature were much more valued by posterity than the generalizations of
bookish men.

I still wince with shame at the grandiose scholasticism of my thesis,
but I never forgot the lesson. I got a clearer vision of what true scholarship is, and I came at length to try to be a scholar in my own period.

After various editorial rovings I landed in London with the Encyclopedia Britannica company and soon was assigned to the *Historians'
History of the World*. For four years my job from 9 A.M. to 5 P.M. was
to read history, searching particularly the original sources and the
latest historical verdicts.

I spent months in the British Museum, made two trips to Paris for
work in the Bibliothèque Nationale and later spent years in the libraries
about New York.

I am not so foolish as to pretend that this constitutes me a historian,
but it gave me, I think, the privilege of taking Mr Cabell's measure as
a chronicler. It also taught me that from ancient Assyria to modern
Guatemala people always have been people; also that Cabells always
have existed to speak with disdain of everything modern and native
and rhapsodize only over an imaginary golden age.

The past-praiser is found in the most archaic papyrus. Even Horace
roasted him in the well-known phrase, "Laudator temporis acti," for
the Romans suffered from those who thought that only Greek was
artistic. Dante was considered cheap for writing in the dialect of his
town instead of in Latin and for putting his neighbors into hell and
heaven. Gower and Chaucer apologized for not writing in polite
French. And Mr Cabell thinks I am a mere sensationalist because I try
to make faithful portraits of New York City, in as many of its phases—
rich, poor, gentle, criminal, tragic, gay, lazy and swirling—as I can reveal without forgetting that as a novelist it is a duty and an art to
build a plot and tell a story.

Mr Cabell speaks with amusement of my *Music Lover's Cyclopedia*,
a work on which I spent three fierce years of toil, and which contains
thousands more of names and definitions than any other musical direc-
tory in any language. He does not mention the research among manuscripts shown in my pioneer work, *American Composers*, nor the vast
amount of reading involved in the very serious work, *The Love Affairs
of Great Musicians*. He does not mention my volume of poetry, *Gyges'*

Ring, a dramatic monolog in blank verse, nor my sonnets and other verse contributed to the *Century, Scribner's,* etc.

But he mocks *The Lady Who Smoked Cigars,* plainly knowing nothing about it. It is a very short story, hardly more than the transcription of what I heard a very wealthy American woman tell at a London dinner table of her early experiences when she and her husband were penniless prospectors. She was a very quaint and beautiful character, and I am proud to have given her beautiful deed what publication it has had.

Among my plays he mentions *Tommy Rot,* with which I had little to do except to get the deservedly bad notices, and *Excuse Me,* for which I do not apologize. He ignores *Alexander the Great,* a poor thing, but very ambitious, and *The Bridge,* a serious treatment of the gulf between capital and labor.

I quote all this autobiography because Mr Cabell presents me in his ignorance and indifference as a man of "an ingenuity hitherto devoted to the contrivance of mysterious murders and an indignation until this reserved for the iniquity of millionaires." As usual he has not read the work he so gayly dismisses—not that I blame him, though it is surprising to find him among the millions.

As a matter of fact, I have contrived only one mysterious murder (Shakespeare used many), and I have never attacked the iniquity of millionaires. I have always defended them from the usual literary cartoonists.

Mr Cabell next destroys me thus: "It is undeniable that there have always been writers who were unable to venture in imagination beyond the orbit of their daily lives and substitutes for thought; and so have devoted their talents to the making of ephemeral chronicles of ephemeral conditions, to the delight of a vast number of equally unimaginative readers." He goes on to refer to *What Will People Say?* and *Empty Pockets* as types of that sort of work, not alluding to the many books, poems, stories, plays and essays far beyond the orbit of my daily life.

I can't say, of course, till long after both Mr Cabell and I are dead which one of us has written ephemeral chronicles; doubtless both of us have. But I insist that the spiritual conditions I describe are not ephemeral, and I can honestly say that my novels of modern American life are written with all the scholarship I have, all the indefatigable urge to research, all the longing for truth which impels me, and which Mr Cabell despises. And I am happy to say that my heartiest support comes from scholars and men of high literary ideals, who realize that my program is earnest and honest, and have compared it with Balzac's.

Mr Cabell simply will not use the truth. In implying my "vast number of unimaginative readers," he flatters me outrageously. I have not a vast number of any sort of readers, except in so far as the magazines I contribute to have big circulations. I wish I had more readers. I should esteem it an honor. Mr Cabell seems to assume that the more readers a man has the less worthy he is an artist.

Let me warn him solemnly that if he does not choke off Mr Burton Rascoe, Mr Cabell will find himself eternally disgraced, for the *Tribune* has a vast number of readers who will buy almost anything the book page recommends. I love Mr Rascoe's enthusiasm, and I think he is doing American letters a service in crying up Mr Cabell, who really ought to have several more readers.

One final personal word: Mr Cabell keeps harping on my captaincy and refers to me as one of "these bluff military fellows." He likes this so well that he uses it again, and a third time refers to my "sturdy military humor."

I wish to God I were indeed a bluff military fellow, for then I should be in the regiment I served twelve years with and now in France suffering the gas attacks of the enemies of our country, instead of being kept back here by a slight damned deafness and undergoing the perfume of asphyxiation of Mr Cabell and a bombardment of tuberoses by one who affects a learning he lacks and proclaims himself an imaginative artist because he is superior to the truth about either the past or the present. Since he will have it that I am a bluff military fellow, I may say that his writings in this field give me the Cabelly-ache.

As for the rest of his answer, he alternately ridicules me with lah-de-dah flippancies and pretends that I have stated truisms which he was about to pronounce artistically in future essays. This is the usual method of argument, but it does not correct the particular misstatements to which I objected in the essay in question. They are just as glaring now as before he pooh-pooh'd me to death.

Just once he answers a specific charge specifically, and that is when he protests against my allusions to lost dramas and to the satyric farces of Athens. He insists that neither I nor anyone else "can pretend to speak with authority save that of casual mentions."

But what I said was none the less true for his denying it. I said that the three names he mentioned as summing up Greek dramatic art—Æschylus, Sophocles and Aristophanes—did not adequately represent Athenian dramatic art as it was, because there were other playwrights far more popular than any of them, and because the indecent knock-about farces were so prevalent.

He points out "some trivial difference" between the choruses of "The Clouds" and of "I May Be Gone for a Long, Long While," and thinks me answered. I might pick out some of our best lyric poetry and contrast it with some of Aristophanes' more characteristic lines and business, but the *Tribune* would not print them.

Mr Cabell seems to feel that imagination and truth have some horrible quarrel. But there is a logic of fantasy and a logic of history. I, too, have an imagination, and I can enjoy *A Midsummer Night's Dream* as well as the next one, both elfin poetry and horseplay. I enjoyed *The Rivet in Grandfather's Neck* immensely.

But I think that I have said enough and more than enough about both of us. As Theocritus might have ended an idyll: "And now, Captain, do you return to your mysterious murders, and you, Cabellus, to your reveries by the pool of the lotuses."

An Epilogue

By James Branch Cabell

WITH PARDONABLE GUSTO I have read every word of Capt. Rupert Hughes' painstaking and enthusiastic article dealing with himself from the time he left his mother's knee, and I congratulate the captain upon his strategic removal to a topic concerning which he speaks with authority.

For nobody can well deny his dicta to be unanswerable now that Capt. Hughes confines himself so rigidly to the accomplishments and exploits of Capt. Hughes and meddles not at all with the makers of literature as to whom I had erroneously assumed the captain intended to favor the *Tribune* readers with some ideas.

Instead, it seems that nothing of the sort has ever entered his head or else the captain has quite unaccountably transferred the exposition of his literary notions to the *Cosmopolitan* magazine, wherein we have the captain's standards stated in gratifying directness. In the June number one discovers that Capt. Hughes' ideal of a really "brilliant artist" in literature is Mr Robert W. Chambers, whose "masterpieces" and "triumphs of art" have aroused the captain to a three-page outburst of naïve and touching reverence, but little inferior to that with which he speaks of the fruitage of his own fierce years of toil.

So I elect to return good for evil and, in spite of his harsh words, I shall even now magnanimously indorse, in addition to Capt. Hughes' fair-minded tribute to himself, his paper upon "The Art of Robert W. Chambers." With this I obediently return to my reveries and wish him all prosperity in the commission of yet other amiable crimes.

ON A CERTAIN CONDESCENSION IN OUR NATIVES

By Burton Rascoe

A SITUATION somewhat different now obtains from that which once caused James Russell Lowell with admirable restraint to write: "It is not merely the Englishman; every European admits in himself some right of primogeniture in respect to us, and pats his shaggy continent on the back with a lively sense of generous unbending.

"The German who plays the bass viol has a well-founded contempt, which he is not always nice in concealing, for a country so few of whose children ever take that noble instrument between their knees. . . . The Frenchman feels an easy mastery in speaking his mother tongue, and attributes it to some native superiority of parts that lifts him high above us barbarians of the west. The Italian prima donna sweeps a courtesy of careless pity to the overfacile pit which unsexes her with the *bravo!* meant to show a familiarity with foreign usage."

They are not foreigners, in especial, now who slander us, though it was only recently that the scholarly A. B. Walkley left off reading his Bohn's *Handbook of Classical Quotations* long enough to counsel Englishmen to forget, in the interest of the duty which Great Britain and the United States are allied in fulfilling, the disagreeable fact that America is the raucous region of vulgarity and illiteracy that it is. These unpleasantries we condone, assenting in the general belief that from Mr Walkley's unapproachable standards they are justified. Further, we are purring over the nice things the French are saying about us—their insistence that with Poe, Whitman and Emerson, at least, we have given great names to literature, and their assurances that reciprocal literary relations are now being fostered between the two countries.

Why Masks and Disguises?

What we are beginning to bear with indifferent fortitude is the self-alienation of many of our native born, the assumption of superiority by the very "hicks" among us. We have Iowans who annoy us with boarding-school French when they could be nearly as intelligible in

English. We have Chicagoans who affect the contraband English of Boston in preference to their less anomalous patois of State Street.

We meet those who will have in their libraries nothing except English editions and those to whom Mark Twain is a vulgar bounder they would not think of reading. We have collectors (through agents) of Italian *objets d'art* (as they invariably refer to them) who would shudder on being apprised that ceramics have, in this country, been developed to a remarkably satisfying degree of esthetic perfection. There exists a wide acquaintance (through postcards and imported folios) with the paintings and sculpture of the Louvre, the Uffizi and the Dresden galleries among those who have never spent an hour at a time in the Art Institute.

Everywhere is to be seen the partial accomplishment of that amusing desire of human beings to seem otherwise than they are. And just now to be an American, above all a Midwest American, with a liking for American books, American art, American language, and American traditions is to be a pariah to the gentleman who is eager to forget that he was born on a Nebraska farm, the young lady who has spent three years at an Eastern finishing school, and the matron whose salon is furnished with an astonishing admixture of the bizarre of all periods.

The Same in Literature

This state of affairs is reflected in our literary no less than in our social life. We who have done some intensive cultivation in the narrow patch of esthetics that our infertile country has apportioned us stand without the pale. It matters not that we have, so far as our limited time allowed, gone to other fields for exotic fruits, acquiring a taste for the best that Russia, England, the Romance countries and Scandinavia have produced: sufficing to damn us is the fact that we read and enjoy American literature.

Have you enjoyed the finished subtleties, the cultured cosmopolitanism of Henry Blake Fuller's novels, the essays of Edgar Saltus, the intense human drama of Stephen Crane, the wry cynicism of Ambrose Bierce? If you have, keep it a dark secret from the enterprising Hoosier to your right, who is making a study of the Russians and who can quote you long passages from the reviews of the latest translation.

Did you read with keen enjoyment, as a quite accurate picture of an American boy's life, Booth Tarkington's *Penrod* and *Seventeen*? Refrain from saying so to the Buckeye you meet at dinner. It seems that he acquired his present intellectuality from obliging Mother Nature, who omitted from her curriculum, in his case, that span of years he would find embarrassing to recall. He has a fine misunderstanding of

Huysmans, Baudelaire, Stendhal, and Freud which he has acquired through dint of several glances at translations.

There is an American conspiracy in effect to keep hidden the disturbing idea that literature has been, is being and will be produced in this country. Among the "established" critics of the various literary journals there is a tacit agreement to up and clout every American who shows signs of producing anything approaching literary excellence. If he is bad enough to insure his dropping out of sight within a month or so, they pass him a generous meed of praise, conscious that he will not, in the future, arise and trouble them.

A Case in Point

It may be the enchantment of distance; it may be the almost universal habit of acquiring matters of intellect and taste at second hand. Certain it is that an inferior Russian, French or English writer can be assured deference from our native critics, while a worthy American can expect only a snub. According to their narrow lights of esthetic judgment, our native critics (excepting, here, such men as James Huneker, H. L. Mencken, John Macy and a few others) will rule an American writer out as immoral and incompetent and let in a foreign writer whose subject matter, technique and point of view are hardly to be differentiated from that of the outlawed American.

The Folletts have just published *Some Modern Novelists*. In it are some fair estimates, some accurate placing of novelists on the shelves where they belong. But for the most part, these novelists had been placed there long ago, and to perform their duty it became necessary for the Folletts to take the novelists down and then replace them.

There is, for instance, a fairly general understanding of the worth of Thomas Hardy, George Meredith and Henry James, even of Galsworthy, Bennett and Wells. But the Folletts omit to mention an American who is as great as the greatest of them—James Branch Cabell. Cabell's recency cannot be offered in extenuation, for the very novel upon which this claim to literary excellence rests, *The Rivet in Grandfather's Neck,* was published two years ago.

U. S. Has Just as Good

The Folletts make kind mention of the younger English novelists, J. D. Beresford, Gilbert Cannan, Hugh Walpole and D. H. Lawrence. These men have gone in wholeheartedly for naturalism, naturalism of the most unwavering kind. Sex is their theme, sex and the conflict it brings to the aspiring individual. Therein they differ but little from Theodore Dreiser. Yet the Folletts take up the domestic cry against Dreiser as a false philosopher of degrading animal behavior and pat the

[398]

young Englishman on the back. Moreover, they leave out of consideration Sherwood Anderson, Waldo Frank, W. H. Wright and Joseph
Hergesheimer, Americans who have employed the same themes as do
the Englishmen and with equal skill.

Elsewhere among the critics hypermetropy is evident. They can see
Anatole France, probably the greatest literary figure on the European
continent, but they cannot see James Branch Cabell, who is under their
noses. The viewpoint of the two men is much the same; they have the
same tolerant irony, the same refinement of taste, the same sanity of
judgment and much the same subtlety of expression. They can see
Gilbert Chesterton's huge bulk in Fleet Street, but they cannot descry
Frank Moore Colby, who is cleverer, at their elbow. They pass up our
most cosmopolitan writer and our most discursive essayist, James
Huneker—but that may be ascribed to jealousy.

H. L. Mencken, whose *A Book of Burlesques* strikes with fine precision many notes as fundamental as themes from Swift, Molière and
Aristophanes, is unread save by a few and is avoided mention by those
who write of books. But Stephen Leacock, a Canadian clown, whose
burlesques are no more rereadable than the jokes of vaudeville, is invited to give lectures at American universities.

A bearded Bengalese in a kimono, whose translated poems read like
paraphrases of Ossian, is taken seriously; an American experimenting
in unrhymed verse is greeted with derision. Europeans are accorded
praise by our critics for the very virtues they account as vices in an
American. An Icelander, a Polynesian, a Spaniard, a Pole, a Peruvian,
a Turk, has by the very fact of his being such, a carte blanche at our
tables, while an American, by the very fact of being such, must beg his
bread. Our generous hospitality knows no gauches excepting home-
folk. (February 16, 1918.)

OUR VICIOUS ZEAL

By Burton Rascoe

*This is one of several editorials I wrote against specific acts of censor-
ship and against censorship in general for the Saturday page of Book
News and Reviews of the Chicago* Tribune *during 1918–19, when
censorship of literature by private organizations was rife. I reprint the
piece because I think it has a certain historical value as do all the*

phases and steps in the war for the freedom of expression, phases and steps largely ignored, by the way, by Morris Ernst and William Seagle in their shoddy and superficial book, To the Pure: A Study of Obscenity and the Censor. *B. R.*

OUR PECULIARLY AMERICAN form of the Inquisition, the Society for the Suppression of Vice, has bestirred itself to one more grotesque act of highhanded tyranny. It has seized Dr Sigmund Freud's monograph on Leonardo da Vinci and haled the publishers into court on a charge of publishing and disseminating an immoral book.

A costly litigation, no doubt, will ensue. The publishers, if pilloried to no greater extent than as affects their time and pocketbooks, will suffer for having, with little if any profit to themselves, made procurable to specialists and students a much-talked-of quasi-scientific work. And once more fear will descend into the hearts of publishers and caution will dictate their refusal of translated works of high scientific and literary value and the bowdlerizing of others until they are scarcely more than scenarios of the original.

Thus will our national literature be kept at that skimmed-milk consistency which makes us the laughingstock of civilized Europeans and the object of sneers even from the English, whose censorship is only a trifle less barbarous.

It happens that Dr Freud's *Leonardo da Vinci* is less a contribution to psychoanalytic data than a weapon in the hands of the critics of Freud and his followers. In the history of thought, probably, there is no more elaborate generalization from a flimsy premise than this attempt of Dr Freud to trace the erotic genesis of Leonardo's masterpieces in painting.

Freud conceives the idea that Leonardo's libido was incestuous in character, and, obsessed by the notion, wholly abandons the skeptical and analytical attitude necessary for scientific thinking in his desperate attempt to prove his point. The result, of course, is not only entirely unconvincing; it is an actual boomerang. The anti-Freudians can with glib certainty fling Freud's own terminology in his face; his *Leonardo* they can show is actually only a realization of the Freudian "wish," and Freud himself the victim of a suppressed desire of an unhealthy and irregular kind. Which, in fact, can be said of most of the psychoanalysts when they venture beyond the narrow confines in which their virgin and undeveloped theories permits them legitimately to speculate.

But the lack of scientific merit in the book was not the Vice society's reason for suppressing it. There is not that much intelligence in the organization. The Freud treatise, couched in a terminology intelligible only to educated adults, is seized by them two years after publication on the same grounds upon which they seized the world-renowned classics of Rabelais, Boccaccio, Balzac, Daudet, Thomas Hardy and Gautier; to quote from the court decisions (from data compiled by H. L. Mencken): because it might "excite 'impure thoughts' in the 'minds of persons that are susceptible to impure thoughts'" or "tend to deprave the minds of the young and inexperienced," or "arouse a libidinous passion . . . in the mind of a modest [sic] woman."

To all this pious naïveté, this confession of infantile mentality, this avowal of a prepossession for smut and an interest in books solely dependent upon the erotic excitation to be got out of it, the artist, the critic, the scientist and the intelligent reader can only shrug in despair and wonder how much further the will of the illiterate, the obsessed-by-vice, the self-elected guardians of the welfare of others will be worked to reduce our literature to that which may be read in young ladies' seminaries without provoking giggles.

The actual effect of all this pernicious activity has been, of course, to make the current reading matter and amusement in America un-exampled in its nastiness as well as unique in its utter vacuity. Instead of the healthy obscenity of Rabelais and the frankly critical works of the French literary psychologists and the exquisite prose and poetic compositions of other countries, we have the discreetly and hence emphatically pornographic—nudity clothed in a chemise and black silk stockings, bedroom farces, the Victory Loan poster by H. C. Christy, the art of innuendo, the short stories of two thirds of our magazines, the Junior Leg show, and the Follies, "a national institution." In this no other country is our equal. Our literature is for "the young and in-experienced" and for "modest women" to read—in secret.

We draw the literature of other nations into this cesspool of a nationally suppressed libido. We make conscientious artists conform to our unhealthy inversion. The Galsworthy of *The Patrician* and *The Man of Property* is induced by rich offers to become the Galsworthy of *The Saint's Progress.* Our successes are *Scandal,* and *Virtuous Wives,* cheap art, and sentimental movies "for adults only."

Meanwhile Flaubert's exquisite *La Tentation de Saint-Antoine* comes to us with more than a third of the original left untranslated and the rest bungled. Huysmans' tremendous novel, *En Route;* Stendhal's *Le Rouge et Le Noir,* Barbusse's terrible *L'Enfer,* the unsurpassed novels of Anatole France, the works of French, Flemish, Dutch, Italian,

Russian, Spanish and Scandinavian masters come to us expurgated, toned down, innocuous, ready for the nursery.

What is worse, the work of men of unquestioned genius in other countries, Rémy de Gourmont, Pierre Louÿs, Camille Lemonnier, Georges Rodenbach, Arthur Schnitzler, Ludwig Thoma, Pierre Mille, Louis-Philippe and any number of such eminent artists, remains untranslated (or unavailable to the public) for the very reason that such an enterprise is too dangerous to the publishers. A mere phrase may strike the ferret eyes of smut-seeking readers for the Vice society and result in a costly trial and a jail sentence for the publisher.

George Moore finds it necessary to publish his works privately, in subscription editions. "Athenian" societies, "Benares" societies, fake Gaelic societies spring up to publish unexpurgated translations of Aristophanes, Casanova, Petronius, the *Arabian Nights,* Aphrodite, and other classics, at exorbitant prices, and these, with Lucian and Apuleius, are classed as "erotica" and sold surreptitiously, along with the works of the infamous Marquis de Sade, villainous pseudopathological studies, and stuff frankly for morons!

That, then, is the net result of the activities of the Society for the Suppression of Vice, excepting only its legitimate suppression of such things as vile post cards: it has forced literary masterpieces into a classification with the bawdy and obscene; it has turned many of our writers toward an unhealthy eroticism; and it has kept this nation the most ignorant of all civilized nations with the work of the genius of other countries. And there seems no way to end it.

"EXCUSE THE GLOVE"

By Burton Rascoe

The appetite of the American lecture-attending public for lectures by foreigners appeared to be insatiable during the first two decades of the century. Georg Brandes, Maurice Maeterlinck and Blasco Ibáñez, each speaking a gibberish which he imagined to be English, drew huge audiences, not one of whom could understand a word the lecturer said; William Butler Yeats recited his beautiful poems in a singsong, beating time with his hands, destroying all their value to the enraptured reader of these same poems; English authors, many of them third rate, presumed to lecture American audiences on American literature, of which they were appallingly ignorant. In time we, in

*Chicago, got fed up with this; and the newspaper reporters among us
began to treat the foreign visitors with something less than reverence.
Charley MacArthur on the* Herald and Examiner *wrote such a comical
interview with Blasco Ibáñez that the Spaniard gave out the story
that he was going to challenge MacArthur to a duel, until it was
pointed out that duelling was illegal in this country. The platform
antics of Lord Dunsany were a scandal. The reference in the subjoined
article to the Prince of Wales has to do with the furor that arose when
William Hale Thompson, mayor of Chicago, publicly refused to issue
an invitation to Prince Albert Edward to visit the city and announced
that there would be no public reception for him, on the ground that
this is a democratic country wherein the people do not kowtow to
royalty. B. R.*

WE HAVE, IT SEEMS, been remiss in hospitality to our distinguished
guests. When we should have greeted them with bay and laurel and
made them privy to our private stock, we have met them with guffaw
and snicker and made coarse comments on their hands and feet. A
noble lord of an ancient barony and a Spanish don whose work is read
from Archangel to the Argentine and is feared by king and pope
are among those who have thus been by us very grievously affronted.

Only the etiquette of composure demanded of a guest and a sense
of pity for so gauche a carcass restrained the eloquent Don Vicente
Blasco-Ibáñez from challenging a Chicago reporter to a pistol duel. The
provocation, it appears, was considerable enough: the reporter insisted
upon an interview after the don had gone to bed; the don offered him
what courtesy and comfort he might find in a hotel room and listened
with patience to the reporter's childish questions, answering them as
intelligently as he could manage. The reporter fixed his attention not
upon the author's words but upon the author's toes (which were revealed beneath his pajamas) and made them and not the author's
opinions the theme and recurrent motif of a jesting article. *Caspita!
Canastos!*

Lord Dunsany was equally mistreated. One literary editor as much as
told him in print that his monkeyshines were a public nuisance and
his lectures a bore and that he ought to sneak home as quickly as
possible. Another more or less literary editor intimated that the whole
caboodle of foreign authors, with one exception, ought to be run
out of the country because they hadn't paid us enough compliment
and didn't know the works of American authors whom Americans
themselves do not read.

This, of course, is the most distressing sort of provincialism. It is on a par with the sentiment, publicly expressed, which kept the young Prince of Wales away from Chicago—"We don't want nothing to do with them princes and dooks; they don't mean nothing good by us." It preserves our self-esteem; but it gives us a black eye. It marks us out as a self-willed, frank and industrious people; but also marks us out as a people of deplorable manners, lacking all suavity, tact, grace and cosmopolitanism.

And yet . . . and yet there is something to be said on the other side. Experience has repeatedly proved that the most fatal thing an author can do is to show himself. An author's essential and commendable being is in his work, not in his squat or ungainly flesh or in his funny gestures and fatuous grimace. What authors feel and write, that intangible beauty they express or that mood which they invoke, is really what there is of them to offer us. To see them always is something of a disillusion.

The reason is that, having greatly admired an author through his work, we frequently imagine him with the physique of the Farnese Hercules and the brilliant speech of Jimmy Whistler. We expect him to be courteous and cultured, brilliant, daring and attired like the impeccables in a ready-made-clothing ad, or, failing that, in the colorful costume of a bal masqué.

Of course they are usually quite otherwise. They look often like the little tailor around the corner. They are fat and dumpy, with faces like an unshaven full moon, or they are lean and hatchet faced, with thinning hair and trousers that bag badly at the knees. They stutter frightfully, like Arnold Bennett; they forget you are there, like William Butler Yeats; they gesticulate, like a fruit peddler (or like Blasco-Ibáñez); or they utter platitudes as though they had mush in their mouths, like Lord Dunsany. In all my experience with authors I have met but few who talked more than passably well. And I have met none at all who reminded me of the Farnese Hercules, the Donatello David, or the Apollo Belvedere. On the other hand, I have met many who set me to thinking of a Briggs or a Goldberg cartoon.

The ugliest and most ineffectual-looking man in all Europe is Gabriele d'Annunzio. He is only a little over five feet tall and is as bald as an egg. Yet he has written the finest Italian poetry since Dante, and he has made the premiers of three countries obey his whim.

The point is that with authors nearly all of their reserve vitality, their brilliance, their perceptions of beauty are committed to paper in the lonely privacy of their workrooms. The energy which others spend in making themselves easy and agreeable with their fellows, in learning to orate in public, in acquiring social graces, is expended by authors in the more arduous and exacting work of writing novels, poems, plays, essays.

Well, the answer is that when they show themselves in public, address provincial literary societies and women's clubs, they do themselves and their reputations irreparable injury. They spoil the illusion their readers have of them. A shadowy and somewhat mystical creative figure, working amid romantic surroundings 'way off yonder, intrigues the interest. When that figure emerges as something not much to look at and spends two hours telling a bored audience that "art makes life pleasanter," the effect is disastrous. Whereas the audience had previously imagined the author as a compound of his heroes, it begins to regard him as a harmless sort of nincompoop who needs more exercise. Thus does familiarity breed contempt and the wine of astonishment turn from sweet to bitter.

Lord Dunsany has written some of the most exquisite tales in the language. He has the magic of words to evoke in grown-up and sophisticated people the wonder they experienced as children on reading their first fairy tales. His work has the charm of beautiful prose, of pity and irony, of suggestive power, and his plays are miracles of strange beauty. But Dunsany reading a bad paper on art and dumping a pitcher of ice water over his head while he reads is not precisely an inspiring figure.

Vicente Blasco-Ibáñez is one of the great melodramatists of fiction of the school of Hugo, Sienkiewicz, and, to drop a notch, say, our Lew Wallace. In pictorial facility he has no superior in modern literature. He writes, apparently, a brilliant journalese, vivid, racy and interesting. In character development he is weak, in character sketching he is superb. His centaur of the plains in *The Four Horsemen of the Apocalypse,* his Hannibal in *Sonnica,* his old captain in *Mare Nostrum,* his old toreador in *Blood and Sand* are magnificent and finely realized romantic conceptions.

His most salient weakness, probably, is that he wearies of his own novel before he is through writing it. The result is that the first half of every one of his novels is invariably superior to the latter half. Another weakness is his tendency to propagandize in each novel—always disastrous to art—against the Church, against the monarchy, against alcohol, against the bull fight or against the Germans.

And yet he is unquestionably a considerable figure in contemporary literature. His *Sonnica* compares favorably with Flaubert's *Salammbô.*

His *Blood and Sand* is a finely conceived and excellently written novel: the chapters dealing with the spell of the Mediterranean in *Mare Nostrum* are the pictorial and suggestive art of fiction at its best.

And yet when he applauded himself under the apprehension that he was honoring the name of Victor Hugo, and when he gave vent to outbursts of temperament, and when he told us that we did not properly appreciate Edgar Allan Poe and Upton Sinclair, somehow we were amused rather than edified, and courtesy failed us. But had we laughed up our sleeve instead of in his face, the laugh would have been no less a laugh, and a laugh at the most conspicuous literary man of Spain is not seemly. And we might have gone on imagining him as the distinguished-looking personage of Sorolla's portrait had he not stepped out of character.

Good authors should be neither seen nor heard. They should be read.

PROF. SHERMAN GIVES ASYLUM TO HIS BROOD

By Burton Rascoe

PROF. STUART PRATT SHERMAN, to propitiate Posterity, has rescued some of his brain children from the precarious orphanage of a weekly gazette, clothed them anew, fed them out of the generosity of his talent, and lodged them permanently in a domicile over the doorpost of which he has, for some esoteric reason, inscribed the words *On Contemporary Literature* [Holt].

We must cloak this act with the wings of our charity. That these children were conceived in error, that they are aberrant and defective, and that beauty and strength grace them not, should elicit our sympathy rather than our censure. Contrition is in the dedication, which is to Mr Paul Elmer More; and atonement is in the frankness with which the author admits his dereliction. "I have been accused," says he, "of being a besotted mid-Victorian." *Oremus pro sibi.*

It is unfortunate, of course, that these offspring should need bear names at all; but it is more so that Prof. Sherman was not more decorous in selecting them. The unhappy manner in which he cast about and filched prominent names must surely cause embarrassment. It were better, if such were possible, that these unfortunates might forego prænomens altogether, and answer simply to the name of Sherman. As it is, they, who might otherwise escape attention, draw curious eyes and painful comment. The late Mr Dixon Scott is Prof. Sherman's bad precedent in this.*

As a case in point: one wizened, emaciated, joyless creature, deeply serious in his pubescent preoccupation with the moral law, Prof. Sherman rather heartlessly burdens with the ludicrous handle "The

---

*Dixon Scott, a brilliant young English critic killed at Gallipoli during the war, had written a number of critical essays which were collected and published under the title *Men of Letters* in 1916. Some of his titles were: "The Innocence of Bernard Shaw," "The Meekness of Mr Rudyard Kipling," "The Commonsense of Mr Arnold Bennett," etc. Professor Sherman quite shamelessly and, without credit, lifted this titular form by calling his essays "The Utopian Naturalism of H. G. Wells," "The Æsthetic Idealism of Henry James," "The Complacent Toryism of Alfred Austin," etc.

Æsthetic Naturalism of George Moore." Now, Mr Moore, in the autumn of his happy years, may be indifferent to the dubious honor of standing namesake for children who in nowise resemble him. In fact, a vicarious Euphorion in Texas might amuse him. But what of the child?

Mr Moore is sprightly of speech, engaging in conversation; the child is inarticulate and a stutterer. Mr Moore is a Dionysian; the child is unnaturally concerned with hell fire and the rewards of the pure in heart. Mr Moore is oblivious of anything that may be said for or against him; the child is morbidly sensitive, anxious to be thought nice, ambitious of being some day accepted in polite society.

And there is a pitiable mite Prof. Sherman has most indelicately called "The Democracy of Mark Twain." How much more humanely might the waif have been named "Wherein I Curry Favor with the Boston Back Bay Set," or "Wherein I Demonstrate Myself a Superior Person and a Conceited Prig."

One belligerent blockhead, unconscious of the ridicule his antics inspire, Prof. Sherman has named "The Barbaric Naturalism of Theodore Dreiser." This practical joker, who dumps the critical slop pail over the heads of all the French realists, Balzac, Flaubert and Maupassant included, were more happily named "Wherein I Convict Myself of Being One with the Unctuous Southey and the Clownish Lockhart, without the Wit of Either."

There are other hapless progeny in this ménage, all destined to suffer unnecessary pangs because of their father's heedless nomenclature—a Wells, a James, a Bennett, even a Shakespeare, about whose doings Prof. Sherman seems vaguely to have heard. One tolerable youngster, "The Skepticism of Anatole France," I fear, is not Prof. Sherman's: he resembles a French critic, M. Jules Lemaître, very much, indeed. And so, though I dislike to suggest it, I am afraid Prof. Sherman has been imposed upon.*

On the whole, setting aside the French chap, I suggest sterilization for this brood of delinquents, lest they propagate their kind and become a burden and a menace to our letters. (Chicago *Tribune,* January 12, 1918.)

*This veiled reference to what I considered a heavy indebtedness of Professor Sherman to Lemaître's essay on Anatole France in *Les Contemporaines* disturbed Professor Sherman more than anything else I ever wrote against him; cf. p. 338 in *Life and Letters of Stuart P. Sherman.*

"JIM AND JOE, AUTHORS," A ONE–ACT PLAY
WHICH LACKS PUNCH OR POINT

By Burton Rascoe

As a professional judge of books I must, in critical honesty, say that this, my maiden playwriting effort, is very shoddy stuff. Willard Mack or Maurice Maeterlinck could do better. It possesses none of the dramatic virtues; it has no beginning and no end, no point, no punch, no anything. But the actors in the initial, and only, production were artists, and by the very realistic interpretation of their roles, somehow saved the thing from utter failure.

TIME: February 1919. Place: New York. Scene: At a table in the rear of a Thirty-sixth Street restaurant, famous for its collection of long-stemmed pipes which no one ever smokes and its gallery of historical theater programs which no one ever reads. Cast of characters:

JAMES BRANCH CABELL, whose *Beyond Life* has just been published and who is now at work on a book of excursions from and for the library chair.

JOSEPH HERGESHEIMER, whose *Java Head* is somehow a best seller, though radically to the contrary in theme and treatment of what is currently supposed to requite the popular demand, and who is now tidying up the sentences and paragraphs of a new romance of modern times.

A scribe, a publisher, waiters, bus boys, etc., complete the ensemble. Hergesheimer is, say, 5 feet 9, possibly less, rather heavily built; in the thirties (or looks it), with a rotund mouth, full-lipped, somewhat protruding, which helps to give him a look of puzzled and anxious inquiry when he directs his gaze toward you from those small, blue, keen (yes, keen) eyes with which he regards you altogether absorbedly through the thick-lensed, horn-rimmed glasses. His nose is ample. You are rather startled by his voice at first: it has a tenor pitch and becomes the more nasalized the more interested he gets in the conversation. His hair is dark and his color is good, though he is not what you would call a handsome man.

Nor would the discriminating observer apply the word "handsome" to Cabell; his nose is long, but it has a squatty aspect at the tip; it looks snubbed, but isn't, as a profile view would instantly reveal. And his hair is thinning on the sides of his forehead, where it might be parted if he didn't roach it back. This impoverishment of the hirsute heritage of his youth gives him an appearance of a more than normal expanse of brow. If he loses much more hair his cupola will suggest the droll wig worn by the Irish comedian of the old burlesque school. His mouth is distinctly Southern—if you know what I mean—the sort of mouth that cannot pronounce "rs" without difficulty, a mouth with few motions. But if there is a lassitude in his mouth, there is not in his eyes—grayish blue, quizzical eyes which observe you from the angle of a depressed chin, and then from the angle of a thrust-out chin, and then from the corners. When he talks you don't at first know whether he is jesting or is speaking in sober earnest. You learn later that he is doing both. He speaks with his head thrown back, and he listens with it bowed. He and Hergesheimer are of a height and almost of a build: Hergesheimer says they are of a mind, but that remains to be seen.

Hergesheimer is easily the better talker—one of the best, in fact, I have ever heard, and I only trust that I report him with appreciable accuracy. Expertness in shorthand would be necessary to record his minute, suggestive, colorful descriptions of people and places. I wish I could remember how he described the mouth of a certain woman dramatist: If I ever see her I shall recognize her instantly, though the wording of his portrait has left me.

Cabell says little, but he is vastly interested, and there is an agreeable touch of humor to all he says. Throughout the scene Cabell smokes cheap, domestic cigarettes, and Hergesheimer smokes excellent cigars. The latter offers the contents of his case to the others, and there are encomiums for the flavor of the weed.

The Dialogue

HERGESHEIMER: Mr Cabell, Rascoe here says we have little in common; but he's wrong. You and I are traversing somewhat the same ground. We are both interested in the theme of romantic love, in projecting that aspect of love against a background of color and beauty, which exists only in the imagination. I am very fond of *The Soul of Melicent,* a beautiful thing. Why don't you do another *Melicent?*

CABELL: But *Melicent* is already written.

HERGESHEIMER: Yes, but I should like to see you write some more in that vein. I am saying that because it is inevitable that a man should desire more of that which gives him especial pleasure. That, after all, is the ultimate criticism: Does a thing of beauty give the specific pleasure the author intended? I write a book and it is written. I couldn't change it, no matter what's said about it. To write it differently would mean that I should have to feel differently; it is not a matter of what anybody else wants or expects, it is what I want or it wouldn't be true. If Rascoe thinks the ending of *Java Head* is bad, it can't be helped. I wrote it that way, and that way it stays.

CABELL: I told Rascoe he was wrong about that ending. I like it.

HERGESHEIMER: No, the value of literary criticism to an author is in proportion to the communicated enthusiasm, whatever its value to the public. If a critic reveals in what he writes that he actually derives pleasure from even a portion of a novel, or the aim of a novel, he is of infinite help to the author. He may be suggestive in what he says against certain technicalities, but criticism of the essential substance of a novel is no help at all. Every author who appeals to anyone must write *himself*. There must be that self-confidence or it doesn't get across. I regard what I write as highly important, and it *is* highly important to me. It is the one necessary thing for an author. Mrs Gene Stratton-Porter, I think, has that same feeling. She must have it or she would not retain the hold she has upon the limited imaginations of so many people whose views of life are as naïve as hers. . . . *Beyond Life* is a marvelous book. I read it through the other night at a single sitting. It is one of the few books I have ever read from beginning to end without leaving my chair.

CABELL: I am gratified to hear you say that. I didn't know it was a book anyone would willingly read at a sitting.

THE PUBLISHER: I regret to acknowledge that I haven't got around to read *Beyond Life* yet.

CABELL: There is no cause for you to feel isolated. There are a lot like you.

HERGESHEIMER: When are you going to write another mediæval romance, another story involving the platonic idea of love? You should write some more of those. My next novel is to be about the daydream romance of a young girl, that love which a young girl carries about in her imagination and which colors all things for her. There again we have themes in common. All of your books embody the platonic concept of love.

CABELL: I am afraid that my next book scarcely deals with love on the platonic order. It seems to me I have heard intimations from

Rascoe and others who have read the manuscript that it is even a trifle improper here and there.

HERGESHEIMER: But all of your books deal with platonic love. Have you read Plato?

CABELL: No, I got a set of Plato once, but, like Mr Cook here in regard to *Beyond Life,* I have never got around to read it yet, with the exception of the *Crito,* which I didn't find very remarkable.

HERGESHEIMER: *Beyond Life* and *The Cream of the Jest* contain many derivatives from the platonic dialogues, interpreted in the terms of your own temperament and personality.

CABELL: How do you write your books—do you ever dictate?

HERGESHEIMER: I first write the novel through from beginning to end, usually in longhand, and then I turn it over to my secretary to copy out with triple spacing. Then I take the copy and go over it bit by bit, tinkering with it and polishing it up. When I have finished with that there are changes and corrections on every page. I have it copied again and again, tinker with it until I am absolutely satisfied that there is nothing more I can do with it, then my secretary copies it again and it is ready for publication. Of course, I often make many changes in proof. How do you work?

CABELL: I do all my own typewriting, even my letters. When I have finished the first draft I go over it and make so many corrections that no one else could read it. Then I do all my copying and recopying. I seem never to be able to leave my manuscript alone. I am still making some changes in a book I wrote the first draft of last summer. I was looking it over and found a lot of sentences beginning with "and." I have got to go through it again and take out about a bushel of them.

HERGESHEIMER: The first sentence of the first chapter is the hardest to write. The beginning is always my greatest worry.

CABELL: I usually begin about the middle and write the beginning later on. It always seems to be easier to do it that way. What do you do with your manuscripts?

HERGESHEIMER: I save them all, all drafts of them. Had a request the other day for them from a museum.

CABELL: I have always burned mine.

HERGESHEIMER: You ought to keep them. They will be valuable in years to come.

JOHN BUTLER YEATS ON HIS SON AND ON VARIOUS MATTERS

By Burton Rascoe

"You will find him every evening at the little French restaurant of the Mlles. Petitpas in West Twenty-ninth Street," a friend had told me in New York, and at 6:30 I was awaiting the answer to my ring at the puzzling iron grating beneath the high stoop of an old residence which is architecturally identical with the rows of others on each side of the street. One of the mesdemoiselles, an anomaly to the eyesight by reason of her gingham dress with leg-of-mutton sleeves and her exaggerated pompadour of the period of the early Charles Dana Gibson, unlocked the gate and with a friendly greeting ushered me to a table.

Here and there were French sailors in their blue uniforms, piped with white, and colorful further in splotches of red, I don't recall exactly where—pompons, I remember, on their small blue tams and another dab of red somewhere about their blouses. A French officer or so, a veteran poilu with the Croix de Guerre, here to aid in the Fourth Liberty loan, and the rest, for the most part, middle-aged civilians—not the Brevoort crowd, or that of the Village sinkholes, or of the Plaza, Jack's, Child's or Keane's. And there in a far corner, surrounded by his evening audience, the white-bearded old gentleman I had come to see.

At demitasse and cognac I sent a note asking a few minutes in conversation. While I was thinking what I should ask John Butler Yeats, the father of William Butler Yeats, and himself a portrait painter and the author of a series of letters to his son which had piqued my curiosity about the man, he arose from his table, looked around the room and, when I stood up, came over to me smiling pleasantly.

"They are out of print," he told me when I asked him about his published correspondence. "The London catalogues quote them at fifteen dollars apiece now. I have been unable to get any of them. Haven't a copy myself. When my son left here to return to Dublin he told me to write him anything that came into my head. I wrote him off and on, just anything I happened to be thinking about. And then one day Ezra Pound selected a number of them for publication by my daughters.

"One might get the impression from those letters," he continued, "that I know all about all the arts and literature that ever existed. But I don't at all. I had a pontifical air in them, as though I were speaking ex cathedra with a profound knowledge of Greek and Latin, but I really know very little about either. You see, I could do that because I had no notion that the letters would ever be printed. My son wasn't being flimflamed by my pretensions and my oracular manner, but those who don't know my actual limitations might be. My son knew just what I had read and what I hadn't, just how much I knew and how much I didn't, so he could discount here and there and arrive at their actual value.

"But the letters are better than my essays, which the Macmillans are going to publish in this country shortly. I had to be careful in the essays, so I wouldn't be caught up. I spoke only of subjects I was acquainted with. But when you are confined like that and can't be expansive and pretentious, as I can be to my son, you lose something. No, the essays aren't quite as good as the letters, but they more accurately reflect what I actually know."

I found it wasn't necessary to ask questions.

"Did you see my son's poem in memory of Robert Gregory printed in the *Little Review?*" (I had.) "It is a beautiful thing, isn't it?" (It is.) "My son, I think, is the only real poet left. This is the great critical age. All the high creative intellects are going into criticism of one form or another. The poets, the creators of pure beauty, are out of date.

"People ask me why my son doesn't write about the war, and I answer that it is impossible for him. The war is too big; he can't grasp it; it is foreign to him, entirely out of his experience or imagination. A man can write only what he is fit to write, what he feels, what is in him.

"Pound's a great fellow. Got a lot in him. I don't like his insulting people and his insolence and his bombastic tricks; but I suppose he has to do that to attract attention. He would be lost if he weren't vulgar and insolent and full of braggadocio. It is necessary these days, I suppose; some of it at least. But beneath it all Pound is a clever fellow, a good critic. He hasn't any creative genius, and he's not much of a poet. All his talent is critical. And this is a critical age."

The elder Yeats paints an occasional portrait—"to keep me in bread and cheese," he said—and discourses on art and life every evening to a little gathering of students and friends at the far corner table of the restaurant of the Mlles. Petitpas.

UNCONVENTIONAL PORTRAITS

With Some Details Concerning Frank Moore Colby, Joseph Hergesheimer, Sherwood Anderson, Carl Sandburg and H. L. Mencken, as
They Were at the Beginning of the 1920s.

By Burton Rascoe

FRANK MOORE COLBY

THREE CONTRIBUTORS TO THE early issues of the *New Republic* after its
founding in 1914 made that publication one which I looked forward
to with eagerness. They were Clarence Day, Jr., Philip Littell and
Frank Moore Colby, and the greatest of these, to my mind, was Colby.

Colby had taught history for a year at Amherst, lectured in history
at Columbia while teaching economics at Barnard and had taught
economics at New York University. He had been the literary critic of
Harper's Weekly for precisely three months and had written reviews
and essays for the *Bookman* and *Vanity Fair*. He had been an editorial
writer for the New York *Commercial Advertiser* (later the *Globe*),
and when I first encountered his work he had published *Outlines of
General History* (1909), *Imaginary Obligations* (1904) and *Constrained
Attitudes* (1910).

These two latter books of essays caused me, in my first blast as
literary editor of the Chicago *Tribune,* to lash out against the myopia
of domestic critics who had failed to recognize Colby's genius and
proclaim it. Week in and week out I used Colby as a stick wherewith
to beat Richard Watson Gilder, Hamilton Wright Mabie, Paul Elmer
More, Irving Babbitt, William Dean Howells, Henry Mills Alden,
Brander Matthews, Dr Clifford B. Smythe, of the *Times* literary supplement, and William Lyon Phelps, of Yale, *Scribner's* and the women's
clubs (all the literary arbiters of the time), and what I then considered
their successors, Christopher Morley, Robert Cortes Holliday, Richard-
son Wright, Logan Pearsall Smith and Grant Overton. The older men
seemed to me almost illiterate, petty, provincial bigwigs, kowtowing
to the self-satisfied insular ignorance of the writers for the London
literary reviews, such as the *Spectator,* the *Athenaeum,* the *Nation* and

the *New Statesman,* whereas Chris Morley and the men about him, with their little Lambsian whimsies, seemed to me like so many Rhodes Scholar Oxonians with affected accents, twiddling their thumbs or playing tag-you-are-it. The whole caboodle of them did not seem to be aware that the coach-and-six had been displaced by the locomotive and the automobile as a means of transportation, nor did they seem to know that vital things in literature and life were happening in America and in Continental Europe, unbeknownst to the dried-up turnips of the British reviews.

One Edgar Jepson, a fatheaded English literary mediocrity, wrote a screed against American taste and intelligence which was widely quoted and which infuriated me. I dug through the envelope on Jepson in the *Tribune* "morgue" and came upon a clipping in which this same Edgar Jepson had once invented a one-piece suit and had patented it. There was a photographic reproduction of Jepson clad in this sartorial monstrosity. I sent a satirical contribution to B. L. T., embodying the information, and followed my contribution up with this lead to my Saturday article, quoting Colby to devastating effect:

PRESUMING YOU ARE INTERESTED IN SUCH MATTERS

By Burton Rascoe*

Mr Edgar Jepson, the inventor of the one-piece suit which was to be "the first step toward the realization of that greatest of all human ideals—one man, one garment"—is, of course, being English, entirely in character when he speaks of us as "fatheaded Western ruck" whose only distinctive contributions to the arts have been made by the Negroes among us.

We have grown to expect nothing else from these penny-a-line fifth-raters who are so visibly annoyed by the fact that we in the United States can read and write, however imperfectly, that they must occasionally turn an honest shilling in disparaging our attempts. But they have long since ceased to wound our feelings: their squawks merely amuse us. Frank Moore Colby in a delightful essay once expressed our attitude perfectly:

"'It would be churlish to deny,' said an editorial writer for the London *Bombardinian* at the end of a severe rebuke of American taste in novels—'it would be churlish to deny that America has produced great writers who can hold their own with any European

*February 1919.

or Asiatic.' Why 'churlish,' I wonder, and to whom? Is the country, then, so tender or the writer so Olympian that the cruel words must be withheld for fear of crushing? Would they not be the words of a simple, harmless, unknown, perspiring man with space to fill and possibly a printer's devil waiting and ideas hanging back and no means of making sure of anything under the sun, and only some haphazard personal tastes and private guesses to rely upon? Why, then, that Atlantean manner, as if responsible to the man in the moon for letting the world slip?

"Surely readers must understand the situation. There is nothing papal about that well-known editorial chair wherein he wriggles, nor is he by any magic transformed into an ecumenical council, vox populi, enlightened public opinion, consensus of the learned, fourth estate, moral bulwark, or anything else more representative or apostolic or numerous than a man with a pen and an inkpot. Nowhere, it would seem, could a literary opinion be expressed with less concern for the susceptibilities of nations than in the unsigned pages of a British magazine. Yet nowhere do words imply a more awful sense of their own consequences . . ."

One of the dire results of our alliance with England in the war may be the disappearance of these thoughtproof, opinion-tight, unconscious humorists who episcopate in the pages of British periodicals. It would be pure vandalism to remove them, a desecration of a time-honored institution. To install Irishmen or educated young Englishmen in the places held by these hard-shelled Podsnaps would be to destroy Stonehenge to install a munitions plant.*

In writing about Colby I did not hesitate to say that Colby was one of the finest essayists living or dead (an opinion I hold unmodified

---

*Author's note, 1937: In my "Notes and Comment" for March 15, 1919, I find this:

"Edgar Jepson, the inventor of that one-piece suit which was to realize 'that greatest of all human ideals—one man, one garment,' writes to the London *Egoist* to complain that instead of controverting his contention that all contemporary American poetry is, as he with infinite poetic delicacy expresses it, punk, Miss Harriet Monroe, editor of *Poetry: A Magazine of Verse*, and I merely abuse him.

"We did just that. And we abused him because the presumptuous noodle wrote such idiotic drivel as to expose himself exclusively to ridicule and not to controversy. When a British nobody displays such colossal conceit as to condemn all modern American poetry out of hand and to write about American poetry when he doesn't even know that Mr Frost's first name is Robert, not Edgar, the more logical thing to do would be to send for a psychiatrist, not to argue with him. The symptoms are rather those of paranoia than of critical insight." I did not know the names of any of Jepson's novels, so I continued to refer to him not as a novelist but as the inventor of a one-piece suit.

today). He was urbane, analytical, subtle and concise. He was a man of great learning who took his learning lightly and made quiet pointed fun of fact gatherers and pedants. He was so sound a scholar in Greek that he could, and did, in four paragraphs, blast utterly A. S. Way's and Gilbert Murray's translation of Euripides and Professor Butler's translation of Quintilian in the Loeb Classics series. Of Way's translation he wrote:

"Patience with Way's Euripides is almost a proof of illiteracy. I suppose no man outside a government bureau at Washington ever wrote worse English than Professor A. S. Way, and he wrote it out of sheer love of bad English, for page after page of it has not the slightest excuse in the Greek. . . . Professor Gilbert Murray's Euripides has so little to do with Euripides that all compliments paid to it belong to Professor Murray himself. . . . Professor Way's method resulted in murder, and Professor Gilbert Murray's in oblivion."

And of Professor Butler he wrote:

"Loquacity is a native quality in Professor Butler. He had rather use sixty-eight words than thirty-five, and he will say the same thing twice over in order to do so. This is shown on page after page, when the thought is simple and the way to brevity perfectly open. Professor Butler takes the longest way because he likes it. When he sees seven words by Quintilian, he says to himself, 'Why does the old chap waste his opportunity? I can put the same idea in forty.' It is a difference in temperament. Quintilian likes to pack things into small space, skip an explanation, leave a little to inference. Professor Butler hates that kind of thing—thinks it selfish and secretive. He dislikes Quintilian for it and thwarts him when he can. If there is any man in the world that I should hate to resemble, said Professor Butler, when he began this version, it's Quintilian, and his whole text is a demonstration of this incompatibility. Not once does he let Quintilian have his own way about anything. There is no doubt that Quintilian becomes modern by this method. You would swear he was a contributor to the London *Spectator.*"

On a trip to New York in March 1918 I called upon Colby in response to an invitation to come to see him when I was next in New York (a correspondence between us had arisen out of my writings about him) and found him occupying a tiny bit of desk room in the crowded office of Dodd, Mead & Co., as editor of the *New International Encyclopedia* and the *International Year Book*. The desk was a battered, rolled-top antique, with papers sticking out of the pigeonholes and every available inch of space, except a few square inches in the center, crowded with papers. On top of the desk was a large tin cracker box. Not until years afterward did I learn from his daughter, Harriet, the usages of that cracker box. It was for articles comprising the text of the *International Year Book*. It was also a measuring gauge: he knew how far along he was with his work of editing by the height of the pile in the cracker box and, he said, he knew his job was done when the papers were level with the top edge. When this achievement had been accomplished, he said, he threw all remaining articles into the wastebasket, tied up his cracker box and sent it to the printer.

Colby was a stalwart man of fifty-three when I first saw him. He was over six feet in height, broad-shouldered and ruddy. His sandy hair was curly and gray only around the temples; his sandy mustache was not gray at all. His face was squarish, with high cheekbones and square jaw. He had a handsome, aggressive appearance, although he was not aggressive in the least—diffident, rather.

He took me to the University Club for lunch, and it was not until after the meal was finished that I overcame my shyness in the presence of the man whose work I admired so much. But he put me at my ease, and we conversed for more than an hour, during which time he told me he rarely had a chance to talk to young men and could talk only banalities to the men he knew of his own age. He asked me if we couldn't "play around a little, have something to eat in a quiet little French restaurant and wander about the parts of town that have long been unfamiliar to me. I spend so much time among the dodos of the club that I begin to feel like a dodo myself. This has been a refreshing experience. I have had a most jolly good time."

He asked me to name an evening, but I was going to Boston the next day, and when he repeated the invitation on later occasions I was too shy to accept it. I thought he was merely being polite, and although up to the time of his death in 1925 I occasionally had lunch with him, I still had that deference toward him which made me afraid to intrude upon his time. When I told this to Philip Littell after Colby's death he said, "You deprived Frank of a genuine pleasure, something he wanted to do. He probably never proposed to anyone else that they wander around seeing the interesting quarters of New York, for Frank himself was a shy man. He would have enjoyed it, otherwise he would not have suggested it to you."

APPENDICES

On that first meeting with Colby I did succeed in my mission, which was to get him to write a weekly article for the "highbrow" page of the Chicago *Tribune*. He was meticulous about details, and when he asked me how long each article should be I said offhandedly, "About twelve hundred words," meaning anywhere between one thousand and fifteen hundred. When the articles came to my desk they were always exactly twelve hundred words long. On the margins were penciled notations of his count, and there were evidences that he had gone through his copy, taking out a word here and a word there so that the article should be twelve hundred words exactly.

What Colby said of Quintilian applied to himself: "Quintilian likes to pack things into small space, skip an explanation, leave a little to inference." In the two volumes of selected work edited by Clarence Day, Jr., after Colby's death under the title *The Colby Essays,* many of the pieces are only two or three paragraphs long, and Colby's sense of the paragraph was exact. He was one of the very few writers we have had who possessed the sense of humor that is defined in George Meredith's *The Comic Spirit.* It was that unusual and true sense of humor, so different from a sense of fun which characterizes so much American humor, that throughout his career he was to meet with annoyed incomprehension when he displayed it in his writings. I was soon to brush against this incomprehension, and I have already related two other displays of it; for Colby's articles had hardly begun on the "highbrow" page before Percy Hammond began to knock them to me as being vague, pointless and uninteresting, whereas they were extremely pointed, even barbed, and to me by far the most interesting stuff in the whole newspaper. Hammond may have merely been jealous of Colby (he was capable of this), but he must have communicated his criticism of Colby to E. S. Beck, the managing editor, for soon Beck was knocking Colby's articles to me in practically the same words Hammond had used; and finally he took out a Colby article which had been run in the "bull-pup" edition (the out-of-town Sunday edition made up on Thursday night and run off on Friday morning) and made me dig up something to put in its place, saying it was dull and did not make sense (it was a biting piece of irony about what public-school teachers had to knuckle to in order to keep their jobs). I wrote Colby what had occurred and regretfully told him that inasmuch as the managing editor did not understand the meaning of the articles it was probably futile to hope that many of the *Tribune's* readers would.

In 1921, after I had gone from Chicago to New York to become as-

sociate editor of *McCall's* magazine, I was drawn into the group that
had been summoned by Harold Stearns for a symposium to be called
Civilization in the United States. The purpose of the book was to stir
up the ineffable complacency America had fallen into. Mencken and
Nathan had each written to me about it while I was still in Chicago,
and both of them took the symposium as a huge practical joke upon
the professional patriots, the reformers and the public in general.
Mencken wrote me that it was a buffoonery in which "some professors
and New Republicans" were to be dragged in as contributors to make
the thing sound authentic.

Stearns was not of this opinion: it was a serious affair with him.
Meetings to discuss the book and the best ones to write the various
articles were held in Stearns's dingy quarters at Barrow and Jones
streets. At the meetings I attended were Elsie Clews Parsons,
Katharine Anthony, Lewis Mumford, Van Wyck Brooks, Walter Pach,
George Soule, Robert Lowie, John Macy, Clarence Britten, Ernest
Boyd and sometimes Thorne Smith. Rarely was anything discussed for
more than fifteen minutes, because everybody seemed to be eager to
get off for a party. When the subject came up as to who could do the
chapters on sport and humor, I suggested Ring Lardner for the first
and Frank Moore Colby for the latter and said I would undertake to
get the articles from these men because I knew them both and no one
else there did.

In his autobiography, *The Street I Know,* Stearns writes:

"No Harvard pride or vestigial Boston correctness prevented
me from going after Ring Lardner hammer and tongs for the essay
on sport and play—he was the man I wanted, and I wanted him
badly. He could write in his 'Americanese', if he wanted to? Why
not? That was his natural style of writing anyway; he would be
self-conscious had he tried to do anything else. . . . Even to this
day I don't exactly know what Ring thought of being in such
'highbrow' company, but I do know how he felt—that he was
doing us an honor, not we him. Anyway, I managed to persuade
him finally, although I had to see him several times."

Stearns never approached Lardner for the article. I doubt that he
ever met him. I asked Ring to write the article at the bar of the old
Waldorf-Astoria, told him the general scheme of the book; and there
was no trouble about it at all: he sent me the article the next day, and
I turned it over to Stearns. Stearns implies that Lardner habitually and
naturally wrote in the style of his bushers, which shows that Stearns

did not know the least thing about Lardner except possibly by hearsay, for Lardner wrote a great number of short stories, articles and sports accounts in fluid and correct English prose; and moreover, so little would Lardner have been awed by Stearns and his highbrows that he would have needed to see and hear them only once to have comic material for a long time to come.

Stearns also says:

> "I contrived to convince Frank M. Colby to do the piece [on humor], which, although it was rather slight in substance and almost flippant in tone, was really a much subtler bit of work than too many hasty critics gave it credit for being."

Stearns did not see Colby. I got Colby to write the article, and when I turned it over to Stearns and watched him while he read it over I could see that Stearns could not make head or tail of it. He shook his head and said he was disappointed in it. As a matter of fact it was the soundest and subtlest piece of writing in the entire book.

It was Colby's contention in that article that "the literary upper classes" did not understand a sense of humor even when it was explained to them; but that Americans of all classes had a very good sense of fun. When Stearns's co-editors read the Colby essay they were as puzzled by it as Stearns was and were all for rejecting it, because they and Stearns did not understand that Colby was using them as a conspicuous example of his thesis, that he was using the occasion of the publication of a denigration of American civilization to point out that the editors themselves and their collaborators had, for a time at least, forsaken their sense of humor. They wanted him to be lambasting something because that was the scheme of the book; they could not understand that Colby was exercising a superior sort of humor to their piddling inquietudes.

Colby's fame has never been commensurate with his deserts, because he wrote painfully and with exactness, sometimes spending a whole day over a single paragraph. His friend and associate, Philip Littell, once told me of an occasion when the editor of the *Globe* had asked Colby to write the editorial obituary on Hamilton Wright Mabie when that literary panjandrum died. Days passed, and the editorial was not turned it; a week passed, and the editor became anxious. He called Colby and asked him what about that piece on Mabie; Colby replied that he had been struggling hard with the article but had not been able to get any further than the first sentence. The editor asked to see the sentence. Colby produced it. It read: "Hamilton Wright Mabie conducted young women into the suburbs of literature and left them there."

One can understand that, having achieved that sentence, Colby had had his say about Mabie: that was all there was, there wasn't any more.

In the office of the *Globe* the editorial writers were daily assembled in the office of the editor for the purpose of discussing the various topics that were to be written about by the editorial writers. At these meetings, Mr Littell said, Colby always sat sprawled in his chair, with his eyes glued to the floor, never contributing anything to the discussion. One day as he sat thus, after about thirty different subjects had been brought up as possible meat for editorial comment, the editor turned to Colby and said, "Frank, do any of these subjects we've been discussing appeal to you to write about?" Colby straightened up and fixed the editor with his steady eyes, slumped down again and said, "Me? Heavens no!"

When the *New Republic* was about to be launched Colby was called in as an adviser on the editorial policy to be pursued by the paper. His one contribution was this: "Manage somehow to have at least one article in every issue which *nobody* can understand. That will give you a reputation for being very profound. Once having achieved that reputation, you can be wrong on everything and nobody will ever believe that you are."

"I am not sure just how far we carried out that suggestion," said Mr Littell.

Joseph Hergesheimer

Joseph hergesheimer is an exquisite, thwarted by adiposity and malicious circumstance. He is at heart an eighteenth-century dandy in plush pants and ruffled lace; but he looks like a bread-and-pastry dealer with eyebrows arched in perpetual inquiry as to what the customer will have today. His soul is the soul of William Hickey, groomed by a Wetzel of a former day, his satin boots spattered by spurting blood in a duet of rapiers, as an entr'acte between epigrams and cocktails. And he lives in West Chester, Pennsylvania, a settlement of Quakers and Scots Presbyterians.

He has his compensations for this disparity between essence and exterior, spirit and flesh, desire and circumstance. He dresses three times a day. He reads *Vogue,* the *Gazette du Bon Genre,* and the memoirs of the court of Louis XIV.

He writes beautiful books, luscious with pretty words, about marionettes whose charm is a matter of fragility, cosmetics, and linen carefully draped. He winks at women with an air of self-confidence and smiles at them as if there were something between him and them. He has assignations with adjectives, love affairs with nouns, and capricious liaisons with adverbs and prepositions. He believes he is an authority on women.

He never wearies of repeating that art comes from the heart and not from the mind. What he means by the heart, one is hard put to conjecture. Certainly it is not tenderness and compassion and pity, for his work has the cold shimmer of the glazed surface of a porcelain trinket. He is a momentarian in his philosophy, with a polite and airy skepticism about the worth and value of character and steadfastness, denial and sacrifice.

Like that fanciful philosophic nihilist, Santayana, he is an advocate of "fluttering tiptoe loves," and when he depicts passion it is always with a left impression that it is wasting and a little messy.

He has an Oriental's attraction to fabrics, spices, essences and tinsel items of indulgence. Silks and stained glass, wrought silver and carved panelings catch his eye not only in ensemble but in minutiae. This suggests an artistic strain at war with a chill impulse to respond reverently to the plastic loveliness of the Winged Victory and the Cytherean goddess.

There results at once a balance and an anomaly: his work is neither austere nor hedonistic; it is decorative and Schnitzleresque, with the sub-acid pathos of a Punch and Judy show. It has the ironic sentiment of banjo chords on a moonlit lake while a child of eighteen out of finishing school is drowning herself for love of a gardener.

Hergesheimer's sensory impressions are predominately tactile and visual. There are no odors in his books: he describes even perfumes in terms of sight, as liquids of certain hues and exotic names in be-ribboned bottles pleasingly shaped.

His sense of taste is rudimentary; food interests him only as an arrangement of words in the depiction of a dinner party, and drink is to him a fluid in graceful glasses and with a connotation of luxury.

In *Cytherea* he describes a champagne bottle in detail and expatiates upon the process involved in releasing the cork; but he is not concerned with taste and savor.

His ear is as deficient as Meredith's, which explains their affinity in style,—thought as a sequence of two-dimensional pictures, set off as conversation that is elliptical and funambulesque and is meant to be precise.

[424]

He thinks in terms of sight and touch; and should one seek to reduce his search and interest in life to two words, they would be "elegance" and "charm."

He takes vast liberties with accuracy of statement. That is one of his chiefest virtues. He bathes and basks in flattery, and from the reticent he provokes it by the disingenuous way he has of piling compliment upon compliment. He is extremely sensitive to criticism, and this sketch will make him hopping mad. It shouldn't, because it is written by one of his most loyal admirers, by one who thinks that, without question, Hergesheimer is one of the best craftsmen among novelists now writing in English. But it will. To him there is no other occupant of the peak of Teneriffe, and he whose goddesses have unearthy feet would have you confine your gaze to his own less peccable aspects.

Four years ago he talked entirely about himself, and the subject became a little shopworn after two hours and a half. But of late he has got about and has achieved a more general fund of ideas. His conversation is brilliant and witty, keen, amusing, and to the point. He talks less about himself, and even when he is his theme, he endows it with a glamour and an interest that is stimulating and entertaining.

He is an impatient auditor, but a perfect companion. Believing nothing, he first senses and then feeds one's tastes and biases. He is a facile sophist and the soul of reassurance. Still, in some moods he delights in saying the thing that will irritate; and half the time he doesn't believe what he is saying. He talks always from a point of view. And he changes his point of view almost as often as he changes his underwear.

His dress is chosen for smartness and for comfort. In the mornings he wears flannel shirts and tweed knickers, in the afternoon a lounge suit, not too snugly tailored, and in the evening dinner dress with a shirt and soft collar of thick silk.

One of his favorite expressions in speech is "utterly charming," and utterly charming describes perfectly his home in West Chester. It is an ancient house built of boulder stones, with huge fireplaces and heavy, seasoned timbers. It sits away from the road on a rounded knoll, a little sombre and commanding.

Airedales disport themselves on the lawn. Two cars, one Joe's and the other Dorothy's, are in the ample barn, now equipped as a garage. Servants perfectly trained; furnishings a continual surprise and delight, inevitably placed; and plenty of hot water, a rarity in country homes.

APPENDICES

Over this demesne rules Dorothy, frank, cordial, unaffected, wholesome, pretty and lovable. An agile and alert little bundle of energy, her
most constant thought is to make her scribbling husband comfortable
and happy. Her job is not easy: he is a moody, grumpy, unruly, self-
centered child, plagued by insomnia, nervous and fidgety. To her,
though, he is ever gracious and considerate, even a little humble, as if
abashed by her uncommon good sense, her forbearance, her perfect
poise.

With such a home one would think that Hergesheimer would do all
his writing there, isolated and quiet, among familiar surroundings.
Instead he rents a small office opposite the courthouse in West Chester
and arrives there at nine o'clock in the morning, like a business man.
He has steel filing cabinets in which he keeps his notes, his correspondence and the manuscripts of everything he writes. He uses a stub
pen and writes the first draft carefully in a grade-school composition
book. Then his secretary makes a triple-spaced copy on the typewriter.
He goes through it patiently, making innumerable changes and corrections. She copies it again, and again he makes corrections. The third
draft and even the printer's proof are not free from his rearrangement
of words.

He is naïve about these manuscripts. He refuses to part with them,
because he believes, rightly, that they will someday be of high
monetary value. He is a shrewd businessman; knows how to think in
terms of money. One of his recent hobbies is the collection of rare
books and first editions.

He plays this game, I believe, because it is less expensive and
pleasanter than playing the stock market. But at bottom it is the same
sort of gambling with him. He gets catalogs from the rare-book dealers
in every mail, and he reads these through for the rise or fall in the
quotations on certain books, just as a gambler in stocks watches the
market quotations. He spends at least an hour every morning studying
these catalogs, making out his orders to dealers and figuring out what
some of his books are worth. Most of them he has never read.

Hergesheimer inherited a bit of money and a weak constitution. As
a boy he was a bookworm, shy and reserved. When money fell into his
hands he forthwith got married and lived in Florence. There he suffered a nervous breakdown and was nursed back to health by Dorothy
after months of care and anxiety.

He wrote for fourteen years, urged on by a dogged belief in himself,
without having a single manuscript accepted. He and Dorothy bore
the pinch of adversity and the rebuffs of editors with fortitude, and

the final triumph was therefore all the sweeter. In these years of apprentice work, his masters were Conrad, Henry James, Meredith and Flaubert. His style, even yet, is not fixed and inflexible. It varies between a highly tenuous and involuted prose and a smoothly cadenced manner which is simple and clear. To my mind the very finest writing he has yet published is to be found in two pieces which are widely dissimilar in manner: one of them, "A Scots Grandfather" in the *Reviewer;* the other, "Eight Novels" in *Vanity Fair.*

One of Hergesheimer's weaknesses is that of speaking before women's clubs. He is in great demand for that sort of thing. But usually he does not get a second invitation to speak before the same club. He has a faculty for getting himself in bad; he is a consummate egotist, and he takes a sadistic delight in saying things which make his audience uncomfortable. Probably nine tenths of his readers are women, but when he has an audience of women, he usually asperses their intelligence categorically and in detail.

That is a cultivated attitude which feeds his own vanity. When he was in Chicago, he felt called upon to upbraid the citizens for the physical unloveliness of the city. He lamented that the architecture there was not the same as that of Florence. He was invited to speak before a certain club and in sheer perversity failed to show up. When no one later showed concern for his negligence, he called up his hostess five times, trying to get her to arrange another lecture date for him.

Hergesheimer's talents, I believe, are just maturing. He is just now arriving at a mastery of his media of expression. He has only recently attained an aesthetic attitude. He has produced, to date, only two novels with themes which were not factitious: *The Three Black Pennys* and *Cytherea.* The others are full of sensuous beauty, colorful, more carefully and more exquisitely written than these two. But it is safe to predict that his forthcoming novels will be novels wherein a finished and polished style will be wedded to a content which itself shall command an interest.

SHERWOOD ANDERSON

I HAVE NEVER KNOWN a man who was worth his salt who was not in some way vain, proud, puffed up or conceited. There are vanities and vanities, and the sagacious mind will not resent the one and be taken in by the other.

Sherwood Anderson has the most gorgeous vanity of any writer I have ever seen. It is gorgeous because on the surface he is the least vain of men. On the surface he displays a charming modesty and a sweet humility, a companionable deference and a willingness to listen.

Many are taken in by this. They speak of him as a delightful and lovable fellow, which he is, indeed, but for reasons beyond this gracious exterior. These same people upon encountering Ben Hecht, say, or Joseph Hergesheimer are often repelled and disconcerted by the elaborate surface vanity of these men and are soothed and comforted by the much more extensive vanity of Sherwood Anderson.

Hecht and Hergesheimer wear their vanity like a chip on the shoulder, but it is not so deep and significant as Sherwood's vanity, which he conceals from all but the most penetrant eye. Hecht cocks his hat on the side of his head, cultivates a repertoire of gestures and facial expressions and speaks with a swagger that has overtones of insolence. This is because he has not at bottom a self-assurance half so sure as Sherwood's. Hergesheimer dresses for morning, for afternoon and for evening even when he is alone, and he talks at you rather than with you, except when he remembers that Meredith or someone once said that conversation must not be a monologue but a spontaneous exchange of ideas, at which time he tells you that he dislikes people who orate but do not converse, and gives you all of two minutes to get a word in.

These two men pass for vain and conceited while Sherwood escapes. In sheer truth they are amusing and entertaining, and their vanity is a matter of ingenuous surfaces while Sherwood's is a question of his whole being, his very existence. Both Hecht and Hergesheimer are capable of viewing their work in a critical and disinterested light; they are capable of maintaining a certain skepticism as to its ultimate worth. Sherwood is not. He would, however, valiantly deny this contention of mine. When he is brought to speak of his work he does it in a modestly evasive manner, very pleasing for the gullible to see. Hecht would have no hesitancy in *telling* you that he is the greatest writer living; but Sherwood *believes* that *he* is.

I doubt whether Sherwood, when the time comes for him to be embalmed in a uniform collected edition, will alter a line that he has written. He's that much stuck on himself as a writer. Mind you, I think that is an excellent and by no means a reprehensible thing. It accounts for the phenomenon that is Sherwood Anderson, a great and original figure in American literature. It is a beautiful vanity, but it is a vanity no less. I would not, for one, have him be otherwise.

To illustrate: Sherwood's *New Testament*, which ran in the *Little*

Review, and some of his poems in *Mid-American Chants* are often unintelligible, incoherent and disconcerting. He wrote these things down without effort of will, without a plan, simply as they came to him while he sat alone in his room. They are uncorrelated, crotchety mental associations, unraveling under a personal stimulus. The usual artist's point of view would be to regard this material as the makings of poems which should be rounded, traditional and comprehensible. Not Sherwood. They are, as he regards them, the unhampered, free progeny of a rich, untutored, creative urge. They are Sherwood Anderson, and you can take them or leave them, call them art or nonsense; but he will not change them to suit your preconceptions of what art should be, and he will not cease to regard them as important and significant. And I think perhaps he is right.

Again, take his paintings. Until that summer he stayed down in Alabama near Mobile Bay he had never painted anything except wagon spokes and barns. And he can't draw a better likeness than I can. But he had the urge to paint—to express himself in form and color—so he sent north for paint and canvas and started feverishly to work. He did not paint what he saw before him: that is, he did not attempt to reproduce what he saw as photographic reality. He painted what was in his mind's eye. He put reds on and smeared greens and dabbed yellows where something inside him told him to place these colors. It was a sort of automatic painting, undirected, unguided by will, except the will to create.

He had the effrontery to exhibit these paintings. Again his superb vanity; the vanity of a man who believes that nothing that he does is shallow, weak, useless or unimportant because he is absolutely honest and sincere in expressing himself. His paintings met with ridicule, incomprehension, derision; but this did not faze him. He sent them on from Chicago to New York to be exhibited. In New York two of them were sold, fetching a hundred dollars apiece. Sherwood was grateful that there were two who appreciated his work. Maybe they didn't. Maybe they bought them out of curiosity or out of sentimental regard for the handiwork of a man they considered a fine writer of stories. But, whether anyone thought well of the paintings or not, you may be sure Sherwood does not underestimate their value. He rates this value pretty high. So do I. It may be that I am under the spell of him as a writer and as a personality; but I think that these paintings are not only interesting, but strangely, curiously beautiful. And I know there is no insincerity, hokum or trickery in them.

No, Sherwood is not modest. His vanity peeps out, like those atrocious socks he wears with red and black checks in them, each block of color two inches square. Most people are not likely to notice these socks, because his suit is usually a quiet and comfortable tweed. They are not likely to pay close attention to the violent multicolored muffler he wears, because his overcoat is a decorous raglan. They are not likely to notice the guinea feather in his hatband, because his hat is cleverly chosen to show off his head most effectively and unostentatiously. They are not likely to notice that his hair is trimmed more often than a movie star's, because it looks so unkempt, unwieldy and romantic. They are not likely to observe that he is fastidious, because he so adroitly conveys the opposite impression.

You see, Sherwood is a Scotsman with the uncanny canniness that is traditional with the race. He is shrewd as well as talented; he has social sense as well as genius. People are charmed by his conversation, because he sets them up a bit. Anyone who gives assurance to another always wins his admiration, sympathy and championship, especially if the latter is suffering from a sense of inferiority. Sherwood always gives that assurance to everyone. Not, however, because he is particularly interested in everybody, but because he is particularly interested in himself and that presupposes a definite, disinterested but assumed interest in the petty opinions, worries and convictions of others.

Sherwood will spend hours listening to doddering and garrulous old men who lie about their early escapades, adventurous enterprises and deeds of strength, amour and bravery. I have seen him listen in apparent fascination to a windy old fraud backed up to a building on the busiest street in Chicago. In the Kentucky mountains, where he has gone for several years on business connected with the advertising company he occasionally works for, he is the most popular "furriner" who ever went into those parts. This is because he interrogates everyone in a pleasing fashion, draws them all out, displays an interest and a sympathy with them. He listens to isolated men and women, who for years have been shut up in the silence of routine monosyllables, without the stimulus to talk of a sympathetic ear.

He is a sort of lay confessor to all and sundry. A wise and tolerant priest, he violates the confessional only in an unmalicious and disguised way. There is something about him that makes people want to recount their life histories to him. He is the confidant of enterprising businessmen who tell him their dissatisfaction with life, their secret aspirations, the difficulties they get into over their sweethearts. Hardups and frustrated geniuses, neurotics and racehorse touts tell him all about themselves. Give Sherwood twenty minutes in the corner with a married woman and he knows every blessed grievance she has against her husband, from his habit of wearing nightgowns to his silly preferences in women, from his humming idiotic snatches of song in his bath to his shallow lies, petty trickeries and empty vanities.

What is more, he has a sinister talent for telling you just what is wrong with you, for diagnosing your case with amazing accuracy. He is like a clever mind reader or an Indian fakir. His intuitions are so sure that they act as prompters to your own easy disclosures. He has acquired this talent by a persistent and patient interest in people, by an insatiable curiosity, by an early Christian belief in the profound significance of all human life.

To get back to his vanity: His vanity is such that it presupposes that his own life and work are important, significant and invaluable. Such is his profound belief in himself that this belief precludes his active sympathy with the work of any other writer, especially of anyone working in a different field from his own. Thus he may profess in an amiable fashion that he likes the work of Hecht, of Hergesheimer, of Waldo Frank, of this or that one he meets; but actually he not only dislikes it and can't read it, but is very suspicious of it. He has hurt the feelings of many a fellow writer by telling him, in effect, that in his opinion the inquiring and hopeful writer wasn't honest or sincere. A novelist should know better than to ask another novelist what he thinks of his work: in reply, if the questioned is truthful, he must either admit that he considers the other fellow's work bad or have doubts about the value of his own work. And Sherwood has absolutely no doubts whatever.

He is, indeed, one of the few consistent artists in America, one of the very few men who have had the courage to deny the American god of monetary success and devote themselves to their highest self-realization as artists. Even at the height of his present run of acclamation, he has refused to be lionized. While lesser men would be accepting every tea and dinner, every opportunity to appear before women's clubs and school societies, every chance to give readings in arty eating places, Sherwood sticks to his shack in Palos Park, Illinois, and works. Once a week he goes into Chicago and has lunch at Schlogl's with Harry Hansen, Carl Sandburg, Ben Hecht, Keith Preston, T. K. Hedrick, Llewellyn Jones and Gene Markey (the true and only claim Chicago has to be the literary center of America, the only group of people who are vitally interested in literature in the whole sprawly town). That is about the extent of his social activities.

Sherwood rents a small shack for twenty dollars a month in Palos

Park, cooks most of his own meals, does his own housework and even some of his laundry. He goes into Chicago occasionally and works long enough with an advertising agency to lay by sufficient money for his meager needs when he is ready to write again. He has refused to tie himself for any protracted length of time to any industrial endeavor, because money means nothing to him beyond its power to purchase the few necessities of life and give him the leisure in which to write. It is for this reason that the *Dial* award means much more to him than it would to most writers, accustomed to expensive scales of living, self-indulgence and extravagance. Sherwood knows how to use the money so that it will, in very truth, give him the opportunity to write.

But had he not got the award, had his books never sold beyond a number affording him a pitiable royalty, he would yet have done perhaps precisely what he is doing now. He would continue to create, for he has the soul of an artist, a soul uncorrupted by the exigencies of a material civilization. He began to write late in life, to keep himself, so he says, from "going crazy." Writing was a relief from the strain of years of bitter experience and trying hours in the cutthroat, nerveracking game of commercial competition. He wrote, and he writes now, from an inner necessity, and even did he never get his work between covers he would still continue to write and still continue to keep his faith in its very high personal (and that is, ultimate) value. Such is the triumph and the apology for Sherwood's inordinate, magnificent vanity.

Anderson is by nature a mystic. He has intimations of things beyond his power to comprehend or to articulate. That accounts for the tenebrous quality of much of his writing. His *Mid-American Chants* and *New Testament,* wherein he has written prose poetry of a deep, resonant, organ-music type, which is moving and impressive without conveying any concrete ideas or definite, describable impression to the reader, are but the sort of thing Anderson would write altogether if he did not find that he must make his writing less idiosyncratic if he would find an audience of any size for his work. Between *New Testament* and the comparatively realistic and factual *Windy McPherson's Son* there is his half-mystical, half-realistic novel, *Many Marriages,* which represents the confusion of tendencies of his own mind, and the difficulty he has in keeping the mystically poetic and the realistically prosaic apart in his fiction. The fusion of the two is most successful in the short stories of *Winesburg, Ohio* and *Horses and Men,* two books of fiction which are certainly to be counted among the finest contributions to literature in our period.

Knowing this mystical, almost religious asceticism in Anderson, I am amused, when I am not annoyed, by the critical denunciations he has received from people who look upon him as immoral and corrupting. One night Anderson was at my house, and it pleased me for the moment to espouse the cause of individualism, intelligent self-interest, and a modified Nietzscheism more for the effect of bringing out Anderson's ideas than anything else. I was not surprised to find a deep religious streak in him. He told me that I intellectualized life too much, that I sought causes and traced effects and did not "lie fallow" enough.

Anderson rarely seeks the company of writing folk, preferring the company of simple and guileless people. He will stand on a street corner for hours listening to a garrulous old man of the shiftless, imaginative, vagabond sort, encouraging the old fellow to fall back upon his memory of his past life and yield up to Anderson the secrets of his ambitions, his views of life. Often, indeed usually, such fellows will grow expansive, for they are lonely people and rarely find anyone who will listen to them, and they lie and exaggerate about their past, tell fantastic yarns about themselves, and so for a little while achieve importance in their own eyes. For this privilege they are grateful to Anderson, and Anderson is rewarded by material for his stories. He has the manner which inspires confidence, like an old priest who has listened to many confessions; he is sympathetic and kindly and, though he rarely offers advice, he so contrives to encourage those who confess to him to do what they were going to do anyhow that he is looked upon by many people as a man infallibly wise in human understanding. People hurt by life, women intangled with psychic conflicts, bruised, saddened and disillusioned spirits find in him a consoler.

He has, however, another more expansive side of his nature. He is one of the finest yarn spinners I have ever heard. His story of "Mama Geighen" is an epic now famous in all the circles in which Anderson has moved. It is a story about a huge, muscular, Chaucerian woman who ran a countryside saloon in Wisconsin before prohibition and about how Anderson and a newspaperman who went with him on a fishing trip spent a Rabelaisian evening with the farmhands at Mama Geighen's place. He has numerous such stories, though none quite so good as "Mama Geighen," and they are all, curiously, gay and comical, not at all like the stories with somber overtones which he writes. He loves to tell these stories, and given the right sort of receptive audience, one not easily shocked or embarrassed, and he is one of the most delightful of entertainers.

CARL SANDBURG

CARL SANDBURG'S FEATURES aren't finely chiseled; they look as if they might have been hacked out with an adze and mattock. His countenance is not only rugged, it is rough and weatherworn. He has high cheekbones and precipitous brows, widely brambled. Two deep furrows run down his face and around the corners of his mouth, like gullies on a clay hillside. His chin juts out from square jaws, and, save for his nose and forehead, he might serve as a model for a reconstructed bust of a Neanderthalman. He parts his gray-streaked, wiry hair in the middle, but it hangs in bangs to his eyebrows. He is square-shouldered, powerfully built. There is probably Viking blood in his veins, and he was bequeathed a manual laborer's physique by his father, who was a Swedish immigrant, Johnson by name. The elder Sandburg was a section hand who adopted the name of Sandburg when another Johnson claimed his check one week at the railroad's pay window.

Carl Sandburg, the poet, has a brooding, glowering look, though his soul is kindly and his nature sentimental in its tenderness. He talks with a slow, organ-toned sententiousness, like a medieval bishop describing the wrath of God. His cerebral processes are a series of intimations which leave him vague and troubled. He thinks in images which have blurred outlines and an aspect either sinister or sorrowful. He has hates, but they are of abstract social nature; they are not hates really, but resentments against the exploitation of the proletarian class from which he comes, and against the mechanical brutishness of that aspect of industrial civilization which stamps out beauty and simple, joyous living.

But the soul of man, he is convinced, is good at bottom, and that in the heart of everyone there is an aspiration toward righteousness, beauty and justice. When he meets a capitalist his prejudices are dissolved; and about men who had hitherto personified to him greed and cruelty I have heard him, once he had talked with them, say in his august and kindly voice: "Now, they are pretty good guys when you get right down inside of them."

He once had a profound distrust and disrespect for colleges, though he is a Lombard graduate himself. That is all changed now. He has lectured and recited to college students in all parts of the country. The students, and members of the faculty no less, have been from the first warmly enthusiastic over his singing "Frankie and Johnnie," playing his banjo and reciting his poems. He has revised his opinions about colleges and college students. He once spoke with contempt of the Rotary Clubs and Kiwanis; but one time he was asked to lecture before such a club in one of the large cities of the Middle West, and when the largest crowd that had ever turned out for him applauded him vigorously, he changed his mind about Rotary Clubs and Kiwanis also.

He is naïve and simple. Like Will Rogers, his handsome homeliness is irresistible, and he wins his way into the hearts of his audience the moment he appears on the stage. So great, indeed, has been his success during the past three years that his innumerable and varied social contacts will inevitably wash away every vestige of his reforming temper and conquer his distress over social and economic conditions. More and more his poetry is freeing itself of its burden of social criticism and propaganda; more and more it is becoming fanciful, imaginistic and elegiac. Hitherto he has sung mostly one dolorous tune with numerous variations; he has sung the imminence of death and the ironic futility of human endeavor; and he has bidden men be kind to one another. He is growing more and more fanciful, more interested in line and color, mists and lights. He is growing less and less the protester against the social order and more and more the painter and etcher with a special, impressive vision.

Sandburg's experience during the formative years of his life was such as would breed in him a humanitarian radicalism. He left school when he was thirteen. He worked at odd jobs in Galesburg, Ill.— driving a milk wagon, portering in a barber shop, shifting scenes in a theater, working in a brick factory. He threshed wheat in Colorado, labored with pick and shovel with railroad construction gangs, washed dishes in hotels and returned to Galesburg to learn the painter's trade.

He served in the Spanish-American War, tried for entrance at West Point, failed, and matriculated at Lombard College, where he edited the college paper and became interested in poetry. He got into newspaper work, reporting for a while on the adless daily newspaper which the Scripps organization tried out in Chicago. When the paper died Sandburg went to work for the Chicago *Daily News* as a reporter. He went abroad for a year as a correspondent in the Scandinavian countries and returned to the *News,* where he is now employed as an editorial writer. His first book was *Chicago Poems,* which appeared

[435]

in 1916. By the time he had published *Corn Huskers* he was described by some not overcautious critics as the successor to Walt Whitman.

Sandburg is charmingly naïve, almost childlike. One time I dropped in to see him at his desk in the *Daily News* office in Chicago, after I had been on a farm in the Southwest for several months. I had not changed, really, in appearance and had not put on more than a few pounds in weight. But Sandburg knew I had been on the prairies, and the prairies have a profound poetic meaning for him, a meaning which he contrasts with the cramped ugliness of growth-stunting cities. He wears a slouchy cap, which he does not remove at the office because the visor shades his eyes against the glare of the light.

Turning around in his swivel chair, beaming upon me his frank and homely smile, he said: "Now you look like something! You've got the wind of the prairies in your face, and the soul-curing sun of the broadlands has stamped its O. K. on you. You used to look like one of these Greenwich Village poets, pale and haggard. Now you look like something."

He was only making phrases: he never allows anything, reality or factuality, to interfere with his Biblical sonority and imagery in conversation. He likes to talk in parables and to use metaphors so fanciful that you have to ask him the meaning of them. He likes to give an ominous twist to his simplest, most matter-of-fact conversation, and he is always intimating profound enigmas when he hasn't anything particular in mind. He used to talk or hint portentously about the coming of a revolution, and even after he had ceased to believe wholeheartedly in the possibility, he would continue to make such hints as a method of humorous mystification, hoaxing his auditor, playing on his credulity and having fun out of doing so.

He carries around in his pockets great batches of newspaper clippings of reviews. He shows these to his friends with a happy pride. About these clippings he shows no discrimination, no snobbery, so long as they are favorable. He will pull out a long clipping and say, "Here's a nice send-off the London *Times* gave *Corn Huskers*"; and when you have glanced through it he will pull out another and say, "And here's a nice write-up the Grenfell, Idaho, *Weekly Democrat* gave me."

One clipping means just as much to him as another. A critical analysis of his work or a technical aesthetic study of his effects is lost upon him, for he writes what he writes without understanding the why of it, and is not only puzzled but pleased when he reads what others discern in his work.

He has a love for all things which are close to the heart of average humanity. He cuts out and preserves clippings of love letters that are introduced into divorce and alienation suits, letters of query to advisers to the lovelorn and such things. He finds pathos and beauty in them. He responds to all that is in the most modernistic art with a response that is wholly emotional.

When he sets down his impressions they are poetic and curious, but they might just as well apply to one thing as another, for they are not concrete. He wrote a prose poem about Brancusi, describing him as a "galoot," and wrote that Brancusi doesn't "know where he is going, but is on his way." He mixes slang, colloquialisms and Middle Western idioms into his poems with great effectiveness.

Sandburg has the most deficient critical sense of any writer I know. He is a man almost entirely of intuitions about which he is more or less inarticulate. That accounts for much of the charm and impressiveness of his best poems. If he had a keener discrimination, a finer sense of word values and more general information—in a word, if he were more sophisticated—he would not display that genius for inappropriate analogy which makes the line "Shovel 'em in!" in his poem, "Cool Tombs," and the whole poem directed against Billy Sunday so startlingly distinctive.

Whitman hoped to write poems which would be read by the man in the street, by laborers, by "the bone and sinews of democracy"; and it has been his fate to be read, when he is read at all, only by shut-in and sedentary men, by scholars, students and poets. He failed to learn the secret of the appeal of poetry to simple and unlettered hearts.

That secret is that the poet must express what they feel, must give words to sentiments which they understand. He must not write about them, he must write for them; he must not flatter them, he must be their voice.

Robert Burns understood this; Whitman did not (which is not to avow that Whitman was not a great poet). Sandburg understands it, or, probably more properly speaking, Sandburg speaks for the people to whom Whitman wished to appeal, for Sandburg has remained at heart one of them. Nothing has ever made him "literary." Read some of his poems to teamsters or truckmen (as I have done), and the response in them is immediate, affectionate and enthusiastic. He speaks a language they understand and expresses emotions they are capable of feeling, even when his poems are not clear and his images not concrete.

Sandburg's peasantlike deficiency in a critical sense causes him to see analogies where they do not exist. And by drawing analogies that were unflattering he used to infuriate Sherwood Anderson. When Sandburg was given the sinecure as motion-picture critic for the Chicago *Daily News* (that kindly orphanage for so much literary talent), he soon began to take the movies with a heavy seriousness. He saw in them the modern substitute for folk tales, heroic legends and *chansons de geste* (which, in a way, they are). This led him to see in them much more than there is. He would encounter Sherwood Anderson on the street and say, with his slow, ponderous, drawling bass: "I have just seen a real, typical, sure-enough Sherwood Anderson movie. It was real Winesburg, Ohio, stuff. It had guts to it, and the breath of the sage country breezed through it. It was Bill Hart in ———" And he would mention some terrible title like *Hearts Astray,* whereupon Anderson's lips would quiver. He would say nothing, for he loves "Old Carl" with a profound affection.

In Sandburg's poetry this confused critical sense becomes a shining virtue. Suggestion rather than explicit delineation and exposition is, of course, frequently the function of the highest poetry. And Sandburg's poetry usually intimates, or gives the impression of intimating, much more than what you see before your eyes when you read him. What he intimates, when you come right down to it, is that soon or late we are all going to die.

H. L. MENCKEN

PICTURE A BUTCHER'S BOY with apple cheeks, who parts his hair in the middle and laughs out of the side of his mouth, and you have a fair idea of the facial aspect of Heinie Mencken. He is forty-one, but there are moments when he looks fifteen. These moments are frequent when he is with George Jean Nathan. He never knows when Nathan is kidding him and, although he has been associated with Nathan for over twelve years, Nathan remains to him an enigma past resolving.

Nathan has been trying to get him to dress like an Algonquin ham ever since the day they met. At the present rate of progress he will have achieved success about the time Mencken becomes professor of English literature at Western Reserve University. Nathan got him to discard suspenders in favor of a belt and after years of persuasion prevailed upon him to carry a cane. Heinie backslid on the cane after tripping himself on the thing for weeks and catching it between his bowlegs every time he boarded a street car. During the interlude he used to carry the cane with an anguished air of affected jauntiness. In Baltimore he always left it at home until after nightfall, when he could practise carrying it without braving the guffaws of the yokelry. . . . And last August Nathan badgered him into buying a new hat in place of the battered relic he had been having annually renovated by a Greek bootblack. Nathan has yet to persuade him to turn over to the Salvation Army the faded cravenette which hangs from his champagne-bottle shoulders in folds like the skin on McAdoo's cheek.

It would be a mistake to assume from this that Mencken is a sloppy dresser. To the contrary, he is one of the best-dressed men I have ever seen. He learned early that the secret of dressing well is to wear nothing which will attract attention either by its smartness or its shabbiness. In fewer words, to quote a memorable phrase, he has risen above his tailor. He would no more wear yellow gloves than he would wear a rubber collar. His clothes fit him; they are of excellent material; and they are always in subdued colors. When Belmont collars first came into style, he discovered that they effectively covered up his Adam's apple and felt all right on his neck, so he has worn them ever since. When he was in school, it was the style for youths to part their hair in the middle. He parted his hair thus, and, being a creature of habit, he never changed it.

A relentless opponent of Christianity, Mencken is the most Christian of men. A verbal flouter of the bourgeois virtues, he practices them all. He is thoroughly honest; he discharges his obligations promptly; he keeps his appointments; he is a man of his word; and he is a dutiful and affectionate son. I have never seen a man who is so ridden by relatives. He has scores of them, and to them all he is obliging and courteous. He is always doing something for them: assisting at weddings, arranging for proper hospital service, meeting them at trains, taking them for automobile rides, or minding their babies when they are off to the theater. He lives with his mother and sister in the old family home in Baltimore, and he is a model householder. He built a garden wall of which he is proud and boastful. He sees that the bin is full of coal, and he can mend a leak in the plumbing.

He used to belong to a club in Baltimore which met every Saturday night in the back room of a dealer in musical instruments. The club had to be abandoned after Prohibition because two members died of the ill effects of near-beer. Expenses for floral horseshoes and Rocks of Ages exhausted the club funds. But during brighter days than these it was a happy gathering. For exactly one hour every Saturday night they made an awful din with two violins, a cello, piccolo and bass tuba, with Mencken at the piano, pressing with might and main on the loud pedal and pounding like Percy Grainger.

"Sweet noises," was Mencken's invariable comment after each debauch, "I'm as thirsty as a bishop." Then they would bundle away a few blocks to the top floor of a restaurant whereat a long table was ready with filled steins and a patent meat chopper. Mention of that meat chopper is important, for it was the instrument used in preparing the weirdest victual ever devised by the human mind. Into it went raw meat, onions, and other ingredients which no stomach not made of cast iron could hold longer than five seconds.

Just as a guest of the evening would get the first mouthful down, Mencken would lean over and impart this jolly little bit of information: "That fellow there at the meat chopper is a surgeon at Johns Hopkins. He discovered that the rump and loin of unembalmed cadavers is both highly nutritious and palatable. He has been able to obtain some choice cuts without expense to the club, through his hospital connections." . . . I succeeded in forking three helpings into my vest and two into my hat without being detected and earned thereby hearty commendation as a gentleman and an epicure. It wasn't for long. It was, by mistake, Mencken's hat.

He is an inveterate practical joker, and in this he is not always the soul of honor that he might be. He and Nathan once engaged to write some sweet and bitter facts about each other to be printed in a pamphlet. Mencken got Nathan pickled and wrote both of them, handing himself all the berries in the world and libeling Nathan scurrilously. He has stolen, to date, fifty-eight Gideon Bibles and presented them to friends. He collects religious leaflets and tracts, especially those announcing the second coming of the Lord, and passes them on to his correspondents, urging them to repent of their sins.

He has his house cluttered up with prints of funny-looking fellows he calls his ancestors. He bought the lot of them at curio shops in Germany.

The erroneous notion sometimes obtains that Mencken is a Jew. His physiognomy belies it. He has the blond, broad features of a typical Saxon. One trait, though, suggests that some remote ancestor was Semitic: he washes his hands fifteen or twenty times a day. That is a Jewish trait which probably had its origin in the days when— but it is best not to go into that here.

The healthiest individual you could possibly imagine, he is always complaining of ills in such a manner that you would think he was dying. Probably this comes from reading too much medical literature.

His technical knowledge of anatomy and therapy is amazingly large; probably no man living has a vaster vocabulary of medical jargon. He reads all the medical journals, quack and legitimate, from table of contents to lost-vigor ads. As a residuum of so much reading, he has come to believe that all doctors are quacks. Still, he has tried sixty-seven "cures" for hay fever and confidently announces every spring that he is rid of it. Just as regularly he begins to sneeze about the middle of August. He satirizes prophylaxis in an amusing play but he is a bug on bacteria. He is tidy and clean. When he has a stag party at his house, he sends his mother and sister away. After the fellows have gone, he sweeps the floors, dusts the furniture, washes and dries the dishes, puts everything in place and leaves the rooms orderly and immaculate.

Once he engaged in a book-length debate, in the form of letters, with Robert Rives La Monte on the subject "Men vs. the Man." Mencken argued fiercely for individualism, *les droits de seigneur,* aristocracy, and the right of the few to exploit the weak. La Monte argued with equal heat for the rights of the proletariat, the need for socialism and the blessings of altruism and the equal chance. The joke of it is that Mencken at the time was sweating away in his shirt sleeves at a newspaper job while La Monte was taking his ease on a beautiful country estate in Connecticut.

All this only goes to show that the Freudians are right and that all literary expressian is merely a projection of subconscious wishes. For all that Mencken disparages American civilization, he would be profoundly uncomfortable if the sort of society he presents as desirable should happen to exist. I was right when I wrote that Mencken in any other country would be unthinkable and am right again when I say that Mencken is America's most ardent patriot. Nine tenths of his life is given over to denunciation, and were there nothing to denounce he would be profoundly unhappy. As it is he is as happy as Pollyanna. No one gets more fun out of living. Indeed, such a jolly time does he have dancing about "with arms and legs," goosing solemn and serious people and playing ribald jokes, that for six years he has been repeating himself, progressing far too little, developing almost not at all. For two years he has not bothered to vary his startling vocabulary, and it is becoming a little stale. This is, perhaps, the penalty of getting a reputation based upon a manner. An audience is created by it, and an audience demands repetition. It is hard to imagine cynical Ecclesiastes writing the Psalms of David or Jeremiah singing another Song of Songs.

APPENDICES

But whatever Mencken's destiny or place may become in American literature he will always remain, you may be sure, a warmly human figure. All women, without exception, like him. And all men do too, who have ever met him—scholars, pedants, boozers, preachers, teamsters, politicians, highbrows, lowbrows and medium brows. That is a test and an achievement. The secret of this is that he is frank and unaffected, courteous, gentle, amiable, wise, jovial and a gentleman.